Get started in Hindi

Rupert Snell

edited by
Florence Kerns and Bruno Paul

First published in Great Britain in 2003 by Hodder & Stoughton. An Hachette UK company.
First published in US in 2003 by The McGraw-Hill Companies, Inc.
This edition published 2014

British Library Cataloguing in Publication Data: a catalogue record for this title is available from the British Library.

Library of Congress Catalog Card Number: on file.

ISBN 978 1 444 17468 7

10 9 8 7 6 5 4 3 2 1

Typeset by Aptara

Printed and bound in Great Britain by CPI Group (UK) Ltd., Croydon, CRO 4YY.

John Murray Learning policy is to use papers that are natural, renewable and recyclable products and made from wood grown in sustainable forests. The logging and manufacturing processes are expected to conform to the environmental regulations of the country of origin.

John Murray Learning
338 Euston Road
London NW1 3BH
www.hodder.co.uk

Contents

Meet the author

My contact with Indian culture began in about 1967, when I first heard Hindustani music – Ravi Shankar's recording of Raga Khamaj – in a booth in a provincial record shop in England. This musical encounter led me eventually to begin a BA in Hindi at the School of Oriental and African Studies, University of London, in 1970. From the outset, I forced myself to use my faltering Hindi whenever the chance came along, although not always with great success: one day in Anwar's Delicacies in London I asked for a *paṛosī* (*neighbour*) when I meant a *samosā*! But Hindi speakers proved to be nothing if not neighbourly, and as soon as I started valuing communication above grammar, my conversations in Hindi began to be more meaningful. Numerous trips to India helped build my confidence. My interest in Hindi literature took me back in time to the old dialect of Braj Bhasha and eventually I wrote a PhD dissertation on a 16th-century text from the Braj devotional tradition. Teaching and researching both early and modern Hindi kept me gainfully employed at SOAS for more than three decades, after which I moved to the University of Texas at Austin, happily plying the same trade but now in the context of UT's Hindi Urdu Flagship. For me personally, Hindi has been the key to a rich and wonderful cultural world. Over the years I have learned to distinguish *samosās* from *paṛosī* with a ready confidence; but, thankfully, not everything has changed, and the Raga Khamaj that I listened to on that vinyl LP more than 40 years ago sounds just as good nowadays played on my MP3 player.

Rupert Snell

How to use this book

WELCOME TO *GET STARTED IN HINDI!*

This course is designed for people who want a structured but user-friendly introduction to Hindi, whether studying alone or in a class. It aims to get you into the world of real Hindi as quickly as possible.

Each of the twelve units prepares you for some new social or practical situations while also introducing the grammar gradually and simply. We begin with simple statements and questions using the verb *to be*; then the various tenses and other structures are explained, steadily increasing the range of contexts that you can deal with.

There are plentiful examples and exercises; all numbered questions are provided with answers in the **Key to the exercises** at the back of the book. The activities often address you directly, asking questions about you and encouraging you to use the language as you learn it. The carefully graded **Vocabulary builder** for each unit comes at the end, with full **Hindi–English** and **English–Hindi vocabulary** lists bringing it all together at the back of the book.

THE SHARMA FAMILY

Most of the dialogues come in a loose **Storyline** and are based on the various members of the Sharma family, who live in Agra: Geeta (a doctor) and her husband Raju (a teacher), their children Manoj, Ram, and Meena – and a dog, Moti. Because we're dealing with a set of known characters, it's easy to see the different levels of formality that are an important feature of Hindi: for example, we hear the children being addressed less formally than adults and strangers.

Most conversations are accompanied by comprehension questions to focus your attention as you listen.

Language discovery questions guide you to consider language points in the conversations. Look to the light bulb icon to *discover* how the language works, whether it is a grammar rule or a way of saying things.

SCRIPT AND PRONUNCIATION

The Hindi script, called 'Devanagari', is an extremely systematic writing system: each character represents a particular sound, making it the perfect guide to pronunciation. Although a 'roman' transliteration is given throughout the book, the small effort required to learn Devanagari is very well worthwhile! You may have noticed that all the Hindi in this book is transliterated into the roman script and this may tempt you not to bother to learn Devanagari. ***Don't give in to this temptation!*** Devanagari is really very easy to learn, and with a character for every sound and a sound for every character, it is extremely helpful in developing good pronunciation and learning new words.

Listen out for two important contrasts in pronunciation. The first is between *retroflex* consonants (pronounced with the tongue touching the roof of the mouth, giving a 'hard' sound of the kind associated with Indian pronunciations of words like *doctor*) and *dental* consonants (pronounced with the tongue touching the upper teeth, giving a 'soft' sound as in the Italian pronunciation of *Italia*). The second contrast is between 'unaspirated' and 'aspirated' consonants, such as the pair क *ka* and ख *kha* – the first is much less 'breathy' than the second. Vowel sounds are very 'clean': the vowel ए *e* is more like the vowels in French *été* than in English *payday*.

THE AUDIO PROGRAMME

This book is accompanied by an audio programme which will help bring the language alive for you. It introduces the sounds of Hindi, presents the **Storyline** and other features from the book, and goes beyond the book with further listening and speaking exercises that will build your confidence in using Hindi in real conversations. Pause the audio whenever you need time to think and practise imitating the Hindi voices as closely as possible, speaking out loud.

WHERE DOES THIS COURSE LEAD?

After finishing this course, you may like to look at *Complete Hindi*, by Rupert Snell with Simon Weightman: this gives more detail on the grammar, and plenty of reading practice. Further resources by Rupert Snell and others are available at www.hindiurduflagship.org. The web-based course *A Door into Hindi* (www.ncsu.edu/project/hindi_lessons) has an interactive approach to the learning process; and Hindi films also offer a brilliant way of getting to know the language and the culture it expresses. Most important of all, you will find some 400 million Hindi speakers waiting to talk to you: start speaking Hindi today!

Dictionaries: Rupert Snell's *Essential Hindi Dictionary* is designed for learners and gives a lot of help with sentence formation, while the *Oxford Hindi–English Dictionary* by R.S. McGregor is what you need if you want to start reading Hindi newspapers and magazines, many of which are available on the internet.

Learn to learn

The Discovery method

There are lots of approaches to language learning, some practical and some quite unconventional. Perhaps you know of a few, or even have some techniques of your own. In this book we have incorporated the **Discovery method** of learning, a sort of DIY approach to language learning. What this means is that you will be encouraged throughout the course to engage your mind and figure out the language for yourself, through identifying patterns, understanding grammar concepts, noticing words that are similar to English, and more. This method promotes *language awareness*, a critical skill in acquiring a new language. As a result of your own efforts, you will be able to better retain what you have learned, use it with confidence, and, even better, apply those same skills to *continuing* to learn the language (or, indeed, another one) on your own after you've finished this book.

Everyone can succeed in learning a language – the key is to know *how to learn* it. Learning is more than just reading or memorizing grammar and vocabulary. It's about being an *active* learner, learning in real contexts, and, most importantly, *using* what you've learned in different situations. Simply put, if you **figure something out for yourself**, you're more likely to understand it. And when you use what you've learned, you're more likely to remember it.

And because many of the essential but (let's admit it!) dull details, such as grammar rules, are taught through the **Discovery method**, you'll have more fun while learning. Soon, the language will start to make sense and you'll be relying on your own intuition to construct original sentences *independently*, not just listening and repeating.

Enjoy yourself!

Be successful at learning languages

1 MAKE A HABIT OUT OF LEARNING

Study a little every day, between 20 and 30 minutes if possible, rather than two to three hours in one session. Give yourself short-term goals, e.g. work out how long you'll spend on a particular unit and work within your time limit. This will help you to create a study habit, much in the same way you would a sport or music. You will need to concentrate, so try to create an environment conducive to learning which is calm and quiet and free from distractions. As you study, do not worry about your mistakes or the things you can't remember or understand. Languages settle differently in our brains, but gradually the language will become clearer as your brain starts to make new connections. Just give yourself enough time and you will succeed.

2 EXPAND YOUR LANGUAGE CONTACT

As part of your study habit, try to take other opportunities to **get exposure to the language**. As well as using this course you could try listening to the radio and watching television programmes or reading online articles and blogs. Many learners of Hindi find that they can learn a lot through watching film clips and listening to film songs, all accessible on the internet. Web searches in the Devanagari script will bring examples of real-life Hindi usage direct to your screen: for example, you could look up train times from Mathura Junction to Agra City and learn useful expressions like *leaving at…* and *arriving at…* Perhaps you could find information in Hindi about a personal passion or hobby or even a news story that interests you. In time you'll find that your vocabulary and language recognition deepen and you'll become used to a range of writing and speaking styles.

3 VOCABULARY

- To organize your study of vocabulary, group new words under:
  - **a** generic categories, e.g. *food, furniture*.
  - **b** situations in which they occur, e.g. under *market* you can write *fruit, vegetable, fresh, price*.
  - **c** functions, e.g. greetings, parting, thanks, apologizing.
- Say the words out loud as you read them.

- Write the words over and over again. Remember that if you want to keep lists on your smartphone or tablet you can usually switch the keyboard language to make sure you are able to include all accents and special characters.
- Listen to the audio several times.
- Cover up the English side of the vocabulary list and see if you remember the meaning of words.
- Learn new nouns along with an adjective to help you remember their gender, e.g. बड़ी मेज़ *baṛī mez*, काला बाज़ार *kālā bāzār*.
- Associate the words with similar sounding words in English, e.g. जंगली *janglī* (*wild*) with *jungle*, a place where wild animals live.
- Silly mnemonic devices are a good way to remember vocabulary. Create phrases to associate with vocabulary items to help you remember. For example, पुल *pul* means *bridge*: ***Pull** the bridge down*; सब्ज़ी *sabzī* means *vegetable*: *Vegetables stay fresh at **sub-zero** temperatures*. These phrases might help you remember the words' meanings.
- Create flash cards, drawings and mind maps.
- Write words for objects around your house and stick them to objects.
- Pay attention to patterns in words, e.g. all question words begin with क: क्या *kyā what*, कौन *kaun who*, कब *kab when*, क्यों *kyõ why*, etc.
- **Experiment with words.** Use the words that you learn in new contexts and find out if they are correct. For example, you learn in Unit 5 that चाहिए *cāhie* is used to express needing and wanting, e.g. मुझे पानी चाहिए *Mujhe pānī cāhie, I want water*. Experiment with मुझे नहीं चाहिए ! *Mujhe nahī̃ cāhie! I don't want (it)!*, मुझे मदद चाहिए *Mujhe madad cāhie I need help*, and आपको क्या चाहिए ? *āpko kyā cāhie? What do you want?* Check the new phrases either in this book or with Hindi speakers.

4 GRAMMAR

- To organize the study of grammar write your own grammar glossary and add new information and examples as you go along.
- **Experiment with grammar rules.** Sit back and reflect on the rules you learn. See how they compare with your own language or other languages you may already speak. Try to find out some rules on your own and be ready to spot the exceptions. By doing this you'll remember the rules better and get a feel for the language.
- Try to find examples of grammar in conversations or other articles.
- Keep a 'pattern bank' that organizes examples that can be listed

under the structures you've learned. For example, how to make nouns plural can be organized as patterns: मकान *makān house* stays unchanged in the plural (like *sheep*); but कमरा *kamrā room* becomes कमरे *kamre rooms*, खिड़की *khiṛkī window* becomes खिड़कियाँ *khiṛkiyā̃ windows*, and छत *chat roof* becomes छतें *chatẽ roofs*.

- Use old vocabulary to practise new grammar structures.
- When you learn a new verb form, write the conjugation of several different verbs you know that follow the same form.

5 PRONUNCIATION

- When organizing the study of pronunciation, keep a section of your notebook for pronunciation rules and practise those that trouble you.
- Repeat all of the conversations, line by line.
- Listen to yourself and try to mimic what you hear.
- Record yourself and compare yourself to a native speaker.
- Make a list of words that give you trouble and practise them.
- Study individual sounds, then full words.
- Don't forget, it's not just about pronouncing letters and words correctly, but using the right intonation. So, when practising words and sentences, mimic the rising and falling intonation of native speakers.

6 LISTENING AND READING

The conversations in this book include questions to help guide you in your understanding. But you can go further by following some of these tips.

- **Imagine the situation.** When listening to or reading the conversations, try to imagine where the scene is taking place and who the main characters are. Let your experience of the world help you guess the meaning of the conversation, e.g. if a conversation takes place in a snack bar you can predict the kind of vocabulary that is being used.
- **Concentrate on the main part.** When watching a foreign film you usually get the meaning of the whole story from a few individual shots. Understanding a foreign conversation or article is similar. Concentrate on the main parts to get the message and don't worry about individual words.
- **Guess the key words; if you cannot, ask or look them up.** When there are key words you don't understand, try to guess what they mean from the context. If you're conversing with a speaker of Hindi and cannot get the gist of a whole passage because of one word or phrase, try to repeat that word with a questioning tone; the speaker

will probably paraphrase it, giving you the chance to understand it. If for example you wanted to find out the meaning of the word मेहमान *mehmān* (*guest*) you would ask मेहमान का क्या मतलब है ? *Mehmān kā kyā matlab hai?*

7 SPEAKING

Rehearse in the foreign language. As all language teachers will assure you, the successful learners are those students who overcome their inhibitions and get into situations where they must speak, write, and listen to the foreign language. Here are some useful tips to help you practise speaking Hindi:

- Hold a conversation with yourself, using the conversations of the units as models and the structures you have learnt previously.
- After you have conducted a transaction with a sales assistant, clerk, or waiter in your own language, pretend that you have to do it in Hindi, e.g. *buying groceries, ordering food, getting a rickshaw*, and so on.
- Look at objects around you and try to name them in Hindi.
- Look at people around you and try to describe them in detail.
- Try to answer all of the questions in the book out loud.
- Say the dialogues out loud then try to replace sentences with ones that are true for you.
- Try to role play different situations in the book.

8 LEARN FROM YOUR ERRORS

- Don't let errors interfere with getting your message across. Making errors is part of any normal learning process, but some people get so worried that they won't say anything unless they are sure it is correct. This leads to a vicious circle as the less they say, the less practice they get and the more mistakes they make.
- Many errors are not serious as they do not affect the meaning, for example if you use the wrong possessive marker (की *kī* instead of का *kā*), forget to make your adjective and noun agree (बड़ी मेज़ *baṛī mez* instead of बड़ी मेज़ *baṛī mez*), or forget to put nouns in the oblique before a postposition (कमरा में *kamrā mẽ* instead of कमरे में *kamre mẽ*). So concentrate on getting your message across and learn from your mistakes.

9 LEARN TO COPE WITH UNCERTAINTY

- **Don't over-use your dictionary.**
  When reading a text in the foreign language, don't be tempted to look up every word you don't know. Underline the words you do not understand and read the passage several times, concentrating on trying to get the gist of the passage. If after the third time there are still words which prevent you from getting the general meaning of the passage, look them up in the dictionary.
- **Don't panic if you don't understand.**
  If at some point you feel you don't understand what you are told, don't panic or give up listening. Either try and guess what is being said and keep following the conversation or, if you cannot, isolate the expression or words you haven't understood and have them explained to you. The speaker might paraphrase them and the conversation will carry on.
- **Keep talking.**
  The best way to improve your fluency in the foreign language is to talk every time you have the opportunity to do so: keep the conversations flowing and don't worry about the mistakes. If you get stuck for a particular word, don't let the conversation stop; paraphrase or replace the unknown word with one you do know, even if you have to simplify what you want to say. Hindi speakers frequently use English words in their Hindi, and you can do the same.

Hindi script and sounds

Although a roman transliteration is provided for all the Hindi in this book, learning to read and write the Devanagari script is extremely worthwhile. Its phonetic basis makes it really easy to learn; and if you're in India, being able to read the Hindi all around you in signs and posters will bring its own reward, even before you start reading more ambitiously.

As you begin to learn Devanagari, there's a very useful 'Hindi script tutor' to help you learn the characters and their sounds: **http://www.avashy.com/hindiscripttutor.htm**. This website, devised by Richard Woodward, teaches and tests the script interactively and demonstrates the sounds of Hindi. And for a detailed introduction to Devanagari, see Rupert Snell, *Read and write Hindi script* (Hodder & Stoughton, 2010).

The best way to learn the script is to copy out each character several times, pronouncing its sound as you do so. Start with the consonants. Each basic consonant is actually a complete syllable: for example the sign क stands for not just the consonant *k* but the whole syllable *ka*; it will sound similar to the first syllable of the word *cup*. The *a* vowel is always there unless replaced by some other vowel indicated by a special vowel sign. More on this later: for now, concentrate on copying and learning the consonants.

Write on lined paper, with the top line of the character falling on the printed line and the rest of the character hanging below.

ASPIRATION

In the descriptions of the Hindi sounds you'll see many references to 'aspiration' – the amount of breath that escapes from the mouth when a sound is spoken. In English, the initial *k* of *kick* is strongly aspirated, the closing '*ck*' much less so. In Hindi, such differences are represented by pairs of consonants such as क *ka* (unaspirated) and ख *kha* (aspirated). English consonants fall halfway between the two, so you'll have to make a special effort to cut back your aspiration for one and increase it for the other! All these things are best dealt with by listening to the audio and/or by asking a Hindi speaker to demonstrate them for you.

You'll find all the main characters of the script set out in the table that follows; then each character is set out separately with its handwritten equivalent and a note on pronunciation. The consonants are dealt with first (as is the tradition), although in dictionary order the vowels precede the consonants.

Devanagari: the basic characters

Independent vowel forms ('vowel characters')

अ *a*	आ *ā*	इ *i*	ई *ī*
उ *u*	ऊ *ū*	ऋ *ṛ*	
ए *e*	ऐ *ai*	ओ *o*	औ *au*

Consonants

क *ka*	ख *kha*	ग *ga*	घ *gha*	
च *ca*	छ *cha*	ज *ja*	झ *jha*	
ट *ta*	ठ *ha*	ड *ḍa*	ढ *ḍha*	ण *ṇa*
त *ta*	थ *tha*	द *da*	ध *dha*	न *na*
प *pa*	फ *pha*	ब *ba*	भ *bha*	म *ma*
य *ya*	र *ra*	ल *la*	व *va*	
श *śa*	ष *ṣa*	स *sa*	ह *ha*	

Dependent vowel forms ('vowel signs', based on क as an example)

क *ka*	का *kā*	कि *ki*	की *kī*
कु *ku*	कू *kū*	कृ *kṛ*	
के *ke*	कै *kai*	को *ko*	कौ *kau*

THE CONSONANTS

00.03

क	*ka*	As in *skin*; minimum aspiration.
क़	*qa*	Further back in the throat than undotted क (many speakers say *ka* for both).
ख	*kha*	Aspirated version of क *ka*.
ख़	*<u>kh</u>a*	Like the *ch* in Scottish *loch*.
ग	*ga*	As in *gift*.
ग़	*ga*	A more guttural version of the above.

घ	*gha*	Aspirated version of ग; like the *g h* in *doghouse*. A single sound.
च	*ca*	As in *cheap*, but with the tongue positioned as for the *ty* sound in *tube*.
छ	*cha*	Aspirated form of the above.
ज	*ja*	As in *jeep*.
ज़	*za*	As in *zip*.
झ	*jha*	Aspirated form of ज *ja*.

The next seven consonants are 'retroflex': the tongue curls back to the palate (front part of the roof of the mouth), making a hard sound.

ट	*ṭa*	As in *try*, but harder.
ठ	*ṭha*	Aspirated version of the above.
ड	*ḍa*	As in *dry*, but harder.
ड़	*ṛa*	The tongue flicks past (rather than resting on) the retroflex position.
ढ	*ḍha*	Aspirated version of ड *ḍa*.
ढ़	*ṛha*	Aspirated version of ड़ *ṛa*.
ण	*ṇa*	An *n* sound in the retroflex position.

The next five consonants are 'dental': the tongue touches the upper teeth, making a soft sound.

त	*ta*	As the first *t* in *at the*, very soft.
थ	*tha*	Aspirated version of the above.
द	*da*	As in *breadth*, very soft.
ध	*dha*	Aspirated version of the above.
न	*na*	As in *anthology*.

'SONI DENTAL CHAMBER: [FALSE-] TEETH AND SPECTACLE-MAKER'

Ironically, the English word *dental* is spelt with retroflex ड *ḍ* and ट *ṭ* in this signboard, whereas the Hindi word दाँत *dā̃t tooth* has two dentals!

Now we come to *labials*, consonants produced with the lips.

प	*pa*	Much less aspiration than in *pin*.
फ	*pha*	Aspirated version of the above.
ब	*ba*	As in *bun*.
भ	*bha*	Aspirated version of the above.
म	*ma*	As in *moon*.

Now for a sequence of four characters called semi-vowels:

य	*ya*	As in *yes*.
र	*ra*	As in *roll* – but lightly rolled!
ल	*la*	As in *lullaby*, but softer, more dental.
व	*va*	Neither a buzzy sound as in *visa* nor as rounded as in *we*, but halfway between.

We're nearly done. Here are three sibilants:

श	*śa*	As *sh* in *ship*; pronounced *s* in some regional accents.
ष	*ṣa*	Strictly speaking a 'cerebral' (in which the tongue touches a high point in the roof of the mouth); but usually pronounced *sh*, the same as the previous character, श *śa*. It occurs in loanwords from Sanskrit only.
स	*sa*	As in *sip*.

And finally an aspirate:

ह	*ha*	As in *help*.

You'll have noticed that some characters have 'dotted' versions: these are for sounds which go beyond the range of Sanskrit, the classical language for which the script was first devised. They are क़ *qa*, ख़ *kha*, ग़ *ga*, ज़ *za*, and फ़ *fa* (typically for words borrowed from Arabic and Persian) and ड़ *ṛa*, ढ़ *ṛha* (late developers in the long history of Indian languages). These characters are not distinguished in dictionary order from their undotted equivalents. The showing of dots in print is often rather haphazard – but not in this book!

Remember that each consonant contains an inherent *a* vowel as part of the deal. But it's important to notice that this 'inherent vowel' is not pronounced at the end of a word: thus the word for *all*, सब, reads *sab* (not *saba*), and the word for *simple*, सरल, reads *saral* (not *sarala*). Armed with this information you can now read and write these words:

00.04

कब	*kab*	*when?*	क़लम	*qalam*	*pen*
जब	*jab*	*when*	गरम	*garam*	*warm*
तब	*tab*	*then*	तरफ़	*taraf*	*direction*
पर	*par*	*but; on*	नमक	*namak*	*salt*
फल	*phal*	*fruit*	महल	*mahal*	*palace*
मन	*man*	*mind*	शहर	*śahar*	*town*
सब	*sab*	*all*	सड़क	*saṛak*	*street*
हम	*ham*	*we, us*	सरल	*saral*	*simple*

In the words महल *mahal* and शहर *śahar*, the ह *ha* has the effect of 'lightening' the adjacent vowels, making them sound more like the *e* in *mend* than the *u* in *mundane* (this will vary somewhat from speaker to speaker). Elsewhere, Hindi is remarkably free of such contextual changes: the Hindi script is a 'what you see is what you get' system.

THE VOWELS

Now we move on to look at vowels. Each vowel has two different forms: one is the 'vowel sign', used after a consonant; the other is the 'vowel character', used in other positions. First, vowel signs.

00.05

A vowel sign is used when a vowel follows a consonant. It's a small mark that is added to the consonant and it replaces the *a* sound that is otherwise present as the inherent vowel. The following examples show the vowel *e* added to the consonants क *ka*, ख *kha*, ग *ga*, and घ *gha*.

के *ke* खे *khe* गे *ge* घे *ghe*

Here now is the full range of such vowel signs, based on क

का	*kā*	A long vowel, as in *calm*.
कि	*ki*	A short vowel, as in *kip*.
की	*kī*	A long version of the above, as in *keep*.
कु	*ku*	Short, as in *put*.

कू	*kū*	A long version of the above, as in *food*.
कृ	*kṛ*	A very short *ri* sound, as in *thrill*. It only occurs in Sanskrit loanwords.
के	*ke*	

Like the French *é* in *été; not* a rounded sound as in English *payday*.

कै	*kai*	Similar to the vowel in *cap*, but flatter.
को	*ko*	A pure *o*, less rounded than in *cold*.
कौ	*kau*	Similar to the vowel in *hot*.

And here's some more reading and writing practice:

00.06

कान	*kān*	*ear*	पानी	*pānī*	*water*
कृपा	*kṛpā*	*kindness*	भारत	*bhārat*	*India*
खड़ा	*khaṛā*	*standing*	मकान	*makān*	*house*
चाय	*cāy*	*tea*	वाराणसी	*vārāṇasī*	*Varanasi*
तोता	*totā*	*parrot*	सितार	*sitār*	*sitar*
दुकान	*dukān*	*shop*	सौ	*sau*	*hundred*
दूर	*dūr*	*far*	है	*hai*	*is*

00.07

At this point you should practise writing out these vowel signs attached to all the consonants until they become really familiar.

These vowel signs can only be used when they have a consonant sign to cling to. In other positions, such as at the beginning of a word, the vowel is written with a vowel character. The first in the list is the 'inherent' vowel:

अ	*a*	अब	*ab*	*now*
आ	*ā*	आज	*āj*	*today*
इ	*i*	इधर	*idhar*	*over here*
ई	*ī*	ईरान	*īrān*	*Iran*
उ	*u*	उधर	*udhar*	*over there*
ऊ	*ū*	ऊपर	*ūpar*	*up*
ऋ	*ṛ*	ऋण	*ṛṇ*	*debt*
ए	*e*	एक	*ek*	*one*

ऐ	*ai*	ऐसा	*aisā*	*such*
ओ	*o*	ओर	*or*	*direction*
औ	*au*	और	*aur*	*and*

And here are three words in which vowel characters appear as the second of two sequential vowels (i.e. neither at the beginning of a word nor after a consonant):

कई	*kaī*	*several –*	ई	*ī*	follows the syllable	क	*ka.*
उबाऊ	*ubāū*	*boring –*	ऊ	*ū*	follows the syllable	बा	*bā.*
बनाओ	*banāo*	*make –*	ओ	*o*	follows the syllable	ना	*nā.*

CONJUNCT CHARACTERS

00.08

When two consonant sounds come together without an intervening vowel, we have to cancel or 'kill off' the inherent vowel of the first consonant. For example, in the word *Hindi* there is no *a* between the *n* and the *d*, so a shortened form of the first consonant, न, is physically joined to the second consonant, द, giving हिन्दी *hindī*.

क + य =	क्य	क्या	*kyā*	*what?*
च + च =	च्च	बच्चा	*baccā*	*child*
च + छ =	च्छ	अच्छा	*acchā*	*good*
ल + ल =	ल्ल	बिल्ली	*billī*	*cat*
स + त =	स्त	हिन्दुस्तानी	*hindustānī*	*Indian*

Conjuncts beginning with द *da* can be hard to recognize:

द + द =	द्द	रद्द	*radd*	*cancelled*
द + म =	द्म	पद्म	*padma*	*lotus*
द + य =	द्य	विद्या	*vidyā*	*knowledge*
द + व =	द्व	द्वार	*dvār*	*gateway*

When र is the first character of a compound it turns into a little curl (called रेफ *reph*) above the second character:

र + क़ =	र्क़	फ़र्क़	*farq*	*difference*
र + थ =	र्थ	अर्थ	*arth*	*meaning*
र + द =	र्द	दर्द	*dard*	*pain*

र	+	मा	=	र्मा	शर्मा	*śarmā*	Sharma
र	+	थी	=	र्थी	विद्यार्थी	*vidyārthī*	student

The reph comes at the very end of the syllable in words like शर्मा *śarmā* (where it's above the vowel sign ा) and विद्यार्थी *vidyārthī* (where it's above the vowel sign ी).

When र is the second character of a compound it turns into a little slanting line, tucked into a convenient nook of the first character:

ग	+	र	=	ग्र	सिग्रेट	*sigreṭ*	cigarette
द	+	र	=	द्र	द्रोही	*drohī*	hostile
प	+	र	=	प्र	प्रदेश	*pradeś*	state, region

See what happens when no nook is available:

ट	+	र	=	ट्र	ट्रेन	*ṭren*	train
ड	+	र	=	ड्र	ड्रामा	*ḍrāmā*	drama

Some conjuncts stack vertically:

ट	+	ट	=	ट्ट	छुट्टी	*chuṭṭī*	holiday
ट	+	ठ	=	ट्ठ	चिट्ठी	*ciṭṭhī*	letter

Most conjuncts are easy to read, but there are some in which the conjunct has limited resemblance to its component parts, and these have to be learnt as new characters in their own right:

क	+	त	=	क्त	भक्ति	*bhakti*	devotion
क	+	ष	=	क्ष	रक्षा	*rakṣā*	protection
त	+	त	=	त्त	कुत्ता	*kuttā*	dog
त	+	र	=	त्र	मित्र	*mitr*	friend
द	+	भ	=	द्भ	अद्भुत	*adbhut*	wondrous
श	+	र	=	श्र	श्री	*śrī*	Mr
ह	+	म	=	ह्म	ब्रह्मा	*Brahmā*	Brahma (a deity)

The rare character ज्ञ *jña* is a conjunct of ज with ञ् *ña*, a nasal consonant (like the first *n* in *onion*) that is not shown in our table because it never occurs alone; ज्ञ *jña* is usually pronounced *gy*.

When pronouncing doubled consonants, just 'hold' the sound momentarily, as in distinguishing *night train* from *night rain*. Practise with कुत्ता *kuttā dog*, बिल्ली *billī cat*, बच्चा *baccā child*.

NASALS

00.09

A nasalized vowel is produced by diverting part of the breath through the nose: speak while pinching your nose to hear what it sounds like! Nasalization is marked with a sign called *candrabindu*, *moon-dot*:

हाँ	*hā̃*	*yes*
कहाँ	*kahā̃*	*where?*
यहाँ	*yahā̃*	*here*

If there's a vowel sign above the top line, there won't be room for the moon (*candra*), so the dot (*bindu*) is used alone:

नहीं	*nahī̃*	*no*
कहीं	*kahī̃*	*somewhere*
यहीं	*yahī̃*	*right here*

Nasalizing a vowel can change the meaning, as with है *hai is* and हैं *haĩ are*. Similarly, while यहीं *yahī̃* means *right here*, यही *yahī* means *this one, this very one* – a completely different word!

Our little dot has a second function also (here with a new name – *anusvār*); it can be used to indicate an *n* or *m* when such a letter is the first element of a conjunct:

अंडा	=	अण्डा	*aṇḍā*	*egg*
हिंदी	=	हिन्दी	*hindī*	*Hindi*
लंबा	=	लम्बा	*lambā*	*long, tall*

OTHER SIGNS

The word दुःख *duḥkh sorrow* includes the colon-like sign called *visarga*; this rare sign indicates a lightly pronounced *h* sound.

In situations where it's not possible or convenient to write or print a conjunct, an inherent vowel can be cancelled by hanging a little line called *virām* below it: चड्डी *caḍḍī underpants*.

The 'full stop' is a standing line, as seen from Unit 1 onwards. Most other punctuation follows English usage.

Here are the numerals from 0 to 9:

० १ २ ३ ४ ५ ६ ७ ८ ९

LOANWORDS FROM ENGLISH

When writing non-Indian words, transcribe the sounds, not the spelling; thus *cycle* (*bicycle*) is written साइकिल *sāikil*. English *t* and *d* usually become retroflex: doctor is डाक्टर *ḍākṭar*.

Sometimes a little 'moon' sign is used to designate the Hindi pronunciation of an English *o* like the first vowel in *chocolate* – चॉकलेट. It doesn't have a standard transliteration in the roman script, and the sound isn't really affected: most people say चाकलेट *cākleṭ*, with the standard long *ā* vowel.

SILENT 'INHERENT VOWELS'

The inherent vowel *a* is silent at the end of a word in Hindi – although not in Sanskrit, Hindi's classical ancestor. Thus the name राम is pronounced *Rām* in Hindi, *Rāma* in Sanskrit.

At the end of a word whose last syllable is a conjunct character, the inherent vowel is pronounced lightly in order to make the conjunct easier to say: अवश्य *avaśya certainly*, जन्म *janma birth*.

Sometimes an inherent vowel is silent in the middle of a word, even though the spelling involves no conjunct. Here is a general (if imperfect) pair of rules:

In a word of three or more syllables that ends with a vowel other than the inherent vowel, the penultimate inherent vowel is not pronounced. Thus समझ *samajh*, but समझा *samjhā* (because it ends in long *ā*); रहन *rahan*, but रहना *rahnā* (likewise).

In a word that has three syllables in which the third is a long vowel and the second is the inherent vowel, the inherent vowel is not pronounced. Thus सोमवार *somvār* Monday, लिखता *likhtā* write, writing.

00.10

You will gradually get used to the script and sounds of Hindi, and the roman transliteration is always there for help. To practise linking sound with script, here is the Vocabulary builder from Unit 1. Practise reading along as you listen, and as you progress through the course, you can try writing down the new words you hear.

1 नमस्ते *namaste*

Greetings

In this unit you will learn how to:

- ***say who you are, greet people, and say goodbye.***
- ***ask questions about things and people.***

Language points

- *the verb* to be
- *basic sentence construction*
- *question formation*

Language discovery 1 *Introductions*

SAYING HELLO

The universal greeting in Hindi is the word नमस्ते *namaste*, which means both *hello*, *good morning*, etc. and also *goodbye*. It comes from India's classical language of Sanskrit, where it means *Salutation to you*. Although this literal meaning is now remote (like the *God be with you* that underlies the English *goodbye*), it is part of the elaborate code of respect that runs through the Hindi language.

To communicate well in Hindi, good clear pronunciation is as important as grammar and the word नमस्ते *namaste* gives an ideal chance to practise right from the start. Your tongue should touch your upper teeth as you say the *n* and the *t*; and in the last syllable, aim for the *é* of French *été* – the vowel is not the rounded *ay* sound heard in English *stay*.

In formal contexts the word नमस्ते *namaste* is accompanied by a gesture in which the palms are put together (although many people are more likely to offer a handshake these days). It's considered polite to say नमस्ते *namaste* to an older or senior person first, before he or she says it to you. Sometimes you will hear नमस्कार *namaskār* (in which the **s** may be pronounced **sh**); this means the same thing.

What are the two meanings of नमस्ते *namaste* in English?

INTRODUCING YOURSELF

01.01 Here we meet Raju and Geeta, a married couple from Agra; later we'll meet their children Manoj (boy, 16), Meena (girl, 10), and Ram (boy, 8), and their dog Moti (male, age unknown).

I am is मैं हूँ *maĩ hū̃*, and *I am not* is मैं नहीं हूँ *maĩ nahī̃ hū̃*. Notice how the verb हूँ *hū̃ am* comes at the end of the sentence.

मैं राजू हूँ ।	*maĩ Rājū hū̃.*	*I am Raju.*
मैं ठीक हूँ ।	*maĩ ṭhīk hū̃.*	*I am OK.*
मैं बीमार नहीं हूँ ।	*maĩ bīmār nahī̃ hū̃.*	*I am not ill.*
मैं गीता हूँ ।	*maĩ Gītā hū̃.*	*I am Geeta.*
मैं हिन्दुस्तानी हूँ ।	*maĩ hindustānī hū̃.*	*I am Indian.*
मैं अँग्रेज़ नहीं हूँ ।	*maĩ ãgrez nahī̃ hū̃.*	*I am not English.*

In this last sentence, मैं अँग्रेज़ नहीं हूँ, where does the negation go: before or after the verb?

MY AND MINE

01.02 The word मेरा *merā* means both *my* and *mine*; है *hai* means *is*.

मेरा नाम राजू है ।	*merā nām Rājū hai.*	*My name is Raju.*
मैं अध्यापक हूँ ।	*maĩ adhyāpak hū̃.*	*I'm a teacher.*
गीता डाक्टर है ।	*Gītā ḍākṭar hai.*	*Geeta is a doctor.*
सीता नर्स है ।	*Sītā nars hai.*	*Sita is a nurse.*

YES/NO QUESTIONS

01.03 A statement is turned into a question by simply adding the question word क्या *kyā* at the beginning of the sentence; क्या *kyā* isn't translatable here; it just turns what follows into a question. There's no change in the word order: just add क्या *kyā* to make a question.

क्या मैं अध्यापक हूँ ?	*kyā maĩ adhyāpak hū̃?*	*Am I a teacher?*
क्या गीता डाक्टर है ?	*kyā Gītā ḍākṭar hai?*	*Is Geeta a doctor?*
क्या सीता नर्स है ?	*kyā Sītā nars hai?*	*Is Sita a nurse?*

Because these questions can all be answered either जी हाँ *jī hā̃ yes* or जी नहीं *jī nahī̃ no*, we'll call them *yes/no* questions. Here are two more, with their answers:

क्या राजू ठीक है ?	*kyā Rājū ṭhīk hai?*	*Is Raju OK?*
जी हाँ, राजू ठीक है ।	*jī hā̃, Rājū ṭhīk hai.*	*Yes, Raju is OK.*
क्या गीता बीमार है ?	*kyā Gītā bīmār hai?*	*Is Geeta ill?*
जी नहीं, गीता बीमार नहीं है ।	*jī nahī̃, Gītā bīmār nahī̃ hai.*	*No, Geeta isn't ill.*

Can you turn this statement into a question? राम डाक्टर है । *Rām ḍākṭar hai.*

YOU

01.04 In order to begin real conversations, we need to add the word आप *āp you* and the verb हैं *haĩ are* – आप हैं *āp haĩ you are*. Notice the difference between है *hai is* and हैं *haĩ are*: the second is nasalized (a nasal sound is produced when some of the breath comes through the nose rather than through the mouth).

LEARNING TIP

Read aloud! You will find that you actually *learn* what you read – rather than simply *understanding* it – if you make it your own, proclaiming each sentence boldly to the world. Go for the Oscar!

Now we're really talking:

क्या आप गीता हैं ?	*kyā āp Gītā haĩ?*	*Are you Geeta?*
जी हाँ, मैं गीता हूँ ।	*jī hā̃, maĩ Gītā hū̃.*	*Yes, I am Geeta.*
क्या आप डाक्टर हैं ?	*kyā āp ḍākṭar haĩ?*	*Are you a doctor?*
जी हाँ, मैं डाक्टर हूँ ।	*jī hā̃, maĩ ḍākṭar hū̃.*	*Yes, I'm a doctor.*
क्या मैं बीमार हूँ ?	*kyā maĩ bīmār hū̃?*	*Am I ill?*
जी नहीं, आप बीमार नहीं हैं ।	*jī nahī̃, āp bīmār nahī̃ haĩ.*	*No, you're not ill.*
क्या मैं ठीक हूँ ?	*kyā maĩ ṭhīk hū̃?*	*Am I all right?*
जी हाँ, आप बिलकुल ठीक हैं !	*jī hā̃, āp bilkul ṭhīk haĩ!*	*Yes, you're quite all right!*

Start reading Devanagari: which of these two words is the plural form of *to be*: हैं *haĩ* or है *hai*?

SPEAKING

01.05 Practise these questions by speaking them out loud (and answering them) until you're completely at home with the format. Stay with this pattern until new words and phrases have been introduced.

क्या आप अँग्रेज़ हैं ?	*kyā āp ãgrez haĩ?*	*Are you English?*
क्या आप डाक्टर हैं ?	*kyā āp ḍākṭar haĩ?*	*Are you a doctor?*
क्या आप अध्यापक हैं ?	*kyā āp adhyāpak haĩ?*	*Are you a teacher?*
क्या आप विद्यार्थी हैं ?	*kyā āp vidyārthī haĩ?*	*Are you a student?*
क्या आप ठीक हैं ?	*kyā āp ṭhīk haĩ?*	*Are you OK?*
क्या आप बीमार हैं ?	*kyā āp bīmār haĩ?*	*Are you ill?*
क्या आप खुश हैं ?	*kyā āp khuś haĩ?*	*Are you happy?*
क्या आप नाराज़ हैं ?	*kyā āp nārāz haĩ?*	*Are you angry?*

You may have noticed that Hindi doesn't have a word for *a* (although sometimes the word एक *ek* – the number *one* – serves this purpose). There isn't a word for *the* either.

Language discovery 2 *Talking about others*

THIS AND *THAT*; *HE*, *SHE*, AND *IT*

01.06 So far we've seen the pronouns मैं *maĩ I*, and आप *āp you*. Now we move on to the two words that mean *this, that, he, she, it*.

यह *yah* (often pronounced *ye*) means *this* and वह *vah* (often pronounced *vo*) means *that*.

यह लड़का राम है ।	*yah laṛkā Rām hai.*	*This boy is Ram.*
यह लड़की मीना है ।	*yah laṛkī Mīnā hai.*	*This girl is Meena.*
वह लड़का नाराज़ है, लेकिन ...	*vah laṛkā nārāz hai, lekin ...*	*That boy is angry, but ...*
वह लड़की ख़ुश है ।	*vah laṛkī <u>kh</u>uś hai.*	*That girl is happy.*

यह *yah* and वह *vah* also mean *he, she, it*. If the person referred to is near at hand (*this person here*), use यह *yah*; otherwise, use वह *vah*. Only use यह *yah* when indicating quite specifically *this person/thing here*: when referring to *he, she, it* generally, वह *vah* is better.

राम ठीक नहीं है । वह बीमार है ।

Rām ṭhīk nahī̃ hai. vah bīmār hai. Ram isn't well. He's ill.

यह मोती है ।	*yah Motī hai.*
यह कुत्ता है ।	*yah kuttā hai.*
यह खुश है ।	*yah khuś hai.*
यह मेरा है ।	*yah merā hai.*

There's no *he/she* gender distinction in the Hindi pronoun. Later on you'll see that gender is distinguished by some verb endings.

In the plural, यह *yah* becomes ये *ye* (*these, they*), and वह *vah* becomes वे *ve* (*those, they*). And remember है *hai is* and हैं *haĩ are*.

यह आदमी अँग्रेज़ है ।	*yah ādmī ãgrez hai.*	This man's English.
ये लोग अँग्रेज़ हैं ।	*ye log ãgrez haĩ.*	These people are English.
वह आदमी अँग्रेज़ है ।	*vah ādmī ãgrez hai.*	That man's English.
वे लोग अँग्रेज़ हैं ।	*ve log ãgrez haĩ.*	Those people are English.

What is the plural of यह *yah* (this) and वह *vah* (that)?

WHAT? AND *WHO*?

01.07 We saw just now that क्या *kyā* turns a statement into a question, without changing the word order: आप ठीक हैं *āp ṭhīk haĩ You are OK* becomes क्या आप ठीक हैं ? *kyā āp ṭhīk haĩ? Are you OK?*

But in a second meaning, क्या *kyā* has the sense *what?* Similarly कौन *kaun* means *who?*

क्या	*kyā*	what?
यह क्या है ?	*yah kyā hai?*	What is this?
वह क्या है ?	*vah kyā hai?*	What is that?
कौन	*kaun*	who?
यह कौन है ?	*yah kaun hai?*	Who is this?
वह कौन है ?	*vah kaun hai?*	Who is that?

Notice how a reply copies the word order of the question, the answer word simply replacing the question word. In the following pair of sentences, कौन *kaun who?* is replaced by the answer मेरा दोस्त *merā dost my friend.*

वह कौन है ?	*vah kaun hai?*	Who is he?
वह मेरा दोस्त है ।	*vah merā dost hai.*	He is my friend.

Our conversation possibilities are growing rapidly:

आप कौन हैं ?	*āp kaun haĩ?*	*Who are you?*
मैं राजू हूँ ।	*maĩ Rājū hũ.*	*I am Raju.*
यह कौन है ?	*yah kaun hai?*	*Who is this?*
यह मीना है ।	*yah Mīnā hai.*	*This is Meena.*
वह क्या है ?	*vah kyā hai?*	*What is that?*
वह सितार है ।	*vah sitār hai.*	*That is a sitar.*
वह कौन है ?	*vah kaun hai?*	*Who is that?*
वह मनोज है ।	*vah Manoj hai.*	*That is Manoj.*
मनोज कौन है ?	*Manoj kaun hai?*	*Who is Manoj?*
मनोज मेरा भाई है ।	*Manoj merā bhāī hai.*	*Manoj is my brother.*

Using what you already know, how would you say in Hindi: *This is my sitar*, and *That is my dog*?

LANGUAGE TIP

Question words in English mostly begin with *wh*, as in *what?*, *who?*, *when?* etc. In Hindi the equivalent words begin with क् *k*, as in क्या *kyā what?*, कौन *kaun who?*, and – a little later in the book – कब *kab when?*, कहाँ *kahā̃ where?*, and क्यों *kyõ why?*.

Listen and understand

WHAT'S THIS?

01.08 Here's a chance for you to practise a very useful question-and-answer pattern – *What's this? It's a...*

यह क्या है ? *yah kyā hai?*
यह किताब है । *yah kitāb hai.*

यह क्या है ? *yah kyā hai?*
यह कलम है । *yah qalam hai.*

यह क्या है ? *yah kyā hai?*
यह रेडियो है । *yah reḍiyo hai.*

यह क्या है ? *yah kyā hai?*
यह कुरसी है । *yah kursī hai.*

यह क्या है ? *yah kyā hai?*
यह मेज़ है । *yah mez hai.*

यह क्या है ? *yah kyā hai?*
यह मकान है । *yah makān hai.*

यह क्या है ? *yah kyā hai?*
यह कुत्ता है । *yah kuttā hai.*

यह क्या है ? *yah kyā hai?*
यह बिल्ली है । *yah billī hai.*

Remember that when क्या *kyā* comes at the beginning of the sentence, it turns a following statement into a question.

01.09 **Answer the following questions. You'll find the answers in the Key to the activities at the back of the book.**

a क्या मोती बिल्ली है ? *kyā Motī billī hai?*
b क्या गीता डाक्टर है ? *kyā Gītā ḍākṭar hai?*

c क्या आप डाक्टर हैं ? *kyā āp ḍākṭar haĩ?*

d क्या राजू और गीता हिन्दुस्तानी हैं ? *kyā Rājū aur Gītā hindustānī haĩ?*

e क्या हिंदी आसान है ? *kyā hindī āsān hai?*

Make up more questions and answers of your own, using any everyday words from the glossary. How would you say in Hindi, *Are you sick? Is Neha happy? Is that girl a student?*

Storyline

RAJU MEETS HIS NEW NEIGHBOUR, JAVED

You'll see a new pronoun here: उसका *uskā* his, her/hers, its.

01.10 **Listen to the following conversation between Raju and Javed, and answer the questions.**

1 How does Javed introduce himself?

राजू	नमस्ते । मैं राजू हूँ । आप कौन हैं ?
जावेद	नमस्ते । मेरा नाम जावेद है ।
राजू	क्या आप ठीक हैं ?
जावेद	जी हाँ, शुक्रिया, मैं ठीक हूँ ।
राजू	वह लड़की कौन है ?
जावेद	उसका नाम बानो है ।
राजू	आपका पूरा नाम क्या है ?
जावेद	मेरा पूरा नाम जावेद ख़ाँ है ।
Rājū	*namaste. maĩ Rājū hū̃. āp kaun haĩ?*
Jāved	*namaste. merā nām Jāved hai.*
Rājū	*kyā āp ṭhīk haĩ?*
Jāved	*jī hā̃, śukriyā, maĩ ṭhīk hū̃.*
Rājū	*vah laṛkī kaun hai?*
Jāved	*uskā nām Bāno hai.*
Rājū	*āpkā pūrā nām kyā hai?*
Jāved	*merā pūrā nām Jāved Khā̃ hai.*

2 Listen to the conversation again and answer the following questions:

a Who is the girl Raju asks about?

b What is Javed's full name?

Practice

1 Translate:

Javed	What is this?
Manoj	This is my radio.
Javed	Who is that boy?
Manoj	He is my brother.
Javed	What's his name?
Manoj	His name is Ram.
Javed	Who is that girl?
Manoj	Her name is Meena.
Javed	Is she ill?
Manoj	No, she isn't ill. She's OK.

2 Answer the questions about the people described in the table. (New words: शादी–शुदा *śādī-śudā* married, दोनों *donõ* both.)

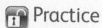

सुरेश खन्ना Suresh Khanna	उमा देवी Uma Devi	विनोद कुमार Vinod Kumar
student	teacher	doctor
Indian	Indian	American
not married	not married	married
not happy	happy	happy

a क्या सुरेश शादी-शुदा है ? *kyā Sureś śādī-śudā hai?*

b क्या वह हिन्दुस्तानी है ? *kyā vah hindustānī hai?*

c क्या वह अध्यापक है ? *kyā vah adhyāpak hai?*

d उसका पूरा नाम क्या है ? *uskā pūrā nām kyā hai?*

e क्या उमा हिन्दुस्तानी है ? *kyā Umā hindustānī hai?*

f क्या वह डाक्टर है ? *kyā vah ḍākṭar hai?*

g क्या वह शादी-शुदा है ? *kyā vah śādī-śudā hai?*

h क्या वह सुखी है ? *kyā vah sukhī hai?*

i क्या विनोद अँग्रेज़ है ? *kyā Vinod ãgrez hai?*

j क्या वह अध्यापक है ? *kyā vah adhyāpak hai?*

k उसका पूरा नाम क्या है ? *uskā pūrā nām kyā hai?*

l क्या वह शादी-शुदा है ? *kyā vah śādī-śudā hai?*

m क्या विनोद और सुरेश दोनों हिन्दुस्तानी हैं ?
kyā Vinod aur Sureś donõ hindustānī haĩ?

n क्या उमा और विनोद दोनों शादी-शुदा हैं ?
kyā Umā aur Vinod donõ śādī-śudā haĩ?

o क्या सुरेश और उमा दोनों अध्यापक हैं ?
kyā Sureś aur Umā donõ adhyāpak haĩ?

3 01.11 **Listen to two short conversations. In the first one, try to catch the name of the doctor who is being talked about. In the second conversation, try to catch the first names of the doctor and his son.**

1 वह आदमी कौन है ? *vah ādmī kaun hai?*
वह मेरा डाक्टर है । *vah merā ḍākṭar hai.*
क्या वह डाक्टर शर्मा है ? *kyā vah ḍākṭar śarmā hai?*
जी नहीं, वह डाक्टर शर्मा नहीं है, वह डाक्टर वर्मा है । *jī nahī̃ vah ḍākṭar śarma nahī̃ hai, vah ḍākṭar Varmā hai.*

2 क्या आप डाक्टर वर्मा हैं ? *kyā āp ḍākṭar Varmā haĩ?*
जी हाँ, मैं वर्मा हूँ । *jī hā̃, maĩ Varmā hū̃.*
आपका पूरा नाम क्या है ? *āpkā pūrā nām kyā hai?*
मेरा पूरा नाम मोहनलाल वर्मा है । *merā pūrā nām Mohanlāl Varmā hai.*
वह लड़का कौन है ? *vah laṛkā kaun hai?*
वह मेरा बेटा है । *vah merā beṭā hai.*
उसका नाम क्या है ? *uskā nām kyā hai?*
उसका नाम मुन्ना है । *uskā nām Munnā hai.*

Vocabulary builder

00.10 **You heard these words once before, in the Pronunciation section at the beginning of the book. Listen to them again, then try to imitate the native speaker.**

अँग्रेज़	*ãgrez* m., f.	*English person*
अध्यापक	*adhyāpak* m.	*teacher*
अमरीकन	*amrīkan*	*American*
आदमी	*ādmī* m.	*man*
आप	*āp*	*you*
आपका	*āpkā*	*your, yours*
आसान	*āsān*	*easy*
इसका	*iskā*	*his, her/hers, its*
उसका	*uskā*	*his, her/hers, its*
एक	*ek*	*a; one*
और	*aur*	*and*
औरत	*aurat* f.	*woman*
क़लम	*qalam* m./f.	*pen*
किताब	*kitāb* f.	*book*
कुत्ता	*kuttā* m.	*dog*
कुरसी	*kursī* f.	*chair*
कौन	*kaun*	*who?*
क्या	*kyā*	*what?; and question marker*
खुश	*khuś*	*pleased, happy*
जी नहीं	*jī nahī̃*	*no*
जी हाँ	*jī hā̃*	*yes*
ठीक	*ṭhīk*	*OK, all right*
डाक्टर	*ḍākṭar* m.	*doctor*
दोनों	*donõ*	*both*
दोस्त	*dost* m., f.	*friend*
नमस्कार	*namaskār*	*hello, goodbye*
नमस्ते	*namaste*	*hello, goodbye*
नर्स	*nars* m., f.	*nurse*

नहीं	*nahī̃*	*not, no*
नाम	*nām* m.	*name*
नाराज़	*nārāz*	*angry, displeased*
पूरा	*pūrā*	*full, complete*
बिलकुल	*bilkul*	*quite, completely*
बिल्ली	*billī* f.	*cat*
बीमार	*bīmār*	*ill, sick*
बेटा	*beṭā* m.	*son*
भाई	*bhāī* m.	*brother*
मकान	*makān* m.	*house*
मेज़	*mez* f.	*table*
मेरा	*merā*	*my, mine*
मैं	*maĩ*	*I*
यह	*yah*	*he, she, it, this*
ये	*ye*	*they, these*
रेडियो	*reḍiyo* m.	*radio*
लड़का	*laṛkā* m.	*boy*
लड़की	*laṛkī* f.	*girl*
लेकिन	*lekin*	*but*
लोग	*log* m. pl.	*people*
वह	*vah*	*he, she, it, that*
विद्यार्थी	*vidyārthī* m.	*student*
वे	*ve*	*they, those*
शादी-शुदा	*śādī-śudā*	*married*
शुक्रिया	*śukriyā*	*thank you*
सुखी	*sukhī*	*happy*
सितार	*sitār* m.	*sitar*
हाँ	*hā̃*	*yes*
हिन्दी	*hindī* f.	*Hindi*
हिन्दुस्तानी	*hindustānī*	*Indian*
हूँ	*hū̃*	*am*
हैं	*haĩ*	*are*
है	*hai*	*is*

Test yourself

1 How do we say both *hello* and *goodbye* in Hindi?
2 Where does the verb come in a typical Hindi sentence?
3 How would you say *Suresh is OK but his friend is sick*?
4 How is a statement turned into a *yes/no* question?
5 How would you say *My name is X*, using your own name?
6 What *two* main pronunciation points should an English speaker remember when saying नमस्ते *namaste*?
7 What is the difference between यह *yah* and वह *vah* (both of which mean *he/she/it*)?
8 What are the meanings and genders of the words किताब *kitāb*, मकान *makān*, and मेज़ *mez*?
9 If उसका नाम क्या है ? *uskā nām kyā hai?* means *What is his name?*, how do we ask *What is her name?*
10 What are the words for *yes* and *no*?

SELF CHECK

	I CAN...
○	... say who I am, greet people and say goodbye.
○	... ask questions about things and people.

2 हमारा परिवार

hamārā parivār

Our family

In this unit you will learn how to:

- ***use masculine and feminine forms.***
- ***use formal and informal ways of speaking to people.***

Language points

- *agreement of number and gender*
- *cardinal and ordinal numbers*

Language discovery 1

GENDER MATTERS

02.01 We saw earlier that लड़का *laṛkā* means *boy* and लड़की *laṛkī* means *girl*. This contrast between *-ā* in the masculine and *-ī* in the feminine appears in many nouns, adjectives, etc. – in fact it's a characteristic feature of Hindi. See how both adjective and noun change in the following:

मनोज बड़ा लड़का है ।	*Manoj baṛā laṛkā hai.*	*Manoj is a big boy.*
मीना बड़ी लड़की है ।	*Mīnā baṛī laṛkī hai.*	*Meena is a big girl.*

Masculine बड़ा *baṛā* becomes feminine बड़ी *baṛī*. Watch again:

मनोज लंबा और पतला है ।	*Manoj lambā aur patlā hai.*	*Manoj is tall and thin.*
मीना लंबी और पतली है ।	*Mīnā lambī aur patlī hai.*	*Meena is tall and thin.*
राम छोटा है ।	*Rām choṭā hai.*	*Ram is little.*
क्या राम अच्छा लड़का है ?	*kyā Rām acchā laṛkā hai?*	*Is Ram a good boy?*
मोती मोटा नहीं है ।	*Motī moṭā nahī̃ hai.*	*Moti isn't fat.*
क्या मनोज पतला है ?	*kyā Manoj patlā hai?*	*Is Manoj thin?*
क्या मीना लंबी है ?	*kyā Mīnā lambī hai?*	*Is Meena tall?*

02.02 Similarly, मेरा *merā my, mine* becomes मेरी *merī* when describing a feminine noun:

यह लड़का मेरा छोटा भाई है ।
yah laṛkā merā choṭā bhāī hai.
This boy is my little brother.

यह लड़की मेरी छोटी बहिन है ।
yah laṛkī merī choṭī bahin hai.
This girl is my little sister.

मेरा बेटा ठीक है लेकिन मेरी बेटी बीमार है ।
merā beṭā ṭhīk hai lekin merī beṭī bīmār hai.
My son is well but my daughter is sick.

Say if the following words are masculine or feminine:

लड़का
बेटी
कुत्ता
बिल्ली
खिड़की

The speaker of these three sentences could be either male or female: the gender of मेरा/मेरी *merā/merī* depends on the thing or person possessed, *not* the possessor. It behaves just like any other adjective. Similarly आपका *āpkā* becomes आपकी *āpkī* in the feminine:

आपका बेटा काफ़ी लंबा है ।
āpkā beṭā kāfī lambā hai.
Your son is quite tall.

आपकी बेटी बहुत सुंदर है ।
āpkī beṭī bahut sundar hai.
Your daughter is very beautiful.

But be careful! Not all *-ī* words are feminine (आदमी *ādmī man* is masculine!), and not all *-ā* words are masculine (माता *mātā mother* is feminine!).

WRITING

Think of a neighbour and answer these questions about him or her:

A male neighbour	A female neighbour
क्या आपका पड़ोसी लंबा है ? *kyā āpkā paṛosī lambā hai?*	क्या आपकी पड़ोसिन लंबी है ? *kyā āpkī paṛosin lambī hai?*
क्या आपका पड़ोसी पतला है ? *kyā āpkā paṛosī patlā hai?*	क्या आपकी पड़ोसिन पतली है ? *kyā āpkī paṛosin patlī hai?*
क्या आपका पड़ोसी अँग्रेज़ है ? *kyā āpkā paṛosī ãgrez hai?*	क्या आपकी पड़ोसिन अँग्रेज़ है ? *kyā āpkī paṛosin ãgrez hai?*
क्या वह नाराज़ है ? *kyā vah nārāz hai?*	क्या वह नाराज़ है ? *kyā vah nārāz hai?*
क्या वह बीमार है ? *kyā vah bīmār hai?*	क्या वह बीमार है ? *kyā vah bīmār hai?*
क्या वह सुंदर है ? *kyā vah sundar hai?*	क्या वह सुंदर है ? *kyā vah sundar hai?*

ALL NOUNS HAVE A GENDER

You must learn the gender of every new noun you meet – it's not only animate beings that have gender. The words आशा *āśā hope*, अलमारी *almārī cupboard*, and तस्वीर *tasvīr picture* are all feminine, while कमरा *kamrā room*, मकान *makān house*, and आदमी *ādmī man* are all masculine. Try learning nouns with an appropriate adjective:

बड़ा कमरा, बड़ा आदमी	*baṛā kamrā, baṛā ādmī*	big room, big man
बड़ी तस्वीर, बड़ी किताब	*baṛī tasvīr, baṛī kitāb*	big picture, big book
बड़ा कुत्ता, छोटी बिल्ली	*baṛā kuttā, choṭī billī*	big dog, small cat

How would you say in Hindi: *small daughter, big table, fat dog*?

SOME ADJECTIVES NEVER CHANGE

02.03 Only those adjectives that end in *-ā* in the masculine change to *-ī* in the feminine. Other adjectives never change and so are called *invariable;* ठीक *ṭhīk OK* is a good example.

यह किताब ठीक है ।	*yah kitāb ṭhīk hai.*	*This book is OK.*
यह कमरा ठीक है ।	*yah kamrā ṭhīk hai.*	*This room is OK.*
मनोज ठीक है ।	*Manoj ṭhīk hai.*	*Manoj is OK.*

A few adjectives ending in *-ā* are invariable in spite of this ending. Examples are ज़िन्दा *zindā alive* and शादी-शुदा *śādī-śudā married.* A few adjectives ending in *-ī,* such as ख़ाली *khālī vacant, empty, free,* are also invariable.

क्या बिल्ली ज़िन्दा है ?	*kyā billī zindā hai?*	*Is the cat alive?*
गीता शादी-शुदा है ।	*Gītā śādī-śudā hai.*	*Geeta is married.*
यह कमरा ख़ाली है ।	*yah kamrā khālī hai.*	*This room is free.*

SPEAKING

02.04 In this role play, your name is Geeta Sharma and you are married to Raju Sharma; you have a brother, Rakesh, and a sister, Sita – she's unwell, but everyone else is OK. Answer these questions:

a क्या आप गीता हैं ? *kyā āp Gītā haĩ?*
b आपका पूरा नाम क्या है ? *āpkā pūrā nām kyā hai?*
c क्या आप शादी-शुदा हैं ? *kyā āp śādī-śudā haĩ?*
d राकेश कौन है ? *Rākeś kaun hai?*
e सीता कौन है ? *Sītā kaun hai?*
f क्या आपकी बहिन ठीक है ? *kyā āpkī bahin ṭhīk hai?*
g क्या आपका भाई बीमार है ? *kyā āpkā bhāī bīmār hai?*
h क्या आप बीमार हैं ? *kyā āp bīmār haĩ?*

Language discovery 2

NUMBER

English usually makes nouns singular plural by adding an *s*, as in *one book, two books.* In Hindi, it's a bit more complicated, because masculine and feminine nouns behave differently. We'll look at masculine nouns first.

Two types of masculine noun

Most masculine nouns ending in *-ā* in the singular change to *-e* in the plural. The same happens with most adjectives ending in *-ā*.

बड़ा कमरा	*baṛā kamrā*	*big room*
बड़े कमरे	*baṛe kamre*	*big rooms*

Other masculine nouns don't change at all in the plural – they behave like the English word *sheep*. In the following, although the noun आदमी *ādmī* doesn't change, its singular or plural (number) is revealed by the adjective changing from singular *-ā* to plural *-e*:

बड़ा आदमी	*baṛā ādmī*	*big man*
बड़े आदमी	*baṛe ādmī*	*big men*

You'll sometimes find that neither the adjective *nor* the noun is of the changing type. As with the numerically ambiguous English phrase *fat sheep*, you can only tell the number from the context:

आसान काम	*āsān kām*	*easy work/easy jobs*
साफ मकान	*sāf makān*	*clean house/clean houses*

A handful of nouns ending in *-ā* belong to this non-changing group: पिता *pitā father,* चाचा *cācā uncle,* राजा *rājā king,* नेता *netā leader, politician.*

मेरे पिता और चाचा दोनों नेता हैं।
mere pitā aur cācā donõ netā haĩ.
My father and uncle are both politicians.

Can you give the plural of these nouns? मकान *makān,* लड़का *laṛkā,* कमरा *kamrā,* पिता *pitā*

Two types of feminine noun

Feminine nouns ending in *-ī* (like लड़की *laṛkī girl*) or *-i* (शक्ति *śakti power*) change this ending to *-iyā̃* in the plural, but feminine adjectives stay the same in the plural:

छोटी लड़की	*choṭī laṛkī*	*little girl*
छोटी लड़कियाँ	*choṭī laṛkiyā̃*	*little girls*

Other feminine nouns are made plural by adding -एँ *-ẽ*.

एक मेज़	*ek mez*	*one table*
दो मेज़ें	*do mezẽ*	*two tables*
एक औरत	*ek aurat*	*one woman*

तीन औरतें	*tīn auratẽ*	*three women*
एक मोटी महिला	*ek moṭī mahilā*	*one fat lady*
चार मोटी महिलाएँ	*cār moṭī mahilāẽ*	*four fat ladies*
मेरी बड़ी बहिन	*merī baṛī bahin*	*my big sister*
मेरी बड़ी बहिनें	*merī baṛī bahinẽ*	*my big sisters*

Are these words in the singular or plural form?

किताबें *kitābẽ* कुर्सियाँ *kursiyā̃* बिल्ली *billī*

An adjective that refers to mixed genders is masculine, as in लंबे *lambe*:

मनोज और मीना दोनों लंबे हैं ।
Manoj aur Mīnā donõ lambe haĩ.
Manoj and Meena are both tall.

(Manoj is male, Meena female: the adjective लंबे *lambe* is masculine plural.)

Practice 1

1 Complete the sentences with the appropriate word(s).

क्या	*kyā*	बहुत पतला है	*bahut patlā hai*				
कौन	*kaun*	वे लड़के	*ve laṛke*			लंबी	*lambī*

a ये औरतें बहुत __________ हैं ।
ye auratẽ bahut __________ *haĩ.* These women are very tall.

b __________ बहुत मोटे हैं ।
__________ *bahut moṭe haĩ.* Those boys are very fat.

c आपका दोस्त __________ ।
āpkā dost __________ Your friend is very thin.

d सीता __________ है ?
Sītā __________ *hai?* Who is Sita?

e __________ मोती ठीक है ?
__________ *Motī ṭhīk hai?* Is Moti OK?

02.05 Making nouns plural is an essential skill: practise singular/plural contrasts out loud, pronouncing every word as clearly as you can, and you'll feel the music of the language as you learn it.

एक आदमी	*ek ādmī*	*one man*
दो आदमी	*do ādmī*	*two men*

एक लड़का	*ek laṛkā*	*one boy*
दो लड़के	*do laṛke*	*two boys*
एक लड़की	*ek laṛkī*	*one girl*
दो लड़कियाँ	*do laṛkiyā̃*	*two girls*
एक मेज़	*ek mez*	*one table*
दो मेज़ें	*do mezẽ*	*two tables*

Do this with a variety of different nouns and you'll soon get the hang of it – a certain amount of parrot-like repetition is essential when learning a new language! Throw in an adjective too:

एक बड़ा आदमी	*ek baṛā ādmī*	*one big man*
दस बड़े आदमी	*das baṛe ādmī*	*ten big men*, etc.

Being able to pluralize nouns correctly is an essential skill for a language learner. We see here that different groups of nouns in Hindi form their plurals in different ways – just as English does with its *ship* > *ships*, *sheep* > *sheep*, *child* > *children*, *baby* > *babies*, etc.

Language discovery 3

SOME NUMBERS

02.06 Talking of numbers – you should learn to count! Learn the numbers from 1 to 20 in groups of five as they're set out here. (You'll find a full list of numbers in Unit 12. Hindi uses both the Arabic set of numerals (1, 2, 3, etc.) and the Devanagari set (१, २, ३, etc.).

१	*1*	एक	*ek*	११	*11*	ग्यारह	*gyārah*
२	*2*	दो	*do*	१२	*12*	बारह	*bārah*
३	*3*	तीन	*tīn*	१३	*13*	तेरह	*terah*
४	*4*	चार	*cār*	___	*14*	चौदह	*caudah*
५	*5*	पाँच	*pā̃c*	१५	*15*	पंद्रह	*pandrah*
६	*6*	छह	*chah*	१६	*16*	सोलह	*solah*
७	*7*	सात	*sāt*	१७	*17*	सत्रह	*satrah*
८	*8*	आठ	*āṭh*	___	*18*	अठारह	*aṭhārah*
९	*9*	नौ	*nau*	१९	*19*	उन्नीस	*unnīs*
१०	*10*	दस	*das*	२०	*20*	बीस	*bīs*

Devanagari numbers follow a predictable pattern. Can you place these numerals in the table: १४ and १८?

ORDINAL NUMBERS: FIRST, SECOND, THIRD

02.07 Ordinal numbers are made by adding *-vã̃* to the cardinal number, as in पाँचवाँ *pā̃cvā̃* *fifth*; but *first, second, third, fourth, sixth* and *ninth* are irregular:

पहला	*pahlā*	*first*	छठा	*chaṭhā*	*sixth*
दूसरा	*dūsrā*	*second, other*	सातवाँ	*sātvā̃*	*seventh*
तीसरा	*tīsrā*	*third*	आठवाँ	*āṭhvā̃*	*eighth*
चौथा	*cauthā*	*fourth*	नवाँ	*navā̃*	*ninth*
पाँचवाँ	*pā̃cvā̃*	*fifth*	दसवाँ	*dasvā̃*	*tenth*

The ordinal numbers agree as adjectives: दसवाँ कमरा *dasvā̃ kamrā* *tenth room*, दसवीं तस्वीर *dasvī̃ tasvīr* *tenth picture*.

How would you say in Hindi: *first neighbour* (m), *third daughter*? If मंज़िल *manzil* is the word for *floor*, how would you say *tenth floor*?

Practice 2

1 Bingo – if you have people you can practise with, have a game of bingo: everyone selects ten numbers of their choice (between 1 and 20) as shown, then the caller calls out random numbers in Hindi between 1 and 20 until the winner declares a victory. No cheating!

2 02.08 Numbers quiz: Listen to the numbers and give the corresponding ordinal. For example, if you hear पाँच *pā̃c* *five*, say पाँचवाँ *pā̃cvā̃* *fifth*.

दस	*das*	उन्नीस	*unnīs*
बारह	*bārah*	बीस	*bīs*
पंद्रह	*pandrah*		

3 02.09 Numbers quiz: Answer the questions about these five fine fellows:

गणेश **Ganesh**

सुरेश **Suresh**

महेश **Mahesh**

दिनेश **Dinesh**

राजेश **Rajesh**

a क्या पहला लड़का मोटा है ? *kyā pahlā laṛkā moṭā hai?*

b पहला लड़का कौन है ? *pahlā laṛkā kaun hai?*

c क्या तीसरा लड़का ख़ुश है ? *kyā tīsrā laṛkā <u>kh</u>uś hai?*

d पाँचवाँ लड़का कौन है ? *pā̃cvā̃ laṛkā kaun hai?*

e क्या चौथा लड़का पतला है ? *kyā cauthā laṛkā patlā hai?*

f चौथा लड़का कौन है ? *cauthā laṛkā kaun hai?*

g क्या दूसरा लड़का महेश है ? *kyā dūsrā laṛkā Maheś hai?*

Language discovery 4

GETTING FAMILIAR

We've already seen that आप *āp* means *you* and आप हैं *āp haĩ* means *you are*. But in an informal context (talking to a friend, or with someone perceived by the speaker to be in some way close or socially 'junior'), the pronoun तुम *tum you* is used instead. तुम *tum* has its own verb form: तुम हो *tum ho you are*.

तुम कौन हो ?	*tum kaun ho?*	*Who are you?*
क्या तुम राम हो ?	*kyā tum Rām ho?*	*Are you Ram?*

When addressing someone as तुम *tum*, the word for *your* is तुम्हारा *tumhārā*. Remember that such words must agree with the person or thing 'possessed'.

तुम्हारा भाई	*tumhārā bhāī*	*our brother*
तुम्हारी बहिन	*tumhārī bahin*	*your sister*

The important point here is that तुम *tum* is much more familiar and informal than आप *āp*. Used in the wrong context, तुम *tum* and तुम्हारा *tumhārā* could sound presumptuous or offensive, so you have to tread carefully here.

LANGUAGE TIP

Use the आप *āp* form when addressing anybody except close friends or relatives. It's better to sound overly formal than too familiar. And listen out for how others choose between आप *āp* and तुम *tum* when talking to *you*.

Even greater familiarity is shown by yet another pronoun, तू *tū you*, whose verb is है *hai* (the same as for यह *yah* and वह *vah*): तू है *tū hai you are*. This is very intimate and is restricted to the closest of relationships, such as with partners, small children – and God.

राजू, तू मेरी जान है !	*Rājū, tū merī jān hai!*	*Raju, you are my darling!*
गीता, तू मेरी जान है !	*Gītā, tū merī jān hai!*	*Geeta, you are my darling!*

We won't be seeing much of तू *tū* in this book. Its intimacy restricts its usage; and if you know a Hindi speaker well enough to use it, he or she will happily teach you all you need to know! Used in the wrong context, it can be insultingly blunt. All its verb forms (except the commands – see 4.1) are the same as for यह *yah* and वह *vah*.

Here then is the full range of 'you' words, with their verbs:

आप हैं	*āp haĩ*	*you are* (formal and polite)
तुम हो	*tum ho*	*you are* (familiar and casual)
तू है	*tū hai*	*you are* (intimate or blunt)

So which pronoun would you use to speak to your mum? How about a friend's younger sibling? A shop assistant? A sweetheart?

Grammatically, तू *tū* is singular, and both आप *āp* and तुम *tum* are plural – whether addressing one person or more than one.

02.10 **Now here is a newcomer whom you haven't met yet. Listen out for this information: what's his name, what does he do, and where does he live?**

नमस्ते । मेरा नाम प्रताप है । मैं विद्यार्थी हूँ । मैं आपका पड़ोसी हूँ ।

namaste. merā nām Pratāp hai. maĩ vidyārthī hũ. maĩ āpkā paṛosī hũ.

HOW ARE YOU?

02.11 This is a good moment to introduce another new word, the very important कैसा *kaisā how?*, as in *how are you?*. (Later we'll see that it can also mean *what kind of?*.)

राजू, आप कैसे हैं ?	*Rājū, āp kaise haĩ?*	*Raju, how are you?*
गीता, आप कैसी हैं ?	*Gītā, āp kaisī haĩ?*	*Geeta, how are you?*
आपका भाई कैसा है ?	*āpkā bhāī kaisā hai?*	*How is your brother?*
आपकी बहिन कैसी है ?	*āpkī bahin kaisī hai?*	*How is your sister?*
आपके माता-पिता कैसे हैं ?	*āpke mātā-pitā kaise haĩ?*	*How are your parents?*
राम, तुम कैसे हो ?	*Rām, tum kaise ho?*	*Ram, how are you?*
मीना, तुम कैसी हो ?	*Mīnā, tum kaisī ho?*	*Meena, how are you?*

Language discovery 5

GETTING FORMAL

As we have seen in the आप-तुम-तू *āp-tum-tū* distinction, Hindi has a hierarchy of formality: calling someone आप *āp* shows respect and sets them 'above' people referred to as तुम *tum*, who, in turn, have higher status than those addressed as तू *tū*.

You may be familiar with similar systems in languages such as French, with its distinction between *vous* and *tu* in the second person (*you*). But in Hindi, the system extends to the third person: *he/she* can be expressed with the plural pronouns ये *ye* and वे *ve* instead of यह *yah* and वह *vah*. In effect, it's like referring to an individual person as *they* rather than as *he* or *she*. The bad news is that verbs and adjectives must be plural to match!

As there's no difference between this 'honorific' plural and a numerical plural, some statements could be ambiguous:

वे अच्छे आदमी हैं।	*ve acche ādmī haĩ.*	*He is a good man./They are good men.*
मेरे भाई लंबे हैं।	*mere bhāī lambe haĩ.*	*My brother is tall./My brothers are tall.*

But this ambiguity only occurs in the masculine. In the feminine, only *numerically* plural nouns show plural forms. Compare the following:

ये लंबी महिला कौन हैं ? *ye lambī mahilā kaun haĩ?* Who is this tall lady?

(Here the pronoun ये *ye* and verb हैं *haĩ* are honorific plural, but the noun महिला *mahilā* stays singular.)

ये लंबी महिलाएँ कौन हैं ?
ye lambī mahilāẽ kaun haĩ? Who are these tall ladies?

(Here ये *ye*, महिलाएँ *mahilāẽ*, and हैं *haĩ* are all plural.)

In each pair of sentences, decide which is more formal.

a	मेरा दोस्त मोटा है ।	*merā dost moṭā hai.*
	क्या आप राजू के भाई हैं ?	*kyā āp Rājū ke bhāī haĩ?*
b	मेरी बड़ी बहिन सुंदर हैं ।	*merī baṛī bahin sundar haĩ.*
	वह लंबी लड़की कौन है ?	*vah lambī laṛkī kaun hai?*

RAJU JI, GEETA JI

Respect can also be shown by adding जी *jī* to a name – written as one word or two (गीताजी *Gītājī*, or गीता जी *Gītā jī*). It's used with first names of both genders, or with surnames for males; also with titles and relationship terms (e.g. पिता जी *pitā jī* father). It's sometimes a bit like *Mr* or *Mrs*, but manages to combine respect and warmth more successfully than these rather stuffy English equivalents.

ये सीता जी हैं ।	*ye Sītā jī haĩ.*	This is Sita ji.
शर्मा जी अच्छे अध्यापक हैं ।	*Śarmā jī acche adhyāpak haĩ.*	Sharma ji is a good teacher.

Used alone, जी *jī* can be used as a polite way of addressing someone: नमस्ते जी ! *namaste jī!* English has no single equivalent.

How would you translate: हम राजू की बहनें हैं । ***ham Rājū kī bahinẽ haĩ*** वह बिल्ली हमारी है । ***vah billī hamārī hai?***

WE AND *OUR*

Finally: *we* and *us* is हम *ham*, and *our, ours* is हमारा *hamārā*.

हम आपके पड़ोसी हैं ।	*ham āpke paṛosī haĩ.*	We're your neighbours.
मोती हमारा कुत्ता है ।	*Motī hamārā kuttā hai.*	Moti is our dog.
मोती हमारा है ।	*Motī hamārā hai.*	Moti is ours.

Storyline

JAVED ASKS RAJU ABOUT HIS FAMILY

02.12 **Listen to the following conversation between Javed and Raju and answer the questions.**

1 What are the names of Raju's family members?

जावेद	राजू जी, मनोज कौन है ?
राजू	मनोज हमारा बड़ा बेटा है ।
जावेद	अच्छा । मीना और राम कौन हैं ?
राजू	मीना हमारी बेटी है और राम हमारा दूसरा बेटा है ।
जावेद	और गीता जी आपकी पत्नी हैं ?
राजू	जी हाँ, गीता मेरी पत्नी है ।
जावेद	क्या आपके भाई डाक्टर हैं ?
राजू	जी नहीं । वे अध्यापक हैं ।
जावेद	वे कैसे अध्यापक हैं ?
राजू	वे बहुत अच्छे अध्यापक हैं ।

Jāved	*Rājū jī, Manoj kaun hai?*
Rājū	*Manoj hamārā baṛā beṭā hai.*
Jāved	*acchā. Mīnā aur Rām kaun haĩ?*
Rājū	*Mīnā hamārī beṭī hai aur Rām hamārā dūsrā beṭā hai.*
Jāved	*aur Gītā jī āpkī patnī haĩ?*
Rājū	*jī hā̃, Gītā merī patnī hai.*
Jāved	*kyā āpke bhāī ḍākṭar haĩ?*
Rājū	*jī nahī̃. ve adhyāpak haĩ.*
Jāved	*ve kaise adhyāpak haĩ?*
Rājū	*ve bahut acche adhyāpak haĩ.*

2 Listen to the conversation again and answer these questions.

a How many sons does Raju have?

b Is Geeta Raju's wife?

c What does Raju's brother do?

Practice 3

1 02.13 Listen to Pratap talking and concentrate on understanding three things: Who is his friend? Who's his teacher? What's his teacher like?

मेरा नाम प्रताप है । क्या ? क्या मनोज मेरा भाई है ? जी नहीं । वह मेरा भाई नहीं है । मेरा दोस्त है । शर्मा जी मेरे अध्यापक हैं । वे बहुत अच्छे अध्यापक हैं । लेकिन... लेकिन... नहीं । वे बहुत अच्छे अध्यापक हैं ।

merā nām Pratāp hai. kyā ? kyā Manoj merā bhāī hai? jī nahī̃. vah merā bhāī nahī̃ hai. merā dost hai. Manoj acchā laṛkā hai. Śarmā jī mere adhyāpak haĩ. ve bahut acche adhyāpak haĩ. lekin...lekin...nahī̃. ve bahut acche adhyāpak haĩ.

2 Translate these sentences into Hindi.

(NB: *There are* is हैं *haĩ*; *only* is सिर्फ़ *sirf.*)

- **a** My name is Manoj. Raju and Geeta Sharma are my parents.
- **b** Meena is my little sister and Ram is my little brother.
- **c** Moti is our dog. He's very cute.
- **d** This is Meena. She is OK. She is little.
- **e** Our house isn't very big. There are only five rooms.
- **f** That boy is my friend; his name is Pratap (प्रताप *Pratāp*).
- **g** Javed Sahab is our neighbour. (Use honorific plural.)

3 Here are some sentences with singular subjects. Make them all numerically plural. (Make sure that all verbs, pronouns, and adjectives agree!)

a यह लड़का बहुत प्यारा है ।	*yah laṛkā bahut pyārā hai.*
b यह कुत्ता हमारा नहीं है ।	*yah kuttā hamārā nahī̃ hai.*
c वह लड़का कौन है ?	*vah laṛkā kaun hai?*
d यह आदमी कौन है ?	*yah ādmī kaun hai?*
e मेरा दोस्त पंजाबी है ।	*merā dost panjābī hai.*
f क्या यह कुत्ता आपका है ?	*kyā yah kuttā āpkā hai?*
g वह औरत कौन है ?	*vah aurat kaun hai?*
h हमारा बेटा अच्छा लड़का है ।	*hamārā beṭā acchā laṛkā hai.*
i मेरी बेटी बीमार है ।	*merī beṭī bīmār hai.*
j क्या यह किताब महँगी है ?	*kyā yah kitāb mahãgī hai?*
k यह मेज़ गंदी है ।	*yah mez gandī hai.*

4 Change the sentences from आप *āp* to तुम *tum,* or vice versa, making sure that all the verb agreements (तुम हो *tum ho,* आप हैं *āp haĩ,* etc.) work properly.

- **a** तुम कौन हो ?
  tum kaun ho?
- **b** तुम्हारा नाम क्या है ?
  tumhārā nām kyā hai?
- **c** तुम्हारे माता-पिता बहुत अच्छे लोग हैं ।
  tumhāre mātā-pitā bahut acche log haĩ.
- **d** तुम्हारा भाई सुंदर नहीं है ।
  tumhārā bhāī sundar nahī̃ hai.
- **e** तुम दोनों लड़के लंबे हो ।
  tum donõ laṛke lambe ho.
- **f** तुम कैसे हो ?
  tum kaise ho?
- **g** आपका नाम क्या है ?
  āpkā nām kyā hai?
- **h** क्या आप ठीक हैं ?
  kyā āp ṭhīk haĩ?
- **i** आप नाराज़ नहीं हैं ?
  āp nārāz nahī̃ haĩ?
- **j** आप कैसी हैं ?
  āp kaisī haĩ?

Finally, go through all the sentences in exercises 2–4, underlining the subject of the verb, and make sure you can understand why each verb is singular or plural.

Vocabulary builder

(NB: Cardinal numbers up to 10 (and ordinals up to *sixth*) are included here. Higher cardinal numbers are given in Unit 12.)

अच्छा	*acchā*	*good, nice*
अलमारी	*almārī* f.	*cupboard*
आठ	*āṭh*	*eight*
आशा	*āśā* f.	*hope*
औरत	*aurat* f.	*woman*
कमरा	*kamrā* m.	*room*
काफ़ी	*kāfī*	*quite, very; enough*
काम	*kām* m.	*work; job, task*
कैसा	*kaisā*	*how?*
ख़ाली	*khālī*	*empty, free, vacant*
गंदा	*gandā*	*dirty*
चाचा	*cācā* m.	*uncle* (father's younger brother)
चार	*cār*	*four*
चौथा	*cauthā*	*fourth*
छठा	*chaṭhā*	*sixth*
छह	*chah*	*six*
छोटा	*choṭā*	*small*
ज़रूर	*zarūr*	*of course*
जान	*jān* f.	*life, soul*
ज़िंदा	*zindā*	(invariable -*ā* ending) *alive*
जी	*jī*	word of respect used after names, etc. and as a short form of जी हाँ *jī hā̃* yes
तस्वीर	*tasvīr* f.	*picture*
तीन	*tīn*	*three*
तीसरा	*tīsrā*	*third*
तुम	*tum*	*you* (familiar)
तुम्हारा	*tumhārā*	*your, yours*
तू	*tū*	*you* (intimate)
दस	*das*	*ten*
दूसरा	*dūsrā*	*second; other*
दो	*do*	*two*
नेता	*netā* m.	*leader; politician*
नौ	*nau*	*nine*
पड़ोसी	*paṛosī* m.	*neighbour*
पड़ोसिन	*paṛosin* f.	*neighbour*

पतला	*patlā*	*thin*
पत्नी	*patnī* f.	*wife*
पहला	*pahlā*	*first*
पाँच	*pā̃c*	*five*
पाँचवाँ	*pā̃cvā̃*	*fifth*
पिता	*pitā* m.	*father*
प्यारा	*pyārā*	*dear, sweet, cute*
बड़ा	*baṛā*	*big*
बहिन	*bahin* f.	*sister*
बहुत	*bahut*	*very*
बेटी	*beṭī* f.	*daughter*
महँगा	*mahã̄gā*	*expensive*
महिला	*mahilā* f.	*lady*
माता	*mātā* f.	*mother*
माता-पिता	*mātā-pitā* m. pl.	*parents*
मोटा	*moṭā*	*fat*
राजा	*rājā* m.	*king, raja*
लंबा	*lambā*	*tall*
शक्ति	*śakti* f.	*power*
सात	*sāt*	*seven*
साफ़	*sāf*	*clean, clear*
साहब	*sāhab*	*sahib*
सिर्फ़	*sirf*	*only*
सुंदर	*sundar*	*beautiful, handsome*
हम	*ham*	*we, us*
हमारा	*hamārā*	*our, ours*
हो	*ho* (with तुम *tum*)	*are*

Test yourself

1 What word can be added to a personal name to indicate politeness and respect?

2 All Hindi nouns ending in *-ī* are feminine. True or false?

3 Convert the cardinal numbers दस *das ten* and बीस *bīs twenty* into ordinal numbers (*tenth, twentieth*).

4 All nouns change their form in the plural. True or false?

5 आप हैं *āp haĩ* means *you are*. Give the equivalent verb forms for तुम *tum* and for तू *tū*.

6 Give the Hindi for: *two girls, three boys, four pictures, five men.*

7 If यह मेरा कमरा है *yah merā kamrā hai* means *this is my room*, how do we say *this room is mine*?

8 वह पतली किताब मेरी है *vah patlī kitāb merī hai that thin book is mine.* What does this sentence tell us about the gender of the speaker?

9 Give four examples of invariable adjectives (those that don't change with gender).

10 Transcribe the following place names: वाराणसी, जयपुर, भोपाल, लंदन, शिकागो.

SELF CHECK

	I CAN...
○	... use masculine and feminine forms.
○	... use formal and informal ways of speaking to people.

3 कमरे में
kamre mẽ
In the room

In this unit you will learn how to:

- ***say where people and things are.***
- ***describe things.***
- ***talk about ownership.***

Language points

- *postpositions and case*
- *word order*

Language discovery 1 *Describing people and things*

HOW MUCH, HOW MANY? WHAT KIND OF ...? HOW IS IT?

03.01 You'll have noticed that question words in Hindi begin with a *k* – क्या *kyā*, कौन *kaun*, etc. A further selection of such words will give us much more to talk about. We've already met कैसा *kaisā*, used in asking *how* someone is; but it also means *what kind of...?* And कितना *kitnā* means *how much?*

कैसा मकान ?	*kaisā makān?*	*what kind of house?*
यह कैसा मकान है ?	*yah kaisā makān hai?*	*What kind of house is this?*
कितना पानी ?	*kitnā pānī?*	*how much water?*
कितना पानी है ?	*kitnā pānī hai?*	*How much water is there?*

Note that कैसा *kaisā* usually precedes the noun when it means *what kind of...?* कैसी किताब है ? *kaisī kitāb hai? What kind of book is it?*, and follows it when asking about how someone is or what something is like राम कैसा है ? *Rām kaisā hai? How is Ram?*, किताब कैसी है ? *kitāb kaisī hai? What's the book like?*

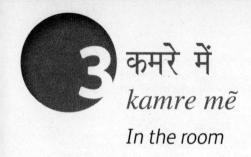

Both कैसा *kaisā* and कितना *kitnā* inflect (OK, change their endings!) like adjectives: कैसा-कैसे-कैसी *kaisā-kaise-kaisī*, कितना-कितने-कितनी *kitnā-kitne-kitnī*.

यह कैसा कमरा है ?	*yah kaisā kamrā hai?*	*What kind of room is this?*
यह कैसी किताब है ?	*ye kaisī kitāb hai?*	*What kind of book is this?*
ये कैसे कमरे हैं ?	*ye kaise kamre haĩ?*	*What kind of rooms are these?*
कितने कमरे हैं ?	*kitne kamre haĩ?*	*How many rooms are there?*
कितनी दुकानें हैं ?	*kitnī dukānẽ haĩ?*	*How many shops are there?*
कितना पैसा है ?	*kitnā paisā hai?*	*How much money is there?*
कितने लोग हैं ?	*kitne log haĩ?*	*How many people are there?*
कितना समय है ?	*kitnā samay hai?*	*How much time is there?*

Using what you know, how would you say in Hindi: *How many students are there?* and *What kind of house is it?*

WHAT'S THIS LIKE?

When कैसा *kaisā* comes *after* the noun, it means *what is X like?* Remember that it's also the usual way of asking about someone's health – such a commonly used expression that we'll look at some more examples:

यह कमरा कैसा है ?	*yah kamrā kaisā hai?*	*What's this room like?*
मनोज कैसा है ?	*Manoj kaisā hai?*	*How is Manoj?*
माता जी कैसी हैं ?	*mātā jī kaisī haĩ?*	*How is Mother?*
राम, तुम कैसे हो ?	*Rām, tum kaise ho?*	*Ram, how are you?*
शर्मा जी, आप कैसे हैं ?	*Śarmā jī, āp kaise haĩ?*	*Sharma ji, how are you?*
गीता जी, आप कैसी हैं ?	*Gītā jī, āp kaisī haĩ?*	*Geeta ji, how are you?*

SPEAKING

03.02 Answer the questions about the picture, using words from the list:

बूढ़ा	*būṛhā*	*elderly*
पुराना	*purānā*	*old* (of things)
कुल मिलाकर	*kul milākar*	*in total*
चूहा	*cūhā* m.	*mouse, rat*
तोता	*totā* m.	*parrot*

a कितने आदमी हैं ? *kitne ādmī haĩ?*

b यह कैसा आदमी है ? *yah kaisā ādmī hai?*

c मेज़ कैसी है ? *mez kaisī hai?*

d कितनी लड़कियाँ हैं ? *kitnī laṛkiyā̃ haĩ?*

e कुल मिलाकर कितने लोग हैं ? *kul milākar kitne log haĩ?*

f क्या दोनों लड़कियाँ लंबी हैं ? *kyā donõ laṛkiyā̃ lambī haĩ?*

g कितने चूहे हैं ? *kitne cūhe haĩ?*

h कितनी कुरसियाँ हैं ? *kitnī kursiyā̃ haĩ?*

i क्या चूहे बहुत बड़े हैं ? *kyā cūhe bahut baṛe haĩ?*

j कितने तोते हैं ? *kitne tote haĩ?*

LEARNING TIP

Take a short sentence, such as कितनी मेज़ें हैं ? *kitnī mezẽ haĩ? How many tables are there?* and practise it with many different nouns until it rolls off the tongue.

WHERE? ON THE TABLE

03.03 The word कहाँ *kahā̃* means ***where?*** In order to say ***where*** something is, we need the words for ***on, in,*** and so on. Here's a little list:

पर	*par*	*on, at*
में	*mẽ*	*in*
से	*se*	*from, with, by*
तक	*tak*	*up to, until*
को	*ko*	*to* (and other meanings)

And here are some phrases:

मेज़ पर	*mez par*	*on the table*
कुरसी पर	*kursī par*	*on the chair*
घर पर	*ghar par*	*at home*
घर में	*ghar mẽ*	*in the house*
दिल्ली में	*dillī mẽ*	*in Delhi*
भारत में	*bhārat mẽ*	*in India*
आज तक	*āj tak*	*until today*

As you can see, the words पर *par,* में *mẽ*, etc. come *after* the noun. Because of this they're called *post*positions rather than *pre*positions.

SPEAKING

03.04 Answer these questions, using the postposition में *mẽ in.*

a दिल्ली कहाँ है ? *dillī kahā̃ hai?*

b काठमांडु कहाँ है ? *kāṭhmāṇḍu kahā̃ hai?*

c कराची कहाँ है ? *karācī kahā̃ hai?*

d मुम्बई कहाँ है ? *mumbaī kahā̃ hai?*

e लंदन कहाँ है ? *landan kahā̃ hai?*

f आप कहाँ हैं ? *āp kahā̃ haĩ?*

Your answers should be दिल्ली भारत में है *dillī bhārat mẽ hai,* etc.; and my answer to the last one is मैं लंदन में हूँ *maĩ landan mẽ hū̃.*

Language discovery 2

AT HOME, AT SCHOOL, AT WORK

पर *par* usually means *on*, but it means *at* in phrases like घर पर *ghar par at home*.

> आज मनोज घर पर नहीं है ।
> *āj Manoj ghar par nahī̃ hai.*
> *Manoj isn't at home today.*
>
> राम स्कूल पर नहीं है ।
> *Rām skūl par nahī̃ hai.*
> *Ram isn't at school.*
>
> मेरे दोस्त काम पर हैं ।
> *mere dost kām par haĩ.*
> *My friends are at work.*
>
> शर्मा जी काम पर हैं ।
> *Śarmā jī kām par haĩ.*
> *Sharma ji is at work.*

WORD ORDER

Look very closely at the difference between these two sentences:

मेज़ पर पंखा है ।	*mez par pankhā hai.*	*There's a fan on the table.*
पंखा मेज़ पर है ।	*pankhā mez par hai.*	*The fan is on the table.*

You'll see that the main piece of new information comes *just before the verb*. Another way of looking at these sentences is to see them as the answers to particular questions, with the new information simply slotting into the space that had been occupied by the question word:

मेज़ पर क्या है ?	*mez par kyā hai?*	*What is on the table?*
मेज़ पर पंखा है ।	*mez par pankhā hai.*	*There's a fan on the table.*
पंखा कहाँ है ?	*pankhā kahā̃ hai?*	*Where is the fan?*
पंखा मेज़ पर है ।	*pankhā mez par hai.*	*The fan is on the table.*

If the answer is राम स्कूल पर है *Ram skūl par hai*, what would the question be?

SPEAKING

Answer the questions about the picture:

a	बिल्ली कहाँ है ?	*billī kahā̃ hai?*
b	कुत्ता कहाँ है ?	*kuttā kahā̃ hai?*
c	तस्वीर में कितनी कुरसियाँ हैं ?	*tasvīr mẽ kitnī kursiyā̃ haĩ?*
d	तस्वीर में कितनी बिल्लियाँ हैं ?	*tasvīr mẽ kitnī billiyā̃ haĩ?*
e	छोटी कुरसी पर क्या है ?	*choṭī kursī par kyā hai?*
f	बड़ी कुरसी पर क्या है ?	*baṛī kursī par kyā hai?*
g	मेज़ पर क्या है ?	*mez par kyā hai?*
h	क्या कुत्ता और बिल्ली प्यारे हैं ?	*kyā kuttā aur billī pyāre haĩ?*

Language discovery 3

DO YOU HAVE ...

03.05 One postposition that you'll often need is के पास *ke pās*. We'll meet it more fully later, but we need to know how it's used now. Its first meaning is *near*:

हमारी दुकान स्टेशन के पास है ।
hamārī dukān sṭeśan ke pās hai. Our shop is near the station.

But के पास *ke pās* can also indicate *ownership* of goods and chattels (or even time) – it's used in the meaning of *to have*:

मनोज के पास नया रेडियो है ।
Manoj ke pās nayā reḍiyo hai. Manoj has a new radio.

राम के पास कई नई किताबें हैं ।
Rām ke pās kaī naī kitābẽ haĩ. Ram has several new books.

मीना के पास कुछ नए कपड़े हैं ।
Mīnā ke pās kuch nae kapṛe haĩ. Meena has some new clothes.

राजू के पास कम्प्यूटर नहीं है ।
Rājū ke pās kampyūṭar nahī̃ hai. Raju doesn't have a computer.

पिताजी के पास समय नहीं है ।
pitājī ke pās samay nahī̃ hai. Father doesn't have time.

आपके पास कितना पैसा है ?
āpke pās kitnā paisā hai? How much money do you have?

When के पास *ke pās* is used with मेरे *mere,* तुम्हारे *tumhāre,* or हमारे *hamāre,* the के *ke* is dropped:

मेरे पास समय नहीं है ।	*mere pās samay nahī̃ hai.*	I don't have time.
तुम्हारे पास क्या है ?	*tumhāre pās kyā hai?*	What have you got?
हमारे पास कुछ नहीं है ।	*hamāre pās kuch nahī̃ hai.*	We have nothing.

Think about the two different meanings of के पास *ke pās* you just learned. What would be the meanings of these two sentences?

मेरे पास अस्पताल की तस्वीर है ।	*mere pās aspatāl kī tasvīr hai.*
अस्पताल मेरे घर के पास है ।	*aspatāl mere ghar ke pās hai.*

Although के पास *ke pās* is used widely for a variety of possessions, it's not usually used with relatives (*I have a son*, etc.); we'll come to a way of saying this in Unit 6.

SPEAKING

03.06 **Now the time has come to answer questions about yourself. Listen and speak in the pauses. You will then hear a sample answer.**

क्या आप के पास ...	*kyā āp ke pās ...*
a ... साइकिल है ?	*sāikil hai?*
b ... बहुत पैसे हैं ?	*bahut paise haĩ?*
c ... नया रेडियो है ?	*nayā reḍiyo hai?*
d ... नए हिन्दुस्तानी कपड़े हैं ?	*nae hindustānī kapṛe haĩ?*
e ... नई गाड़ी है ?	*naī gāṛī hai?*

CASE

In the English phrase *he speaks to him*, the two pronouns can't be exchanged: *him speaks to he* isn't impressive English! This is an example of a difference of *case* – a system that shows how words relate to each other in a sentence. Stand by for a really important piece of grammar here.

Hindi has two main cases – the *oblique*, always used before postpositions, and the *direct*, used elsewhere.

In the following sentences, the underlined words are postpositions, and the **bold** words are oblique, because they're followed by those postpositions.

हम लोग घर में हैं । *ham log **ghar** mẽ haĩ.*	*We (we people) are in the house.*
दिल्ली भारत में है । *dillī **bhārat** mẽ hai.*	*Delhi is in India.*
क्या आप लंदन से हैं ? *kyā āp **landan** se haĩ?*	*Are you from London?*
शर्माजी दुकान पर हैं । *Śarmājī **dukān** par haĩ.*	*Sharma ji is at the shop.*

In the first example, में *mẽ in* affects only घर *ghar house*, giving the sense *in the house* – it doesn't affect हम लोग *ham log we* because this is the subject and not part of the location. The same principle applies with the other examples.

Why say that these words are oblique, when they haven't changed their form at all? Because in the singular, only *some* nouns change in the oblique. Masculine *-ā* endings are the culprits here: they change to *-e*, as shown in the following list.

कमरा	*kamrā*	*room*
कमरे में	*kamre mẽ*	*in the room*
लड़का	*laṛkā*	*boy*
लड़के से	*laṛke se*	*by the boy*
आगरा	*āgrā*	*Agra*
आगरे तक	*āgre tak*	*as far as Agra*

Masculine -*ā* adjectives describing oblique nouns change similarly:

छोटा कमरा	*choṭā kamrā*	*small room*
छोटे कमरे में	*choṭe kamre mẽ*	*in a/the small room*
मोटा लड़का	*moṭā laṛkā*	*fat boy*
मोटे लड़के से	*moṭe laṛke se*	*by the fat boy*
मेरा बग़ीचा	*merā bag̱īcā*	*my garden*
मेरे बग़ीचे में	*mere bag̱īce mẽ*	*in my garden*

An -*ā* adjective changes like this with *all* types of masculine noun. So although घर *ghar house* does not end in -*ā* and therefore cannot change visibly in the oblique, -*ā* adjectives qualifying it must change all the same:

बड़े घर में	*baṛe ghar mẽ*	*in the big house*
छोटे मकान में	*choṭe makān mẽ*	*in the little house*

Feminine nouns and adjectives are easier to deal with – they don't change at all in the oblique singular:

छोटी मेज़ पर	*choṭī mez par*	*on the little table*
मेरी बहिन को	*merī bahin ko*	*to my sister*

PLURAL NOUNS IN THE OBLIQUE CASE

In the oblique plural, all nouns take the ending -*õ* as shown:

मेज़	*mez*	*table*
मेज़ों पर	*mezõ par*	*on tables*
कमरा	*kamrā*	*room*
कमरों में	*kamrõ mẽ*	*in rooms*
लड़का	*laṛkā*	*boy*
लड़कों को	*laṛkõ ko*	*to boys*
कुत्ता	*kuttā*	*dog*
कुत्तों को	*kuttõ ko*	*to dogs*

… and masculine -*ā* adjectives keep their *usual* oblique -*e* ending:

कमरा	*kamrā*	*room*
छोटे कमरों में	*choṭe kamrõ mẽ*	*in small rooms*
लड़का	*laṛkā*	*boy*
बड़े लड़कों को	*baṛe laṛkõ ko*	*to big boys*
हमारा कुत्ता	*hamārā kuttā*	*our dog*
हमारे कुत्तों को	*hamāre kuttõ ko*	*to our dogs*

Nouns of either gender that end in *-ī* change this to *-iy* before adding the *-õ* ending. So they end in *-iyõ*.

आदमी	*ādmī*	*man*
आदमियों से	*ādmiyõ se*	*from men*
लड़की	*laṛkī*	*girl*
लड़कियों से	*laṛkiyõ se*	*from girls*

Using what you've learned, how would you say the phrases *to the tall boys* and *on the big table*?

Well, after all that grammar you probably feel the need to sit or even lie down for a bit, so …

SITTING AND LYING

Sitting is बैठा *baiṭhā* and *standing* is खड़ा *khaṛā*; *lying* is पड़ा *paṛā* for an inanimate object (e.g. a book lying on the table), but लेटा *leṭā* for a person who is *lying down*. These words need to agree with their nouns, like adjectives:

मनोज कमरे में बैठा है ।
Manoj kamre mẽ baiṭhā hai. — *Manoj is sitting in the room.*

गीता बग़ीचे में खड़ी है ।
Gītā bag̱īce mẽ khaṛī hai. — *Geeta is standing in the garden.*

आपके कपड़े कुरसी पर पड़े हैं ।
āpke kapṛe kursī par paṛe haĩ. — *Your clothes are lying on the chair.*

दोनों लड़कियाँ फ़र्श पर लेटी हैं ।
donõ laṛkiyā̃ farś par leṭī haĩ. — *The two girls are lying on the floor.*

Reading

A Hindi-speaking friend has seen an advertisement in an English newspaper and needs your help in understanding it. Read the advertisement and then answer her questions.

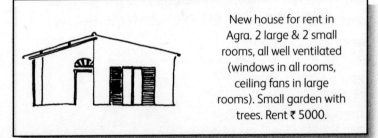

New house for rent in Agra. 2 large & 2 small rooms, all well ventilated (windows in all rooms, ceiling fans in large rooms). Small garden with trees. Rent ₹ 5000.

a घर कहाँ है ? *ghar kahā̃ hai?*

b क्या वह बहुत पुराना है ? *kyā vah bahut purānā hai?*

c कितने कमरे हैं ? *kitne kamre haĩ?*

d क्या सब कमरों में खिड़कियाँ हैं ? *kyā sab kamrõ mẽ khiṛkiyā̃ haĩ?*

e क्या पंखे भी हैं ? *kyā pankhe bhī haĩ?*

f बाहर क्या है ? *bāhar kyā hai?*

g किराया कितना है ? *kirāyā kitnā hai?*

LANGUAGE TIP

The house advertisement contains the rupee sign ₹. In Hindi, *rupee/rupees* is रुपया/रुपये *rupayā/rupaye*; 'thirty-five thousand' is पैंतीस हज़ार *paĩtīs hazār* – see p. 215.

Storyline

GEETA'S HOME

03.07 **Geeta is telling us about her husband and her home. As you listen, underline all the words in the oblique case in Geeta's statement.**

मेरा नाम गीता है – श्रीमती गीता शर्मा । मैं वाराणसी से हूँ । मेरे पति श्री राजकुमार शर्मा हैं । वे दिल्ली से हैं । राजू अध्यापक हैं । यह हमारा घर है । हमारा घर आगरे में है । घर में एक बड़ा कमरा और चार छोटे कमरे हैं । यह हमारा बड़ा कमरा है । कमरे में एक बड़ी मेज़ है । मेज़ पर मेरा कम्प्यूटर है । एक पंखा भी है । फ़र्श पर कुछ किताबें पड़ी हैं । बग़ीचे में दो-तीन लंबे पेड़ हैं ।

merā nām Gītā hai – śrīmatī Gītā Śarmā. maĩ vārāṇasī se hū̃. mere pati śrī Rājkumār Śarmā haĩ. ve dillī se haĩ. Rājū adhyāpak haĩ. yah hamārā ghar hai. hamārā ghar āgre mẽ hai. ghar mẽ ek baṛā kamrā aur cār choṭe kamre haĩ. yah hamārā baṛā kamrā hai. kamre mẽ ek baṛī mez hai. mez par merā kampyūṭar hai. ek pankhā bhī hai. farś par kuch kitābẽ paṛī haĩ. bagīce mẽ do-tīn lambe peṛ haĩ.

03.08 Now listen again, then answer these questions:

a	गीता कहाँ से है ?	*Gītā kahā̃ se hai?*
b	क्या गीता शादी-शुदा है ?	*kyā Gītā śādī-śudā hai?*
c	क्या राजू दिल्ली से है ?	*kyā Rājū dillī se hai?*
d	क्या राजू डाक्टर है ?	*kyā Rājū ḍākṭar hai?*
e	क्या यह घर दिल्ली में है ?	*kyā yah ghar dillī mẽ hai?*
f	घर में कितने कमरे हैं ?	*ghar mẽ kitne kamre haĩ?*
g	बड़े कमरे में क्या है ?	*baṛe kamre mẽ kyā hai?*
h	कम्प्यूटर कहाँ है ?	*kampyūṭar kahā̃ hai?*
i	किताबें कहाँ हैं ?	*kitābẽ kahā̃ haĩ?*
j	बग़ीचे में क्या है ?	*bag̱īce mẽ kyā hai?*

Go further

भी *bhī* : A WORD THAT HATES TO BE MISPLACED

The little word भी *bhī also, too* is simple enough in itself, but it's incredibly fussy about where it goes in the sentence – it insists on following the word it emphasizes. Look closely at the difference between these two statements, both of which could be translated as *this cloth is cheap too*, leaving the emphasis ambiguous in English:

यह कपड़ा भी सस्ता है ।
yah kapṛā bhī sastā hai.
This cloth too is cheap (i.e. as well as the other cloth we were just looking at).

यह कपड़ा सस्ता भी है ।
yah kapṛā sastā bhī hai.
This cloth is cheap too (i.e. in addition to its other advantages – colour, texture, and so on).

Storyline

AT SCHOOL

1 03.09 **Listen to the following conversation between Ram and his teacher. What is on Ram's chair?**

अध्यापक	राम, तुम्हारी किताबें कहाँ हैं ?
राम	जी, मेरी किताबें यहाँ मेज़ पर पड़ी हैं ।
अध्यापक	तुम्हारी कुरसी पर क्या पड़ा है ?
राम	जी, मेरी कुरसी पर मेरे क़लम हैं ।
अध्यापक	तुम्हारे हाथों में क्या है ?
राम	मेरे हाथों में कुछ नहीं है ।
अध्यापक	आज तुम्हारी बहिन मीना कहाँ है ?
राम	जी, वह घर पर है । वह बीमार है ।
adhyāpak	*Rām, tumhārī kitābẽ kahā̃ haĩ?*
Rām	*jī, merī kitābẽ yahā̃ mez par paṛī haĩ.*
adhyāpak	*tumhārī kursī par kyā paṛā hai?*
Rām	*jī, merī kursī par mere qalam haĩ.*
adhyāpak	*tumhāre hāthõ mẽ kyā hai?*
Rām	*mere hāthõ mẽ kuch nahī̃ hai.*
adhyāpak	*āj tumhārī bahin Mīnā kahā̃ hai?*
Rām	*jī, vah ghar par hai. vah bīmār hai.*

2 Listen again and answer these questions:

a What is Ram holding in his hands?

b Where is Ram's sister today? Why?

AT HOME

1 03.10 Raju asks Geeta where various people are at this moment. Where are Manoj and Ram?

राजू	गीता, मनोज कहाँ है ?
गीता	वह स्कूल पर है ।
राजू	और राम कहाँ है ?
गीता	वह भी स्कूल पर है ।
राजू	अच्छा ! और मीना ?
गीता	मीना बग़ीचे में बैठी है ।
राजू	मेरा भाई कहाँ है ?
गीता	मालूम नहीं !
Rājū	*Gītā, Manoj kahā̃ hai?*
Gītā	*vah skūl par hai.*
Rājū	*aur Rām kahā̃ hai?*
Gītā	*vah bhī skūl par hai.*
Rājū	*acchā! aur Mīnā?*
Gītā	*Mīnā bag̠īce mẽ baiṭhī hai.*
Rājū	*merā bhāī kahā̃ hai?*
Gītā	*mālūm nahī̃!*

2 Listen again and answer the following questions:

- **a** Who is in the garden?
- **b** Is Raju's brother in the garden, too?

Practice

1 Translate into Hindi:

- **a** My books are lying on the table.
- **b** Your brother is sitting in the garden.
- **c** I am standing in the big room.
- **d** Your books are in the little cupboard.
- **e** His house is not far from here.
- **f** How many people are there in your family?
- **g** How much money does your husband have?
- **h** How is your wife today? And how are you?
- **i** The children aren't at home, they're at school.
- **j** Is this little girl your sister?

2 **Role play. You are Geeta Sharma (a doctor, remember), at home in Agra with your husband and children; they're in the garden and your husband's indoors. Answer these questions for a local government survey. (Say *no* to item *i*, *yes* to *m* and *n*.)**

a आपका पूरा नाम क्या है ?
āpkā pūrā nām kyā hai?

b क्या आप डाक्टर हैं ?
kyā āp ḍākṭar haĩ?

c क्या आपके पति भी डाक्टर हैं ?
kyā āpke pati bhī ḍākṭar haĩ?

d क्या आपके पति घर पर हैं ?
kyā āpke pati ghar par haĩ?

e क्या आप लोग दिल्ली से हैं ?
kyā āp log dillī se haĩ?

f आपके मकान में कितने कमरे हैं ?
āpke makān mẽ kitne kamre haĩ?

g आपके परिवार में कितने बच्चे हैं ?
āpke parivār mẽ kitne bacce haĩ?

h क्या आपका छोटा लड़का आज स्कूल पर है ?
kyā āpkā choṭā laṛkā āj skūl par hai?

i क्या उसका स्कूल यहाँ से दूर है ?
kyā uskā skūl yahā̃ se dūr hai?

j आपके दूसरे बच्चे कहाँ हैं ?
āpke dūsre bacce kahā̃ haĩ?

k क्या वह कुत्ता भी आपका है ?
kyā vah kuttā bhī āpkā hai?

l बहुत प्यारा है ! उसका नाम क्या है ?
bahut pyārā hai! uskā nām kyā hai?

m क्या आपके पास गाड़ी है ?
kyā āpke pās gāṛī hai?

n क्या आपके पास कम्प्यूटर है ?
kyā āpke pās kampyūṭar hai?

धन्यवाद ! बहुत धन्यवाद !
dhanyavād! bahut dhanyavād!

Vocabulary builder

अस्पताल	*aspatāl* m.	*hospital*
आज	*āj*	*today*
आजकल	*ājkal*	*nowadays, these days*
कई	*kaī*	*several*
कपड़ा	*kaprā* m.	*cloth, garment*
कम्प्यूटर	*kampyūṭar* m.	*computer*
कराची	*karācī* f.	*Karachi*
काठमांडु	*kāṭhmāṇḍu* m.	*Kathmandu*
कहाँ	*kahā̃*	*where?*
कितना	*kitnā*	*how much/many?*
किराया	*kirāyā* m.	*rent; fare*
कुछ	*kuch*	*some; something*
कुछ और	*kuch aur*	*some more*
कुछ नहीं	*kuch nahī̃*	*nothing*
कुल मिलाकर	*kul milākar*	*in total, all together*
के पास	*ke pās*	*near; in the possession of*
को	*ko*	*to*
खड़ा	*kharā*	*standing*
खिड़की	*khiṛkī* f.	*window*
गाड़ी	*gāṛī* f.	*car; train; vehicle*
घर	*ghar* m.	*house, home*
चूहा	*cūhā* m.	*mouse, rat*
छुट्टी	*chuṭṭī* f.	*holiday; free time, time off*
तक	*tak*	*up to, until, as far as*
तोता	*totā* m.	*parrot*
दफ़्तर	*daftar* m.	*office*
दिल्ली	*dillī* f.	*Delhi*
दुकान	*dukān* f.	*shop*
दूर	*dūr*	*far, distant*
धन्यवाद	*dhanyavād*	*thank you*
नया	*nayā* (f. नई *naī;* m. pl. नए *nae*)	*new*
नेपाल	*nepāl* m.	*Nepal*
पंखा	*pankhā* m.	*fan*
पड़ा	*paṛā*	*lying*
पति	*pati* m.	*husband*
पर	*par*	*on (and at in at home, etc.)*

परिवार	*parivār* m.	*family*
पाकिस्तान	*pākistān* m.	*Pakistan*
पानी	*pānī* m.	*water*
पास	*pās*, पास में *pās mẽ*	*nearby*
पुराना	*purānā*	*old* (only for inanimates)
पेड़	*peṛ* m.	*tree*
पैसा	*paisā* m.	*money*
फ़र्श	*farś* m.f.	*floor*
फूल	*phūl* m.	*flower*
बग़ीचा	*bag̱īcā* m.	*garden*
बाहर	*bāhar*	*outside*
बूढ़ा	*būṛhā*	*elderly, old* (only for animates)
बैठा	*baiṭhā*	*seated, sitting*
भारत	*bhārat* m.	*India*
भी	*bhī*	*also; even*
मालूम नहीं	*mālūm nahī̃*	*(I) don't know*
मुंबई	*mumbaī* f.	*Mumbai, Bombay*
में	*mẽ*	*in*
यहाँ	*yahā̃*	*here*
या	*yā*	*or*
लन्दन	*landan* m.	*London*
लेटा	*leṭā*	*lying, lying down*
रास्ता	*rāstā* m.	*road*
वहाँ	*vahā̃*	*there*
वाराणसी	*vārāṇasī* f.	*Varanasi, Banaras*
श्री	*Śrī*	*Mr*
श्रीमती	*Śrīmatī*	*Mrs*
सब	*sab*	*all*
समय	*samay* m.	*time*
सस्ता	*sastā*	*cheap*
साइकिल	*sāikil* f.	*bicycle*
से	*se*	*from*
सोमवार	*somvār* m.	*Monday*
स्कूल	*skūl* m.	*school*
हज़ार	*hazār* m.	*thousand*
हाथ	*hāth* m.	*hand*

Test yourself

1 कितना *kitnā* means *how much/many*. Give the appropriate form with the Hindi of: chairs, people, trees, water, husbands.

2 What's the difference in meaning between बूढ़ा *būṛhā* and पुराना *purānā*?

3 To what Hindi question is this statement the answer? – मेज़ पर पैसा है *mez par paisā hai.*

4 To what Hindi question is this statement the answer? – पैसा मेज़ पर है *paisā mez par hai.*

5 Give the Hindi for: *in the house, on the chair, at home, from Delhi.*

6 Give two different senses for the expression के पास *ke pās*, with examples.

7 What is the oblique case for?

8 What is the final vowel of all oblique plural nouns? Give three examples.

9 If पड़ा *paṛā* and लेटा *leṭā* can both be translated as *lying*, what's the difference between them?

10 What's the rule about the position of भी *bhī also*?

SELF CHECK

	I CAN...
○	... say where people and things are.
○	... describe things.
○	... talk about ownership.

4 चाय पीजिए

cāy pījie

Have some tea

In this unit you will learn how to:

▶ ***make requests and give commands.***
▶ ***describe everyday events and habits.***

Language points

▶ *imperative verbs*
▶ *imperfective present tense*

Language discovery 1 *Commands and requests*

Giving commands and making requests is easy in Hindi: but what you say depends on whom you're speaking to, because the imperative (command-giving) verb has different forms for तू *tū*, तुम *tum*, and आप *āp* people. We're going to concentrate on the तुम *tum* and आप *āp* forms here. First, we have to define a couple of terms.

Dictionaries list verbs in their *infinitive* form: बैठना *baiṭhnā to sit*. Take away the –ना *-nā* ending and you are left with बैठ *baiṭh*, which is the basic building block of the verb; it's called the *verb stem*. Remember these terms, because we'll be using them quite often.

For commands to someone you call तुम *tum*, just add *-o* to the stem: बैठो *baiṭho sit*, etc.

For commands to someone you call आप *āp*, add *-ie* to the stem: बैठिए *baiṭhie sit*, etc. Because this is inherently polite, it more or less implies the sense *please*.

As in English, the pronoun is optional: you can say either तुम बैठो *tum baiṭho you sit*, or just बैठो *baiṭho sit*.

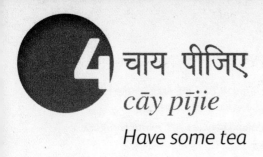

Spend some time getting to know these very common commands:

INFINITIVE		तुम	***tum***	आप	***āp***
बैठना *baiṭhnā*	to sit	बैठो *baiṭho*	sit	बैठिए *baiṭhie*	please sit
बोलना *bolnā*	to speak	बोलो *bolo*	speak	बोलिए *bolie*	please speak
जाना *jānā*	to go	जाओ *jāo*	go	जाइए *jāie*	please go
आना *ānā*	to come	आओ *āo*	come	आइए *āie*	please come
कहना *kahnā*	to say	कहो *kaho*	say	कहिए *kahie*	please say
खाना *khānā*	to eat	खाओ *khāo*	eat	खाइए *khāie*	please eat

Four of the commonest verbs are irregular:

करना *karnā*	to do	करो *karo*	do	कीजिए *kījie*	please do
देना *denā*	to give	दो *do*	give	दीजिए *dījie*	please give
लेना *lenā*	to take	लो *lo*	take	लीजिए *lījie*	please take
पीना *pīnā*	to drink	पियो *piyo*	drink	पीजिए *pījie*	please drink

Commands to someone you call तू *tū* just use the verb stem – बैठ *baiṭh*, बोल *bol*, जा *jā*, आ *ā*, कह *kah*, खा *khā*, कर *kar*, दे *de*, ले *le*, पी *pī*. As their shortness suggests, these तू *tū* commands are very blunt (or, if you prefer, sharp!) – *Speak! Sit!*; used out of context, they could easily give offence. Care needed here!

Commands are made negative by न *na* or मत *mat* *don't*. The latter is blunter.

यहाँ न बैठिए ।	*yahā̃ na baiṭhie.*	*Please don't sit here.*
कुछ मत बोलो !	*kuch mat bolo!*	*Don't say anything!*

Which of the following commands are positive, and which are negative?

a यहाँ आइए । *yahā̃ āie.*

b मिठाई मत खाओ । *miṭhāī mat khāo.*

c मेरा इंतज़ार न कीजिए । *merā intazār na kījie.*

d वह किताब दीजिए । *vah kitāb dījie.*

Listening and speaking

1 04.01 **Let's practise giving some basic commands. Listen and turn the verbs you hear into तुम *tum* commands.**

2 04.02 **Continue transforming the infinitives into commands, but this time use the आप *āp* command. Remember that irregular verbs undergo a stem change.**

3 04.03 **Here are some आप *āp* commands for you to change into तुम *tum* commands. You'll find the new verbs in the Vocabulary builder at the end of the unit.**

a मत जाइए! आइए, बैठिए । *mat jāie! āie, baiṭhie.*

b बताइए, आप कैसे हैं ? *batāie, āp kaise haĩ?*

c समोसा खाइए, पानी पीजिए । *samosā khāie, pānī pījie.*

d यह दूसरा समोसा भी लीजिए । *yah dūsrā samosā bhī lījie.*

e मोती को समोसा न दीजिए । *Motī ko samosā na dījie.*

f और खाइए ! *aur khāie!* (Have some more!)

g ख़ाली प्लेट मेज़ पर रखिए । *khālī pleṭ mez par rakhie.*

h अरे! सिग्रेट न पीजिए ! *are! sigreṭ na pījie!*

i और चाय लीजिए । *aur cāy lījie.* (Have some more tea)

Language discovery 2

THE INFINITIVE AS A COMMAND

The infinitive too can be used as a command: हिन्दी में बोलना ! *hindī mẽ bolnā! Speak in Hindi!* Such commands are often meant to be obeyed at some time in the future, or generally at all times, rather than immediately.

झूठ मत बोलना ।	*jhūṭh mat bolnā.*	*Don't tell lies.*
घर में सिग्रेट न पीना ।	*ghar mẽ sigreṭ na pīnā.*	*Don't smoke in the house.*
आगरे से ख़त भेजना ।	*āgre se khat bhejnā.*	*Send (me) a letter from Agra.*

SOME CONVERSATIONAL GAMBITS

V 04.04 When you're learning Hindi you may find that people speak quite fast – you'll need to ask them to repeat things or to speak slowly etc. This section gives you some useful phrases to help you out!

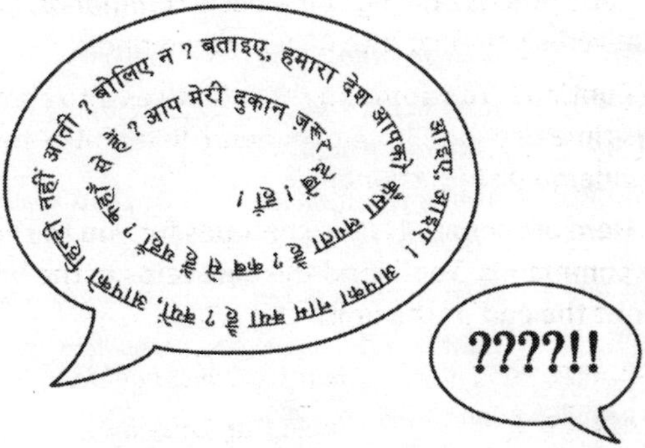

फिर से पूछिए ।	*phir se pūchie.*	*Please ask (me) again.*
फिर से कहिए ।	*phir se kahie.*	*Please tell (me) again, say (it) again.*
ज़ोर से बोलिए ।	*zor se bolie.*	*Please speak loudly.*
धीरे धीरे बोलिए ।	*dhīre dhīre bolie.*	*Please speak slowly.*
हिन्दी में बोलिए ।	*hindī mẽ bolie.*	*Please speak in Hindi.*
हिन्दी में बोलिएगा ।	*hindī mẽ boliegā.*	*Be so kind as to speak in Hindi.*

This last sentence adds *-gā* to the command: बोलिए *bolie* becomes बोलिएगा *boliegā*. This gives a particularly polite command.

मैं नहीं समझा ।	*maĩ nahī̃ samjhā.*	*I don't/didn't understand.* (male speaker)
मैं नहीं समझी ।	*maĩ nahī̃ samjhī.*	*I don't/didn't understand.* (female speaker)

These sentences use the past tense, introduced in Unit 10.

TELLING, SAYING, SPEAKING, ASKING

When using verbs like *to tell* and *to ask*, you may want to specify the person being spoken to. Most *saying, asking* verbs make this link with से *se*, and here's a list of the common ones that do so:

कहना	*kahnā*	*to say, tell*
बोलना	*bolnā*	*to speak*
बात करना	*bāt karnā*	*to converse*
पूछना	*pūchnā*	*to ask*
माँगना	*mā̃gnā*	*to ask for, demand*
मिलना	*milnā*	*to meet*
राम से कहो।	*Rām se kaho.*	*Tell Ram.*
राम से बात करो, मनोज से नहीं ।	*Rām se bāt karo, Manoj se nahī̃.*	*Talk to Ram, not to Manoj.*
मनोज से न पूछो, राम से पूछो ।	*Manoj se na pūcho, Rām se pūcho.*	*Don't ask Manoj, ask Ram.*
राम से पैसा माँगो ।	*Rām se paisā mā̃go.*	*Ask Ram for money.*
राम से मिलो ।	*Rām se milo.*	*Meet Ram.*

But the verb बताना *batānā to tell* uses को *ko*:

राम को बताओ ।	*Rām ko batāo.*	*Tell Ram.*

Can you say the following requests and commands in Hindi?

a *Please say that again.*

b *Ask my brother.*

c *Please speak slowly.*

d *Don't tell my mother!*

Writing

Using both तुम *tum* and आप *āp* forms, make up some requests and commands from the following lists. Make some of your examples negative by using न *na* or मत *mat*. Here are a few examples:

यह किताब ध्यान से पढ़िए	*yah kitāb dhyān se paṛhie.*	*Read this book carefully.*
ठंडा पानी न पीना ।	*ṭhaṇḍā pānī na pīnā.*	*Don't drink cold water.*
ज़ोर से मत बोलो ।	*zor se mat bolo.*	*Don't speak loudly.*

Objects

समोसा	*samosā* m.	*samosa*
किताब	*kitāb* f.	*book*
हिन्दी	*hindī* f.	*Hindi*
पानी	*pānī* m.	*water*
खाना	*khānā* m.	*food*
और चाय	*aur cāy* f.	*more tea*
घर	*ghar*	*home*
मेरी बात	*merī bāt* f.	*what I say, my words*
यह	*yah*	*this*
ये	*ye*	*these*

Adverbs

अब	*ab*	*now*
अभी	*abhī*	*right now*
जल्दी से	*jaldī se*	*quickly*
ज़ोर से	*zor se*	*loudly*
धीरे धीरे	*dhīre dhīre*	*slowly*
यहाँ	*yahā̃*	*here*
यहीं	*yahī̃*	*right here*
ध्यान से	*dhyān se*	*carefully*
फिर से	*phir se*	*again*

Verbs

कहना	*kahnā*	*to say*
खाना	*khānā*	*to eat*
चलाना	*calānā*	*to drive* (vehicle)
जाना	*jānā*	*to go*
देखना	*dekhnā*	*to see, look at*
पढ़ना	*paṛhnā*	*to read*
पीना	*pīnā*	*to drink*
पूछना	*pūchnā*	*to ask*

बताना	*batānā*	*to tell*
बात करना	*bāt karnā*	*to talk, converse*
बैठना	*baiṭhnā*	*to sit*
बोलना	*bolnā*	*to speak*
रखना	*rakhnā*	*to put; to keep*
सीखना	*sīkhnā*	*to learn*
सुनना	*sunnā*	*to listen, hear*

Language discovery 3

ROUTINE EVENTS

04.05 We now take a big step forward by learning how to describe present-tense events and actions – starting with the verbs बोलना *bolnā to speak* and समझना *samajhnā to understand*:

मैं हिन्दी बोलता हूँ ।	मैं हिन्दी समझता हूँ ।
maĩ hindī boltā hū̃.	*maĩ hindī samajhtā hū̃.*
I speak Hindi. (male speaker)	*I understand Hindi.* (male speaker)

This is a present tense that describes actions that are done regularly or habitually. It is called the imperfective and it consists of two parts. First, the word describing the action is बोलता *bolta*, which consists of the stem बोल *bol* plus the ending -ता *-tā*).

बोल + ता = बोलता	*bol + tā = boltā*
समझ + ता = समझता	*samajh + tā = samajhtā*

The second part is the verb *to be* – here हूँ *hū̃* – already familiar to us from मैं हूँ *maĩ hū̃ I am*. Its purpose here is to show that the verb is in the present tense (*I speak*, rather than *I used to speak*).

As you might expect, बोलता *boltā* changes to बोलते *bolte* in the masculine plural, and to बोलती *boltī* in the feminine; the part of the verb *to be* also changes with the subject – वे बोलती हैं *ve boltī haĩ*, etc.

मैं हिन्दी बोलती हूँ ।	*maĩ hindī boltī hū̃.*	*I speak Hindi.* (female)
तुम हिन्दी बोलते हो ।	*tum hindī bolte ho.*	*You speak Hindi.* (male)

तुम हिन्दी बोलती हो । *tum hindī boltī ho.* You speak Hindi. (female)

वह हिन्दी बोलता है । *vah hindī boltā hai.* He speaks Hindi.

वह हिन्दी बोलती है । *vah hindī boltī hai.* She speaks Hindi.

हम/आप/वे हिन्दी बोलते हैं ।
ham/āp/ve hindī bolte haĩ. We/you/they speak Hindi. (male)

हम/आप/वे हिन्दी बोलती हैं ।
ham/āp/ve hindī boltī haĩ. We/you/they speak Hindi. (female)

Speaking, saying, talking/conversing: these three actions are generally covered by बोलना *bolnā*, कहना *kahnā*, and बात करना *bāt karnā* respectively, though there's some overlap between them. In all three, the person addressed takes से *se*: राम से बात करो *Rām se bāt karo* Talk to Ram.

The verb पढ़ना *paṛhnā to read* follows the same pattern as बोलना *bolnā to speak*. How would you say *She reads, He reads, They (female) read*, and *We (male) read*?

WHERE DO YOU LIVE? WHAT DO YOU DO?

04.06 Let's look at examples of the imperfective tense using other verbs:

आप कहाँ रहती हैं ? *āp kahā̃ rahtī haĩ?* Where do you live?

मैं दिल्ली में रहती हूँ । *maĩ dillī mẽ rahtī hū̃.* I live in Delhi.

आप क्या काम करती हैं ? *āp kyā kām kartī haĩ?* What work do you do?

मैं संगीतकार हूँ; सितार बजाती हूँ ।
maĩ sangītkār hū̃; sitār bajātī hū̃. I'm a musician; I play the sitar.

क्या आपके पति भी सितार बजाते हैं ?
kyā āpke pati bhī sitār bajāte haĩ? Does your husband play the sitar too?

जी नहीं, वे अँग्रेज़ी पढ़ाते हैं ।
jī nahī̃, ve ãgrezī paṛhāte haĩ. No, he teaches English.

आपकी बेटी क्या करती है ? *āpkī beṭī kyā kartī hai?* What does your daughter do?

वह अभी छोटी है। वह स्कूल जाती है ।
vah abhī choṭī hai. vah skūl jātī hai. She's still young; she goes to school.

Using what you've learned, how would you say *She lives in India, I speak English, He works in a hospital*?

WHAT'S THIS CALLED?

The verb कहना *kahnā to say* is useful in asking what something is called – a frequent event when learning a new language! Point to something and say:

इसको क्या कहते हैं ?
isko kyā kahte haĩ?
What's this called?

You'll get answers like:

इसको किताब कहते हैं ।
isko kitāb kahte haĩ.
This is called a book.

इसको मेज़ कहते हैं ।
isko mez kahte haĩ.
This is called a table.

The question literally means *What do (they) call this?*, leaving the *they* unexpressed because it's an impersonal kind of question. (The word इसको *isko this* will be explained in Unit 5.)

Listen and understand

1 04.07 **It's time to meet another newcomer. Listen and try to find out who she is, where she lives, and where she and her husband work.**

नमस्ते । मेरा नाम उर्वशी है । मैं मुंबई में रहती हूँ । मैं एक बहुत बड़े बैंक में काम करती हूँ । मेरा पती भी वहाँ काम करता है । उसका नाम बंटी है ।

namaste. merā nām Urvaśī hai. maĩ Mumbaī mẽ rahtī hū̃. maĩ ek bahut baṛe baink mẽ kām kartī hū̃. merā pati bhī vahā̃ kām kartā hai. uskā nām Banṭī hai.

2 04.08 **Each sentence numbered 1–7 matches up with one from the sequence A–G. Find the matching pairs. Then, listen to confirm your answers.**

1 मनोज और राम सिनेमा जाते हैं ।
Manoj aur Rām sinemā jāte haĩ.

2 शर्मा जी अध्यापक हैं ।
Śarmā jī adhyāpak haĩ.

A लेकिन वह बहुत ध्यान से नहीं पढ़ता ।
lekin vah bahut dhyān se nahī̃ paṛhtā.

B लेकिन हम को कुछ नहीं देते हो ।
lekin ham ko kuch nahī̃ dete ho.

3 राम स्कूल जाता है ।
Rām skūl jātā hai.

4 कभी कभी मनोज और मीना चाय बनाते हैं ।
kabhī kabhī Manoj aur Mīnā cāy banāte haĩ.

5 गीता बहुत अच्छा खाना बनाती है ।
Gītā bahut acchā khānā banātī hai.

6 मीना बग़ीचे में बैठती है ।
Mīnā bagīce mẽ baiṭhtī hai.

7 तुम हमेशा हम से पैसा माँगते हो ।
tum hameśā ham se paisā mā̃gte ho.

C वे हिन्दी पढ़ाते हैं ।
ve hindī paṛhāte haĩ.

D वे हिन्दी फ़िल्में देखते हैं ।
ve hindī filmẽ dekhte haĩ.

E पर मनोज नहीं बनाता, सिर्फ़ खाता है !
par Manoj nahī̃ banātā, sirf khātā hai!

F वे काफ़ी भी बनाते हैं ।
ve kāfī bhī banāte haĩ.

G वह वहाँ बिल्ली से बात करती है ।
vah vahā̃ billī se bāt kartī hai.

Go further

THE IMPERFECTIVE PRESENT

Because the tense introduced in this chapter describes events that haven't been completed, it's called the *imperfective present*. The form बोलता *boltā* is called the *imperfective participle*.

The verb *to be* (हूँ *hū̃*, है *hai*, etc.) as used here is called the *auxiliary*, because it helps complete the meaning of the verb by specifying its time frame. (English uses auxiliaries too: *will* in the future tense *I will go* is an example.)

NEGATIVE VERBS

A final point here: the auxiliary can be dropped when the verb is in the negative – it's often optional, as shown by the brackets:

क्या तुम गोश्त खाते हो ?
kyā tum gośt khāte ho? — *Do you eat meat?*

नहीं, मैं गोश्त नहीं खाता (हूँ) ।
nahī̃, maĩ gośt nahī̃ khātā (hū̃). — *No, I don't eat meat.*

क्या वे शराब पीते हैं ?

kyā ve śarāb pīte haĩ? — Do they drink alcohol?

नहीं, वे शराब नहीं पीते (हैं) ।

nahī̃, ve śarāb nahī̃ pīte (haĩ). — No, they don't drink alcohol.

LANGUAGE TIP

I'm a teacher, she's a doctor – in statements like these, the *a* can be expressed in Hindi with एक *ek* (literally *one*), but it's not necessary.

Based on what you've just learned, how would you say *She doesn't go to school* in Hindi?

Storyline

JAVED AND RAJU GET TO KNOW ONE ANOTHER

04.09 *Javed asks Raju some personal questions.*

1 What is the main topic of the conversation: work or marriage?

जावेद	राजू जी, आप एक कालेज में पढ़ाते हैं, न ?
राजू	जी हाँ, मैं इतिहास पढ़ाता हूँ ।
जावेद	और आपकी पत्नी ? क्या वे भी काम करती हैं ?
राजू	हाँ ज़रूर, हम दोनों काम करते हैं ।
जावेद	वे क्या काम करती हैं ?
राजू	वे अस्पताल में काम करती हैं । डाक्टर हैं ।
Jāved	*Rājū jī, āp ek kālej mẽ paṛhāte haĩ, na?*
Rājū	*jī hā̃, maĩ itihās paṛhātā hū̃.*
Jāved	*aur āpkī patnī? kyā ve bhī kām kartī haĩ?*
Rājū	*hā̃ zarūr, ham donõ kām karte haĩ.*
Jāved	*ve kyā kām kartī haĩ?*
Rājū	*ve aspatāl mẽ kām kartī haĩ. ḍākṭar haĩ.*

2 Now listen to the conversation again and answer these questions:

a Which subject does Javed teach?

b Where does Javed's wife work?

c What is her job?

Notice that a pronoun can be dropped when its reference is clear from what's come before: डाक्टर हैं *ḍakṭar haĩ (she) is a doctor*. Look out for further examples of this in the second and third line below:

04.10 *The two men switch the conversation to what they, and Geeta, eat and drink.*

3 What do Javed and Raju both eat on occasion?

जावेद	यह बताइए राजू जी, आप गोश्त खाते हैं ?
राजू	जी हाँ, कभी कभी खाता हूँ । और आप ?
जावेद	मैं भी खाता हूँ । लेकिन शराब नहीं पीता ।
राजू	आप शराब नहीं पीते ? मैं पीता हूँ , लेकिन बहुत कम ।
जावेद	क्या गीता जी भी पीती हैं ?
राजू	जी नहीं, वे नहीं पीतीं ।
Jāved	*yah batāie Rājū jī, āp gośt khāte haĩ?*
Rājū	*jī hā̃, kabhī kabhī khātā hū̃. aur āp?*
Jāved	*maĩ bhī khātā hū̃. lekin śarāb nahī̃ pītā.*
Rājū	*āp śarāb nahī̃ pīte? maĩ pītā hū̃, lekin bahut kam.*
Jāved	*kyā Gītā jī bhī pītī haĩ?*
Rājū	*jī nahī̃, ve nahī̃ pītī̃.*

4 Listen again and answer these questions:

- **a** Who eats meat and enjoys an alcoholic drink every once in a while?
- **b** Who eats a little meat but doesn't drink alcohol?
- **c** How about Geeta, how often does she drink alcohol?

वे नहीं पीतीं *ve nahī̃ pītī̃* – when पीती हैं *pītī haĩ* becomes negative it can drop the auxiliary हैं *haĩ*, leaving just वे नहीं पीतीं *ve nahī̃ pītī̃*. The nasal from the dropped हैं *haĩ* has been made homeless by this, so it jumps onto the participle पीती *pītī* ! This only happens with the feminine plural, and only in this tense.

Now look back at the list of verbs in **Language discovery 1** and make up sentences from as many as you can, with yourself as subject (e.g. मैं हिन्दी बोलता हूँ *maĩ hindī boltā hū̃*). Then do the same with other subjects such as *she* or *they*. Be sure to say your sentences out loud, with conviction; this will help you get used to this very important tense.

Food restrictions: many people particularly avoid गाय का गोश्त, *gāy kā gośt* (*'cow's meat'*, i.e. *beef*) and सूअर का गोश्त *sūar kā gośt* (*'pig's meat'*, i.e. *pork*); some strict vegetarians also abstain from लहसुन *lahsun* (*garlic*) and प्याज *pyāz* (*onions*) as being 'fervent' foods.

Practice

1 Translate, using first तुम *tum* commands and then आप *āp* commands:

a Don't drink alcohol in the house.
b Listen carefully.
c Send this letter to Manoj.
d Go home.
e Tell me his name.
f Eat these two samosas.
g Play the sitar.
h Ask my neighbour.
i Give this money to my wife.
j Don't drive the car today.
k Speak slowly.

2 Complete the sentences with the right postposition, से *se* or को *ko*. Then translate them into English.

a राम... पूछिए । *Rām _______ pūchie.*
b बच्चों... मत बताना । *baccõ_______ mat batānā.*
c चाचा जी... हिन्दी बोलो । *cācā jī _______ hindī bolo.*
d मनोज... बात कीजिए । *Manoj _______ bāt kījie.*
e गीता... पैसा माँगना । *Gītā _______ paisā mā̃gnā.*

3 Translate all the variations shown in these sentences:

a My brother/sister lives in Delhi.
b I/we understand Hindi.
c The boy/girl drives the car very fast.
d My husband/wife speaks Hindi.
e Who (male/female) speaks English?

4 04.11 We end this unit with a short listening task. Can you figure out who plays the sitar, who plays the sarangi, and who plays the tabla?

मेरे दोस्त सुरेश और महेश दोनों संगीतकार हैं । वे दिल्ली में रहते हैं । सुरेश तबला बजाता है और रेडियो में काम करता है । महेश सितार बजाता है । मैं संगीतकार नहीं हूँ, लेकिन मैं सारंगी बजाता हूँ । मेरा नाम ? मेरा नाम दिनेश है । मैं भी दिल्ली में रहता हूँ ।

mere dost Sureś aur Maheś donõ sangītkār haĩ. ve Dillī mẽ rahte haĩ. Sureś tablā bajātā hai aur reḍiyo mẽ kām kartā hai. Maheś sitār bajātā hai. maĩ sangītkār nahī̃ hū̃, lekin maĩ sārangī bajātā hū̃. merā nām? merā nām Dineś hai. maĩ bhī Dillī mẽ rahtā hū̃.

Vocabulary builder

अभी	*abhī*	*right now; still*
अरे	*are*	*hey! oh!*
आना	*ānā*	*to come*
इतिहास	*itihās* m.	*history*
और	*aur*	*more*
कभी	*kabhī*	*ever*
कभी कभी	*kabhī kabhī*	*sometimes*
कम	*kam*	*little, less*
करना	*karnā*	*to do*
कहना	*kahnā*	*to say*
काफ़ी	*kāfī* f.	*coffee*
काम	*kām*	*work*
काम करना	*kām karnā*	*to work*
कालेज	*kālej* m.	*college*
ख़त	*k̲h̲at* m.	*letter* (correspondence)
खाना[1]	*khānā* m.	*food*
खाना[2]	*khānā*	*to eat*
गाना[1]	*gānā* m.	*song, singing*
गाना[2]	*gānā*	*to sing*
गोश्त	*gośt* m.	*meat*
चलाना	*calānā*	*to drive*
चाय	*cāy* f.	*tea*
जाना	*jānā*	*to go*
ज़ोर से	*zor se*	*with force, loudly*
झूठ	*jhūṭh* m.	*a lie*
तबला	*tablā* m.	*tabla* (drum)
देखना	*dekhnā*	*to look, to see*
देना	*denā*	*to give*
धीरे धीरे	*dhīre dhīre*	*slowly*
ध्यान	*dhyān* m.	*attention*
ध्यान से	*dhyān se*	*attentively*

न	*na*	*don't; not*
पढ़ना	*paṛhnā*	*to read; to study*
पढ़ाना	*paṛhānā*	*to teach*
पीना	*pīnā*	*to drink; to smoke*
पूछना	*pūchnā*	*to ask*
प्लेट	*pleṭ* f.	*plate*
फिर; फिर से	*phir; phir se*	*again*
फ़िल्म	*film* f.	*film*
बजाना	*bajānā*	*to play* (music)
बताना	*batānā*	*to tell*
बनाना	*banānā*	*to make*
बात	*bāt* f.	*thing said, idea*
बात करना	*bāt karnā*	*to talk, converse*
बैठना	*baiṭhnā*	*to sit*
बोलना	*bolnā*	*to speak*
भेजना	*bhejnā*	*to send*
मत	*mat*	*don't*
माँगना	*mā̃gnā*	*to ask for, demand*
मिलना	*milnā*	*to meet*
यहीं	*yahī̃*	*right here*
रखना	*rakhnā*	*to put, place, keep*
लेना	*lenā*	*to take*
शराब	*śarāb* f.	*alcoholic drink, liquor*
संगीत	*saṅgīt* m.	*music*
संगीतकार	*saṅgītkār* m.	*musician*
समझना	*samajhnā*	*to understand*
समोसा	*samosā* m.	*samosa*
सिग्रेट	*sigreṭ* m.	*cigarette*
सिनेमा	*sinemā* m.	*cinema*
सीखना	*sīkhnā*	*to learn*
सुनना	*sunnā*	*to hear, to listen*
हमेशा	*hameśā*	*always*

Test yourself

How would you do the following?

1 Give the infinitive and stem forms of the Hindi verbs *to sit, to send, to eat.*

2 और *aur* usually means *and*; but what else does it mean?

3 When an infinitive verb is used as a command, what shade of meaning is likely to be implied?

4 Speaking to a person you don't know well, how do you say *(Please) speak slowly*?

5 The verbs कहना *kahnā to say*, बात करना *bāt karnā to converse*, मिलना *milnā to meet*, पूछना *pūchnā to ask* and माँगना *mā̃gnā to ask for* all use the same postposition to mark the person addressed. What is it?

6 How do you say, *What's this called*?

7 Turning a sentence such as वह झूठ बोलता है *vah jhūṭh boltā hai he tells lies* into a negative sentence would involve adding नहीं *nahī̃*. But which word could be dropped from the negative version of the sentence?

8 मनोज सिग्रेट पीता है, पर अरुण जी सिग्रेट नहीं पीते *Manoj sigreṭ pītā hai, par Aruṇ jī sigreṭ nahī̃ pīte.* Their smoking habits apart, what does this sentence tell us about the attitude of the speaker to the two protagonists?

9 How would you say to a child, *Don't sit on the floor*?

10 Give the Hindi for *to study* and *to teach.*

SELF CHECK

	I CAN...
○	... make requests and give commands.
○	... describe everyday events and habits.

5 आपको क्या चाहिए ?

āpko kyā cāhie?

What do you want?

In this unit you will learn how to:

- ***talk about likes and needs.***
- ***Use expressions for to get and to know.***

Language points

- *oblique-case expressions*
- *imperfective of to be*

Language discovery 1 *More obliques*

Just when you thought you'd got things straight, we go oblique again! This time it's with the pronouns. To say *to me*, *from her*, etc., we need to use a postposition, which means that the pronoun must become oblique. (Look back to Unit 3 if you're uncertain about the use of obliques.)

The good news is that हम *ham*, आप *āp*, and तुम *tum* don't change at all in the oblique:

हम को	*ham ko*	*to us*
आप को	*āp ko*	*to you*
तुम को	*tum ko*	*to you*

The bad news is that the others do change – like this:

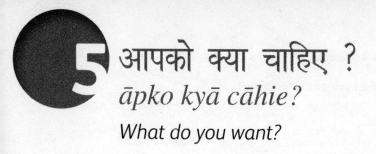

DIRECT		OBLIQUE + को *ko*		
मैं	*maĩ*	मुझ को	*mujh ko*	*to me*
तू	*tū*	तुझ को	*tujh ko*	*to you*
यह	*yah*	इस को	*is ko*	*to him, her, it, this*
वह	*vah*	उस को	*us ko*	*to him, her, it, that*
ये	*ye*	इन को	*in ko*	*to them, these*
वे	*ve*	उन को	*un ko*	*to them, those*
कौन	*kaun*	किस को	*kis ko*	*to whom* (sing.)
कौन	*kaun*	किन को	*kin ko*	*to whom* (pl.)

उस को ये चीज़ें दीजिए ।	*us ko ye cīzẽ dījie.*	Please give these things to him/her.
उन को मेरा पैसा दो ।	*un ko merā paisā do.*	Give my money to them.
मुझ को बताइए ।	*mujh ko batāie.*	Please tell me.
तुम मुझ को कुछ नहीं देती हो ।	*tum mujh ko kuch nahī̃ detī ho.*	You give me nothing.

How would you say *Ask them, don't ask me!* and *Please give me that book*?

Pronoun + postposition are usually written together as one word (उसको *usko*), although they are written as two words above (उस को *us ko*), to show you more clearly what's going on.

Storyline

GEETA TALKS TO HER CHILDREN

05.01 *Geeta is getting Manoj and Ram to help in the house.*
First, some new words:

कौनसा	*kaunsā*	*which?*
जो	*jo*	*which, who*
साफ़ करना	*sāf karnā*	*to clean*
अख़बार	*akhbār* m.	*newspaper*

1 What does Geeta need help with – cooking or tidying the house?

मनोज बेटा, ये किताबें तुम अलमारी में रखो । कौनसी किताबें ? हाँ ये, जो मेरी मेज़ पर पड़ी हैं । मीना कहाँ है ? उसको बुलाओ । अच्छा मीनू , तुम यहाँ हो ? तुम यह कमरा साफ़ करो । राम, तुम पिताजी से पूछो कि अख़बार कहाँ है । उनसे कहो कि चाचाजी बैठे हैं ।

Manoj beṭā, ye kitābẽ tum almārī mẽ rakho. kaunsī kitābẽ? hā̃ ye, jo merī mez par paṛī haĩ. Mīnā kahā̃ hai? usko bulāo. acchā Mīnū, tum yahā̃ ho? tum yah kamrā sāf karo. Rām, tum pitājī se pūcho ki akhbār kahā̃ hai. unse kaho ki cācājī baiṭhe haĩ.

2 Now listen again and answer these questions:

a Where does Geeta ask Manoj to put the books?

b What is Meena's chore?

c What does Ram need to ask his father?

Language discovery 2 *Expressing likes, needs, and wants*

LIKING THINGS

05.02 In English, we can say *I like London*; the subject of this is *I*. But we could also say *London appeals to me*, which makes *London* the subject. Hindi has many such constructions. They work like this:

मुझको दिल्ली पसंद है ।	*mujhko dillī pasand hai.*	*I like Delhi.*
हमको दिल्ली पसंद है ।	*hamko dillī pasand hai.*	*We like Delhi.*

These sentences translate literally as *Delhi is pleasing to me/us*; the word दिल्ली *dillī* is the subject of the verb है *hai is*, with the *me/us* expressed in the oblique with को *ko*. Here are some more examples.

क्या राम को यह जगह पसंद है ?
kyā Rām ko yah jagah pasand hai? — *Does Ram like this place?*

हमको वह आदमी पसंद नहीं है ।
hamko vah ādmī pasand nahī̃ hai. — *We don't like that man.*

मेरे दोस्त को ये तस्वीरें पसंद नहीं हैं ।
mere dost ko ye tasvīrẽ pasand nahī̃ haĩ. — *My friend doesn't like these pictures.*

> IMPORTANT!
> GRAMMATICAL HEALTH WARNING
> Constructions using को *ko* can damage your grammar

Take care: as you learn more Hindi you will see that this switch from English *I* to Hindi मुझ को *mujh ko to me* is very common. The focus of *I* sentences is the person who experiences, but मुझको *mujhko* sentences have the experience itself as the focus. We can call these मुझको *mujhko* constructions.

Using what you've just learned, how would you answer this question (assuming you do like पपीता *papītā, papaya*): क्या आप को पपीता पसंद है ? *kyā āp ko papītā pasand hai?*

NEEDING AND WANTING THINGS

05.03 Another मुझको *mujhko* construction expresses *I need* or *I want*, using the word चाहिए *cāhie* – literally *is wanted*. There's no है *hai* used with चाहिए *cāhie*.

तुमको क्या चाहिए ?	*tumko kyā cāhie?*	*What do you want/need?*
मुझको काफ़ी चाहिए ।	*mujhko kāfī cāhie.*	*I want/need coffee.*
हमको भी काफ़ी चाहिए ।	*hamko bhī kāfī cāhie.*	*We want/need coffee, too.*
किसको चाय चाहिए ?	*kisko cāy cāhie?*	*Who wants/needs tea?*
राजू को चाय चाहिए ।	*Rājū ko cāy cāhie.*	*Raju wants/needs tea.*

Remember that किस *kis* is the oblique of कौन *kaun who?*, as in किसको *kisko to whom?*

If मीना को बिस्कुट चाहिए *mina ko biskut cāhie* is the answer, what is the question?

SAYING I KNOW

05.04 A similar construction means *I know*, using the word मालूम *mālūm* – literally *known*. A difference from the चाहिए *cāhie* construction is that है *hai* is used here (although it can be dropped in the negative).

मुझको मालूम है ।
mujhko mālūm hai. — *I know.*

मुझको नहीं मालूम / मुझको मालूम नहीं ।
mujhko nahī̃ mālūm / mujhko mālūm nahī̃. — *I don't know.*

किसको मालूम है ?
kisko mālūm hai? — *Who knows?*

उनको मालूम है कि मुझको चाबी चाहिए ।
unko mālūm hai ki mujhko cābī cāhie. — *They know that I want/need a key.*

हमको मालूम है कि तुम यहाँ हो ।
hamko mālūm hai ki tum yahā̃ ho. — *We know that you're here.*

मुझको मालूम है कि तुम कहाँ हो ।
mujhko mālūm hai ki tum kahā̃ ho. — *I know where you are.*

उनको मालूम है कि मुझको क्या चाहिए ।
unko mālūm hai ki mujhko kyā cāhie. — *They know what I want.*

How would you say *I don't know what kind of car it is* and *You know what my brother likes?*

From now on we will meet many constructions in which a मुझको *mujhko to me* orientation replaces the *I* orientation of the English. In expressions like *I like*, *I know*, *I have a cold*, etc., the English *I* puts the self at the centre of its own universe, directing and influencing things around it; but Hindi's मुझको *mujhko* type of constructions sees the self as being affected by influences from outside, rather than as being the master of such influences. This point is important and we'll return to it again later.

Storyline

PRATAP GOES SHOPPING

05.05 *Pratap, a visitor from England, is shopping in Delhi. He's forgotten the Hindi for some of the things he needs, but luckily for him, the shopkeeper knows some English and is able to help him out. We join them in the middle of their conversation.*

1 What kind of shop is Pratap in?

प्रताप	मुझको टोर्च भी चाहिए ।
दुकानदार	"टोर्च" नहीं, "टार्च" ! यह लीजिए । और ?
प्रताप	मुझको ... क्या कहते हैं उस को ? ... एक छोटी किताब ... मैं कुछ लिखना चाहता हूँ ...
दुकानदार	अच्छा, आपको कापी चाहिए ।
प्रताप	हाँ, कापी ! एक क़लम भी दीजिए ।
दुकानदार	कैसा क़लम चाहिए ?
प्रताप	काला नहीं ... ब्लू ...
दुकानदार	यह लीजिए, नीला क़लम । और ?
प्रताप	मुझको वह चीज़ भी चाहिए ...
दुकानदार	कौनसी चीज़ ? यह डिब्बा ?
प्रताप	नहीं नहीं, वह लाल चीज़ जो डिब्बे पर पड़ी है ।
दुकानदार	अच्छा, चाक़ू! आपको चाक़ू चाहिए । लीजिए ।

Pratāp	*mujhko ṭorc bhī cāhie.*
dukāndār	*'ṭorc' nahī̃, 'ṭārc'! yah lījie. aur?*
Pratāp	*mujhko ... kyā kahte haĩ us ko? ... ek choṭī kitāb ... maĩ kuch likhnā cāhtā hū̃ ...*
dukāndār	*acchā, āp ko kāpī cāhie.*
Pratāp	*hā̃, kāpī! ek qalam bhī dījie.*
dukāndār	*kaisā qalam cāhie?*
Pratāp	*kālā nahī̃ ... blū ...*
dukāndār	*yah lījie, nīlā qalam. aur?*
Pratāp	*mujhko vah cīz bhī cāhie ...*
dukāndār	*kaunsī cīz? yah ḍibbā?*
Pratāp	*nahī̃ nahī̃, vah lāl cīz jo ḍibbe par paṛī hai.*
dukāndār	*acchā, cāqū! āp ko cāqū cāhie. lījie.*

2 Now listen again and answer these questions:

a What does Pratap need a notebook for?
b What colour pen does he need?
c Where is the penknife that Pratap wants to buy?

SPEAKING

05.06 **It's time to get some role-playing practice. You will hear questions and a prompt for the replies. Speak in the pauses, and then listen to check your answers.**

आपको क्या चाहिए ?	*āpko kyā cāhie?*
आपको कैसा टार्च चाहिए ?	*āpko kaisā ṭārc cāhie?*
और क्या चाहिए ?	*aur kyā cāhie?*
क्या आपको यह कलम पसंद है ?	*kyā āpko yah kalam pasand hai?*
क्या ये चाबियाँ आपकी हैं ?	*kyā ye cābiyā̃ āpkī haĩ?*
क्या आपके दोस्त को भी कुछ चाहिए ?	*kyā āpke dost ko bhī kuch cāhie?*

Language discovery 3 *Where to get things*

AVAILABILITY – *to get, to find*

05.07 Besides meaning *to meet*, मिलना *milnā* also means *to be available*, and is the normal way to express the meaning *to get, to find, to receive*. The subject here is not the person who gets or receives something, but the thing that's available or received.

इस दुकान में अच्छे जूते मिलते हैं ।
is dukān mẽ acche jūte milte haĩ.
You can get good shoes in this shop. (Good shoes are available in this shop.)

दिल्ली में सब कुछ मिलता है ।
dillī mẽ sab kuch miltā hai.
You can get everything in Delhi.

हाथी भी मिलते हैं !
hāthī bhī milte haĩ!
You can even find elephants!

Notice that the sense of *you* in *you can get* is dropped, because the situation is an impersonal one, describing general availability.

सस्ते कपड़े कहाँ मिलते हैं ?

saste kapṛe kahā̃ milte haĩ? Where can you get cheap clothes?

अच्छी साड़ियाँ कहाँ मिलती हैं ?

acchī sāṛiyā̃ kahā̃ miltī haĩ? Where can you get good saris?

WRITING

Match up the items with the locations, as in these examples:

समोसे ढाबे में मिलते हैं ।

samose ḍhābe mẽ milte haĩ. Samosas are available in a roadside café.

सुंदर कपड़े उस दूकान में मिलते हैं ।

sundar kapṛe us dukān mẽ milte haĩ. Lovely clothes are available in that shop.

What's available

समोसे	*samose* m. pl.	samosas
सस्ता खाना	*sastā khānā* m.	cheap food
डाक टिकटें	*ḍāk ṭikaṭẽ* f. pl.	stamps
ताज़ा फल	*tāzā phal* m.	fresh fruit
अच्छा खाना	*acchā khānā* m.	good food
सिग्रेट	*sigreṭ* f.	cigarette
सुंदर कपड़े	*sundar kapṛe* m. pl.	lovely clothes
अच्छे कमरे	*acche kamre* m. pl.	good rooms

Where to find it/them

डाक घर	*ḍāk ghar* m.	post office
मेरा कमरा	*merā kamrā* m.	my room
छोटी दुकान	*choṭī dukān* f.	small shop
यहाँ	*yahā̃*	here
ढाबा	*ḍhābā* m.	roadside café
भारत	*bhārat* m.	India
यह होटल	*yah hoṭal* m.	this hotel/restaurant
वह दुकान	*vah dukān* f.	that shop

THE GENERAL AND THE PARTICULAR

Look closely at these two sentences:

बनारसी साड़ियाँ बहुत अच्छी होती हैं ।	
banārasī sāṛiyā̃ bahut acchī hotī haĩ.	Banarasi saris are very good.
ये साड़ियाँ बहुत अच्छी हैं ।	
ye sāṛiyā̃ bahut acchī haĩ.	These saris are very good.

The participle होता *hotā* (from होना *honā to be*) is used in a statement that relates to a whole class of things: it's a general statement. Thus the first sentence here is about all saris from Banaras (a centre of fine sari making), while the second one is a specific one about a particular selection of saris.

How would you express these two different ideas: *That tree is tall* and *Trees are tall*?

Storyline

RAJU VISITS A HOTEL

05.08 *This section presents a revision dialogue in two parts. Visiting a small town for a teachers' conference, Raju tries his luck at the local hotel. There's no new grammar, but here are some useful new words:*

कोई	*koī*	some, any, a
अच्छा-सा	*acchā-sā*	goodish, decent
दिखाना	*dikhānā*	to show
दिन	*din* m.	day
के लिए	*ke lie*	for
यानी	*yānī*	that is to say
शुक्रवार	*śukravār* m.	Friday
फ़ोन	*fon* m.	phone
शहर	*śahar* m.	town
ऐसा	*aisā*	such, of this kind
किराया	*kirāyā* m.	rent; fare
सौ	*sau* m.	hundred
रुपया	*rupayā* m.	rupee

When the context is clear, it's perfectly OK to drop the pronoun from such sentences as (आपको) क्या चाहिए? *(āpko) kyā cāhie?* and (मुझको) कमरा चाहिए *(mujhko) kamrā cāhie*. Hindi favours crisp economy, and is quick to drop any superfluous words.

1 How many days does Raju need a room for? Which day is he leaving?

शंकर	आइए साहब, आपको क्या चाहिए ?
राजू	मुझको कमरा चाहिए । कोई अच्छा-सा कमरा दिखाइए ।
शंकर	बहुत अच्छा । आपको कैसा कमरा चाहिए ?
राजू	मुझको बड़ा कमरा चाहिए ।
शंकर	बहुत अच्छा । कितने दिनों के लिए चाहिए ?
राजू	चार दिनों के लिए, यानी शुक्रवार तक ।
शंकर	बहुत अच्छा । आज से शुक्रवार तक हमारा एक बहुत अच्छा कमरा ख़ाली है ।
राजू	क्या कमरे में फ़ोन है ? फ़ोन चाहिए ।
शंकर	जी हाँ, है । बहुत अच्छा कमरा है । इस शहर में ऐसे कमरे मुश्किल से मिलते हैं ।
राजू	किराया कितना है ?
शंकर	सिर्फ़ दो हज़ार रुपये ।
राजू	कमरा दिखाइए ।
शंकर	बहुत अच्छा साहब । आइए, मैं कमरा दिखाता हूँ ।
Śankar	*āie sāhab, āpko kyā cāhie?*
Rājū	*mujhko kamrā cāhie. koī acchā-sā kamrā dikhāie.*
Śankar	*bahut acchā. āpko kaisā kamrā cāhie?*
Rājū	*mujhko baṛā kamrā cāhie.*
Śankar	*bahut acchā. kitne dinõ ke lie cāhie?*
Rājū	*cār dinõ ke lie, yānī śukravār tak.*
Śankar	*bahut acchā. āj se śukravār tak hamārā ek bahut acchā kamrā khālī hai.*
Rājū	*kyā kamre mẽ fon hai? fon cahie.*
Śankar	*jī hā̃, hai. bahut acchā kamrā hai. is śahar mẽ aise kamre muśkil se milte haĩ.*
Rājū	*kirāyā kitnā hai?*
Śankar	*sirf do hazār rupaye.*
Rājū	*kamrā dikhāie.*
Śankar	*bahut acchā sāhab. āie, maĩ kamrā dikhātā hū̃.*

2 Now listen again and answer these questions:

a What does Raju insist on having in the room?

b How much is the room per night?

LANGUAGE TIP

In this last line, Shankar's sentence मैं कमरा दिखाता हूँ *maĩ kamrā dikhātā hũ* shows how the present tense can refer to something just about to be done.

The encounter continues, but before we move on to the second part, some more new words:

ऊपर	*ūpar*	*up, upstairs*
दरवाज़ा	*darvāzā* m.	*door*
खोलना	*kholnā*	*to open*
करवाना	*karvānā*	*to get done, caused to be done* (by someone else)
काम करना	*kām karnā*	*to work, to function*
चालू करना	*cālū karnā*	*to turn on, make work*
घूमना	*ghūmnā*	*to turn, revolve*
लाइट	*lāiṭ* f.	*electricity, electrical power*
बिजली	*bijlī* f.	*electricity*
शुभ	*śubh*	*good, auspicious* (mainly used in the formula शुभ नाम *śubh nām good name*)
कोई दूसरा	*koī dūsrā*	*another, some other one*

LANGUAGE TIP

Hindi has a category of verbs called 'causatives' (e.g. करवाना *karvānā to cause to be done*): they speak of getting something done by someone else. Notice in the dialogue when Shankar says मैं कमरा अभी साफ़ करवाता हूँ *maĩ kamrā abhī sāf karvātā hũ* he means, *I'll have it cleaned immediately (by someone else).*

05.09 *All seems to be going fine so far and Shankar is obviously eager to please. But it's when he shows Raju the room that the problems start. Do you notice a change in tone in the way Raju addresses Shankar? (Look out for the pronouns.)*

3 Overall, what is wrong with the room?

(दोनों आदमी ऊपर जाते हैं । शंकर एक दरवाज़ा खोलता है ।)

शंकर आइए जी ।
राजू यह कमरा साफ़ नहीं है ।
शंकर बहुत अच्छा साहब । मैं कमरा अभी साफ़ करवाता हूँ ।
राजू क्या यह पुराना पंखा काम करता है ?
शंकर जी हाँ, पंखा काम करता है । बहुत अच्छा पंखा है । आजकल ऐसे पंखे नहीं मिलते हैं ।
राजू चालू करो ।
शंकर बहुत अच्छा साहब ।

(शंकर स्विच को "ऑन" करता है (turns on the switch) *लेकिन पंखा घूमता नहीं ।)*

राजू पंखा घूमता नहीं ।
शंकर जी हाँ, क्योंकि लाइट नहीं है – बिजली नहीं है ।
राजू तुम्हारा नाम क्या है ?
शंकर जी, मुझको शंकर कहते हैं । और आपका शुभ नाम ?
राजू मेरा नाम शर्मा है । श्री राजकुमार शर्मा ।
शंकर बहुत अच्छा नाम है सर । मुझको आपका नाम बहुत पसंद है ।
राजू शंकर, तुम "बहुत अच्छा" बहुत कहते हो । लेकिन यह कमरा बहुत अच्छा नहीं है । मुझको पसंद नहीं है । कोई दूसरा कमरा दिखाओ ।
शंकर बहुत अच्छा शर्मा जी । आइए ।

(donõ ādmī ūpar jāte haĩ. Śankar ek darvāzā kholtā hai.)

Śankar *āie jī.*
Rājū *yah kamrā sāf nahī̃ hai.*
Śankar *bahut acchā sāhab. maĩ kamrā abhī sāf karvātā hū̃.*
Rājū *kyā yah purānā pankhā kām kartā hai?*
Śankar *jī hā̃, pankhā kām kartā hai. bahut acchā pankhā hai. ājkal aise pankhe nahī̃ milte haĩ.*
Rājū *cālū karo.*
Śankar *bahut acchā sāhab.*

(Śankar svic ko 'ān' kartā hai (turns on the switch) lekin pankhā ghūmtā nahī̃.)

Rājū	*pankhā ghūmtā nahī̃.*
Śankar	*jī hā̃, kyõki lāiṭ nahī̃ hai – bijlī nahī̃ hai.*
Rājū	*tumhārā nām kyā hai?*
Śankar	*jī, mujhko Śankar kahte haĩ. aur āpkā śubh nām?*
Rājū	*merā nām Śarmā hai. Śrī Rājkumār Śarmā.*
Śankar	*bahut acchā nām hai sar. mujhko āpkā nām bahut pasand hai.*
Rājū	*Śankar, tum 'bahut acchā' bahut kahte ho. lekin yah kamrā bahut acchā nahī̃ hai. mujhko pasand nahī̃ hai. koī dūsrā kamrā dikhāo.*
Śankar	*bahut acchā Śarmā jī. āie.*

In the first part of the dialogue, Raju had been calling Shankar आप *āp* (as is apparent from such commands as दिखाइए *dikhāie*); but in the second part, he calls Shankar तुम *tum* – the drop in honorific level indicating his declining patience!

4 Listen again and answer these questions:

a Why doesn't the fan turn?

b What is it that Shankar keeps saying that finally bothers Raju?

Language discovery 4 *Quantities*

Expressing quantities or amounts in Hindi is simplicity itself:

एक किलो चावल	*ek kilo cāval*	*one kilo of rice*
दो चम्मच चीनी	*do cammac cīnī*	*two spoons of sugar*
तीन कप चाय	*tīn kap cāy*	*three cups of tea*

The word 'of' is not used between the amount and the measured substance, as it is in English.

Use what you've learned to answer these two questions:

आप को कितने किलो चावल चाहिए? *āp ko kitne kilo cāval cāhie?* (तीन *tīn*)

आप को कितने चम्मच चीनी चाहिए? *āp ko kitne cammac cīnī cāhie?* (एक *ek*)

Practice

1 05.10 **You're doing some shopping in the market. Reply to the shopkeeper's questions:**

a आइए ! आज आपकी तबियत कैसी है ?
āie! āj āpkī tabiyat kaisī hai?

b घर में सब लोग ठीक हैं ?
ghar mẽ sab log ṭhīk haĩ?

c आपको क्या चाहिए ?
āpko kyā cāhie?

d कितना चाहिए ?
kitnā cāhie?

e आपको और क्या चाहिए ?
āpko aur kyā cāhie?

f साबुन वग़ैरह चाहिए ?
sābun vagairah cāhie?

g चाय, कॉफ़ी, बिस्कुट... ?
cāy, kāfī, biskuṭ...?

h आपका घर कहाँ है ?
āpkā ghar kahā̃ hai?

i क्या ये चीज़ें भी आपकी हैं ?
kyā ye cīzẽ bhī āpkī haĩ?

j आपकी गाड़ी बहुत दूर खड़ी है ?
āpkī gāṛī bahut dūr khaṛī hai?

2 **Translate into Hindi:**

a I need three samosas.
b They don't like this house, they like the small house.
c I don't like this room, show me another room.
d Where do you live? We live in Old Delhi.
e Your house isn't very far from my house. Come tomorrow.
f I know that (कि *ki*) my teacher doesn't live here.
g I know where your teacher lives.
h Houses in Delhi are quite expensive.
i Grandfather speaks very beautiful Hindi.
j We don't want these black shoes.

3 **Complete the requests using these verbs:** आना ***ānā***, बैठना ***baiṭhnā***, पीना ***pīnā***, खाना ***khānā***, देना ***denā***.

a (तुम) इस कुर्सी पर मत ________ । *(tum) is kursī par mat ________.*

b (आप) मुझ को वह कलम ________ । *(āp) mujh ko vah kalam ________.*

c (आप) कुछ और ________ । *(āp) kuch aur ________.*

d (तुम) पानी ________ । *(tum) pānī ________.*

e (आप) यहाँ ________ । *(āp) yahā̃ ________.*

4 **Complete the sentences using the correct form of the words in brackets.**

a मेरी कॉपी ________ पर पड़ी है । (मेज़)
merī kāpī ________ par paṛī hai. (mez)

b ________ को कुछ मत बताओ । (वह लड़का)
________ ko kuch mat batāo. (vah laṛkā)

c खाना ________ में रखता हूँ । (ये डिब्बे)
khānā ________ mẽ rakhtā hū̃. (ye ḍibbe)

d ये फूल ________ को दीजिए । (वे लड़कियाँ)
ye phūl ________ ko dījie. (ve laṛkiā̃)

e ________ में अच्छे कपड़े मिलते हैं । (वह दूकान)
________ mẽ acche kapṛe milte haĩ. (vah dūkān)

Vocabulary builder

आधा	*ādhā* m.	*half*
ऊपर	*ūpar*	*up, upstairs*
ऐसा	*aisā*	*such, of this kind*
क़मीज़	*qamīz* f.	*shirt*
करवाना	*karvānā*	*to get done* (by someone else), *to cause to be done*
कल	*kal*	*yesterday; tomorrow*
काम करना	*kām karnā*	*to work, to function*
काला	*kālā*	*black*
कि	*ki*	*that* (conjunction)
किराया	*kirāyā* m.	*rent; fare*
किलो	*kilo* m.	*kilo, kilogramme*
कुरता	*kurtā* m.	*kurta*
के लिए	*ke lie*	*for*
कोई	*koī*	*some, any, a*
कोई दूसरा	*koī dūsrā*	*some other, another*

कौनसा	*kaunsā*	*which?*
क्यों	*kyõ*	*why?*
क्योंकि	*kyõki*	*because*
खोलना	*kholnā*	*to open*
घूमना	*ghūmnā*	*to turn, revolve*
चम्मच	*cammac* m.	*spoon*
चाक़ू	*cāqū* m.	*knife, penknife*
चाबी	*cābī* f.	*key*
चालू करना	*cālū karnā*	*to turn on*
चावल	*cāval* m.	*rice*
चाहना	*cāhnā*	*to want, wish*
चाहिए	*cāhie*	*(is) wanted, needed*
चीज़	*cīz* f.	*thing*
चीनी	*cīnī* f.	*sugar*
जगह	*jagah* f.	*place*
ज़ुकाम	*zukām* m.	*head cold*
जूता	*jūtā* m.	*shoe*
जो	*jo*	*who, which; the one who/which*
टार्च	*ṭārc* m.	*torch, flashlight*
टिकिया	*ṭikiyā* f.	*cake (of soap)*
डाक	*ḍāk* f.	*post*
डाक घर	*ḍāk ghar* m.	*post office*
डाक की टिकट	*ḍāk kī ṭikaṭ* f.	*stamp*
डिब्बा	*ḍibbā* m.	*box*
ढाबा	*ḍhābā* m.	*roadside café*
तबियत	*tabiyat* f.	*health, disposition*
ताज़ा	*tāzā* m.	*fresh*
तो	*to*	*so, then*
दरवाज़ा	*darvāzā* m.	*door*
दिखाना	*dikhānā*	*to show*
दिन	*din* m.	*day*
नीला	*nīlā*	*blue*
पढ़ना	*paṛhnā*	*to read; to study*
पर	*par*	*but*
पसंद	*pasand*	*pleasing* (यह मुझको पसंद है *yah mujhko pasand hai* *I like this)*
फल	*phal* m.	*fruit*
फलवाला	*phalvālā* m.	*fruitseller*
फ़ोन	*fon* m.	*phone* (फ़ोन करना *fon karnā* *to phone)*

बिजली	*bijlī* f.	*electricity*
बिस्कुट	*biskuṭ* m.	*biscuit*
बुख़ार	*bukhār* m.	*fever*
मालूम	*mālūm*	*(is) known*
मिलना	*milnā*	*to meet; to be available*
मुश्किल	*muśkil*	*difficult*, (मुश्किल से *muśkil se* barely, hardly)
यानी	*yānī*	*in other words, that is to say*
रहना	*rahnā*	*to live, to stay*
रुपया	*rupayā* m.	*rupee*
लाइट	*lāiṭ* f.	*light, electric power*
लाल	*lāl*	*red*
वग़ैरह	*vagairah*	*etc., and so on*
शहर	*śahar* m.	*town, city*
शायद	*śāyad*	*maybe, perhaps*
शुक्रवार	*śukravār* m.	*Friday*
शुभ	*śubh*	*good, auspicious*
सब कुछ	*sab kuch*	*everything*
-सा	*-sā*	*'-ish'* (suffix that qualifies an adjective, as in बड़ा-सा *baṛā-sā* biggish)
साड़ी	*sāṛī* f.	*sari*
साफ़ करना	*sāf karnā*	*to clean*
साबुन	*sābun* m.	*soap*
सौ	*sau* m.	*hundred*
हाथी	*hāthī* m.	*elephant*
होटल	*hoṭal* m.	*hotel, restaurant, café*

Test yourself

1 English uses an identical structure in both *She speaks Hindi* and *She likes Hindi*, but Hindi uses different constructions for each. What are they?

2 In किसको चाय चाहिए ? *kisko cāy cāhie? Who wants tea?*, what is the literal meaning of किसको *kisko*?

3 The sentence हमको दिल्ली बहुत पसंद है *hamko dillī bahut pasand hai*, meaning *We like Delhi very much*, has a singular verb. Why?

4 We have already encountered the verb मिलना *milnā* as meaning *to meet*. What new function does it carry in this unit? Give a simple example.

5 How would you say *I need two more keys*?

6 Why does the verb होता *hotā* appear in sentence A and not in sentence B?

A दिल्ली में मकान बहुत महँगे होते हैं । *Dillī mẽ makān bahut mahãge hote haĩ.*

B ये मकान बहुत महँगे हैं । *ye makān bahut mahãge haĩ.*

7 How would you say *(Please) give us three cups of coffee*?

8 Give the Hindi for: *red saris, good things, little boxes, beautiful elephants.*

9 An ill-tempered man, speaking very abruptly, tells a junior employee to open the door. How might he say it?

10 What's the difference in meaning between कमरा साफ़ करना *kamrā sāf karnā* and कमरा साफ़ करवाना *kamrā sāf karvānā*?

SELF CHECK

I CAN...
... talk about likes and needs.
... use expressions for *to get* and *to know*.

6 आप क्या काम करते हैं ?

āp kyā kām karte haĩ?

What work do you do?

In this unit you will learn how to:

- ***talk about relationships.***
- ***ask about people's ages.***
- ***say 'I can' and 'Let me'.***

Language points

- *possessives*
- *verb stem and infinitive*

Language discovery 1

POSSESSION AND *TO HAVE*

You already know that मेरा *merā* means *my, mine,* आपका *āpkā* means *your, yours,* उसका *uskā* means *his, her/hers, its,* and हमारा *hamārā* means *our, ours.* So much for showing possession with pronouns; now we need to see how possession works with names and nouns, as in *Ram's friend* or *my son's name.*

The phrase राम का कुत्ता *Rām kā kuttā* means *Ram's dog;* मीना का कुत्ता *Mīnā kā kuttā* means *Meena's dog.* So the little word का *kā* works like the apostrophe *s* in English. Some more examples:

मनोज का दोस्त	*Manoj kā dost*	*Manoj's friend*
गीता का पति	*Gītā kā pati*	*Geeta's husband*
राजू का बेटा	*Rājū kā beṭā*	*Raju's son*

This is a very important feature of the language and you should practise it thoroughly! Make some phrases of your own from the items provided:

डाक्टर	*ḍākṭar*		कमरा	*kamrā*
पिता जी	*pitā jī*	का	भाई	*bhāī*
पड़ोसी	*paṛosī*		चाचा	*cācā*
विद्यार्थी	*vidyārthī*	*kā*	नाम	*nām*
मेरी पत्नी	*merī patnī*		पैसा	*paisā*

You'll have made phrases like मेरी पत्नी का पैसा *merī patnī kā paisā* *my wife's money*. Great! Now look carefully at these phrases:

लड़के का दोस्त	*laṛke kā dost*	*the boy's friend*
लड़के की बहिन	*laṛke kī bahin*	*the boy's sister*
लड़के के माँ-बाप	*laṛke ke mā̃-bāp*	*the boy's parents*

Two things have happened: लड़का *laṛkā* has become oblique, and का *kā* has changed like an adjective to agree with the following word.

So का *kā* is a postposition that works like an adjective! This didn't show up earlier (in राम का कुत्ता *Rām kā kuttā*, etc.) because non-inflecting masculine words had been cunningly chosen there. But from now on we'll have to keep an eye on this का *kā* business. For practice, make up phrases from the following lists, remembering to use oblique versions of words from the left-hand column, and to make का *kā* agree with the word chosen from the right-hand column:

वह आदमी	*vah ādmī*		चाबी	*cabī*
मेरा दोस्त	*merā dost*		भाई	*bhāī*
यह लड़का	*yah laṛkā*	का / की / के	दो भाई	*do bhāī*
फलवाला	*phalvālā*	*kā kī ke*	माता	*mātā*
उसका बेटा	*uskā beṭā*		कपड़े	*kapṛe*
ये लोग	*ye log*		गाड़ी	*gāṛī*

How would you say *I like that boy's shoes* and *Please give me Ram's books*?

DO YOU HAVE BROTHERS AND SISTERS?

Some time back we saw that Hindi doesn't have a verb *to have*, and that ownership of goods and chattels is indicated by के पास *ke pās*:

उसके पास दो चाबियाँ हैं । *uske pās do cābiyā̃ haĩ.* He/she has two keys.

But look at the following and notice the difference:

उसके दो भाई हैं । *uske do bhāī haĩ.* He/she has two brothers.

उसकी दो बहिनें हैं । *uskī do bahinẽ haĩ.* He/she has two sisters.

So describing the 'ownership' of relatives involves का *kā* (or a pronoun like मेरा *merā*, or आपका *āpkā*) rather than के पास *ke pās*. The same applies for parts of the body and real estate:

रावण के दस सिर हैं ।
Rāvaṇ ke das sir haĩ.
Rāvaṇ has ten heads.

मेरा एक भाई है । उसके दो मकान हैं ।
merā ek bhāī hai. uske do makān haĩ.
I have one brother. He has two houses.

मेरी कोई बहिन नहीं । *merī koī bahin nahī̃.* I don't have any sister(s).

Imagine you have three sisters and no brother. How would you answer this question?

आप के कितने भाई-बहिन हैं ? *āp ke kitne bhāī-bahin haĩ?*

Listen and understand

1 06.01 **Translate the phrases, then listen and repeat to check your answers.**

a Ram's father
b Ram's mother
c Ram's sister
d Ram's sister's name
e Ram's brother
f Ram's brother's name
g Ram's dog
h The dog's name
i The man's name
j This man's name
k That man's name

2 06.02 **Listen to a man describing his family and decide if the statements are true or false.**

मेरा नाम सुहास है । मेरे दो भाई हैं, एक छोटा, और एक बड़ा । मेरा बड़ा भाई बैंक में काम करता है । छोटा भाई संगीतकार है । दो बहिनें भी हैं । वे दोनों अमरीका में रहती हैं । मेरी दोनों बहिनें शादी शुदा हैं । दोनों काम करती हैं । क्या काम करती हैं ? मालूम नहीं । मेरा एक लड़का है । वह विद्यार्थी है ।

merā nām Suhās hai. mere do bhāī haĩ, ek choṭā, aur ek baṛā. merā baṛā bhāī baink mẽ kām kartā hai. choṭā bhāī sangītkār hai. do bahinẽ bhī haĩ. ve donõ Amrīkā mẽ rahtī haĩ. merī donõ bahinẽ śādī-śudā haĩ. donõ kām kartī haĩ. kyā kām kartī haĩ? mālūm nahĩ merā ek laṛkā hai. vah vidyārthī hai.

a His name is Mohit.
b He has two brothers.
c His younger brother is a musician.
d His two sisters live in India.
e He has a daughter.

Language discovery 2

THE SHARMA FAMILY

Now let's spend some quality time with the Sharmas. Here's their family tree, to remind you of the family relationships.

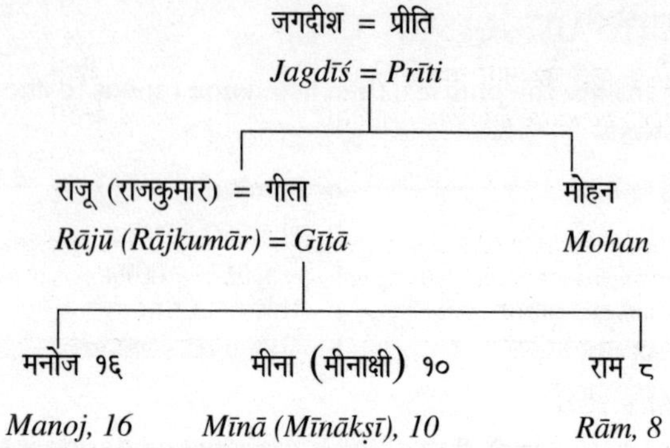

You have to sort out who's who. Test yourself by covering up the answers on the right of the page, then check your answers.

मनोज का छोटा भाई कौन है ? *Manoj kā choṭā bhāī kaun hai?*	राम *Rām*
राम और मनोज की बहिन कौन है ? *Rām aur Manoj kī bahin kaun hai?*	मीना *Mīnā*
बच्चों की माँ का नाम क्या है ? *baccõ kī mā̃ kā nām kyā hai?*	गीता *Gītā*
बच्चों के बाप का नाम क्या है ? *baccõ ke bāp kā nām kyā hai?*	राजू *Rājū*
राजू और गीता की बेटी का नाम क्या है ? *Rājū aur Gītā kī beṭī kā nām kyā hai?*	मीना *Mīnā*
बच्चों के दादा का नाम क्या है ? *baccõ ke dādā kā nām kyā hai?*	जगदीश *Jagdīś*
बच्चों की दादी का नाम क्या है ? *baccõ kī dādī kā nām kyā hai?*	प्रीति *Prīti*
मीना का पूरा नाम क्या है ? *Mīnā kā pūrā nām kyā hai?*	मीनाक्षी शर्मा *Mīnākṣī Śarmā*
बच्चों के चाचा का नाम क्या है ? *baccõ ke cācā kā nām kyā hai?*	मोहन *Mohan*
राजू के पिता का नाम क्या है ? *Rājū ke pitā kā nām kyā hai?*	जगदीश *Jagdīś*

And a final question:

राजू के बच्चों के कुत्ते का नाम क्या है ?	मोती
Rājū ke baccõ ke kutte kā nām kyā hai?	*Motī*

CULTURE TIP

Hindi has a much fuller set of relationship terms than English. For example, the word चाचा *cācā uncle* means specifically *father's younger brother*, while *father's older brother* is ताऊ *tāū*, and so on.

HOW OLD ARE YOU?

06.03 Another use of का-के-की *kā-ke-kī* is to give people's ages. It's used with the word साल *sāl* (m.) *year*:

मनोज सोलह साल का है ।	*Manoj solah sāl kā hai.*	*Manoj is sixteen ('is of sixteen years').*
मीना दस साल की है ।	*Mīnā das sāl kī hai.*	*Meena is ten.*
गीता कितने साल की है ?	*Gītā kitne sāl kī hai?*	*How old is Geeta?*
राम कितने साल का है ?	*Rām kitne sāl kā hai?*	*How old is Ram?*
राम आठ साल का है ।	*Rām āṭh sāl kā hai.*	*Ram is eight.*

The word for *age* is उम्र *umra* (f.), often pronounced as *umar*.

आपकी कितनी उम्र है ?	*āpkī kitnī umra hai?*	*How old are you?*

How would you answer the question: आपकी कितनी उम्र है ? *āpkī kitnī umra hai?*

- **a** If you were a thirteen-year-old girl.
- **b** If you were a nine-year-old boy.

Listening

1 06.04 **Listen to a brief description of four children, then match each child's name with his or her age. (There is an extra name in the list!)**

a *Sunaina*	**1** eleven
b *Mohan*	**2** three
c *Jyoti*	**3** five
d *Sudhir*	**4** six
e *Uma*	**5** nine

2 Which child is not mentioned on the audio? How would you say his or her age in Hindi?

SOMEONE IS HERE

The word कोई *koī any* also means *anyone* or *someone* (and कोई नहीं *koī nahī̃* means *no one*). कोई *koī* can also refer to inanimates, as in कोई दुकान *koī dukān some shop (or other)*. Its oblique form is किसी *kisī*, as in किसी का बेटा *kisī kā beṭā someone's son.*

Don't confuse किसी *kisī* with किस *kis*, which is the oblique of कौन *kaun* and of क्या *kyā*: किसको *kisko to whom/what?*, किसका भाई *kiskā bhāī whose brother?*

कोई है ?	*koī hai?*	*Anyone there?*
घर में कोई नहीं है ।	*ghar mẽ koī nahī̃ hai.*	*There's nobody in the house.*
किसी के घर में कोई चूहा रहता था । *kisī ke ghar mẽ koī cūhā rahtā thā.*		*In somebody's house there lived a certain mouse.*

Here's a very useful little phrase:

कोई बात नहीं । *koī bāt nahī̃.* *Never mind, it doesn't matter, don't mention it.*

Used with a number, कोई *koī* means *about*, just as *some* does in English:

कोई बारह गाड़ियाँ *koī bārah gāṛiyā̃* *some twelve cars*

As we've already seen, कुछ *kuch* means *some* (कुछ पैसा *kuch paisā some money*) or *something*. It doesn't change in the oblique.

क्या मेज़ पर कुछ है ? *kyā mez par kuch hai?*	*Is there something on the table?*
हमको कुछ दूध चाहिए । *hamko kuch dūdh cāhie.*	*We need some milk.*
घर में कुछ नहीं है । *ghar mẽ kuch nahī̃ hai.*	*There's nothing in the house.*
कुछ लोगों के पास कुछ नहीं है । *kuch logõ ke pās kuch nahī̃ hai.*	*Some people have nothing.*

a What is the meaning of the following statement?

किसी को कुछ मत बताइए ।   *kisi ko kuch mat batāie.*

b Suppose someone thanks you for doing them a small favour, how would you say, *No problem, Don't mention it*?

Storyline

MANOJ INTRODUCES PRATAP TO HIS FATHER

06.05

1 Does Raju address Pratap formally or informally?

मनोज	प्रताप, मेरे पिताजी से मिलो ।[1]
प्रताप	नमस्ते जी ।
राजू	हलो प्रताप, क्या हाल है ?[2]
प्रताप	ठीक है, शुक्रिया ।
राजू	तुम्हारी उम्र कितनी है प्रताप ?
प्रताप	मैं इक्कीस साल का हूँ ।
राजू	तुम्हारे कितने भाई और बहिनें हैं ?
प्रताप	मेरा एक भाई है, मेरी कोई बहिन नहीं है ।
Manoj	*Pratāp, mere pitājī se milo.*[1]
Pratāp	*namaste jī.*
Rājū	*halo Pratāp, kyā hāl hai?*[2]
Pratāp	*ṭhīk hai, śukriyā.*
Rājū	*tumhārī umra kitnī hai Pratāp?*
Pratāp	*maĩ ikkīs sāl kā hū̃.*
Rājū	*tumhāre kitne bhāī aur bahinẽ haĩ?*
Pratāp	*merā ek bhāī hai, merī koī bahin nahī̃ hai.*

2 Answer the following questions:

a How old is Pratap?

b How many sisters does he have?

Notes

1 मिलना ***milnā* to meet uses the linking word से *se* with –** पिताजी से मिलो ***pitājī se milo* Meet (with) Father.**

2 क्या हाल है ? ***kyā hāl hai? How's things?* (lit. *what's the condition?*) This is a very common way of asking how someone is – a more colloquial equivalent to** तुम कैसे हो ? ***tum kaise ho? How are you?***

Listening and speaking

1 06.06 **Answer the questions for yourself.**

आपके कितने भाई हैं ? *āpke kitne bhāī haĩ?*

आपकी कितनी बहिनें हैं ? *āpkī kitnī bahinẽ haĩ?*

क्या आपके घर में कोई कुत्ता है ? *kyā āpke ghar mẽ koī kuttā hai?*

2 06.07 **We're going to have another look at the present-tense verbs that we met earlier. First, match the subject with the activity. Then, listen to check your answers.**

a फलवाला *phalvālā*
fruit seller

b अध्यापिका *adhyāpikā*
teacher (female)

c लेखक *lekhak*
writer

d दर्ज़ी *darzī*
tailor

e विद्यार्थी *vidyārthī*
student

f ट्रेन *ṭren*
train

g डाक्टर *ḍākṭar*
doctor

h दुकानदार *dukāndār*
shopkeeper

1 किताबें लिखता है ।
kitābẽ likhtā hai.

2 कालेज में पढ़ता है ।
kālej mẽ paṛhtā hai.

3 फल बेचता है ।
phal bectā hai.

4 मरीज़ों का इलाज करता है ।
marīzõ kā ilāj kartā hai.

5 कालेज में पढ़ाती है ।
kālej mẽ paṛhātī hai.

6 माल बेचता है ।
māl bectā hai.

7 कपड़े बनाता है ।
kapṛe banātā hai.

8 तेज़ चलती है ।
tez caltī hai.

Language discovery 3

YOU CAN GO

06.08 *You can go* is आप जा सकते हैं *āp jā sakte haĩ*. This features the special verb सकना *saknā* – special because it never stands alone, but always follows the stem of the main verb (here जा *jā* from जाना *jānā to go*).

आप मेरी हिन्दी समझ सकते हैं ?
āp merī hindī samajh sakte haĩ? — *You can understand my Hindi?*

मैं यह काम नहीं कर सकता ।
maĩ yah kām nahī̃ kar saktā. — *I can't do this work.*

यह कैसे हो सकता है ?
yah kaise ho sakta hai? — *How can this be?*

06.09 Now turn these *I do* sentences into *I can do* sentences, following this example:

मैं हिन्दी बोलता हूँ ।	*maĩ hindī boltā hū̃.*	*I speak Hindi.*
मैं हिन्दी बोल सकता हूँ ।	*maĩ hindī bol saktā hū̃.*	*I can speak Hindi.*

१ हम सिनेमा जाते हैं ।	*ham sinemā jāte haĩ.*
२ चाचा जी घर पर रहते हैं ।	*cācā jī ghar par rahte haĩ.*
३ मैं अध्यापक से पूछता हूँ ।	*maĩ adhyāpak se pūchtā hū̃.*
४ बच्चे बग़ीचे में खेलते हैं ।	*bacce bag̲īce mẽ khelte haĩ.*
५ मैं अख़बार पढ़ती हूँ ।	*maĩ ak̲h̲bār paṛhtī hū̃.*
६ हम बच्चों को सब कुछ बताते हैं ।	*ham baccõ ko sab kuch batāte haĩ.*
७ तुम शराब नहीं पीते हो ।	*tum śarāb nahī̃ pīte ho.*
८ वह कुछ नहीं कहता है ।	*vah kuch nahī̃ kahtā hai.*

Storyline

THERE'S NOBODY IN THE HOUSE

06.10 *Manoj is talking to Pratap. He thinks they're alone!*

1 What does Manoj want to do?

मनोज	एक सिग्रेट पियो प्रताप ! घर में कोई नहीं है ।
प्रताप	नहीं, मैं सिग्रेट नहीं पीता । तुम पी सकते हो ।
मनोज	हाँ मैं रोज़ दो-तीन सिग्रेट पीता हूँ ।
प्रताप	ये सिग्रेट तुम्हारे हैं ?

मनोज	नहीं, ये मेरे बाप के हैं ।
प्रताप	उनके सिग्रेट क्यों पीते हो ?
मनोज	मेरे पास पैसे नहीं हैं । मैं सिग्रेट नहीं ख़रीद सकता ।
राजू	(दूसरे कमरे से) मनोज ! ओ मनोज ! तुम कहाँ हो ?
प्रताप	तुम्हारे पिताजी की आवाज़ !

(राजू कमरे में आता है)

राजू	अरे, यह क्या ? वह तुम्हारे हाथ में क्या है मनोज ?
मनोज	पिताजी ! देखिए, यह प्रताप का सिग्रेट है ...
राजू	मनोज, बकवास मत कर । प्रताप, तुम जा सकते हो ।
मनोज	लेकिन ... लेकिन ...

Manoj	*ek sigreṭ piyo Pratāp! ghar mẽ koī nahī̃ hai.*
Pratāp	*nahī̃, maĩ sigreṭ nahī̃ pītā. tum pī sakte ho.*
Manoj	*hā̃ maĩ roz do-tīn sigreṭ pītā hū̃.*
Pratāp	*ye sigreṭ tumhāre haĩ?*
Manoj	*nahī̃, ye mere bāp ke haĩ.*
Pratāp	*unke sigreṭ kyõ pīte ho?*
Manoj	*mere pās paise nahī̃ haĩ. maĩ sigreṭ nahī̃ <u>kh</u>arīd saktā.*
Rājū	*(dūsre kamre se) Manoj! O Manoj! tum kahā̃ ho?*
Pratāp	*tumhāre pitājī kī āvāz!*

(Rājū kamre mẽ ātā hai)

Rājū	*are, yah kyā? vah tumhāre hāth mẽ kyā hai Manoj?*
Manoj	*pitājī! dekhie, yah Pratāp kā sigreṭ hai.*
Rājū	*Manoj, bakvās mat kar. Pratāp, tum jā sakte ho.*
Manoj	*lekin ... lekin ...*

2 Now listen to the dialogue again and answer the questions.

a How often does Pratap smoke?

b Why does Manoj smoke his father's cigarettes?

c How does he try to avoid getting in trouble for it?

Listen and understand

06.11 **Are these statements right (सही *sahī correct*, सच *sac true*) or *wrong* (ग़लत *galat*)?**

a प्रताप सिग्रेट पीना चाहता है ।
Pratāp sigreṭ pīnā cāhtā hai.

b मनोज सोचता है कि राजू घर पर नहीं है ।
Manoj soctā hai ki Rājū ghar par nahī̃ hai.

c मनोज के पास उसके पिता के सिग्रेट हैं ।
Manoj ke pās uske pitā ke sigreṭ haĩ.

d मनोज हमेशा सच बोलता है ।
Manoj hameśā sac boltā hai.

e राजू के सिग्रेट प्रताप के हाथ में हैं ।
Rājū ke sigreṭ Pratāp ke hāth mẽ haĩ.

f राजू कहता है कि दोनों लड़के जा सकते हैं ।
Rājū kahtā hai ki donõ laṛke jā sakte haĩ.

Language discovery 4

LET ME

Let me go is मुझको जाने दो *mujhko jāne do*. The sense *to let, to allow* uses the verb देना *denā*, whose literal meaning is *to give*; it's like saying *give me (permission) to go*. As you can see in मुझको जाने दो *mujhko jāne do*, it's used with the infinitive of the main verb. The infinitive ends in *-e* in this construction (here, the infinitive जाना *jānā* changes to oblique जाने *jāne*), and the person who is *allowed to do* takes को *ko*.

हम बच्चों को खेलने देते हैं ।
ham baccõ ko khelne dete haĩ.
We let the kids play.

पर हम उनको सड़क पर खेलने नहीं देते ।
par ham unko saṛak par khelne nahī̃ dete.
But we don't let them play on the road.

हमको सोचने दीजिए ।	*hamko socne dījie.*	*Please let us think.*
मनोज को बाहर जाने दो ।	*Manoj ko bāhar jāne do.*	*Let Manoj go out.*

How would you say *Ram's mother doesn't let him drink coffee* and *Please let me go to the cinema*?

Storyline

MANOJ HAS A DREAM

06.12 *Manoj is dreaming. In this dream, he overhears his mother Geeta talking.*

1 Who is Geeta talking to in the dream?

मनोज का सपना ।

गीता – "मनोज के बाप, मनोज को सिग्रेट पीने दो, उसको शराब भी पीने दो । वह बहुत अच्छा लड़का है; वह स्कूल में बहुत ध्यान से पढ़ता है । उसको गाड़ी क्यों नहीं चलाने देते हो ? और हाँ, छुट्टियों में उसको अमरीका जाने दो !"

Manoj kā sapnā

Gītā – 'Manoj ke bāp, Manoj ko sigreṭ pīne do, usko śarāb bhī pīne do. vah bahut acchā laṛkā hai; vah skūl mẽ bahut dhyān se paṛhtā hai. usko gāṛī kyõ nahī̃ calāne dete ho? aur hā̃, chuṭṭiyõ mẽ usko amrīkā jāne do!'

2 Answer the following questions:

- **a** Why should Manoj's father let him smoke and drink?
- **b** Judging by what his mother says in his dream, where does Manoj want to go on holiday?

Practice

1 Convert the *I want to...* sentences into *Let me...* sentences, following the example:

मैं घर जाना चाहता हूँ ।	मुझको घर जाने दीजिए/दो ।
maĩ ghar jānā cāhtā hū̃.	*mujhko ghar jāne dījie / do.*
I want to go home.	Let me go home.

- **a** मैं अमरीका जाना चाहता हूँ । *maĩ amrīkā jānā cāhtā hū̃.*
- **b** मैं गाड़ी चलाना चाहती हूँ । *maĩ gāṛī calānā cāhtī hū̃.*
- **c** मैं खाना खाना चाहता हूँ । *maĩ khānā khānā cāhtā hū̃.*
- **d** मैं काम करना चाहती हूँ । *maĩ kām karnā cāhtī hū̃.*
- **e** मैं आपसे बात करना चाहता हूँ । *maĩ āpse bāt karnā cāhtā hū̃.*

Continue doing the same with sentences f–j. These feature people other than *I*, as in this example:

वह सोना चाहता है ।	उसको सोने दीजिए/दो ।
vah sonā cāhtā hai.	*usko sone dījie/do*
He wants to sleep.	*Let him sleep.*

f वह सिग्रेट पीना चाहता है ।
vah sigreṭ pīnā cāhtā hai.

g हम अध्यापक से कुछ कहना चाहते हैं ।
ham adhyāpak se kuch kahnā cāhte haĩ.

h वह हिन्दी सीखना चाहती है ।
vah hindī sīkhnā cāhtī hai.

i बच्चे समोसे खाना चाहते हैं ।
bacce samose khānā cāhte haĩ.

j हम यहाँ रहना चाहते हैं ।
ham yahā̃ rahnā cāhte haĩ.

LEARNING TIP

Repeating formulas like this is a very efficient way of learning new expressions. Say them over and over again, out loud. And try making up new examples, choosing any new verbs from the glossary.

2 Answer these questions about occupations:

a	फलवाला क्या बेचता है ?	*phalvālā kyā bectā hai?*
b	अख़बारवाला क्या बेचता है ?	*a<u>kh</u>bārvālā kyā bectā hai?*
c	दूधवाला क्या बेचता है ?	*dūdhvālā kyā bectā hai?*
d	अध्यापक क्या करता है ?	*adhyāpak kyā kartā hai?*
e	स्कूल में बच्चे क्या करते हैं ?	*skūl mẽ bacce kyā karte haĩ?*
f	घर पर बच्चे क्या करते हैं ?	*ghar par bacce kyā karte haĩ?*
g	ड्राइवर क्या करता है ?	*ḍrāivar kyā kartā hai?*
h	दुकानदार क्या करता है ?	*dukāndār kyā kartā hai?*

3 Answer these questions addressed to you:

a आप कहाँ रहते हैं/रहती हैं ?
āp kahā̃ rahte haĩ / rahtī haĩ?

b आप क्या काम करते हैं/करती हैं ?
āp kyā kām karte haĩ / kartī haĩ?

c क्या आप सितार बजाते हैं/बजाती हैं ?
kyā āp sitār bajāte haĩ / bajātī haĩ?

d आप कौनसा अख़बार पढ़ते/पढ़ती हैं ?
āp kaunsā akhbār paṛhte haĩ / paṛhtī haĩ?

e आप कितनी भाषाएँ बोलते हैं/बोलती हैं ?
āp kitnī bhāṣāẽ bolte haĩ / boltī haĩ?

4 Translate the following:

a Jagdish reads Manoj's newspaper.

b My two brothers work in a big office.

c My sister drives my brother's car.

d He only speaks Hindi, he doesn't speak English.

e Our teachers speak three languages.

f His children play cricket in the garden.

g Our parents don't eat meat.

h Where do you work? Where do you live?

i What does your younger (little) brother do?

j How many languages does your mother speak?

5 06.13 **Make *let me* sentences on the model of मुझको जाने दीजिए *mujhko jāne dījie.***

a Let me listen to the radio.
b Let me smoke a cigarette.
c Let me sit here.
d Let me play cricket.
e Let me rest (आराम करना *ārām karnā*).

Vocabulary builder

अख़बार	*a<u>kh</u>bār* m.	*newspaper*
अख़बारवाला	*a<u>kh</u>bārvālā* m.	*newspaper seller*
अध्यापिका	*adhyāpikā* f.	*teacher*
आवाज़	*āvāz* f.	*voice; sound*
इलाज	*ilāj* m.	*cure, treatment*
उम्र	*umra, umar* f.	*age*
ओ	*o*	*oh!*
का-की-के	*kā-kī-ke*	(shows possession, like 's in English)
किसी	*kisī*	oblique of कोई *koī*
कोई	*koī*	*any, some; somebody*
कोई नहीं	*koī nahī̃*	*nobody*
क्रिकेट	*kriket̤* m.	*cricket*
ख़रीदना	*<u>kh</u>arīdnā*	*to buy*
खेलना	*khelnā*	*to play* (a game)
ट्रेन	*t̤ren* f.	*train*
ड्राइवर	*d̤rāivar* m.	*driver*
दर्ज़ी	*darzī* m.	*tailor*
दादा	*dādā* m.	*grandfather* (father's father)
दादी	*dādī* f.	*grandmother* (father's mother)
दुकानदार	*dukāndār* m.	*shopkeeper*
दूध	*dūdh* m.	*milk*
दूधवाला	*dūdhvālā* m.	*milkman*
देना	*denā*	*to give; to allow to, let* (with oblique infinitive: हमको जाने दो *hamko jāne do* Let *us go*)
बकवास	*bakvās* f.	*nonsense, idle chatter*
बच्चा	*baccā* m.	*child*
बाप	*bāp* m.	*dad*
बेचना	*becnā*	*to sell*
भाषा	*bhāṣā* f.	*language*
मरीज़	*marīz* m.	*patient*

माँ	*mā̃* f.	*mother*
माँ-बाप	*mā̃-bāp* m. pl.	*parents*
माल	*māl* m.	*goods, stuff*
रोज़	*roz*	*every day*
लिखना	*likhnā*	*to write*
लेखक	*lekhak* m.	*writer*
सकना	*saknā*	*to be able* (with verb stem: तुम जा सकते हो *tum jā sakte ho You can go*)
सच	*sac* m./adj.	*truth; true*
सड़क	*saṛak* f.	*road, street*
सपना	*sapnā* m.	*dream*
सपना देखना	*sapnā dekhnā*	*to dream, to have a dream*
साल	*sāl* m.	*year*
सोचना	*socnā*	*to think*
सोना	*sonā*	*to sleep*
हाल	*hāl* m.	*condition, state* (in क्या हाल है ? *kyā hāl hai? How's things? How are you?*)

Test yourself

1 His cat is उसकी बिल्ली *uskī billī*. Why oblique उस *us*? And why feminine की *kī*?

2 How would you say *My sister is twelve*?

3 You thank someone for something, and they say कोई बात नहीं *koī bāt nahī̃*. What do they mean?

4 What is the oblique of कोई *koī* ?

5 How would you say, *Someone wants water*?

6 What does this sentence mean, and why doesn't it have हैं *haĩ* at the end? हम अध्यापक जी से नहीं पूछ सकते ! *ham adhyāpak jī se nahī̃ pūch sakte!*

7 पीना *pīnā* means *to drink* – and what else?

8 Give Hindi equivalents for: *ten patients, eleven students, twelve languages, thirteen voices, fourteen children.*

9 देना *denā to give* is used in expressions meaning *to allow, to let*. What's the formula – how does it combine with the verb that relates to the permitted action?

10 What does कोई *koī* mean before a number, as in कोई बीस लोग *koī bīs log*?

SELF CHECK

	I CAN...
○	... talk about relationships.
○	... ask about people's ages.
○	... say *I can* and *Let me*.

7 भूत-काल
bhūt-kāl
The past

In this unit you will learn how to:

- ***talk about memories and routine events in the past.***
- ***add nuance to what you say.***

Language points

- *past imperfective tenses*
- *direct objects*
- *use of emphatics*

Language discovery 1

IN THE PAST

07.01 So far, we've been working in the present all the time. Moving into the past is very easy. It involves these words from the verb 'to be':

	WAS	WERE
MASCULINE	था *thā*	थे *the*
FEMININE	थी *thī*	थीं *thī̃*

We can use this tense in two ways. First, here are *was* and *were* alone:

कल सोमवार था ।	*kal somvār thā.*	*Yesterday was Monday.*
कल आप घर पर थे ।	*kal āp ghar par the.*	*Yesterday you were at home.*
कल वह बीमार थी ।	*kal vah bīmār thī.*	*Yesterday she was ill.*
कल प्रीति जी कहाँ थीं ?	*kal Prīti jī kahā̃ thī̃?*	*Where was Priti ji yesterday?*

Unlike है *hai* and हैं *haī̃*, था-थे-थी-थीं *thā-the-thī-thī̃* distinguish gender as well as number, so we know that the second sentence here refers to males (or one male, honorific plural) and the third to a female.

The second use is in the 'imperfective' tense used for routine actions and introduced in Section 4. Simply changing है *hai* to था *thā* converts present into past – 'I used to ...'.

PRESENT	PAST
मैं यहाँ रहता हूँ । *maĩ yahā̃ rahtā hū̃.* *I live here.*	मैं यहाँ रहता था । *maĩ yahā̃ rahtā thā.* *I used to live here.*
	दादा जी वाराणसी में रहते थे । *dādā jī vārāṇasī mẽ rahte the.* *Grandpa used to live in Varanasi.*
	वे एक दुकान में काम करते थे । *ve ek dukān mẽ kām karte the.* *He used to work in a shop.*
	उनकी बहिनें घर पर खेलती थीं । *unkī bahinẽ ghar par kheltī thī̃.* *His sisters used to play at home.*
	उनके भाई स्कूल जाते थे । *unke bhāī skūl jāte the.* *His brothers used to go to school.*
	वे बहुत ध्यान से पढ़ते थे । *ve bahut dhyān se paṛhte the.* *They used to study very hard.*

Using what you've just learned, change these two sentences from present to past tense:

a मेरे दो भाई दिल्ली में रहते हैं । *mere do bhāī dillī mẽ rahte haĩ.*

b ज्योति अस्पताल में काम करती है । *Jyoti aspatāl mẽ kām kartī hai.*

There are two kinds of dots in Hindi: those that modify a consonant to change its phonetic value (e.g. distinguishing *z* from *j* in ज़ *za* and ज *ja* respectively), and those that mark nasal vowels, as in हैं *haĩ*. Dots of the first kind are often omitted (with ज्यादा and तरफ for ज़्यादा and तरफ़); but dots that mark nasal syllables are essential as they show distinctions of number – as in है *hai* *is* versus हैं *haĩ* *are*, and थी *thī* *was* versus थीं *thī̃* *were*.

How would you say *My sister used to teach English* and *My sisters used to teach English*?

Speaking

07.02 **Listen to five questions and their sample replies, then answer them for yourself. Your own answers may be quite different from the models you will hear.**

a बचपन में आप कहाँ रहते थे या रहती थीं ?
bacpan mẽ āp kahā̃ rahte the yā rahtī thī̃?

b क्या आप स्कूल जाते थे ? जाती थीं ?
kyā āp skūl jāte the?jātī thī̃?

c आप के पिता जी क्या काम करते थे ?
āp ke pita jī kyā kām karte the?

d क्या आप की माता जी भी काम करती थीं ?
kyā āp kī mātā jī bhī kām kartī thī̃?

e घर में खाना कौन बनाता था ?
ghar mẽ khānā kaun banātā thā?

Storyline

MEMORIES OF VARANASI

07.03 *Jagdish Sharma is in nostalgic mood and has begun writing some memories of his childhood. There are notes to help you follow what he's written.*

हम लोग[1] वाराणसी में रहते थे । हमारा घर गंगा[2] के किनारे पर था । बड़ा-सा[3] घर था । हम तीन भाई थे, और चार बहिनें । हम तीनों[4] लड़के स्कूल जाते थे; लड़कियाँ घर पर रहती थीं । उस ज़माने में बहुत कम लड़कियाँ स्कूल जाती थीं । पैसे की कमी थी और लोग यह सोचते थे कि औरतों की जगह घर में है ।

पिताजी स्कूल में पढ़ाते थे – लेकिन हमारे स्कूल में नहीं । उनका स्कूल हमारे घर से काफ़ी दूर था । वे साइकिल से स्कूल जाते थे। सब लोग उनको "मास्टर जी"[5] कहते थे । हम उनको "पापा" कहते थे और माताजी को "माँ" कहते थे ।[6]

कितना सुंदर मकान था हमारा ! कोई बग़ीचा नहीं था, लेकिन हम बच्चे लोग आँगन में ख़ूब खेलते थे । कभी कभी हम सड़कों पर या नदी के किनारे पर भी खेलते थे । शाम को हम नदी पर नाव में सैर करते थे । ठंडी-सी हवा चलती थी । रात को हम छत पर सोते थे । मुझको उन दिनों की यादें बहुत आती हैं ।[7]

ham log[1] *vārāṇasī mẽ rahte the. hamārā ghar gangā*[2] *ke kināre par thā. baṛā-sa*[3] *ghar thā. ham tīn bhāī the, aur cār bahinẽ. ham tīnõ*[4] *laṛke skūl jāte the; laṛkiyā̃ ghar par rahtī thī̃. us zamāne mẽ bahut kam laṛkiyā̃ skūl jātī thī̃. paise kī kamī thī aur log yah socte the ki auratõ kī jagah ghar mẽ hai. pitājī skūl mẽ paṛhāte the lekin hamāre skūl mẽ nahī̃. unkā skūl hamāre ghar se kāfī dūr thā. ve sāikil se skūl jāte the. sab log unko 'māsṭar jī'*[5] *kahte the. ham unko 'pāpā' kahte the aur mātājī ko 'mā̃' kahte the.*[6]

kitnā sundar makān thā hamārā! koī bagīcā nahī̃ thā, lekin ham bacce log ā̃gan mẽ khūb khelte the. kabhī kabhī ham saṛakõ par yā nadī ke kināre par bhī khelte the. śām ko ham nadī par nāv mẽ sair karte the. ṭhanḍī-sī havā caltī thī. rāt ko ham chat par sote the. mujhko un dinõ kī yādẽ bahut atī haĩ.[7]

Notes

1 हम लोग *ham log we, we people, we guys* – the word लोग *log* can indicate a group; compare बच्चे लोग *bacce log the children, the kids.*

2 गंगा *gangā* – like all rivers (and the word for *river*, नदी *nadī*), the Ganges is feminine.

3 The suffix -सा -सी -से *-sā -sī -se* is similar to *-ish* in English: बड़ा-सा घर *baṛā-sā ghar a biggish house,* अच्छी-सी गाड़ी *acchī-sī gāṛī quite a good car,* अच्छे-से लोग *acche-se log quite decent people.*

4 तीनों *tīnõ – all three*; this is a special inclusive use of the oblique plural. Compare दोनों *donõ both,* चारों *cārõ all four.*

5 *Master ji* is a title used for schoolmasters (and for tailors – masters of their craft).

6 When a plural subject comprises both males and females, as here, the verb is masculine.

7 Literally *memories of those days come to me a lot* – a typical मुझको *mujhko* expression.

Listening and speaking

07.04 **Now here are some questions about Jagdish's memories. Listen and speak in the pauses. Then continue listening for the sample answers.**

a जगदीश जी किस शहर में रहते थे ?
Jagdīś jī kis śahar mẽ rahte the?

b उनके परिवार में कितने बच्चे थे ?
unke parivār mẽ kitne bacce the?

c क्या उनकी बहिनें स्कूल जाना नहीं चाहती थीं ?
kyā unkī bahinẽ skūl jānā nahī̃ cahtī thī̃?

d जगदीश के पिता का स्कूल कहाँ था ?
Jagdīś ke pitā kā skūl kahā̃ thā?

e क्या जगदीश के पिता जी पैदल स्कूल जाते थे ?
kyā Jagdīś ke pitā jī paidal skūl jāte the?

Language discovery 2

GETTING SPECIFIC

The word को *ko* means *to:*

यह ख़त गीता को दो ।	*yah <u>kh</u>at Gītā ko do.*	Give this letter to Geeta.
टिकट मुझको दीजिए ।	*ṭikaṭ mujhko dījie.*	Please give the ticket to me.
हम बच्चों को पैसा देते हैं ।	*ham baccõ ko paisā dete haĩ.*	We give money to the children.

In these sentences the *thing given* (e.g. the letter) is the direct object and the recipient (e.g. Geeta) is the indirect object. It's the recipient who is marked with को *ko.*

Usually, को *ko* isn't needed at all with a direct object. In the following, the direct objects are फल *phal fruit* and पानी *pānī water* respectively:

फल खाओ, पानी पियो ।
phal khāo, pānī piyo. Eat fruit, drink water.

The meaning here is a general one – *any fruit, any water*. But if a more specific fruit/water is meant, को *ko* is added (and *the* is used in English):

फल को खाओ, पानी को पियो ।
phal ko khāo, pānī ko piyo. Eat the fruit, drink the water.

The contrast between having को *ko* and not having it isn't always this clear-cut: but in general को *ko* tends to be added to an object that's in some way specific or individualized. For this reason, references to people (and other specific creatures such as animals!) normally *do* take को *ko*:

बच्चों को घर में बुलाओ ।
baccõ ko ghar mẽ bulāo. Call the children inside the house.

मोती को मत मारो !
Motī ko mat māro! Don't hit Moti!

उन लोगों को देखो !
Un logõ ko dekho! Look at those people!

Marking an object with को *ko* doesn't necessarily change the meaning much at all. The two sentences यह ख़त पढ़ो *yah khat paṛho* and इस ख़त को पढ़ो *is khat ko paṛho* both translate as *read this letter*, even though the second version suggests a greater focus on the individual letter (and maybe a closer scrutiny of it also).

How would you say *He reads a newspaper* and *He reads this newspaper*? In which sentence would you use को *ko*?

A SHORTCUT

The word को *ko* is a multi-purpose tool; we saw some of its uses in Unit 5. Whereas English expressions about a person tend to have that person as the grammatical subject (as if individuals were the centre of the universe of experience), Hindi prefers to have the experiences itself as the subject:

आपको बुख़ार है । *āpko bukhār hai.* You have a fever.

तुमको ज़ुकाम है । *tumko zukām hai.* You have a cold.

मुझको मालूम है कि आपको क्या चाहिए ।
mujhko mālūm hai ki āpko kyā cāhie. *I know what you need.*

किसको मालूम है कि यह क्या है ?
kisko mālūm hai ki yah kyā hai? *Who knows what this is?*

उनको नए जूते चाहिए ।
unko nae jūte cāhie. *They need new shoes.*

हमको यह तस्वीर पसंद है ।
hamko yah tasvīr pasand hai. *We like this picture.*

मुझको लिखने का शौक़ है ।
mujhko likhne kā śauq hai. *I'm fond of writing.*

उनको संगीत का शौक़ है ।
unko sangīt kā śauq hai. *They are keen on music.*

This type of construction, with its heavy reliance on को *ko,* is so common that the 'pronoun + को *ko*' combination has an alternative short form: for example, मुझको *mujhko* has the alternative मुझे *mujhe*. Only आपको *āpko* refuses to be shortened. These pairs of forms are completely interchangeable: it makes no difference at all which member of a pair you choose to use.

मुझको *mujhko* = मुझे *mujhe*	इनको *inko* = इन्हें *inhẽ*
हमको *hamko* = हमें *hamẽ*	उसको *usko* = उसे *use*
तुझको *tujhko* = तुझे *tujhe*	उनको *unko* = उन्हें *unhẽ*
तुमको *tumko* = तुम्हें *tumhẽ*	किसको *kisko* = किसे *kise*
इसको *isko* = इसे *ise*	किनको *kinko* = किन्हें *kinhẽ*

Remember that किस *kis* (singular) and किन *kin* (plural) are the oblique forms of कौन *kaun* who and क्या *kyā* what:

किसे मालूम है कि राम कहाँ है ?
kise mālūm hai ki Rām kahā̃ hai? *Who knows where Ram is?*

तुम पत्र किन्हें लिखते हो ?
tum patr kinhẽ likhte ho? *To whom* (plural) *do you write letters?*

The main point to bear in mind here is that many expressions in Hindi are based on a मुझको *mujhko* pattern rather than a मैं *maĩ* pattern. You need to develop the skill of using both types of sentence, switching freely between one and the other. For example, these two sentences have the same meaning:

मुझे मालूम है कि वह कौन है ।
mujhe mālūm hai ki vah kaun hai. I know who he is.

मै जानता हूँ कि वह कौन है ।
maĩ jāntā hū̃ ki vah kaun hai. I know who he is.

When getting to grips with the मुझको *mujhko* pattern, think of the individual as being subjected to the effects of experiences from the world around him or her:

मुझे गाने का बहुत शौक़ है ।
mujhe gāne kā bahut śauq hai.

मुझे तुम्हारा चेहरा बहुत पसंद है !
mujhe tumhārā cehrā bahut pasand hai!

मुझे मालूम है कि तुम कौन हो ।
mujhe mālūm hai ki tum kaun ho.

मुझे हिन्दी आती है ।
mujhe hindī ātī hai.

If the answers are मीना को मालूम है कि गीता कहाँ है *Mīnā ko mālūm hai ki Gītā kahā̃ hai* and मुझे चाई चाहिए *mujhe cāī cāhie*, what are the questions?

Speaking

07.05 **Change the को *ko* constructions to the new pronoun form you've just learnt. For example, change मुझको *mujhko* to मुझे *mujhe*. Then listen to check your answers.**

a मुझको यह होटल पसंद है ।
mujhko yah hoṭal pasand hai.

b यह होटल किसको पसंद नहीं है ?
yah hoṭal kisko pasand nahī̃ hai?

c हमको कमरा चाहिए ।
hamko kamrā cāhie.

d उनको भी कमरा चाहिए ।
unko bhī kamrā cāhie.

e उसको मालूम है कि हमको कमरा चाहिए ।
usko mālūm hai ki hamko kamrā cāhie.

f क्या तुमको यह कमरा पसंद नहीं है ?
kyā tumko yah kamrā pasand nahī̃ hai?

g तुमको कैसा कमरा चाहिए ?
tumko kaisā kamrā cāhie?

Storyline

RAJU RECALLS SOME CHILDHOOD EXPERIENCES

07.06 **While reading this passage, look out for two things in particular: *used to* verbs describing habitual things in the past, and the numerous constructions using को *ko*.**

1 Who did Raju write his letter to?

बचपन में मुझे पत्र लिखने का बहुत शौक़ था । कभी कभी मैं प्रधान मंत्री को भी पत्र लिखता था । मुझे मालूम नहीं था कि उन्हें मेरे पत्र पसंद थे कि नहीं, क्योंकि वे जवाब नहीं देते थे । एक समय मेरा छोटा भाई कई महीनों तक बीमार था । उसे बहुत बुख़ार था इसलिए हमें बहुत चिंता थी । मुझको मालूम था कि उसे दवा की ज़रूरत थी लेकिन हमारे पास पैसे कहाँ थे । लोग कहते थे कि प्रधान मंत्री बहुत दयालु आदमी हैं । इस लिए ...

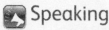

आदरणीय प्रधान मंत्री जी ।

सादर नमस्ते । मुझे मालूम है कि आपको बहुत काम है लेकिन हमें बहुत चिंता है क्योंकि मेरे छोटे भाई को बुख़ार है । हमारे पास पैसे नहीं हैं । क्या आप कुछ कर सकते हैं ? हमको आप पर पूरा भरोसा है ।

शुभकामनाओं सहित

आपका राजकुमार शर्मा

bacpan mẽ mujhe patr likhne kā bahut śauq thā. kabhī kabhī maĩ pradhān mantrī ko bhī patr likhtā thā. mujhe mālūm nahī̃ thā ki unhẽ mere patr pasand the ki nahī̃, kyõki ve javāb nahī̃ dete the. ek samay merā choṭā bhāī kaī mahīnõ tak bīmār thā. use bahut bukhār thā islie hamẽ bahut cintā thī. mujhko mālūm thā ki use davā kī zarūrat thī lekin hamāre pās paise kahā̃ the. log kahte the ki pradhān mantrī bahut dayālu admī haĩ. is lie …

ādaraṇīy pradhān mantrī jī,

sādar namaste. mujhe mālūm hai ki āpko bahut kām hai lekin hamẽ bahut cintā hai kyõki mere choṭe bhāī ko bukhār hai. hamāre pās paise nahī̃ haĩ. kyā āp kuch kar sakte haĩ? hamko āp par pūrā bharosā hai.

śubhkāmnāõ sahit

āpkā Rājkumār Śarmā.

2 Now read or listen again and answer these questions:

a What was wrong with Raju's brother?
b Why couldn't Raju's family get medicine for him?
c Did the Prime Minister enjoy Raju's letters? How can you tell?

Language discovery 3

ADDING EMPHASIS

Three little words can add various kinds of subtle emphasis to a Hindi sentence. We have already met भी *bhī also, even*, and we saw how fussy it was about its position in the word order (see Unit 3). We now add the other two – ही *hī only* etc., and तो *to as for* …. All three follow the words or phrases that they emphasize, but they are *not* postpositions (see Unit 3), so they don't involve any change of case.

First, भी *bhī* means *also, even*, etc.; it gives an *inclusive* emphasis. Look out for the effect of भी *bhī* in these sentences:

अजय पतला है; वह लंबा भी है ।
Ajay patlā hai; vah lambā bhī hai. *Ajay is thin; he's tall too.*

अजय पतला है; विजय भी पतला है ।
Ajay patlā hai; Vijay bhī patlā hai. *Ajay is thin; Vijay is thin too.*

In the first sentence, भी *bhī* emphasizes लंबा *lambā*; in the second it emphasizes the name विजय *Vijay*. Where does the emphasis fall in the following?

मुझे बुख़ार है । मुझे जुकाम भी है ।
mujhe bukhār hai. mujhe zukām bhī hai.
I've got a fever. I've got a cold too.

मुझे बुख़ार है । तुम्हें भी बुख़ार है ।
mujhe bukhār hai. tumhẽ bhī bukhār hai.
I've got a fever. You've got a fever too.

Yes, it's on जुकाम *zukām* and तुम्हें *tumhẽ* respectively. So you see again how sensitive the position of भी *bhī* is.

How would you express these two different thoughts: *I, too, speak Hindi* and *I speak Hindi, too (in addition to other languages)*?

The same applies with our second emphatic word, ही *hī*, which means *only* or stresses what's just been said; it gives an *exclusive* emphasis.

मैं चाय ही पीता हूँ ।
maĩ cāy hī pītā hū̃.
I only drink tea (nothing but tea).

मैं ही चाय पीता हूँ ।
maĩ hī cāy pītā hū̃.
Only I drink tea (or *I drink tea*).

यह चाय बहुत ही अच्छी है !
yah cāy bahut hī acchī hai!
This tea is really good!

Using ही *hī*, how would you say *In our house, we speak only Hindi*?

Third: तो *to* emphasizes one thing by implying a contrast to another; this *contrastive* emphasis may be 'explicit', in the sense that it can name both parts of the contrast:

अजय तो ठीक है, पर विजय थोड़ा पागल है ।
Ajay to ṭhīk hai, par Vijay thoṛa pāgal hai.
Ajay's OK, but Vijay's a bit crazy.

Or it may be merely implied, leaving a *but* ... hanging in the air:

अजय तो ठीक है ।
Ajay to ṭhīk hai.
Ajay's OK (implication: *'but that other guy ...'*).

क़मीज़ तो काफ़ी सुंदर है ।
qamīz to kāfī sundar hai.
The shirt's quite nice (implication: *but the jacket's a nightmare!*).

क़मीज़ सुंदर तो है ।
qamīz sundar to hai.
The shirt is nice (implication: *but have you seen the price tag?*).

Using तो *to*, how would you say *I'm OK, but my sister has a fever*?

Finally, notice how ही *hī* merges with certain words:

यह *yah*	यही *yahī*	*this very one, the same one*
इस *is*	इसी *isī*	*this very one, the same one*
वह *vah*	वही *vahī*	*that very one, the same one*
उस *us*	उसी *usī*	*that very one, the same one*
यहाँ *yahā̃*	यहीं *yahī̃*	*right here, in this very place*
वहाँ *vahā̃*	वहीं *vahī̃*	*right there, in that very place*

For now, it's enough to get a general understanding of how these emphatic words operate: they'll gradually become more familiar.

Practice

1 Translate the following sentences into Hindi.

- **a** Jagdish used to read Manoj's newspaper.
- **b** My two brothers used to work in a big office.
- **c** My sister used to drive my brother's car.
- **d** He only spoke Hindi, he didn't use to speak English.
- **e** Our teachers used to speak three languages.
- **f** His children used to play cricket in the garden.
- **g** Our parents didn't eat meat.
- **h** Where did you use to work? Where did you live?
- **i** What did your younger (little) brother do?
- **j** How many languages did your mother speak?

2 Translate the following, bringing out the emphasis given by तो *to* and ही *hī*.

- **a** जगदीश जी के परिवार में लड़के ही स्कूल जाते थे ।
  Jagdīś jī ke parivār mẽ laṛke hī skūl jāte the.
- **b** उनका स्कूल उनके घर से बहुत ही दूर था ।
  unkā skūl unke ghar se bahut hī dūr thā.
- **c** स्कूल में बच्चे ही नहीं, सब लोग उन्हें "मास्टर जी" कहते थे ।
  skūl mẽ bacce hī nahī̃, sab log unhẽ 'māsṭar jī' kahte the.
- **d** उनकी नौकरी में तनख़्वाह तो बहुत अच्छी नहीं थी ।
  unkī naukarī mẽ tankhvāh to bahut acchī nahī̃ thī.
- **e** जगदीश की माँ हिन्दी ही बोलती थीं ।
  Jagdīś kī mā̃ hindī hī boltī thī̃.
- **f** उस ज़माने में बच्चे तो बहुत ख़ुश थे ।
  us zamāne mẽ bacce to bahut khuś the.
- **g** बग़ीचा तो नहीं था, लेकिन खेलने की जगहें बहुत थीं ।
  bagīcā to nahī̃ thā, lekin khelne kī jagahẽ bahut thī̃.
- **h** बच्चे लोग तो छत पर ही सोते थे ।
  bacce log to chat par hī sote the.
- **i** बचपन में तो राजू को पत्र लिखने का शौक़ था ।
  bacpan mẽ to Rājū ko patr likhne kā śauq thā.
- **j** प्रधान मंत्री दयालु तो थे लेकिन उन्हें बहुत काम होता था ।
  pradhān mantrī dayālu to the lekin unhẽ bahut kām hotā thā.

3 Write a passage of 100 words or so about childhood memories – yours or imagined ones. Try to use a wide range of vocabulary and constructions; remember that you can always supplement your vocabulary from the glossaries at the back of the book.

4 07.07 **This unit had some quite long passages so we'll end with something a bit less taxing. Listen out for just one thing in each sentence as prompted. Then, answer in English.**

a मुझे नौकरी चाहिए ।
mujhe naukrī cāhie.

b मुझे मेहनत करना पसंद नहीं है ।
mujhe mahnat karnā pasand nahī̃ hai.

c मुझे ज़ुकाम है ।
mujhe zukām hai.

d मुझे सितार बजाने का शौक़ है ।
mujhe sitār bajāne kā shauq hai.

e मेरे बाप को पत्र लिखने का शौक़ है ।
mere bāp ko patra likhne kā shauq hai.

f हमें नए घर की ज़रूरत है ।
hamẽ nae ghar kī zarūrat hai.

g मुझे थोड़ा बुख़ार है ।
mujhe thoṛā bukhār hai.

Vocabulary builder

अँग्रेज़ी	*ãgrezī* f.	*English* (language); and adj.
आँगन	*ā̃gan* m.	*courtyard*
आदरणीय	*ādaraṇīy*	*respected* (used for *Dear* in formal correspondence)
इसलिए	*islie*	*so, because of this*
कमी	*kamī* f.	*lack, shortage*
किनारा	*kinārā* m.	*bank, edge*
ख़ूब	*khūb*	*a lot, freely*
गंगा	*gangā* f.	*Ganges*
गरमी	*garmī* f.	*heat*
गरमियाँ	*garmiyā̃* f. pl.	*summer*
चलना	*calnā*	*to move, blow, flow*
चिंता	*cintā* f.	*anxiety*
चेहरा	*cehrā* m.	*face*
छत	*chat* f.	*roof*
ज़माना	*zamānā* m.	*period, time*
ज़रूरत	*zarūrat* f.	*need*
जवाब	*javāb* m.	*answer, reply*
जवाब देना	*javāb denā*	*to reply*
जानना	*jānnā*	*to know*

ज़िंदगी	*zindagī* f.	*life*
टिकट	*ṭikaṭ* m./f.	*ticket; stamp*
ठंडा	*ṭhaṇḍā*	*cold*
ठंडा-सा	*ṭhaṇḍā-sā*	*coldish*
तनख़्वाह, तनख़ाह	*tankhvāh, tankhāh* f.	*pay, wages*
तो	*to*	*as for ...*
थोड़ा	*thoṛā*	*(a) little*
दयालु	*dayālu*	*compassionate, kind*
दवा	*davā* f.	*medicine*
नदी	*nadī* f.	*river*
नाव	*nāv* f.	*boat*
नौकरी	*naukarī* f.	*job, employment*
पत्र	*patr* m.	*letter* (correspondence)
पसंद आना	*pasand ānā*	*to appeal to, to be liked*
पागल	*pāgal*	*mad, crazy*
पापा	*pāpā* m.	*papa, father*
पैदल	*paidal*	*on foot*
प्रधान मंत्री	*pradhān mantrī* m.	*prime minister*
बचपन	*bacpan* m.	*childhood*
भरोसा	*bharosā* m.	*trust, reliance*
महीना	*mahīnā* m.	*month*
मारना	*mārnā*	*to hit, beat, strike*
मेहनत	*mehnat* f.	*hard work*
मेहनती	*mehntī*	*hard-working*
याद	*yād* f.	*memory*
शाम	*śām* f.	*evening*
शुभकामना	*śubhkāmnā* f.	*good wish*
शौक़	*śauq* m.	*liking, hobby, interest*
सहित	*sahit*	*with* (formal)
सादर	*sādar*	*respectful*
सैर	*sair* f.	*trip*
हवा	*havā* f.	*air, breeze*
ही	*hī*	*only* (emphatic)

Test yourself

1 What are the past forms of the verb *to be* in Hindi – that is, what is the Hindi for *was* and *were* in the two genders?

2 वह खेलती थी *vah kheltī thī* – the verb can be pluralized by adding a single dot. Where?

3 चारों बच्चे स्कूल जाते थे । *cārõ bacce skūl jate the*. Why चारों *cārõ*?

4 We can say either दूध को पियो *dūdh ko piyo* or दूध पियो *dūdh piyo*. So why is the को *ko* compulsory in राम को बुलाओ ! *Rām ko bulāo!* ?

5 मुझको मालूम है कि तुमको कुछ पैसा चाहिए । *mujhko mālūm hai ki tumko kuch paisā cāhie*. What substitutes have we learned for the underlined words?

6 राम तो ठीक है । *Rām to ṭhīk hai*. What's implied by the word तो *to* here?

7 What's the difference between यहीं *yahī̃* and यही *yahī*?

8 How do you say *I have a cold*?

9 Translate मुझे हिन्दी आती है *mujhe hindī ātī hai.*

10 Convert the following for use when speaking to an 'आप *āp*' person: फल खाओ, पानी पियो *phal khāo, pānī piyo*.

SELF CHECK

	I CAN...
○	... talk about memories and routine events in the past.
○	... add nuance to what I say.

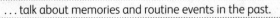

8 क्या हो रहा है ?

kyā ho rahā hai?

What's happening?

In this unit you will learn how to:

- ***make comparisons.***
- ***describe what's going on right now.***
- ***say how things happen.***

Language points

- *comparatives and superlatives*
- *continuous tenses*
- *adverbs and postpositions*

Language discovery 1

COMPARISONS

English has two main ways of showing comparisons, first, as in *harder* (using an *-er* comparative word) and, second, as in *more difficult* (using *more* with the ordinary adjective). Hindi prefers this second type. The word for *more* is ज़्यादा *zyādā* or और *aur*.

यह होटल ज़्यादा/और अच्छा है ।
yah hoṭal zyādā/aur acchā hai. — This hotel is better.

वह होटल ज़्यादा/और महँगा है ।
vah hoṭal zyādā/aur mahãgā hai. — That hotel is more expensive.

When comparing one thing directly to another, the word से *se than* is used, and the ज़्यादा/और *zyādā/aur* can be dropped:

दिल्ली आगरे से बड़ी है । *dillī āgre se baṛī hai.* — Delhi is bigger than Agra.
आगरा दिल्ली से छोटा है । *āgrā dillī se choṭā hai.* — Agra is smaller than Delhi.

Less is कम *kam*:

यह कमरा कम अच्छा है ।
yah kamrā kam acchā hai. — This room is less good.

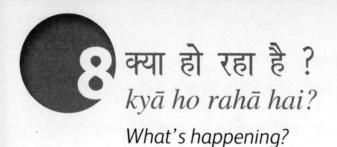

यह किताब (उस किताब से) कम अच्छी है ।
yah kitāb (us kitāb se) kam acchī hai.
This book is less good (than that book).

वह होटल (ताज से) कम महँगा है ।
vah hoṭal (tāj se) kam mahãgā hai. That hotel is less pricey (than the Taj).

LANGUAGE TIP

कम *kam* – this useful little word also means *few* (कम लोग *kam log* few people) and *little, less than expected* (मेरे पास बहुत कम पैसा है *mere pās bahut kam paisa hai* I have very little money).

Superlatives follow the model of सबसे अच्छा *sabse acchā* best of all:

यही दवा सबसे अच्छी है ।
yahī davā sabse acchī hai. This medicine is the best.

मनोज सबसे बड़ा लड़का है ।
Manoj sabse baṛā laṛkā hai. Manoj is the biggest/eldest boy.

राम सबसे छोटा लड़का है ।
Rām sabse choṭā laṛkā hai. Ram is the smallest/youngest boy.

In each of the following sentences, can you tell which are the comparison woxrds?

a यह सबसे सुंदर साड़ी है । *yah sabse sundar sāṛī hai.*

b मनोज मीना से लंबा है । *Manoj Mīnā se lambā hai.*

c वह कमरा ज़्यादा बड़ा है । *vah kamrā zyādā baṛā hai.*

Listening and speaking

08.01 **Answer the questions about these four siblings, shown in age order (Shiv is the eldest).**

शिव m.	रीता f.	ओम m.	शंकर *m.*
Śiv	*Rītā*	*Om*	*Śankar*

a	क्या ओम शंकर से बड़ा है ?	*kyā Om Śankar se baṛā hai?*
b	कितने बच्चे रीता से छोटे हैं ?	*kitne bacce Rītā se choṭe haĩ?*
c	सबसे बड़ा लड़का कौन है ?	*sabse baṛā laṛkā kaun hai?*
d	सबसे छोटा लड़का कौन है ?	*sabse choṭā laṛkā kaun hai?*
e	ओम कितने बच्चों से बड़ा है ?	*Om kitne baccõ se baṛā hai?*
f	क्या रीता शिव से बड़ी है ?	*kyā Rītā Śiv se baṛī hai?*
g	क्या रीता ओम से छोटी है ?	*kyā Rītā Om se choṭī hai?*
h	क्या रीता शंकर से छोटी है ?	*kyā Rītā Śankar se choṭī hai?*
i	आपको किस बच्चे की तस्वीर सबसे ज़्यादा पसंद है ?	*āpko kis bacce kī tasvīr sabse zyādā pasand hai?*

CONTINUOUS TENSE: *-ING* VERBS

I speak Hindi (मैं हिन्दी बोलता हूँ *maĩ hindī boltā hũ*) describes something that's done regularly or habitually; but *I am speaking Hindi* describes something that's going on *at the time*. In Hindi, the *-ing* sense is conveyed like this:

मैं हिन्दी बोल रहा हूँ ।	*maĩ hindī bol rahā hũ.*	*I am speaking Hindi.*
मैं हिन्दी बोल रहा था ।	*maĩ hindī bol rahā thā.*	*I was speaking Hindi.*

This is called the continuous tense. It has three elements:

a the verb stem बोल *bol* (or सीख *sīkh*, कर *kar*, लिख *likh*, कह *kah*, etc.) supplies the basic meaning;

b रहा–रही–रहे *rahā-rahī-rahe* delivers the *-ing* aspect;

c the auxiliary verb 'to be' (हूँ *hũ*, है *hai*, था *thā*, etc.) confirms the timeframe, i.e. past or present.

Some more examples:

वह रो रही है ।
vah ro rahī hai.
She is crying.

पिताजी क्यों मुस्करा रहे हैं ?
pitājī kyõ muskarā rahe haĩ?
Why is Father smiling?

तुम क्यों हँस रहे हो ?
tum kyõ hãs rahe ho?
Why are you laughing?

मेरी बहिन कोई हिन्दी फ़िल्म देख रही थी ।
merī bahin koī hindī film dekh rahī thī
My sister was watching some Hindi film.

क्या तुम तमिल सीख रहे हो ?
kyā tum tamil sīkh rahe ho?
Are you learning Tamil?

दादी जी गुजराती में कुछ पत्र लिख रही थीं ।
dādī jī gujarātī mẽ kuch patr likh rahī thī̃.
Grandma was writing some letters in Gujarati.

Which of these sentences describes a continuous action?

a सारे बच्चे क्रिकेट खेलते थे । *sāre bacce krikeṭ khelte the.*
b सुनीता दादा जी से बात कर रही है । *Sunītā dada jī se bāt kar rahī hai.*
c मेरी बहिन अच्छे समोसे बनाती है । *merī bahin acche samose banātī hai.*

Storyline

GEETA PHONES HOME

08.02 Listen in on a phone conversation between Geeta and Raju with *lots* of verbs in the continuous tense. Here's the new vocabulary:

सहेली	*sahelī* f.	*girl's or woman's female friend*
के साथ	*ke sāth*	*with, in the company of*
आज रात (को)	*āj rāt (ko)*	*tonight*
कब	*kab*	*when?*
देर	*der* f.	*a while, period of time*
रात का खाना	*rāt kā khānā m.*	*dinner*
मदद	*madad* f.	*help*
लाना	*lānā*	*to bring*
बाप रे बाप	*bāp re bāp*	*Oh God!*

1 Where is Geeta calling from?

गीता	हलो राजू, मैं गीता बोल रही हूँ । [१]
राजू	कहाँ से बोल रही हो ? [२]
गीता	ताज होटल से ।
राजू	तुम क्या कर रही हो वहाँ ?
गीता	मैं कुछ सहेलियों के साथ चाय पी रही हूँ !
राजू	बच्चे क्या कर रहे हैं ?
गीता	वे तो यहाँ बग़ीचे में खेल रहे हैं ।
राजू	तो क्या मनोज भी खेल रहा है ?
गीता	नहीं, वह किसी लड़की से बात कर रहा है ।
राजू	ओहो ! तुम लोग घर कब आ रहे हो ? [३]
गीता	हम अभी आ रहे हैं, थोड़ी देर में । क्यों ?
राजू	क्योंकि मैं रात का खाना बना रहा हूँ । मुझे मदद चाहिए ।
गीता	क्यों ? आज रात को कोई आ रहा है ?
राजू	हाँ, जावेद आ रहा है । उसके कुछ दोस्त [४] भी आ रहे हैं ।
गीता	बाप रे बाप ! अच्छा, मैं अभी आती हूँ ।
राजू	वहाँ ताज में ज़्यादा पैसा मत ख़र्च करना !

Gītā	*halo Rājū, maĩ Gītā bol rahī hū̃.* [1]
Rājū	*kahā̃ se bol rahī ho?* [2]
Gītā	*tāj hoṭal se.*
Rājū	*tum kyā kar rahī ho vahā̃?*
Gītā	*maĩ kuch saheliyõ ke sāth cāy pī rahī hū̃!*
Rājū	*bacce kyā kar rahe haĩ?*
Gītā	*ve to yahā̃ bagīce mẽ khel rahe haĩ.*
Rājū	*to kyā Manoj bhī khel rahā hai?*
Gītā	*nahī̃, vah kisī laṛkī se bāt kar rahā hai.*
Rājū	*oho! tum log ghar kab ā rahe ho?* [3]
Gītā	*ham abhī ā rahe haĩ, thoṛī der mẽ. kyõ?*
Rājū	*kyõki maĩ rāt kā khānā banā rahā hū̃. mujhe madad cāhie.*
Gītā	*kyõ? āj rāt ko koī ā rahā hai?*
Rājū	*hā̃, Jāved ā rahā hai. uske kuch dost* [4] *bhī ā rahe haĩ.*
Gītā	*bāp re bāp! acchā, maĩ abhī ātī hū̃.*
Rājū	*vahā̃ tāj mẽ zyādā paisā mat kharc karnā!*

2 Now listen to the dialogue again, and then answer these questions.

a What is Geeta doing?

b What is Manoj doing?

c Why does Raju want Geeta to hurry home?

Notes

1 This is the usual way of announcing yourself on the phone – *I Geeta am speaking*, i.e. 'This is Geeta'.

2 Remember that a pronoun (here तुम *tum*) can be dropped when context makes it clear who is meant.

3 The continuous tense can be used for the immediate future (as in English) – *when are you coming home?*.

4 उसके कुछ दोस्त *uske kuch dost* – *some friends of his*. Note the word order.

LANGUAGE TIP

Words for 'friend': most common is दोस्त *dost*, as in गीता मेरी बहुत अच्छी दोस्त है *Gītā merī bahut acchī dost hai*. मित्र *mitra* has a slightly more formal or bookish ring, and यार *yār* is chummier. सहेली *sahelī* is specifically a female's female friend.

SPEAKING

Look at the pictures, then choose a verb from the list to describe who's doing what. Keep an eye on gender and number! Here's the first answer to show you the format:

जावेद पत्र लिख रहा है

Jāved patr likh rahā hai

Javed is writing a letter.

खाना तैयार करना	*khānā taiyār karnā*	*to prepare food*
शराब पीना	*śarāb pīnā*	*to drink* (alcohol)
ताश खेलना	*tāś khelnā*	*to play cards*
पत्र लिखना	*patr likhnā*	*to write a letter*
दौड़ना	*dauṛnā*	*to run*
बरतन माँजना	*bartan mā̃jnā*	*to wash dishes*
सोना	*sonā*	*to sleep*
फ़ोन पर बात करना	*fon par bāt karnā*	*to talk on the phone*

1

जावेद
Jāved

2

दो लड़कियाँ
do laṛkiyā̃

3

कोई आदमी
koī ādmī

4

कुत्ता
kuttā

5

सीता
Sītā

6

गीता और राजू
Gītā aur Rājū

7

राम
Rām

8

उषा
Uṣā

Language review: verbs summary

08.03 Now that we're more than halfway through the course, here's a summary of all the verb forms we've seen so far, listed by unit and ***Language discovery*** section. Our example verb here is बोलना *bolnā to speak.*

GRAMMAR		EXAMPLES
1.1	होना *honā to be*	है *hai*, हैं *haĩ*
4.1	infinitive	बोलना *bolnā*
4.1	stem	बोल *bol*
4.1	command	बोल, बोलो, बोलिए *bol, bolo, bolie*
4.3	imperfective participle	बोलता *boltā*
4.3	imperfective present	वह बोलता है *vah boltā hai*
7.1	imperfective past	वह बोलता था *vah boltā thā*
8.1	continuous present	वह बोल रहा है *vah bol rahā hai*
8.1	continuous past	वह बोल रहा था *vah bol rahā thā*

Now is the time to look back if you need to review any of these!

Language discovery 2 *One's own*

Consider this statement: *Javed is sitting in Raju's house; Raju is reading his newspaper*. Hmm: *his* is ambiguous here – is Raju reading his own newspaper or Javed's? Hindi has no such ambiguity, because the pronoun अपना *apnā* replaces उसका *uskā* whenever the sense *his/her own* is meant:

राजू अपना अख़बार पढ़ रहा है ।
Rājū apnā akhbār paṛh rahā hai. *Raju is reading his (own) paper.*

राजू उसका अख़बार पढ़ रहा है ।
Rājū uskā akhbār paṛh rahā hai. *Raju is reading his (someone else's) paper.*

अपना *apnā* is not restricted to *his/her*, it can mean *my*, *our*, *your* and so on.

मैं अपना काम कर रहा हूँ ।
maĩ apnā kām kar rahā hū̃. *I am doing my work.*

हम अपना काम कर रहे हैं ।
ham apnā kām kar rahe haĩ. *We are doing our work.*

तुम अपना काम करो !
tum apnā kām karo. *Do your work!*

अपना पैसा लीजिए ।
apnā paisā lījie. *Please take your money.*

When to use अपना *apnā* is a vexing question for all learners of Hindi. As a rule of thumb, it has to be used whenever the 'possessor' is the subject of the main verb. The subjects in the next two sentences (using धोना *dhonā to wash*) are मैं *maĩ I* and वे *ve they* respectively:

मैं अपने कपड़े धो रहा हूँ ।
maĩ apne kapṛe dho rahā hū̃. *I'm washing my clothes.*

वे अपने कपड़े नहीं धोते ।
ve apne kapṛe nahī̃ dhote. *They don't wash their (own) clothes.*

a Where would you use अपना *apnā* in this sentence to make it clear that you are chatting with some of your own friends? मैं कुछ दोस्तों से बात कर रहा हूँ । *maĩ kuch dostõ se bāt kar rahā hū̃.*

b How would you say *Geeta is reading her (own) book*?

Language review: imperfectives

The difference between the continuous and imperfective tenses should be reasonably clear by now. Here's a dialogue to remind you of the imperfective.

08.04 *A young lad called Gopal comes to Jagdish Sharma's shop. Look at the vocabulary, and then listen.*

नौकरी	*naukarī* f.	*job*
पास में	*pās mẽ*	*nearby*
मेहनती	*mehnatī*	*hard-working*
जानना	*jānnā*	*to know*
ज़रूरत	*zarūrat* f.	*need*
थोड़ा	*thoṛā*	*a little*
मुझको X की ज़रूरत है	*mujhko X kī zarūrat hai*	*I need X*
अँग्रेज़ी	*ãgrezī* f.	*English* (language)
मेहनत	*mehnat* f.	*hard work*

1 Why is Gopal coming to Jagdish's shop?

गोपाल	नमस्ते शर्माजी ।
जगदीश	नमस्ते । क्या चाहिए बेटा ?
गोपाल	जी, मुझको आपकी दुकान में नौकरी चाहिए ।
जगदीश	हाँ, मुझको एक मेहनती लड़के की ज़रूरत तो है ।
गोपाल	मैं बहुत मेहनत करता हूँ शर्मा जी !
जगदीश	तुम्हारी उम्र कितनी है ?
गोपाल	जी, मैं सोलह साल का हूँ ।
जगदीश	कहाँ रहते हो ?
गोपाल	पास में । हमारा घर यहाँ से दूर नहीं है ।
जगदीश	क्या तुम पढ़ना-लिखना जानते हो ?
गोपाल	जी हाँ, और मुझे थोड़ी अँग्रेज़ी भी आती है ।
जगदीश	ठीक है, कल से आना ।
गोपाल	बहुत शुक्रिया । शर्माजी, एक बात बताइए ।
जगदीश	बोलो, क्या बात है ?
गोपाल	तनख़्वाह ... ?
जगदीश	यह तुम अभी मत पूछो !
Gopāl	*namaste Śarmājī.*
Jagdīś	*namaste. kyā cāhie beṭā?*
Gopāl	*jī, mujhko āpkī dukān mẽ naukarī cāhie.*
Jagdīś	*hā̃, mujhko ek mahnatī laṛke kī zarūrat to hai.*

Gopāl	*maĩ bahut mehnat kartā hū̃ Śarmā jī!*
Jagdīś	*tumhārī umr kitnī hai?*
Gopāl	*jī, maĩ solah sāl kā hū̃.*
Jagdīś	*kahā̃ rahte ho?*
Gopāl	*pās mẽ. hamārā ghar yahā̃ se dūr nahī̃ hai.*
Jagdīś	*kyā tum paṛhnā-likhnā jānte ho?*
Gopāl	*jī hā̃, aur mujhe thoṛī ãgrezī bhī ātī hai.*
Jagdīś	*ṭhīk hai, kal se ānā.*
Gopāl	*bahut śukriyā. Śarmājī, ek bāt batāie.*
Jagdīś	*bolo, kyā bāt hai?*
Gopāl	*tankhvāh ...?*
Jagdīś	*yah tum abhī mat pūcho!*

थोड़ी अंग्रेज़ी आती है *thoṛī angrezī ātī hai*, literally *a little English comes to me*. This is a common usage with languages: मुझे उर्दू आती है *mujhe urdū ātī hai I know Urdu*; मेरे भाई को चार भाषाएँ आती हैं *mere bhāī ko cār bhāṣāẽ ātī haĩ my brother knows four languages*. Used with an infinitive verb, this construction means *knowing how to do something, having a skill*: मुझे खाना बनाना आता है *mujhe khānā banānā ātā hai, I know how to cook.*

2 Listen to the dialogue again, then answer these questions.

a How old is Gopal?

b Is he well qualified to work with Jagdish? (Name three things he mentions.)

c Does Jagdish agree to take him on as paid help?

Practice 1

1 Are these statements right (सही *sahī*) or wrong (ग़लत *galat*)?

a गोपाल दुकान में कुछ ख़रीदना चाहता है ।
Gopāl dukān mẽ kuch kharīdnā cāhtā hai.

b गोपाल दुकान में काम करना चाहता है ।
Gopāl dukān mẽ kām karnā cāhtā hai.

c गोपाल को मेहनत करना पसंद नहीं है ।
Gopāl ko mehnat karnā pasand nahī̃ hai.

d जगदीश को एक लड़के की ज़रूरत है ।
Jagdīś ko ek laṛke kī zarūrat hai.

e जगदीश गोपाल के बाप से मिलना चाहता है ।
Jagdīś Gopāl ke bāp se milnā cāhtā hai.

f गोपाल तनख़ाह के बारे में जानना चाहता है ।
Gopāl tankhāh ke bāre mẽ jānnā cāhtā hai.

2 08.05 **You will now hear a short conversation, followed by three more examples using आना *ānā* to express knowing a language and knowing how to do things. Match the sentences you hear with their meaning.**

1 क्या तुमको हिंदी आती है ? *kyā tumko hindī ātī hai?*	**a** Wow! I only know Hindi.
2 जी हाँ, आती है । *jī hā̃, ātī hai.*	**b** I know how to cook.
3 तुमको कितनी भाषाएँ आती हैं ? *tumko kitnī bhāṣāẽ ātī haĩ?*	**c** I know three languages: Hindi, Punjabi, and English.
4 मुझको तीन भाषाएँ आती हैं, हिंदी, पंजाबी, और अंग्रेज़ी । *mujhko tīn bhāśāẽ ātī haĩ; hindī, panjābī, aur angrezī.*	**d** Do you know how to play the tabla?
5 अच्छा ! मुझको सिर्फ़ हिंदी आती है । *acchā! mujhko sirf hindī ātī hai.*	**e** Yes, I know it.
6 मुझको खाना बनाना आता है । *mujhko khānā banana ātā hai.*	**f** He knows how to speak, but not how to write.
7 उसको बोलना आता है, लेकिन लिखना नहीं आता । *usko bolnā ātā hai, lekin likhnā nahī̃ ātā.*	**g** Do you know Hindi?
8 क्या तुमको तबला बजाना आता है ? *kyā tumko tablā bajānā ātā hai?*	**h** How many languages do you know?

Storyline

THE PM WRITES BACK

Ah, here's the Prime Minister's reply to the letter that Raju wrote when he was little. (For reasons of confidentiality we can't show the signature.)

1 08.06 **What does the Prime Minister say he can and can't do?**

प्रिय राजू,
तुम जानते हो कि प्रधान मंत्री का जीवन कैसा होता है ? वह अपने लिए तो कुछ नहीं कर सकता है लेकिन दूसरों के लिए कुछ कर सकता है ! तुम अपने भाई की चिंता न करो । मैं अपने ही डाक्टर से तुम्हारे भाई के लिए कुछ दवा भिजवा रहा हूँ । अपने अगले पत्र में उसका हाल लिखना । और अपनी तबियत का भी ध्यान रखना ।

तुम्हारा (...)

priy Rajū,
tum jānte ho ki pradhān mantrī kā jīvan kaisā hotā hai? vah apne lie to kuch nahī̃ kar saktā hai lekin dūsrõ ke lie kuch kar saktā hai! tum apne bhāī kī cintā na karo. maĩ apne hī ḍākṭar se tumhāre bhāī ke lie kuch davā bhijvā rahā hū̃. apne agle patr mẽ uskā hāl likhnā. aur apnī tabiyat kā bhī dhyān rakhnā.

tumhārā (...)

2 Answer these questions:

a Who will send the medicine for Raju's brother?

b What does the Prime Minister ask for in return?

Language discovery 3

ADVERBS WHEN AND HOW

08.07 Here are some sentences with adverbs (words or phrases like *quickly* or *these days*, that describe the *manner* or *context* in which something happens). Look carefully at the underlined words:

इन दिनों तुम क्या कर रहे हो ?
in dinõ tum kyā kar rahe ho? — *What are you doing these days?*

उस दिन हम काम कर रहे थे ।
us din ham kām kar rahe the. — *That day, we were working.*

पिछले हफ़्ते मेरी तबियत ख़राब थी ।
pichle hafte merī tabiyat kharāb thī. — *I was unwell last week.*

वह अगले महीने घर जा रहा है ।
vah angle mahīne ghar jā rahā hai. — *He's going home next month.*

Notice anything? The words in bold print are in the oblique case – as if followed by invisible postpositions. This is usual with adverbs of time; here you have to forget the hard-learned rule that the oblique case is only used when a postposition requires it! Think of the time words as being haunted by the ghosts of dropped postpositions – ghostpositions!

These next sentences involve destinations – *Agra, your house*:

हम आगरे जा रहे हैं ।
ham āgre jā rahe haĩ. — *We're going to Agra.*

वे आपके घर आ रहे हैं ।
ve āpke ghar ā rahe haĩ. — *They're coming to your house.*

Here the obliques (आगरे *āgre*, oblique of आगरा *āgrā*; and आपके घर *āpke ghar*, oblique of आपका घर *āpkā ghar*) are again haunted by the ghosts of postpositions. To put it another way, the oblique case alone is the equivalent for the English *to* in these sentences. It's significant that both sentences involve verbs of motion.

Finally, we find something very similar happening in the following sentences, which use आना *ānā* or जाना *jānā* with a sense of purpose:

वे आपसे मिलने आ रहे हैं । *ve āpse milne ā rahe haĩ.*	*They're coming to meet you.*
हम फ़िल्म देखने जा रहे हैं । *ham film dekhne jā rahe haĩ.*	*We're going to see a film.*

These sentences have a sense of *purpose* or *intention* which is expressed by the मिलने *milne* and देखने *dekhne* (infinitives ending in *-e*) – as if here too some postposition had been dropped.

LANGUAGE TIP

A reminder about 'case' in Hindi grammar: Hindi has two main cases, the direct and the oblique. The oblique is used (a) before a postposition, as in कमरे में *kamre mẽ* in the room, and (b) in the adverbs we've just met, as in उस दिन *us din* (on) that day. Elsewhere, the direct case is used.

How would you say *Next week she is going to Jaipur* and *He is going home to rest*?

ADVERBS AND POSTPOSITIONS

08.08 Now here are some more sentences using adverbs. These ones (underlined) describe place:

मनोज बाहर खड़ा है ।	*Manoj <u>bāhar</u> kharā hai.*	*Manoj is standing outside.*
मीना अंदर बैठी है ।	*Mīnā <u>andar</u> baiṭhī hai.*	*Meena is sitting inside.*
ऊपर देखो ।	*<u>ūpar</u> dekho.*	*Look up.*
नीचे आओ ।	*<u>nīce</u> āo.*	*Come down.*

The thing to notice here is that adverbs and postpositions work differently from one another. Let's take the pair बाहर *bāhar* and के बाहर *ke bāhar*, both meaning *outside*, as an example. बाहर *bāhar* on its own is an adverb that means *outside* without reference to any other place: वह बाहर खड़ा है *vah bāhar kharā hai he's standing outside*. But के बाहर *ke bāhar* is a postposition that means *outside in relation to something*: मकान के बाहर *makān ke bāhar outside the house*. There are many such pairings: for example, the adverb ऊपर *ūpar* means *up, upstairs* (ऊपर जाओ *ūpar jāo go up* or *go upstairs*), while the postposition के ऊपर *ke ūpar* means *on top of, above* (मेज़ के ऊपर *mez ke ūpar on top of the table*).

हमारे मकान के बाहर	*hamāre makān ke bāhar*	*outside our house*
इस कमरे के अंदर	*is kamre ke andar*	*inside this room*
अलमारी के ऊपर	*almārī ke ūpar*	*on top of the cupboard*
इस मेज़ के नीचे	*is mez ke nīce*	*under this table*

There are many such postpositions consisting of two (or even three) words. Grammarians (who are always fond of long names for short things!) call them 'compound postpositions'.

के नज़दीक	*ke nazdīk*	*near*
के पास	*ke pās*	*near; in the possession of*
के अलावा	*ke alāvā*	*as well as*
के यहाँ	*ke yahā̃*	*at the place of, at X's place*
के लिए	*ke lie*	*for*
की तरफ़/ओर	*kī taraf/or*	*towards*
की तरह	*kī tarah*	*like*

When using these with the pronouns मैं *maĩ* (मेरे *mere*), तू *tū* (तेरे *tere*), तुम *tum* (तुम्हारे *tumhāre*), हम *ham* (हमारे *hamāre*), and अपना *apnā* (अपने *apne*) the के/की *ke/kī* component is absent:

उनके यहाँ	*unke yahā̃*	*at their place*
मेरे यहाँ	*mere yahā̃*	*at my place*
मकान की ओर	*makān kī or*	*towards the house*
हमारी ओर	*hamārī or*	*towards us*

You'll find many more of these compound postpositions listed in the Hindi–English glossary under के *ke* and की *kī*.

Using some of the postpositions mentioned above, how would you say the followin g:

a She sings like a nightingale (बुलबुल *bulbul*).

b Go toward the temple. My house is near it.

c Your shoes are under the table.

Practice 2

1 Make up phrases (such as मेरे घर के पीछे *mere ghar ke pīche behind my house*) from the following, remembering to make the first column oblique:

कौन	*kaun* (oblique किस *kis* whom)	के लिए	*ke lie*	*for*
मेरा दोस्त	*merā dost*	के बाद	*ke bād*	*after*
वह बड़ा पेड़	*vah baṛā peṛ*	की तरह	*kī tarah*	*like*
सोमवार	*somvār*	के पहले	*ke pahle*	*before*
हमारा स्कूल	*hamārā skūl*	के पीछे	*ke pīche*	*behind*
यह होटल	*yah hoṭal*	की तरफ़	*kī taraf*	*towards*
पुराना स्टेशन	*purānā sṭeśan*	के नज़दीक	*ke nazdīk*	*near*
मेरा घर	*merā ghar*	के नीचे	*ke nīce*	*under, below*
ये लोग	*ye log*	के यहाँ	*ke yahā̃*	*at the place of*
तुम्हारा घर	*tumhārā ghar*	के चारों ओर	*ke cārõ or*	*all around*

2 Translate the following sentences into Hindi.

- **a** You are not cleverer than them. (*clever*: होशियार *hośiyār*)
- **b** I (f.) am older than my brother but younger than you.
- **c** My other sister is the cleverest.
- **d** Some people say that Hindi is easier than English.
- **e** Mother thinks that my sister is more beautiful than me.
- **f** Father knows more than Mother but he can't say anything.
- **g** Their house is bigger and more beautiful than ours.
- **h** I am cleverer than you.
- **i** Your language is more difficult than my language.

3 Rewrite these sentences in the continuous tense, translating the rewritten version. (Raju is speaking throughout.) Example:

मैं रेडियो सुनता हूँ ।	मैं रेडियो सुन रहा हूँ ।
maĩ reḍiyo suntā hū̃.	*maĩ reḍiyo sun rahā hū̃.*
I listen to the radio.	*I am listening to the radio.*

a हम लोग अपने दोस्तों को खाना खाने बुलाते हैं ।
ham log apne dostõ ko khānā khāne bulāte haĩ.

b मैं खाना तैयार करता हूँ ।
maĩ khānā taiyār kartā hū̃.

c वे लोग शाम को आते हैं ।
ve log śām ko āte haĩ.

d वे अपने बच्चों और दोस्तों को भी लाते हैं ।
ve apne baccõ aur dostõ ko bhī lāte haĩ.

e मेरी पत्नी कहती है कि उनके बच्चे मोती को मारते हैं ।
merī patnī kahtī hai ki unke bacce Motī ko mārte haĩ.

f दादी जी हमारी मदद नहीं करती हैं, सिर्फ़ रेडियो सुनती हैं ।
dādī jī hamārī madad nahī̃ kartī haĩ, sirf reḍiyo suntī haĩ.

g हमारा कुकर ['cooker'] ठीक से काम नहीं करता ।
hamārā kukar ['cooker'] *ṭhīk se kām nahī̃ kartā.*

h हमारे दोस्त कहते हैं कि बाथरूम में पानी नहीं आ रहा है ।
hamāre dost kahte haĩ ki bāthrūm mẽ pānī nahī̃ ā rahā hai.

4 Answer the following questions.

a अपने ख़ाली समय में आप क्या करते/करती हैं ?
apne <u>kh</u>ālī samay mẽ āp kyā karte/kartī haĩ?

b आपको घर पर रहना या बाहर जाना ज़्यादा पसंद है ?
āpko ghar par rahnā yā bāhar jānā zyādā pasand hai?

c आप हिन्दी क्यों सीख रहे/रही हैं ?
āp hindī kyõ sīkh rahe/rahī haĩ?

d क्या हिन्दी अँग्रेज़ी से ज़्यादा आसान है ?
kyā hindī ãgrezī se zyādā āsān hai?

e क्या आपके कुछ दोस्त भी हिन्दी बोलते हैं ?
kyā āpke kuch dost bhī hindī bolte haĩ?

f आज आप क्या कर रहे/रही हैं ?
āj āp kyā kar rahe/rahī haĩ?

g आप अपनी छुट्टियों में कहाँ जाते/जाती हैं ?
āp apnī chuṭṭiyõ mẽ kahā̃ jāte/jātī haĩ?

h अभी आप क्या सोच रहे/रही हैं ?
abhī āp kyā soc rahe/rahī haĩ?

Vocabulary builder

अंदर	*andar*	*inside*
अगला	*aglā*	*next*
अपना	*apnā*	*one's own (my, your, his, etc.)*
आज रात को	*āj rāt ko*	*tonight*
आज शाम को	*āj śām ko*	*this evening*
कब	*kab*	*when?*
की ओर	*kī or*	*towards*
की तरफ़	*kī taraf*	*towards*
की तरह	*kī tarah*	*like*
के अंदर	*ke andar*	*inside*
के अलावा	*ke alāvā*	*as well as*
के ऊपर	*ke ūpar*	*above, on top of*
के नज़दीक	*ke nazdīk*	*near*
के नीचे	*ke nīce*	*below, under*
के बाहर	*ke bāhar*	*outside*
के यहाँ	*ke yahā̃*	*at the place of*
के साथ	*ke sāth*	*with, in the company of*
ख़र्च	*kharc* m.	*expenditure*
ख़र्च करना	*kharc karnā*	*to spend*
गुजराती	*gujarātī* f.	*Gujarati*
ज़रूरत	*zarūrat* f.	*need,*
मुझको X की ज़रूरत है	*mujhko X kī zarūrat hai*	*I need X*
जीवन	*jīvan* m.	*life*
ज़्यादा	*zyādā*	*more, much*
तमिल	*tamil* f.	*Tamil*
ताश *m.*	*tāś* m.	*playing cards*
तैयार	*taiyār*	*ready, prepared*
तैयार करना	*taiyār karnā*	*to prepare*
थोड़ी देर	*thoṛī der* f.	*a little while*
दुखी	*dukhī*	*sad*
दौड़ना	*dauṛnā*	*to run*
धोना	*dhonā*	*to wash*
ध्यान रखना	*dhyān rakhnā*	*to pay attention to, look after*
नीचे	*nīce*	*down, downstairs*
पास में	*pās mẽ*	*nearby*

पिछला	*pichlā*	*previous, last*
प्रिय	*priy*	*dear; Dear* (in informal correspondence)
बरतन	*bartan* m.	*dish, utensil*
बाप रे बाप !	*bāp re bāp!*	*Oh God!*
भिजवाना	*bhijvānā*	*to have sent, to cause to be sent*
मदद	*madad* f.	*help*
किसी की मदद करना	*kisī kī madad karnā*	*to help someone*
माँजना	*mā̃jnā*	*to scour, clean*
मुस्कराना	*muskarānā*	*to smile*
रात	*rāt* f.	*night*
रात का खाना	*rāt kā khānā* m.	*dinner*
लगना	*lagnā*	*to seem*
रोना	*ronā*	*to cry, weep*
सबसे	*sabse*	*of all* (in superlatives, e.g. सबसे अच्छा *sabse acchā best, best of* all)
सही	*sahī*	*correct, true*
सहेली	*sahelī* f.	*female's female friend*
हँसना	*hãsnā*	*to laugh*
हफ़्ता	*haftā* m.	*week*
होशियार	*hośiyār*	*clever*

Test yourself

1 In making comparisons, what Hindi word gives the sense *than*?

2 वह हिन्दी बोलती है/वह हिन्दी बोल रही है *vah hindī boltī hai / vah hindī bol rahī hai* – What's the difference?

3 What do की तरफ़ *kī taraf* and की तरह *kī tarah* mean?

4 हमारा काम *hamārā kām* means *our work*. So why don't we use हमारा *hamārā* when giving the sense *We are doing our work*?

5 What word gives the sense *Dear…* in an informal letter?

6 We'd previously discovered that the oblique case is used only before a postposition. What's the exception?

7 What's the Hindi for: *how many days, how many weeks, how many months, how many years*?

8 What verbs mean *to play* in the contexts of (a) music and (b) games?

9 Translate: *Is Varanasi the oldest city in* (say '*of*') *India?*

10 हम आगरे जा रहे हैं *ham Āgre jā rahe haĩ*. Explain the grammatical case of आगरे *Āgre*.

SELF CHECK

	I CAN…
○	… make comparisons.
○	… describe what's going on right now.
○	… say how things happen.

9 भविष्य में

bhaviṣya mẽ

In the future

In this unit you will learn how to:

- ***talk about the future.***
- ***use 'if' expressions.***
- ***express doubts and possibilities.***

Language points

- *future tenses*
- *conditional clauses*
- *subjunctive mood*

Language discovery 1

THE FUTURE TENSE

The future is quite simple in Hindi. We'll begin with *I will do* and *you will do*, which together will give lots of potential for practice. You already know that *to do* is करना *karnā*, stem कर *kar* – now here are the future forms:

मैं करूँगा/करूँगी	*maĩ karū̃gā/karū̃gī*	*I will do*
आप करेंगे/करेंगी	*āp karẽge/karẽgī*	*You will do*

So the future ending for मैं *maĩ* is *-ū̃gā/-ū̃gī*, and the आप *āp* ending is *-ẽge/-ẽgī*.

Following the pattern above, how would you say *I will speak* (a) if you are a woman and (b) if you are a man?

Storyline

WHAT WILL YOU DO TOMORROW?

09.01 This pair of dialogues uses the future tense of the verbs रहना *rahnā* *to stay* and जाना *jānā to go*.

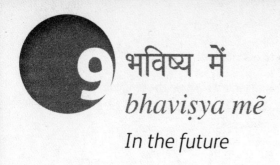

1 What are Raju and Geeta asking their friends about?

राजू	कल आप क्या करेंगे ?
जावेद	कल मैं काम करूँगा । आप क्या करेंगे ?
राजू	मैं घर पर रहूँगा ।
जावेद	आप घर पर क्यों रहेंगे ? काम पर नहीं जाएँगे ?
राजू	नहीं, काम पर नहीं जाऊँगा । कल छुट्टी है ।

Rājū	*kal āp kyā karẽge?*
Jāved	*kal maĩ kām karū̃gā. āp kyā karẽge?*
Rājū	*maĩ ghar par rahū̃gā.*
Jāved	*āp ghar par kyõ rahẽge? kām par nahī̃ jāẽge?*
Rājū	*nahī̃, kām par nahī̃ jāū̃gā. kal chuṭṭī hai.*

गीता	कल आप क्या करेंगी ?
उषा	कल मैं काम करूँगी । आप क्या करेंगी ?
गीता	मैं घर पर रहूँगी ।
उषा	आप घर पर क्यों रहेंगी ? काम पर नहीं जाएँगी ?
गीता	नहीं, काम पर नहीं जाऊँगी । कल छुट्टी है ।

Gītā	*kal āp kyā karẽgī?*
Uṣā	*kal maĩ kām karū̃gī. āp kyā karẽgī?*
Gītā	*maĩ ghar par rahū̃gī.*
Uṣā	*āp ghar par kyõ rahẽgī? kām par nahī̃ jāẽgī?*
Gītā	*nahī̃, kām par nahī̃ jāū̃gī. kal chuṭṭī hai.*

2 Now listen to the dialogues again, then answer the questions.

a What will Javed and Usha do tomorrow?

b Why will Raju and Geeta stay at home tomorrow?

Listening and speaking

09.02 These questions are for you to answer out loud.

a	आज रात को आप क्या खाएँगे/खाएँगी ?	(खाना *to eat*)
	āj rāt ko āp kyā khāẽge/khāẽgī?	*khānā*
b	... और क्या पिएँगे/पिएँगी ?	(पीना *to drink*)
	... aur kyā piẽge/piẽgī?	*pīnā*
c	आज आप क्या करेंगे/करेंगी ?	(करना *to do*)
	āj āp kyā karẽge/karẽgī?	*karnā*
d	कल सुबह आप कहाँ जाएँगे/जाएँगी ?	(जाना *to go*)
	kal subah āp kahā̃ jāẽge/jāẽgī?	*jānā*
e	परसों आप किससे मिलेंगे/मिलेंगी ?	(मिलना *to meet*)
	parsõ āp kisse milẽge/milẽgī?	*milnā*

LANGUAGE TIP

क्या खाएँगे ? *kyā khāẽge?* ... क्या पिएँगे ? *kyā piẽge?* These are useful phrases when offering food or drink; and क्या लेंगे ? *kyā lẽge? What will you take (have)?* is another option. Remember to use feminine forms for female guests: खाएँगी *khāẽgī*, etc.

Language discovery 2

FUTURE VERB ENDINGS

09.03 Now listen out for the future tense again in these sentences and see how it is created for *they*, *we*, *he*, *she*, *it*, and *you* (informal). Read along with the speaker to practise your pronunciation.

The future with *they* and *we* is the same as with आप *āp* – it ends in *-ẽge / -ẽgī*.

वे लोग खाना बनाएँगे ।
ve log khānā banāẽge. — *Those people will make food.*

ये लोग बीयर लाएँगे ।
ye log bīyar lāẽge. — *These people will bring beer.*

हम लोग सिर्फ़ खाएँगे और पियेंगे !
ham log sirf khāẽge aur piyẽge! — *We will just eat and drink!*

The future tense with *he*, *she*, *it* (and also तू *tū you*) has the ending *-ega / -egī*:

वह घर जाएगा ।	*vah ghar jāegā.*	*He will go home.*
वह घर आएगी ।	*vah ghar āegī.*	*She will come home.*

कल कौनसा दिन होगा ?	*kal kaunsā din hogā?*	*What day will it be tomorrow?*
कल सोमवार होगा ।	*kal somvār hogā.*	Tomorrow will be Monday.

Finally, the future with तुम *tum* has the ending *-oge / -ogī*:

राजू, तुम चाय पियोगे ?	*Rājū, tum cāy piyoge?*	*Raju, will you have tea?*
गीता, तुम मेरे साथ चलोगी ?	*Gītā, tum mere sāth calogī?*	*Geeta, will you come with me?*

How would you say *They* (masculine) *will work hard* and *He will come home next week*?

So here's the future tense in all its glory, shown in the verb बोलना *bolnā to speak.*

मैं बोलूँगा/बोलूँगी *maĩ bolū̃gā/bolū̃gī*	हम बोलेंगे/बोलेंगी *ham bolẽge / bolẽgī*
तू बोलेगा/बोलेगी *tū bolegā/bolegī*	तुम बोलोगे/बोलोगी *tum bologe/bologī*
	आप बोलेंगे/बोलेंगी *āp bolẽge/bolẽgī*
यह, वह बोलेगा/बोलेगी *yah, vah bolegā/bolegī*	ये, वे बोलेंगे/बोलेंगी *ye, ve bolẽge/bolẽgī*

Once you've become familiar with the form of बोलना *bolnā,* practise the future by using it in other everyday verbs.

Keeping in mind that Hindi uses pluralization to show respect, what are the two possible translations of this sentence: कल वे हमारे यहाँ आएँगी । *kal ve hamāre yahā̃ āẽgī*?

REPORTED SPEECH AND *WOULD*

In reported speech, the future tense gives the sense *would*:

राजू कह रहा था कि वह नाश्ता तैयार करेगा ।
Rājū kah rahā thā ki vah nāśtā taiyār karegā.
Raju was saying that he would get breakfast ready.

गीता कह रही थी कि वह आराम करेगी ।
Gītā kah rahī thī ki vah ārām karegī.
Geeta was saying that she would rest.

मनोज और राम कह रहे थे कि वे जल्दी नहीं उठेंगे ।

Manoj aur Rām kah rahe the ki ve jaldī nahī̃ uṭhẽge.

Manoj and Ram were saying that they wouldn't get up early.

मोती सोच रहा था कि क्या मुझे भी नाश्ता मिलेगा ?

Motī soc rahā thā ki kyā mujhe bhī nāśtā milegā?

Moti was wondering if he'd get breakfast too.

If Manoj says, 'मीना कह रही थी कि वह गोपाल की मदद करेगी । *Mīnā kah rahī thī ki vah Gopāl kī madad karegī.*' what did Meena tell him directly?

Storyline

THE DAYS AHEAD

09.04 *Manoj is helping Pratap with his Hindi by asking about the coming week.*

1 On which day of the week does their conversation take place?

मनोज	प्रताप, तुम हफ़्ते के दिनों के नाम बताओगे ?
प्रताप	हाँ, ये हैं — सोमवार, मंगलवार, बुधवार, फिर ... फिर ...
मनोज	गुरु ...
प्रताप	हाँ ! गुरुवार या बृहस्पतिवार, शुक्रवार, शनिवार, रविवार ।
मनोज	शाबाश ! कल कौनसा दिन होगा ?
प्रताप	कल मंगलवार होगा ।
मनोज	परसों तुम क्या करोगे ?
प्रताप	परसों, यानी बुधवार को, मैं पिताजी से मिलने जाऊँगा ।
मनोज	गुरुवार को तुम कहाँ जाओगे ?
प्रताप	गुरुवार को मैं घर पर रहूँगा ।
मनोज	शुक्रवार को तुम क्या करोगे ?
प्रताप	शुक्रवार को मैं अपनी पढ़ाई करूँगा ।
मनोज	और शनिवार को तुम आराम करोगे ?
प्रताप	नहीं, शनिवार को मैं बाहर जाऊँगा और मज़े करूँगा !

Manoj	*Pratāp, tum hafte ke dinõ ke nām batāoge?*
Pratāp	*hā̃, ye haĩ – somvār, mangalvār, budhvār, phir ... phir ...*
Manoj	*guru ...*
Pratāp	*hā̃! guruvār yā bṛhaspativār, śukravār, śanivār, ravivār.*
Manoj	*śābāś! kal kaunsā din hogā?*
Pratāp	*kal mangalvār hogā.*
Manoj	*parsõ tum kyā karoge?*
Pratāp	*parsõ, yānī budhvār ko, maĩ pitājī se milne jāū̃gā.*
Manoj	*guruvār ko tum kahā̃ jāoge?*
Pratāp	*guruvār ko maĩ ghar par rahū̃gā.*
Manoj	*śukravār ko tum kyā karoge?*
Pratāp	*śukravār ko maĩ apnī paṛhāī karū̃gā.*
Manoj	*aur śanivar ko tum ārām karoge?*
Pratāp	*nahī̃, śanivār ko maĩ bāhar jāū̃gā aur maze karū̃gā!*

LANGUAGE TIP

Just as कल *kal* means both *yesterday* and *tomorrow*, so परसों *parsõ* means both *the day before yesterday* and *the day after tomorrow*. नरसों *narsõ* and तरसों *tarsõ* both mean *three days earlier* or *three days ahead*.

2 Listen to the conversation again, then answer the questions.

a What will Pratap do on Wednesday?

b On which day will he go out and have fun (मज़े करना *maze karnā*)?

c What will he do on Friday?

GEETA'S DIARY

09.05 **Your next task is to fill Geeta's appointment diary for the coming week, based on what she tells you (notice that she sometimes uses abbreviations for the names of the days). Write the activity using an infinitive verb – Monday has already been completed as an example of the format to use.**

आज सोम है; आज मैं घर पर रहूँगी । कल, यानी मंगल को, हम लोग दिल्ली जाएँगे । परसों, यानी बुध को, हम अपने मकान के लिए कुछ चीज़ें ख़रीदने जाएँगे । गुरुवार को हम घर वापस आएँगे । शुक्रवार को मैं आराम करूँगी । शनिवार की रात को हम सीता के यहाँ जाएँगे । रविवार को मैं अगले हफ़्ते की तैयारियाँ करूँगी ।

āj som hai; āj maĩ ghar par rahū̃gī. kal, yānī mangal ko, ham log dillī jāẽge. parsõ, yānī budh ko, ham apne makān ke lie kuch cīzẽ <u>kh</u>arīdne jāẽge. guruvār ko ham ghar vāpas āẽge. śukravār ko maĩ ārām karū̃gī. śanivār kī rāt ko ham Sītā ke yahā̃ jāẽge. ravivār ko maĩ agle hafte kī taiyāriyā̃ karū̃gī.

सोमवार *somvār*	घर पर रहना ghar par rahnā
मंगलवार *mangalvār*	
बुधवार *budhvār*	
गुरुवार *guruvār*	
शुक्रवार *śukravār*	
शनिवार *śanivār*	
रविवार *ravivār*	

Language discovery 3

IFS AND MAYBES

The sentence आप घर जाएँगे *āp ghar jāẽge* means *you'll go home*. It's a positive statement of something that is clear, certain, definite. But if we remove the last syllable of जाएँगे *jāẽge,* we are left with आप घर जाएँ *āp ghar jāẽ* – which means *you should go home* (suggestion) or *you might go home* (possibility) or even *you may go home* (permission). We've cut off the certainty of the verb with its last syllable.

This form of the verb is called the subjunctive: it expresses a sense of uncertainty, possibility, permission, suggestion, and similar indefinite, imagined, or tentative senses. As we've just seen, it's formed by lopping off the last syllable of the future tense; the distinction between masculine and feminine is lost as a result. You'll often find words like अगर *agar if*, शायद *śāyad maybe, perhaps*, or ज़रूर *zarūr of course* lurking nearby. All the verbs in the next dialogue are in the subjunctive.

In terms of word form, the subjunctive is simply the future minus its final syllable: thus future करेगा *karegā* becomes subjunctive करे *kare*, and जाएँगे *jāẽge* becomes जाएँ *jāẽ*. Buy one, get one free!

मैं अंदर आऊँ ? *maĩ andar āū̃?* *May I come in?* Can you tell if the person asking this question is male or female?

Sentences involving an *if* are quite likely to use a subjunctive verb, but verb forms such as a future tense are also possible:

> अगर वह "हाँ" कहे तो हम शादी करेंगे ।
> *agar vah 'hā̃' kahe to ham śādī karẽge.*
> *If she says 'yes', then we'll marry.*
> (Subjunctive *kahe* – don't count on her agreement.)
>
> अगर वह "हाँ" कहेगी तो हम शादी करेंगे ।
> *agar vah 'hā̃' kahegī to ham śādī karẽge.*
> *If she says 'yes', then we'll marry.*
> (Future *kahegī* – book the photographer!)

These two sentences show how Hindi pairs an अगर *agar* clause with a तो *to* clause: *If X, then Y.*

Using the subjunctive, how would you say *If you tell Rajni, then she will be upset* and *If Ram feeds the dog, then it will come back* (खिलाना *khilānā* to feed)?

Storyline

JAVED CALLS ON RAJU

1 09.06 **Where does their conversation take place, at home or in the office?**

जावेद	मैं अंदर आऊँ ?
राजू	जी हाँ, जी हाँ, आप ज़रूर आएँ !
जावेद	मैं कहाँ बैठूँ ?
राजू	आप इधर बैठें । मैं चाय बनाऊँ ?
जावेद	अगर आप चाहें । या हम बाहर जाएँ ?
राजू	नहीं, हम घर पर ही रहें ।
Jāved	*maĩ andar āū̃?*
Rājū	*jī hā̃, jī hā̃, āp zarūr āẽ.*
Jāved	*maĩ kahā̃ baiṭhū̃?*
Rājū	*āp idhar baiṭhẽ. maĩ cāy banāū̃?*
Javed	*agar āp cāhẽ. yā ham bāhar jāẽ?*
Rājū	*nahī̃, ham ghar par hī rahẽ.*

2 Listen to the conversation again, then answer these questions.

a What does Raju suggest they do?

b Will they stay at home or go out?

Language discovery 4

A SUGGESTION OR A COMMAND?

A subjunctive verb blurs the boundary between a suggestion and a command, offering a nicely diplomatic way of getting someone to comply with your wishes:

आप थोड़ी देर बैठे रहें ।
āp thoṛī der baiṭhe rahẽ.
Kindly remain seated for a while.

कृपया गिलास में हाथ न धोएँ ।
kṛpayā gilās mẽ hāth na dhoẽ.
Please do not wash your hands in the tumbler. (Restaurant sign.)

Where might you find a sign that says गाड़ी धीरे चलाएँ *gāṛī dhīre calāẽ*?

I WANT TO .../I WANT YOU TO ...

Look closely at the difference between the following pair of sentences. How many people are involved in each one?

मैं कुछ कहना चाहता हूँ ।
maĩ kuch kahnā cāhtā hū̃. *I want to say something.*

मैं चाहता हूँ कि आप कुछ कहें ।
maĩ cāhtā hū̃ ki āp kuch kahẽ. *I want you to say something.*

The first sentence involves Person A doing both the wanting and the speaking; the construction uses चाहना *cāhnā to want* with an infinitive verb (here कहना *kahnā to say*). The second involves Person A wanting Person B to do something: the construction uses चाहना *cāhnā to want* with a subjunctive verb (here कहें *kahẽ*). The two clauses are linked by कि *ki that*. Here are two more examples:

मैं चाहता हूँ कि वे यहाँ रहें ।
maĩ cāhtā hū̃ ki ve yahā̃ rahẽ. *I want them to stay here.*

वे चाहते हैं कि मैं यहाँ रहूँ ।
ve cāhte haĩ ki maĩ yahā̃ rahū̃. *They want me to stay here.*

How would you say *Geeta wants her daughter to study* and *He wants to study*?

Listening and speaking

09.07 **Over to you. Make sentences by combining a phrase from the left-hand list with a phrase from the right-hand list, giving meanings such as *I want you to rest*. All the verbs in the right-hand list are subjunctive.**

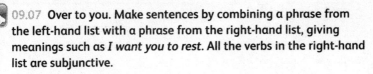

मैं चाहता हूँ कि ... *maĩ cāhtā hū̃ ki ...*	... आप आराम करें । *... āp ārām karẽ.*
हम चाहते थे कि ... *ham cāhte the ki ...*	... तुम हमारे यहाँ ठहरो । *... tum hamāre yahā̃ ṭhahro.*
वे चाहते हैं कि ... *ve cāhte haĩ ki ...*	... तुम्हारा दोस्त भी आए । *... tumhārā dost bhī āe.*

वह चाहता है कि ...	... तुम जाने की तैयारियाँ करो ।
vah cāhtā hai ki ...	*... tum jāne kī taiyāriyā̃ karo.*
मैं चाहती थी कि ...	... वह अपना काम करे ।
maĩ cāhtī thī ki ...	*... vah apnā kām kare.*
मेरी बहिन चाहती है कि ...	... तुम खाना बनाओ ।
merī bahin cāhtī hai ki ...	*... tum khānā banāo.*

Language discovery 5

SO THAT, IN ORDER THAT

The conjunction (or 'linking word') ताकि *tāki* means *so that, in order that*, and is always followed by a subjunctive verb:

मैं उठूँगा ताकि दूसरे लोग बैठें ।
maĩ uṭhū̃gā tāki dūsre log baiṭhẽ.
I'll get up so that others may sit.

अभी आइए ताकि हम काम शुरू करें ।
abhī āie tāki ham kām śurū karẽ.
Come right now so that we can start work.

जल्दी उठो ताकि देरी न हो ।
jaldī uṭho tāki derī na ho.
Get up early so that there won't be any delay.

हम धीरे धीरे बोलेंगे ताकि वे हमारी बात समझें ।
ham dhīre dhīre bolẽge tāki ve hamārī bāt samjhẽ.
We'll speak slowly so that they understand what we say.

How would you properly link these two thoughts using ताकि *tāki*?

राहुल मेट्रो से जाता है ।	*Rahul meṭro se jātā hai.*
वह जल्दी पहुँचता है।	*vah jaldī pahũctā hai.*

HOW LONG DOES IT TAKE?

09.08 To say how long something takes, Hindi uses the versatile verb लगना *lagnā*, here referring to the *time taken*:

एक घंटा लगता है ।
ek ghaṇṭā lagtā hai.
It takes one hour.

दस मिनट लगते हैं ।
das minaṭ lagte haĩ.
It takes ten minutes.

दो दिन लगेंगे ।
do din lagẽge.
It'll take two days.

Notice how the verb agrees with the unit of time – *one hour* (sing.) *ten minutes* (pl.), etc. To specify the action done within the particular time frame, add an infinitive plus में *mẽ*, as in किताब लिखने में *kitāb likhne mẽ in writing the book*:

किताब लिखने में एक साल लगेगा ।
kitāb likhne mẽ ek sāl lagegā.
It'll take a year to write the book.

घर जाने में दो घंटे लगते हैं ।
ghar jāne mẽ do ghaṇṭe lagte haĩ.
It takes two hours to get home.

यह काम ख़त्म करने में मुझे डेढ़ घंटा लगेगा ।
yah kām khatm karne mẽ mujhe ḍeṛh ghaṇṭā lagegā.
It'll take me an hour and a half to finish this work.

How would you say *It takes half an hour to reach the station* and *It will take three hours to prepare dinner?*

Practice 2

1 09.09 **Match up the अगर *agar* (1–6) and तो *to* (a–f) clauses to make meaningful sentences, then listen to check your answers. For additional practice, translate the full sentences.**

1 अगर सब्ज़ी-मंडी आज बंद हो ...
agar sabzī-maṇḍī āj band ho ...

a ... तो आप मेरे यहाँ रहें ।
... to āp mere yahā̃ rahẽ.

2 अगर तुम्हें रास्ता नहीं मालूम ... *agar tumhẽ rāstā nahī̃ mālūm ...*	b ... तो थाने पर जाओ । *... to thāne par jāo.*
3 अगर आप किसी शब्द का मतलब नहीं जानते ... *agar āp kisī śabd kā matlab nahī̃ jānte ...*	c ... तो शब्दकोश में देखिए । *... to śabdkoś mẽ dekhie.*
4 अगर गोलचक्कर पर पुलिसवाला न मिले ... *agar golcakkar par pulisvālā na mile...*	d ... तो नक़्शा ख़रीदना । *... to naqśā <u>kh</u>arīdnā.*
5 अगर होटल में कमरा न मिले ... *agar hoṭal mẽ kamrā na mile ...*	e ... तो कल सुबह को सब्ज़ी लेना । *... to kal subah ko sabzī lenā.*
6 अगर आप उस तंग गली में मुड़ेंगे ... *agar āp us tang galī mẽ muṛẽge ...*	f ... तो बायें हाथ पर ढाबा दिखाई देगा। *... to bāyẽ hāth par ḍhābā dikhāī degā.*

2 You have just arrived at a hotel where you will be staying for several days. Do as instructed:

a Tell the hotel receptionist that you need a room for two people and that you will stay for two days.

b Say that some friends will come to meet you this evening.

c Ask what will be available for breakfast (नाश्ते में *nāśte mẽ*).

d Ask whether dinner will be available as well.

e Ask how long it will take to go on foot from the hotel to the cinema.

f Tell the receptionist that you would like to phone London; ask if you can phone from your room.

g Say that next week you will go to Agra and Delhi.

h Ask if your friends can eat with you in the hotel tonight.

3 **Match both parts of the sentences.**

a कल शनिवार है ... *kal śanivār hai ...*	**1** ...कि वह घर पर रहेगा। *... ki vah ghar par rahegā.*
b हम सोच रहे थे ... *ham soc rahe the ...*	**2** ...हमारे साथ आएँ। *... hamāre sāth āẽ.*
c मेरा भाई कह रहा था ... *merā bhāī kah rahā thā ...*	**3** ...तो हम गाड़ी से जाएँगे। *... to ham gāṛī se jāẽge.*
d अगर आप चाहें ... *agar āp cāhẽ ...*	**4** ...तो हम बाहर जाएँगे। *... to ham bāhar jāẽge.*
e हम जल्दी जाएँगे ... *ham jaldī jāẽge ...*	**5** ...ताकि हमें अच्छी सीटें मिलें। *... tāki hamẽ acchī sīṭẽ milẽ.*
f अगर बारिश हो ... *agar bāriś ho ...*	**6** ...कि हम सिनेमा जाएँगे। *... ki ham sinemā jāẽge.*

Vocabulary builder

अगर	*agar*	*if*
आराम	*ārām* m.	*rest*
आराम करना	*ārām karnā*	*to rest*
इधर	*idhar*	*here, over here*
इधर-उधर	*idhar-udhar*	*here and there, hither and thither*
इमारत	*imārat* f.	*building*
उठना	*uṭhnā*	*to get up, rise*
उधर	*udhar*	*there, over there*
ओर	*or* f.	*side, direction*
कृपया	*kṛpayā*	*please (formal)*
के चारों तरफ़	*ke cārõ taraf*	*all around*
के सामने	*ke sāmne*	*opposite*
गली	*galī* f.	*lane, narrow street*
गिलास	*gilās* m.	*tumbler*
गुरुवार	*guruvār* m.	*Thursday*
गोलचक्कर	*golcakkar* m.	*roundabout*
घंटा	*ghaṇṭā* m.	*hour*
ठंड	*ṭhaṇḍ* f.	*cold*

ठंड लगना	*ṭhaṇḍ lagnā*	*to feel cold*
ठहरना	*ṭhaharnā*	*to stay, remain*
ताकि	*tāki*	*so that, in order that*
तैयारी	*taiyārī* f.	*preparation*
देरी	*derī* f.	*delay*
नक़्शा	*naqśā* m.	*map, plan*
नाश्ता	*nāśtā* m.	*breakfast*
पढ़ाई	*paṛhāī* f.	*studies, studying*
परसों	*parsõ*	*two days away (day after tomorrow; day before yesterday)*
पहुँचना	*pahũcnā*	*to reach, arrive*
पुलिसवाला	*pulisvālā* m.	*policeman*
बंद	*band*	*closed, shut*
बीयर	*bīyar* f.	*beer*
बुधवार	*budhvār* m.	*Wednesday*
बेहतर	*behtar*	*better*
मंगलवार	*maṅgalvār* f.	*Tuesday*
मज़ा	*mazā* m.	*enjoyment, fun*
मज़े करना	*maze karnā*	*to enjoy oneself, have fun*
मतलब	*matlab* m.	*meaning*
मुड़ना	*muṛnā*	*to turn*
रविवार	*ravivār* m.	*Sunday*
लगना	*lagnā*	*time to be taken*
वापस	*vāpas*	*'back'*
वापस आना/जाना/देना	*vāpas ānā/jānā/denā*	*to come/go/give back*
शनिवार	*śanivār* m.	*Saturday*
शब्द	*śabd* m.	*word*
शब्दकोश	*śabdkoś* m.	*dictionary*
शादी	*śādī* f.	*wedding, marriage*
शादी करना	*śādī karnā*	*to marry*
शाबाश	*śābāś*	*bravo*
शुक्रवार	*śukravār* m.	*Friday*
सब्ज़ी	*sabzī* f.	*vegetable(s)*
सब्ज़ी मंडी	*sabzī maṇḍī* f.	*vegetable market*
सब्ज़ीवाला	*sabzīvālā* m.	*vegetable seller*
सुबह	*subah* f.	*morning*

Test yourself

1 A friend says: कल रात आप लोग हमारे यहाँ खाना खाने आएँगे ? *kal rāt āp log hamāre yahā̃ khānā khāne ā̃ege?* What are you being asked to do?

2 In the previous question, the verb आएँगे *ā̃ege* agrees with आप *āp*. What other 'persons' can the form आएँगे *ā̃ege* be used with?

3 आज गुरुवार है । परसों कौनसा दिन होगा ? *āj guruvār hai. parsõ kaunsā din hogā?*

4 What's the difference in tone between the statements आप यहाँ बैठिए *āp yahā̃ baiṭhie* and आप यहाँ बैठें *āp yahā̃ baiṭhẽ*?

5 How do we say, *They* (f.) *want you to come too*?

6 Rewrite your answer to 5, replacing आप *āp* with तुम *tum* (or vice versa).

7 In the sentence आप जल्दी आएँ ताकि अच्छी सीट मिले *āp jaldī āẽ tāki acchī sīṭ mile*, explain the form of the verb मिले *mile*. (सीट *sīṭ* is the English word *seat*.)

8 You're at a hotel. How do you say *Will we get breakfast*?

9 You hear a guest in a hotel asking कमरा साफ़ करने में कितना समय लगेगा ? *kamrā sāf karne mẽ kitnā samay lagegā?* What's being asked?

10 How would you say, *Our room is a little bigger than your room*?

SELF CHECK

	I CAN...
○	... talk about the future.
○	... use *if* expressions.
○	... express doubts and possibilities.

10 क्या हुआ ?

kyā huā?

What happened?

In this unit you will learn how to:

▶ ***describe past events.***

▶ ***link connected actions in a sequence.***

Language points

▶ *perfective tenses*

▶ *transitivity*

▶ *absolutives*

Language discovery 1

THE PAST TENSE

10.01 So far we've seen two kinds of past tense: 'imperfective' (describing **routine or habitual events** of the *I used to* type), and 'continuous' (describing **actions in progress** of the *I was doing* type). Here's an example of each to remind you:

मैं दौड़ता था ।	*maĩ daur̥tā thā.*	*I used to run.*
मैं दौड़ रहा था ।	*maĩ daur̥ rahā thā.*	*I was running.*

The new tense we're going to look at now is this:

मैं दौड़ा ।	*maĩ daur̥ā.*	*I ran.*

This describes a *completed* action in the past and is called the 'perfective' tense. It uses a 'perfective participle' consisting of verb stem plus *-ā/-e/-ī/-ī̃*. Thus दौड़ा *daur̥ā ran*, बोला *bolā spoke*, हँसा *hãsā laughed*, उठा *ut̥hā got up*, पहुँचा *pahũcā arrived*, and so on.

Look carefully at the verb endings in the following three sentences, making sure you can see how they agree with their subjects (for example, the first one is feminine singular to agree with *Meena*):

मीना घर पहुँची ।
Mīnā ghar pahũcī. — Meena arrived home.

फिर मनोज और राजू पहुँचे ।
phir Manoj aur Rājū pahũcī. — Then Manoj and Raju arrived.

बाद में गीता और सीता पहुँचीं ।
bād mẽ Gītā aur Sītā pahũcī̃. — Later Geeta and Sita arrived.

Before going any further, practise using the verbs बोलना *bolnā* and उठना *uṭhnā* (or any others just given) with a range of different subjects, paying attention to the agreements of gender and number.

How would you say *He spoke, She spoke, They* (feminine) *spoke*, and *We spoke*?

COMING AND GOING

You're probably thinking this is all too easy. And you're right: it's time to introduce an exception! The participle from जाना *jānā to go* is गया/गए/गई/गईं *gayā/gae/gaī/gaī̃.* (Don't confuse this with गाया *gāyā*, etc., from गाना *gānā* to sing.)

मीना स्कूल गई, मनोज बाहर गया, राजू और राम बाज़ार गए, गीता और सीता सिनेमा गईं ।

Mīnā skūl gaī, Manoj bāhar gayā, Rājū aur Rām bāzār gae, Gītā aur Sītā sinemā gaī̃.

Meena went to school, Manoj went out, Raju and Ram went to the market, Geeta and Sita went to the cinema.

Participles for the verb आना *ānā to come* are आया, आए, आई, आईं *āyā, āe, āī, āī̃.* Notice how the masculine singular आया *āyā* has a *y* between the stem and the ending. All verbs with *-ā* stems do this.

WHAT HAPPENED THEN?

The perfective from होना *honā to be, to happen* is हुआ, हुए, हुई, हुईं *huā, hue, huī, huī̃ happened.*

तब क्या हुआ ?
tab kyā huā ? — What happened then?

एक दुर्घटना हुई ।
ek durghaṭnā huī. — An accident happened. (There was an accident.)

LANGUAGE TIP

So what? The phrase क्या हुआ *kyā huā* (lit., *what happened?*) is used colloquially with the slightly dismissive sense *So what?*

Which sentence contains an irregular verb?

a मनोज ने एक गाना गाया । *Manoj ne ek gānā gāyā.*

b मनोज सिनेमा गया । *Manoj sinemā gayā.*

Speaking

1 This is all quite easy to understand, but you'll only really learn it when you use it. So make up some short subject-plus-verb sentences using Meena and anyone else (as in the long sentence at the top of this page) as subjects, combined with the following verbs:

आना	*ānā*	*to come*
जाना	*jānā*	*to go*
उठना	*uṭhnā*	*to get up*
दौड़ना	*dauṛnā*	*to run*
पहुँचना	*pahũcnā*	*to arrive*
हँसना	*hãsnā*	*to laugh*

2 Now answer these questions with the data supplied on the right:

a	मनोज कहाँ गया ? *Manoj kahā̃ gayā?*	घर *ghar*
b	राजू और राम कहाँ गए ? *Rājū aur Rām kahā̃ gae?*	बाहर *bāhar*
c	सीता कहाँ गई ? *Sītā kahā̃ gaī?*	दिल्ली *dillī*
d	क्या हुआ ? *kyā huā?*	कुछ नहीं *kuch nahī*
e	मीना कब पहुँची ? *Mīnā kab pahũcī?*	कल *kal*
f	दादीजी कब आईं ? *dādījī kab āī̃?*	परसों *parsõ*
g	मनोज कब आया ? *Manoj kab āyā?*	मंगलवार को *mangalvār ko*

Language discovery 2

TRANSITIVITY

In the perfective, Hindi verbs follow two different patterns depending on whether they are 'intransitive' or 'transitive'. A transitive verb describes an action done to an object, as in *We drank coffee* (in which the drinking was a process done by us to the coffee). We can test its transitivity by asking a question about the object: ***What*** *did we drink?* By contrast, an *in*transitive verb simply describes an action occurring, with no object being involved, as in *we arrived* or *I got up*; here we can't make questions like *What did we arrive?* or *What did I get up?* so these verbs don't pass the transitivity test. The Hindi verbs we've used so far in this unit have all been intransitive; but it's time now to move on transitive verbs, which behave differently in the past tense. Look very closely at the constructions of the following four sentences (a hint: किताब *kitab* is feminine, अख़बार *a<u>kh</u>bar* is masculine):

राजू ने किताब पढ़ी ।
Rājū ne kitāb paṛhī. — *Raju read a book.*

राजू ने दोनों किताबें पढ़ीं ।
Rājū ne donõ kitābẽ paṛhī̃. — *Raju read both books.*

गीता ने अख़बार पढ़ा ।
Gītā ne a<u>kh</u>bār paṛhā. — *Geeta read a newsaper.*

गीता ने दोनों अख़बार पढ़े ।
Gītā ne donõ a<u>kh</u>bār paṛhe. — *Geeta read both newsapers.*

Well, you should have noticed that the verbs agree with the *book/books* and *newspaper/newspapers* rather than with their readers! And also that the readers have sprouted an untranslatable postposition, ने *ne*. This is how transitive verbs always operate in the perfective. A verb that has no object for the verb to agree with stays in the masculine singular:

राम ने खाया । मीनू ने खाया ।
Rām ne khāyā. Mīnū ne khāyā. — *Ram ate. Meenu ate.*

Because we're not told *what* they ate, the verb stays as खाया *khāyā.*

Why do these sentences not take the ने *ne* construction?

a आज राम जल्दी उठा । — *āj Rām jaldī uṭhā.*

b सुनीता मीना के साथ गई । — *Sunītā Mīnā ke sāth gaī.*

c माता-पिता कल रात पहुँचे । — *Mātā-pitā kal rāt pahũce.*

Practice 1

1 10.02 **There was a party at the Sharmas' house. Complete the sentences with the appropriate form of the verb supplied on the right. Then listen to check your answers and repeat in the pauses to practise your pronunciation.**

The agreement of the verb will be with the subject if there's no ने *ne* construction, but with the object if there *is* a ने *ne* construction..

a	गीता ने बढ़िया खाना … *Gītā ne baṛhiyā khānā …*	बनाना *banānā*	*to make*
b	मीना की दो सहेलियाँ पार्टी में … *Mīnā kī do saheliyā̃ pārṭī mẽ ...*	आना *ānā*	to come
c	मनोज के कई दोस्त भी … *Manoj ke kaī dost bhī ...*	आना *ānā*	to come
d	गीता की सहेली ने सितार … *Gītā kī sahelī ne sitār...*	बजाना *bajānā*	to play
e	फिर मोती ज़ोर से … *phir Moti zor se ...*	भौंकना *bhaũknā*	to bark
f	राजू ने पाँच समोसे … *Rājū ne pā̃c samose ...*	खाना *khānā*	to eat
g	सब लोग बड़ी देर तक … *sab log baṛī der tak ...*	रहना *rahnā*	to stay
h	दूसरे दिन बच्चे देर से … *dūsre din bacce der se ...*	उठना *uṭhnā*	to get up

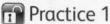

2 How many did you see? Make up sentences on the model of मैंने एक मकान देखा *maĩne ek makān dekhā I saw one house*, to reflect the following objects:

1 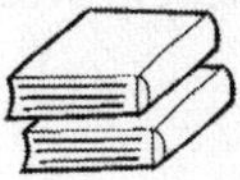

2 

3 

4 

5 

6 

7 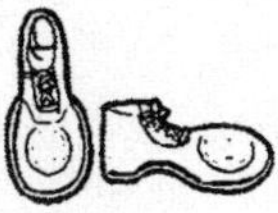

8 

9 

10 

11 

12 

13 

14 

15 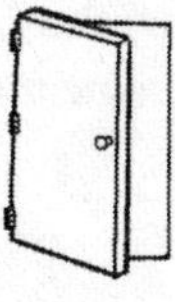

16 

Language discovery 3

SOME SPECIAL PRONOUNS

Some pronouns have special oblique forms for the ने *ne* construction:

PRONOUN	USUAL OBLIQUE	SPECIAL FORM + ने *ne*
मैं *maī̃*	मुझ *mujh*	मैंने *maī̃ne*
तू *tū*	तुझ *tujh*	तूने *tūne*
ये *ye*	इन *in*	इन्होंने *inhõne*
वे *ve*	उन *un*	उन्होंने *unhõne*

SOME SPECIAL VERBS

Some very common verbs have irregular participles:

करना *karnā* to do:	किया, किए, की, कीं *kiyā, kie, kī, kī̃*	did
देना *denā* to give:	दिया, दिए, दी, दीं *diyā, die, dī, dī̃*	gave
लेना *lenā* to take:	लिया, लिए, ली, लीं *liyā, lie, lī, lī̃*	took
पीना *pīnā* to drink:	पिया, पिए, पी, पीं *piyā, pie, pī, pī̃*	drank

Change these two sentences into the perfective tense, keeping in mind the irregular verbs and pronouns you just learned:

a वे इंतज़ार करते हैं । *ve intazār karte haī̃.*

b मैं चाय पीता हूँ । *maī̃ cāī pītā hū̃.*

Listen and understand

10.03 **What did Geeta see? Answer the questions using the data supplied on the right (with which the verb must agree!). Then, listen and repeat to practise your pronunciation, and keep listening to check your answers.**

a गीता ने क्या देखा ? *Gītā ne kyā dekhā?* — एक नई फ़िल्म *ek naī film*

b राजू ने क्या ख़रीदा ? *Rājū ne kyā kharīdā?* — दो अख़बार *do akhbār*

c मोती ने क्या खाया ? — दस चपातियाँ
Motī ne kyā khāyā? — *das capātiyā̃*

d मीना ने क्या पढ़ा ? — दो कहानियाँ
Mīnā ne kyā paṛhā? — *do kahāniyā̃*

e हमने कितने कुरते ख़रीदे ? — चार
hamne kitne kurte kharīde? — *cār*

f उन्होंने मेज़ पर क्या रखा ? — कुछ किताबें
unhõne mez par kyā rakhā? — *kuch kitābẽ*

g आपने दीवार पर क्या लिखा ? — अपना नाम
āpne dīvar par kyā likhā? — *apnā nam*

h तुमने क्या सुना ? — कई बातें
tumne kyā sunā? — *kaī bātẽ*

i तुमने कितनी भाषाएँ सीखीं ? — एक ही
tumne kitnī bhāṣāẽ sīkhī̃? — *ek hī*

All verbs that take the ने *ne* construction are shown with N in the English–Hindi glossary (e.g. देखना *dekhnā* N) at the end of the book. The construction itself may take some time to digest – like Moti's ten chapatties.

Language discovery 4

A PARTICULAR OBJECT

Back in **Language discovery 2** we saw that को *ko* is often added to an object that's particularized in some way. (Go back and review now if you've forgotten this.) If को *ko* is added to the object of a ने *ne* verb, then the verb reverts to a masculine singular.

राम ने चपाती को खाया ।
Rām ne capātī ko khāyā. — *Ram ate the chapatti.*

मैंने उनके बच्चों को देखा ।
maĩne unke baccõ ko dekhā. — *I saw their children.*

उसने किताबों को पढ़ा ।
usne kitābõ ko paṛhā. — *He/She read the books.*

The verbs in these three sentences all end in *-ā* (खाया *khāyā*, देखा *dekhā*, पढ़ा *paṛhā*) because in each one the presence of को *ko* insulates the verb from its object.

How would you add को to this sentence to make it obvious that you saw those particular boys? मैंने लड़के देखे । *maĩne laṛke dekhe.*

OTHER PERFECTIVE TENSES

In English, we differentiate timeframes by saying *I wrote, have written, had written, will have written*, etc. Similarly, in Hindi, all three kinds of perfective verbs can be used in different time frames by adding auxiliary verbs (है *hai*, था *thā*, etc.):

a राजू ने चिट्ठी लिखी ।
Rājū ne ciṭṭhī likhī. — *Raju wrote a letter.*

b राजू ने चिट्ठी लिखी है ।
Rājū ne ciṭṭhī likhī hai. — *Raju has written a letter.*

c राजू ने चिट्ठी लिखी थी ।
Rājū ne ciṭṭhī likhī thī. — *Raju had written a letter (or wrote it some time ago).*

d राजू ने चिट्ठी लिखी होगी ।
Rājū ne ciṭṭhī likhī hogī. — *Raju will have written a letter.*

e राजू ने चिट्ठी लिखी हो ।
Rājū ne ciṭṭhī likhī ho. — *Raju may have written a letter.*

Notes

a लिखी *likhī*, no auxiliary verb; it's the simple past.

b लिखी है *likhī hai has written* (है *hai* is singular because चिट्ठी *ciṭṭhī* is singular), suggesting that the effect of the writing is still felt in the present.

c लिखी थी *likhī thī* (both words are feminine singular, to agree with चिट्ठी *ciṭṭhī*), suggesting that the action happened some time earlier.

d लिखी होगी *likhī hogī will have written*, either referring to some future time (such as *Raju will have written a letter by Monday*) or making an assumption about the present (such as *Presumably Raju will have written a letter by now*).

e लिखी हो *likhī ho may have written*, in which the subjunctive हो *ho* shows that the matter is open to some doubt.

The same range can be used with any perfective verb:

पिताजी मिठाई लाए हैं/थे ।
pitājī miṭhāī lāe haĩ/ the. — *Father has/had brought sweets.*

पिताजी मिठाई लाए होंगे/हों ।
pitājī miṭhāī lāe hõge. Father will/may have brought sweets.

In the last two sentences, the verbs agree with पिताजी *pitājī* (masculine honorific plural) because लाना *lānā,* though transitive, is not a ने *ne* verb.

मोती ने दस चपातियाँ खाई हैं/थीं ।
Motī ne das capātiyā̃ khāī haĩ/ thī̃. Moti has/had eaten ten chapatties.

मोती ने दस चपातियाँ खाई होंगी/हों ।
Motī ne das capātiyā̃ khāī hõgī/ hõ. Moti will/may have eaten ten chapatties.

Put these sentences in chronological order by paying attention to the different perfective tenses of the verbs.

a अब सीमा को भूख लगी है । *ab Sīmā ko bhūkh lagī hai.*

b सुबह सीमा ने नाश्ता किया था । *subah Sīmā ne nāśtā kiyā thā.*

c दिन भर सीमा ने काम किया । *din-bhar Sīmā ne kām kiyā.*

Storyline

RAJU'S VERSION OF THE MORNING

10.04 *Here's Raju's account of his morning, following an evening when he and Geeta had been to see a Hindi film starring Shahrukh Khan. Make sure you can understand all the verb agreements!*

1 Was Raju in a good or bad mood this morning?

आज सुबह मैं पाँच बजे उठा । थोड़ी देर के लिए मैं आँगन में बैठा । कल शाम को जब हम शाहरुख़ खाँ की नई फ़िल्म देखने सिनेमा गए तो बारिश हुई थी लेकिन आज मैंने देखा कि आकाश साफ़ है । *सुबह के समय चारों ओर शान्ति होती है । मुझे सुबह का समय बहुत पसंद है ।

मैंने अपने लिए चाय बनाई । चाय पीने के बाद मैंने अपनी पत्नी को जगाया । चाय बनाना तो दो मिनट का काम है लेकिन मेमसाहब को जगाना दूसरी बात है । आख़िर में जब वह नीचे आई तो मैंने उसका नाश्ता तैयार किया । मैं तो नाश्ता कभी नहीं खाता, लेकिन गीता ज़रूर खाती है । मैंने उसके लिए दो टोस्ट बनाए । उसने चाय पी, आधा केला भी खाया । उसने शिकायत की कि चाय में चीनी ज़्यादा है । *मैंने कहा कि तुम्हारी जिन्दगी में थोड़ी मिठास की ज़रूरत है ।*

āj subah maĩ pā̃c baje uṭhā. thoṛī der ke lie maĩ ā̃gan mẽ baiṭhā. kal śām ko jab ham Śāhrukh Khā̃ kī naī film dekhne sinemā gae to bāriś huī thī lekin āj maĩne dekhā ki ākāś sāf hai. subah ke samay cārõ or śānti hotī hai. mujhe subah kā samay bahut pasand hai.*

maĩne apne lie cāy banāī. cāy pīne ke bād maĩne apnī patnī ko jagāyā. cāy banānā to do minaṭ kā kām hai lekin memsāhib ko jagānā dūsrī bāt hai. ākhir mẽ jab vah nīce āī to maĩne uskā nāśtā taiyār kiyā. maĩ to nāśtā kabhī nahī̃ khātā, lekin Gītā zarūr khātī hai. maĩne uske lie do ṭosṭ banāe. usne cāy pī, ādhā kelā bhī khāyā. usne śikāyat kī ki cāy mẽ cīnī zyādā hai. maĩne kahā ki tumhārī zindagī mẽ thoṛī miṭhās kī zarūrat hai.**

*These three sentences show the use of 'reported speech' in Hindi. Literally, they translate as *Today I saw that the sky is clear; She complained that 'There's too much sugar in the tea'* and *I said, 'In your life a bit of sweetness is needed'*.

2 Listen again and then answer the questions.

a How was the weather the night before? How was it this morning?
b Which is a more difficult task: making tea or waking up Geeta?
c What was wrong with the tea?

Writing

Time for you to try your hand at the past tenses. Translate the following:

a I got up early today.
b My father woke me up at six o'clock.
c He prepared breakfast for me.
d Then I went out to buy a newspaper.
e Near the shop I saw my uncle's car.
f My uncle had gone into the shop.
g My uncle saw me and asked me how I was.
h He came home with me and I made coffee for him.
i My father asked me where the newspaper was.
j I said I hadn't brought the newspaper, I'd brought uncle.

Storyline

GEETA'S VERSION OF THE MORNING

1 10.05 **What was wrong with Geeta's breakfast?**

आम तौर पर राजू मुझे देर से जगाता है लेकिन आज उसने मुझे जल्दी ही जगाया । मैं आराम से सो रही थी और शाहरुख़ ख़ाँ का सपना देख रही थी । इतना मीठा सपना था ! जब मैंने अपने पति की आवाज़ सुनी तो मैंने सोचा कि शाहरुख़ ही मुझे जगाने आया है । लेकिन यह तो सपना ही था । मैं नीचे रसोई में गई । मेरे पति ने मेरे लिए दो टोस्ट बनाए थे । मैंने उसे कितनी बार बताया है कि मुझे टोस्ट पसंद नहीं लेकिन वह तो सुनता ही नहीं । चाय में उसने बहुत ज़्यादा चीनी डाली थी । मेरे सिर में दर्द था इसलिए मैंने दो गोलियाँ खाईं । राजू ने मुझे जगाने से पहले ही नाश्ता किया होगा क्योंकि मेरे साथ तो उसने कुछ नहीं खाया । मैंने उससे पूछा कि तुमने मुझे इतनी जल्दी क्यों जगाया, लेकिन उसने कोई जवाब नहीं दिया । शाहरुख़, तू कहाँ है ?

ām taur par Rājū mujhe der se jagātā hai lekin āj usne mujhe jaldī hī jagāyā. maĩ ārām se so rahī thī aur Śāhruḵẖ Ḵẖā̃ kā sapnā dekh rahī thī. itnā mīṭhā sapnā thā! jab maĩne apne pati kī āvāz sunī to maĩne socā ki Śāhruḵẖ hī mujhe jagāne āyā hai. lekin yah to sapnā hī thā. maĩ nīce rasoī mẽ gaī. mere pati ne mere lie do ṭosṭ banāe the. maĩne use kitnī bār batāyā hai ki mujhe ṭosṭ pasand nahī̃ lekin vah to suntā hī nahī̃. cāy mẽ usne bahut zyādā cīnī ḍālī thī. mere sir mẽ dard thā islie maĩne do goliyā̃ khāī̃. Rājū ne mujhe jagāne se pahle hī nāśtā kiyā hogā kyõki mere sāth to usne kuch nahī̃ khāyā. maĩne usse pūchā ki tumne mujhe itnī jaldī kyõ jagāyā, lekin usne koī javāb nahī̃ diyā. Śāhruḵẖ, tū kahā̃ hai?

2 **After listening to Geeta again, answer these questions.**
 a Who did Geeta dream about and keep thinking about this morning?
 b What was wrong with her this morning, and what did she do about it?

WRITING

Reread Raju and Geeta's accounts and decide which statements are सही *sahī* (right) or ग़लत *galat* (wrong). Then rewrite the incorrect statements to match Raju's or Geeta's version of the facts.

a सबसे पहले गीता उठी ।
 sabse pahle Gītā uṭhī.

b राजू ने गीता के लिए नाश्ता तैयार किया ।
Rājū ne Gītā ke lie nāśtā taiyār kiyā.

c गीता को जगाने से पहले राजू ने चाई पी ।
Gītā ko jagāne se pahle Rājū ne cāī pī.

d गीता ने शिकायत की कि चाई में चीनी कम थी ।
Gītā ne śikāyat kī ki cāī mẽ cīnī kam thī.

e गीता ने रसोई में नाश्ता किया ।
Gītā ne rasoī mẽ nāśtā kiyā.

f राजू ने गोलियाँ खाईं ।
Rājū ne goliyā̃ khāī̃.

g राजू को जल्दी उठना पसंद है ।
Rājū ko jaldī uṭhnā pasand hai.

Speaking

10.06 **Translate these sentences into Hindi, then play the audio, speak at the prompts, and listen to check your pronunciation.**

a Raju made tea.
b He woke up Geeta.
c She came downstairs.
d She ate a banana.
e She also ate two tablets.
f Raju had put too much sugar in the tea.
g Did Raju eat anything?

Language discovery 5

LINKING TWO ACTIONS

English often links two successive actions with *and*, as in *sit and rest*. But Hindi has a neat shortcut for this. Instead of saying बैठो और आराम करो *baiṭho aur ārām karo* we can say बैठकर आराम करो *baiṭhkar ārām karo,* in which बैठकर *baiṭhkar* means literally *having sat*.

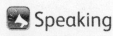

This short verb form has a long name – the 'absolutive'. (The name means that the construction is complete in itself, and has no impact on the surrounding grammar.) It consists of the stem + कर *kar;* thus जाकर *jākar* having gone, देखकर *dekhkar* having seen, etc.

हाथ धोकर खाओ ।	*hāth dhokar khāo.*	*Wash your hands and eat.*
बैठकर आराम करो ।	*baiṭhkar ārām karo.*	*Sit and rest.*
सोचकर बोलो ।	*sockar bolo.*	*Think before you speak.*
चाय पीकर जाइए ।	*cāy pīkar jāie.*	*Have some tea before you go.*

A colloquial form of the absolutive has -के *-ke* instead of -कर *-kar* (आके *āke,* जाके *jāke,* देखके *dekhke,* बुलाके *bulāke*). The verb करना *karnā* always uses this -के *-ke* form: करके *karke* 'having done'.

हाथ धोके खाओ ।	*hāth dhoke khāo.*	*Wash your hands and eat.*
अपना काम ख़त्म करके घर जाओ ।	*apnā kām khatm karke ghar jāo*	*Finish your work and go home.*

How could you combine these two sentences into one using the + कर *kar* construction? सीता उठी । *Sītā uṭhī.* वह बाहर गई । *vah bāhar gaī.*

Storyline

WHAT REALLY HAPPENED THAT MORNING

10.07 Here's a third-person account of Raju's and Geeta's morning. It contains several 'absolutive' expressions – how many can you spot?

1 What are Raju's feelings about Shahrukh Khan – positive or negative?

आज उठकर राजू नीचे गया । फिर चाय बनाकर वह आँगन में बैठने गया । चाय पीकर वह अपने सपनों के बारे में सोचने लगा । सपने में उसने शाहरुख़ ख़ाँ को देखा था । दरवाज़े को तोड़कर शाहरुख़ घर में घुसा था, लेकिन राजू ने मेज़ पर से एक भारी शब्दकोश को उठाकर शाहरुख़ को ख़ूब पीटा था ।

सात बजे राजू ने गीता का नाम पुकारकर उसे जगाने की कोशिश की लेकिन गीता तो घोड़े बेचकर सो रही थी । तब राजू ने खुद चार-पाँच टोस्ट बनाकर खाए । फिर तीन-चार संतरे खाए । आठ बजे उसने गीता के कंधे को हिलाकर उसे जगाया । फिर उसके लिए चाय बनाकर दो टोस्ट भी बनाए । जँभाई लेकर गीता ने कहा कि "संतरा देना" तो राजू ने हँसकर कहा कि "मनोज ने जल्दी उठके सारे संतरे खाए होंगे, उसे तो संतरे बहुत पसंद हैं" ।

āj uṭhkar Rājū nīce gayā. phir cāy banākar vah ā̃gan mẽ baiṭhne gayā. cāy pīkar vah apne sapnõ ke bāre mẽ socne lagā. sapne mẽ usne Śāhrukh Khā̃ ko dekhā thā. darvāze ko toṛkar Śāhrukh ghar mẽ ghusā thā, lekin Rājū ne mez par se ek bhārī śabdkoś ko uṭhākar Śāhrukh ko khūb pīṭā thā.

sāt baje Rājū ne Gītā kā nām pukārkar use jagāne kī kośiś kī lekin Gītā to ghoṛe beckar so rahī thī. tab Rājū ne khud cār-pā̃c ṭosṭ banākar khāe. phir tīn-cār santare khāe. āṭh baje usne Gītā ke kandhe ko hilākar use jagāyā. phir uske lie cāy banākar do ṭosṭ bhī banāe. jā̃bhāī lekar Gītā ne kahā ki santarā denā to Rājū ne hā̃skar kahā ki Manoj ne jaldīuṭhke sāre santare khāe hõge, use to santare bahut pasand haĩ!

2 Listen again and then answer the questions.

- **a** What did Raju eat for his own breakfast?
- **b** What did he prepare for Geeta's breakfast?
- **c** Who really ate the oranges, Manoj or Raju?

Practice 2

1 Link the paired sentences about Raju and Javed, following the model shown. Remember that whether ने *ne* is used will depend on the main verb: in the example, ने *ne* is used when the main verb is पीना *pīnā*, but not when it's जाना *jānā*.

Example:

मैंने चाय पी । मैं घर गया । > मैं चाय पीकर घर गया ।
maĩne cāy pī. maĩ ghar gayā. > maĩ cāy pīkar ghar gayā.

a जावेद ने मुझे फ़ोन किया । उसने कहा कि मेरी तबियत ख़राब है ।
Jāved ne mujhe fon kiyā. usne kahā ki merī tabiyat kharāb hai.

b मैं जावेद के घर गया । मैं उसके कमरे में गया ।
maĩ Jāved ke ghar gayā. maĩ uske kamre mẽ gayā.

c मैंने जावेद का हाल देखा । मैंने डाक्टर को बुलाया ।
maĩne Jāved kā hāl dekhā. maĩne ḍākṭar ko bulāyā.

d थोड़ी देर में डाक्टर आए । उन्होंने कहा कि जावेद बहुत ही कमज़ोर है ।
thoṛī der mẽ ḍākṭar āe. unhõne kahā ki Jāved bahut hī kamzor hai.

e डाक्टर ने जावेद को कुछ गोलियाँ दीं । उन्होंने उससे कहा कि रोज़ दो गोलियाँ लेना ।
ḍākṭar ne Jāved ko kuch goliyā̃ dī̃. unhõne usse kahā ki roz do goliyā̃ lenā.

f जावेद मुस्कराया । उसने डाक्टर से धन्यवाद कहा ।
Jāved muskarāyā. usne ḍākṭar se dhanyavād kahā.

g डाक्टर ने मेरी तरफ़ देखा । उन्होंने कहा कि "अच्छा, तो मैं चलता हूँ" ।
ḍākṭar ne merī taraf dekhā. unhõne kahā ki acchā, to maĩ caltā hū̃.

h मैं ने कहा कि चाय पीजिए । फिर जाइए ।
maĩne kahā ki cāy pījie. phir jāie.

i डाक्टर हँसे । उन्होंने कहा कि मैं चाय नहीं लूँगा, अपनी फ़ीस लूँगा !
ḍākṭar hãse. unhõne kahā ki maĩ cāy nahī̃ lū̃gā, apnī fīs lū̃gā!

2 Translate into Hindi. As this is a longish piece, you may want to do it in two parts. (Check the Vocabulary builder for the words you might need.)

Yesterday morning I got up at six o'clock. After having breakfast I phoned my brother. He was sleeping. When he heard my voice he said, 'Why did you wake me up so early?' I said, 'Don't you remember? Today we are going to Jaipur (जयपुर *jaypur*)!' He asked, 'What time are we going?' I answered, 'We'll catch the ten o'clock train. Get ready quickly!' He yawned and said that he'd had a dream in the night. In the dream an old woman had said to him, 'Don't go anywhere today! Stay right at home!' I laughed and said, 'This was just a dream! Get up, won't you! Get ready.'

The train moved out of the station at exactly ten o'clock. But after 20 or 25 minutes it stopped. The engine had broken down. It was a desolate place; there was no village or house nearby. In the July heat everyone got down from the train and waited for several hours in the shade of some small trees. The heat was terrible. At three o'clock another train came and stopped. This second train had come to bring the passengers back to Delhi.

We heard the story of the train on the radio. We'd taken that old woman's advice! We'll go to Jaipur tomorrow …

Vocabulary builder

अकेलापन	*akelāpan* m.	*loneliness*
आकाश	*ākāś* m.	*sky*
आम[1]	*ām* m.	*mango*
आम[2]	*ām*	*ordinary*
आम तौर पर	*ām taur par*	*usually*
आराम से	*ārām se*	*comfortably, easily*
इंजन	*injan* m.	*engine (train)*
इंतज़ार	*intazār* m.	*waiting, expecting*
का इंतज़ार करना	*kā intazār karnā*	*to wait for*
इतना	*itnā*	*so much, so*
उठाना	*uṭhānā*	*to pick up, raise*
कंधा	*kandhā* m.	*shoulder*
कमज़ोर	*kamzor*	*weak*
कहीं	*kahī̃*	*anywhere*
कुरता	*kurtā* m.	*kurta, loose shirt*
केला	*kelā* m.	*banana*
ख़त्म	*khatm*	*finished*
ख़त्म करना	*khatm karnā*	*to finish*
ख़राब हो जाना	*kharāb ho jānā*	*to break down*
ख़ुद	*khud*	*oneself (myself* etc.)
गाँव	*gā̃v* m.	*village*
गोली	*golī* f.	*tablet, pill; bullet*
घुसना	*ghusnā*	*to enter, sneak in, break in*
घोड़ा	*ghoṛā* m.	*horse*
घोड़े बेचकर सोना	*ghoṛe beckar sonā*	*to sleep like a log*
चपाती	*capātī* f.	*chapati*
चारों ओर	*cārõ or*	*all around*
चिट्ठी	*ciṭṭhī* f.	*letter, note*
चीनी	*cīnī* f.	*sugar*
जँभाई	*jā̃bhāī* f.	*yawn*
जगाना	*jagānā*	*to awaken*
जल्दी	*jaldī* adv.; noun f.	*quickly, early; hurry*
जीतना	*jītnā*	*to win, conquer*
टोस्ट	*ṭosṭ* m.	*toast, piece of toast*
ठीक	*ṭhīk*	*exactly*
डालना	*ḍālnā*	*to put, pour*
तकलीफ़	*taklīf* f.	*suffering, pain, trouble*
तब	*tab*	*then*

तैयार	*taiyār*	*ready, prepared*
तैयार हो जाना	*taiyār ho jānā*	*to get ready*
तोड़ना	*toṛnā*	*to break, smash*
दर्द	*dard* m.	*pain*
दाल	*dāl* f.	*daal, lentil*
दीवार	*dīvār,* दीवाल *dīvāl* f.	*wall*
दुर्घटना	*durghaṭnā* f.	*accident*
देर	*der* f.	*a while, length of time; delay*
देर से	*der se*	*late*
नहाना	*nahānā*	*to bathe*
पकड़ना	*pakaṛnā*	*to catch*
पार्टी	*pārṭī* f.	*party*
पीटना	*pīṭnā*	*to beat, thrash*
पुकारना	*pukārnā*	*to call out*
पेट	*peṭ* m.	*stomach*
प्यास	*pyās* f.	*thirst*
प्यास लगना	*pyās lagnā*	*(thirst to strike) to feel thirsty*
फ़ीस	*fīs* f.	*fee, fees*
बढ़िया	*baṛhiyā (invariable -ā)*	*excellent, really good, fine*
बत्ती	*battī* f.	*light, lamp*
बस	*bas* f.	*bus*
बाज़ार	*bāzār* m.	*market, bazaar*
बार	*bār* f.	*time, occasion*
इस बार	*is bār*	*this time*
कितनी बार	*kitnī bār*	*how many times?*
कई बार	*kaī bār*	*several times*
बारिश	*bāriś* f.	*rain*
बारिश होना	*bāriś honā*	*to rain*
बुलाना	*bulānā*	*to call, invite, summon*
बोतल	*botal* f.	*bottle*
भयंकर	*bhayankar*	*terrible*
भूख	*bhūkh* f.	*hunger*
भूख लगना	*bhūkh lagnā*	*to feel hungry* (hunger to strike)
महसूस करना	*mahsūs karnā*	*to feel*
मिठाई	*miṭhāī* f.	*sweet, sweetmeat*
मिठास	*miṭhās* f.	*sweetness*
मीठा	*mīṭhā*	*sweet*
मेमसाहब	*memsāhab* f.	*memsahib ma'am, good lady, lady of the house*

यात्री	*yātrī* m.	*traveller, passenger*
रसोई	*rasoī* f.	*kitchen*
लौटना	*lauṭnā*	*to return*
शांति	*śānti* f.	*peace*
शिकायत	*śikāyat* f.	*complaint*
शिकायत करना	*śikāyat karnā*	*to complain*
संतरा	*santarā* m.	*orange*
सलाह	*salāh* f.	*advice*
साया	*sāyā* m.	*shade, shadow*
सिर	*sir* m.	*head*
सुनसान	*sunsān*	*desolate, empty*
हिलाना	*hilānā*	*to move, shake*
हुआ	*huā*	*happened* (past tense of होना *honā*)

Test yourself

1 Put the verb दौड़ना *dauṛnā to run* through its paces by saying in Hindi: *we run every day, we are running, we shall run, we may perhaps run, we ran*, using a feminine *we*.

2 When you come back from a trip, a friend asks तुम्हें मज़ा आया ? *tumhẽ mazā āyā?* What does your friend want to know?

3 The sentence ... कल सुबह आईं ... *kal subah āī̃* is missing a word or two at the beginning – it has no subject! How does the verb alone tell us something about who the subject was?

4 What is the main grammatical difference between the two constructions सीता ने खाना खाया *Sītā ne khānā khāyā* and सीता घर गई *Sītā ghar gaī*?

5 How would you say *I learned some Hindi*?

6 Supply the missing verbs for this sentence: मैंने समोसा ..., तुमने चाय ..., और पिताजी ने दो सिग्रेटें ... *maĩne khānā ..., tumne cāy ..., aur pitājī ne do sigreṭẽ ... I ate a samosa, you drank tea, and father smoked two cigarettes.*

7 What does this mean? – हाथ धोकर खाना खाइए *hāth dhokar khānā khāie*.

8 How would you say in informal Hindi *Come over here and sit* without using a word for *and*? Three words only.

9 What two meanings does the word की *kī* have? Give examples of both.

10 If गोपाल ने किताब पढ़ी *Gopāl ne kitāb paṛhī* means *Gopal read a/the book*, how does this meaning change by adding (a) है *hai* (b) थी *thī* (c) होगी *hogī* (d) हो *ho* to the end of the sentence?

SELF CHECK

I CAN...
... describe past events.
... link connected actions in a sequence.

11 कहा जाता है कि...

kahā jātā hai ki ...

It is said that ...

In this unit you will learn how to:

- ***give directions.***
- ***describe things being done.***
- ***say 'should' and 'must'.***

Language points

- *obligation expressions*
- *passive verbs*

Language discovery 1

A VERB WITH MANY MEANINGS

11.01 The verb लगना *lagnā* (literally *to strike*) carries a variety of meanings. Many of these relate to the experiencing of sensations such as heat or cold, hunger or thirst, which *strike* or impinge on the person, but the range of usages is very wide. Here are some of them:

To seem:

लगता है कि वह नहीं आएगी ।
lagtā hai ki vah nahī̃ āegī. — *It seems she won't come.*

तुम बहुत ख़ुश नहीं लगते ।
tum bahut khuś nahī̃ lagte. — *You don't seem too happy.*

Thirst/hunger/cold (etc.) *to strike*:

हमें गरमी/ठंड लग रही है ।
hamẽ garmī/ṭhaṇḍ lag rahī hai. — *We're feeling hot/cold.*

मुझे प्यास/भूख लगी है ।
mujhe pyās/bhūkh lagī hai. — *I'm feeling thirsty/hungry.*

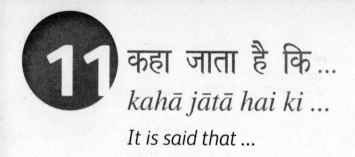

To strike one as good/bad, etc.:

यह जगह मुझे बहुत अच्छी लगती है । *yah jagah mujhe bahut acchī lagtī hai.*	*I really like this place.*
उनकी बातें हमें बुरी लगीं । *unkī bātẽ hamẽ burī lagī̃.*	*We were hurt by what they said.*

To begin (here it follows an oblique infinitive such as होने *hone*):

बारिश होने लगी । *bāriś hone lagī.*	*It began raining.*
मैं सोचने लगा कि अब तो वह नहीं आएगी । *maĩ socne lagā ki ab to vah nahī̃ āegī.*	*I began to think that she wouldn't come now.*

Time to be taken (already seen in Unit 9; *the unit of time* is the subject):

सितार सीखने में सात साल लगेंगे । *sitār sīkhne mẽ sāt sāl lagẽge.*	*Learning the sitar will take seven years.*

How would you use लगना *lagnā* to say: *The boys began to speak* and *Rashmi seems happy today*?

Storyline

GIVING DIRECTIONS

Your first task is to familiarize yourself with the new words relating to *directions*. Here are some useful words and phrases for finding your way. There are more in the unit glossary.

आगे चलना	*āge calnā*	*go straight ahead*
दाहिने मुड़ना	*dāhine muṛnā*	*turn right*
बाएँ मुड़ना	*bāyẽ muṛnā*	*turn left*
चलते जाना	*calte jānā*	*keep going*
दूर	*dūr*	*far*
नज़दीक	*nazdīk*	*near*
दूरी	*dūrī*	*distance*
थोड़ी दूरी पर	*thoṛī dūrī par*	*at a short distance*
सड़क को पार करना	*saṛak ko pār karnā*	*to cross the road*
उस पार	*us pār*	*on the other side*
थोड़ा आगे	*thoṛā āge*	*a little further (ahead)*

FINDING THE WAY IN VILASPUR

11.02 *Come with the Sharmas to the town of Vilaspur, shown on the map. They are going to stay at the Madhuban Hotel and have been given some directions for getting there from the station.*

1 As you listen, you will hear how landmarks are often more useful than street names in giving solid directions. How many landmarks are mentioned? Can you name them?

स्टेशन से निकलकर दाहिने मुड़िए । थोड़ी दूरी पर बायें हाथ पर एक तंग गली आएगी । इस गली में मुड़ना । आगे चलकर एक चौड़ी सड़क आएगी जिसे "चंद्रशेखर आज़ाद रोड" कहते हैं । बाएँ मुड़कर और सड़क को पार करके आप चलते जाएँ । दाहिने हाथ पर स्कूल दिखाई देगा । इसके बाद आप दाहिने मुड़िए । इस सड़क का नाम मुझे याद नहीं लेकिन बायें हाथ पर सिनेमा दिखाई देगा । फिर थोड़ी दूर जाकर एक दूसरी बड़ी सड़क आएगी जिसे शायद "नई सड़क" कहते हैं । बाएँ मुड़िए । फिर गोलचक्कर आएगा । गोलचक्कर के उस पार आपका मधुबन होटल दिखाई देगा ।

स्टेशन से मधुबन होटल ज़्यादा दूर नहीं है । मुश्किल से आठ-दस मिनट का रास्ता है । अगर आपके पास बहुत सामान हो तो बेहतर है कि आप रिक्शा लें । रिक्शेवाले से कहें कि होटल "एम० जी० रोड" पर है । वह तीन सौ रुपये लेगा । आप उसे चार सौ से ज़्यादा न दें ।

sṭeśan se nikalkar dāhine muṛie. thoṛī dūrī par bāyẽ hāth par ek taṅg galī āegī. is galī mẽ muṛnā. āge calkar ek cauṛī saṛak āegī jise 'Candraśekhar Āzād roḍ' kahte haĩ. bāẽ muṛkar aur saṛak ko pār karke āp calte jāẽ. dāhine hāth par skūl dikhāī degā. iske bād āp dāhine muṛie. is saṛak kā nām mujhe yād nahī̃ lekin bāyẽ hāth par sinemā dikhāī degā. phir thoṛī dūr jākar ek dūsrī baṛī saṛak āegī jise śāyad 'naī saṛak' kahte haĩ. bāyẽ muṛie. phir golcakkar āegā. golcakkar ke us pār āpkā madhuban hoṭal dikhāī degā.

sṭeśan se madhuban hoṭal zyādā dūr nahī̃ hai. muśkil se āṭh-das minaṭ kā rāstā hai. agar āpke pās bahut sāmān ho to behtar hai ki āp rikśā lẽ. rikśevāle se kahẽ ki hoṭal 'em. jī. roḍ' par hai. vah tīn sau rupaye legā. āp use cār sau se zyādā na dẽ.

2 Listen to the directions again, then answer these questions.

a What is the name of the first wide road the Sharmas will reach after emerging from the station?

b How long does it take to reach the hotel from the station?

c How much should the trip cost in a rickshaw?

Practice 1

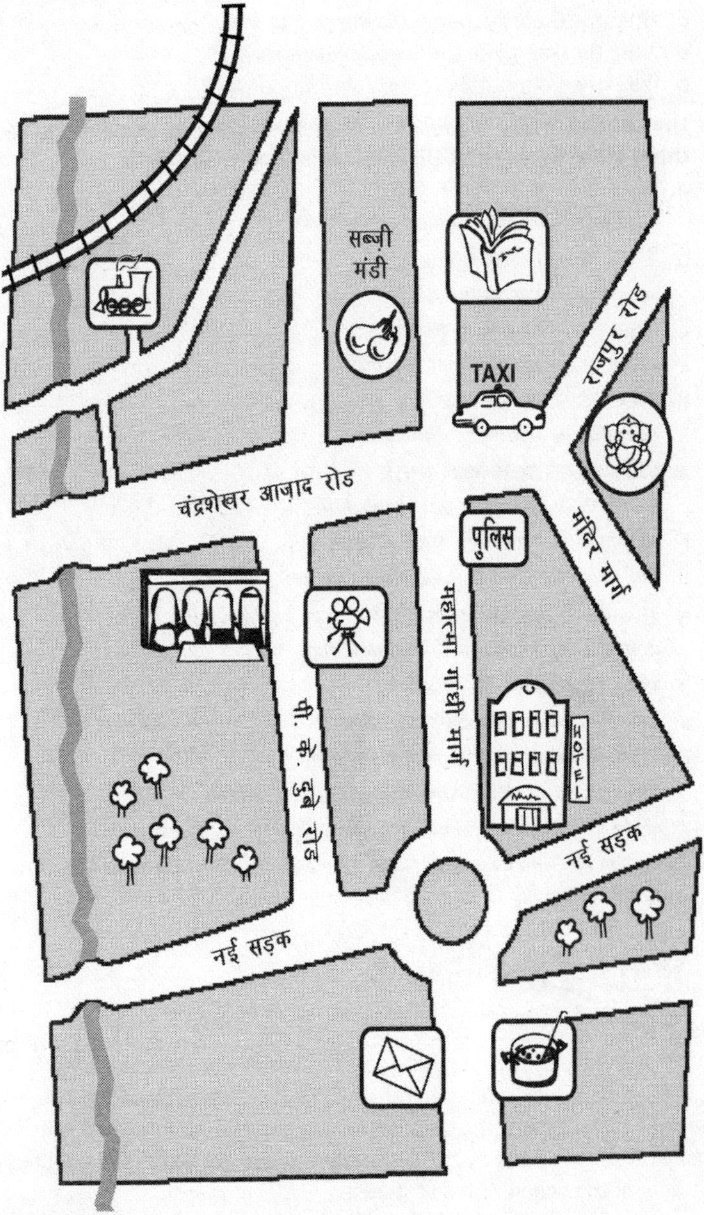
सब्ज़ी मंडी
TAXI
राजपुर रोड
चंद्रशेखर आज़ाद रोड
पुलिस
मंदिर मार्ग
महात्मा गांधी मार्ग
पी. के. दुबे रोड
HOTEL
नई सड़क
नई सड़क

1 How would you give point to point directions? There are sample answers in the Key to the exercises.

a From the Ganesha temple to the post office?

b From the cinema to the vegetable market?

c From the train station to the police station?

2 Look at the map and plot how to go from place to place. Are these statements right (सही *sahī*) or wrong (ग़लत *galat*)?

a मधुबन होटल के सामने एक स्कूल है ।
madhuban hoṭal ke sāmne ek skūl hai.

b सिनेमा थाने की बग़ल में है ।
sinemā thāne kī bagal mẽ hai.

c विलासपुर में तीन छोटे-से पुल हैं ।
vilāspur mẽ tīn choṭe-se pul haĩ.

d डाकघर के सामने एक ढाबा है ।
ḍākghar ke sāmne ek ḍhābā hai.

e सिनेमा गोलचक्कर के बहुत पास है ।
sinemā golcakkar ke bahut pās hai.

f नई सड़क को "एम. जी. रोड" भी कहते हैं ।
naī saṛak ko 'em. jī. roḍ' bhī kahte haĩ.

g इस नक़्शे में कुछ पेड़ दिखाई देते हैं ।
is naqśe mẽ kuch peṛ dikhāī dete haĩ.

h गणेश मंदिर पश्चिम की तरफ़ है ।
Gaṇeś mandir paścim kī taraf hai.

i स्टेशन से पुस्तकालय तक एक घंटे का रास्ता है ।
sṭeśan se pustakālay tak ek ghanṭe kā rāstā hai.

j स्टेशन से गणेश मंदिर पहुँचने में छह-सात मिनट से ज़्यादा नहीं लगेंगे ।
sṭeśan se Gaṇeś mandir pahũcne mẽ chah-sāt minaṭ se zyādā nahī̃ lagẽge.

Language discovery 2

THE PASSIVE VOICE

11.03 A passive verb is one that concentrates on what is done, rather than the person who does it. In other words, its focus is the action, not the doer of the action. Thus *we give money* is active and *money is given* is passive. *Money is given by the government* is also passive, but it identifies the doer of the action with a *by* phrase.

The passive is based on the perfective participle (e.g. दिया *diyā given*). But whereas English forms its passive with *to be*, Hindi uses जाना *jānā* – literally *to go*:

करना	*karnā*	to do	किया जाना	*kiyā jānā*	to be done
देना	*denā*	to give	दिया जाना	*diyā jānā*	to be given
रखना	*rakhnā*	to put	रखा जाना	*rakhā jānā*	to be put

होटल का इंतज़ाम किया जा रहा है ।
hoṭal kā intazām kiyā jā rahā hai.
Arrangements for a hotel are being made.

आपको एक अच्छा कमरा दिया जाएगा ।
āpko ek acchā kamrā diyā jāegā.
You will be given a good room.

आपका सामान टैक्सी में रखा गया है ।
āpkā sāmān ṭaiksī mẽ rakhā gayā hai.
Your luggage has been put into the taxi.

Look at the verb agreements in these two sentences. What is the subject of each sentence?

मेज़ पर किताबें रखी गईं । *mez par kitābẽ rakhī gaī̃.*

उन लोगों को खाना दिया जाएगा । *un logõ ko khānā diyā jāegā.*

Practice 2

INDIA: STATES AND LANGUAGES

The states of India were largely drawn up on the basis of language, an important marker of a sense of regional identity; but the politics of language and identity are much more complex than any map can represent, and language issues frequently make the front page in Indian newspapers.

The map of northern India shows the ten states (shaded) where Hindi is the primary language.

Hindi is closely related to its neighbouring languages, such as Marathi (spoken in Maharashtra), Gujarati (Gujarat), Punjabi (Punjab), Bengali (West Bengal and Bangladesh), and so on. All these languages derive from Sanskrit and share much vocabulary.

In south India – not shown here – are the four major languages of the 'Dravidian' family: Tamil (spoken in Tamil Nadu), Malayalam (Kerala), Kannada (Karnataka), and Telugu (Andhra Pradesh).

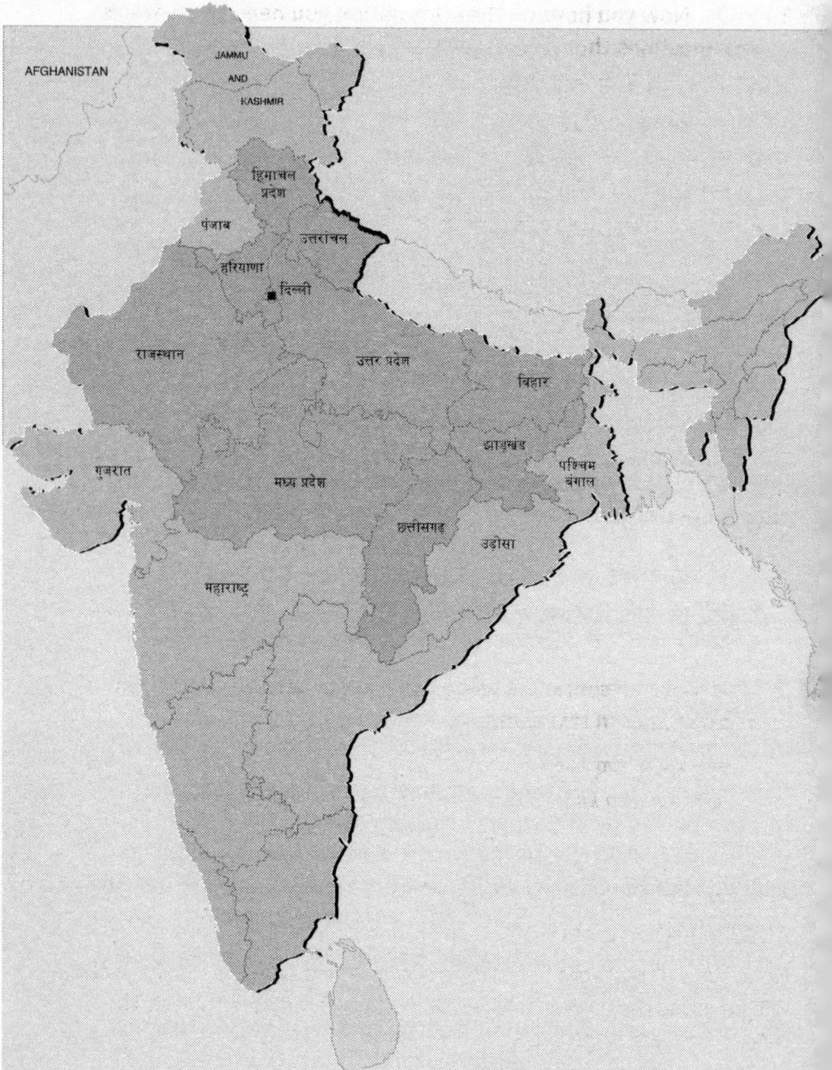
AFGHANISTAN
JAMMU
AND
KASHMIR
हिमाचल प्रदेश
पंजाब
उत्तरांचल
हरियाणा
दिल्ली
राजस्थान
उत्तर प्रदेश
बिहार
झारखंड
पश्चिम बंगाल
गुजरात
मध्य प्रदेश
छत्तीसगढ़
उड़ीसा
महाराष्ट्र

1 11.04 **Now you have all the information you need to answer a few questions that involve passive verbs:**

a तमिल कहाँ बोली जाती है ?
tamil kahā̃ bolī jātī hai?

b मराठी कहाँ बोली जाती है ?
marāṭhī kahā̃ bolī jātī hai?

c केरल में कौनसी भाषा बोली जाती है ?
keral mẽ kaunsī bhāṣā bolī jātī hai?

d हिन्दी कितने प्रदेशों में बोली जाती है ?
hindī kitne pradeśõ mẽ bolī jātī hai?

e दिल्ली और बिहार के बीच कौनसा प्रदेश पाया जाता है ?
dillī aur bihār ke bīc kaunsā pradeś pāyā jātā hai?

2 Work out the passive infinitives of the following verbs (example: बनाना *banānā* to make, बनाया जाना *banāyā jānā* to be made).

a	खाना	*khānā*	to eat	**e**	डालना	*ḍālnā*	to pour
b	पीना	*pīnā*	to drink	**f**	बताना	*batānā*	to tell
c	लाना	*lānā*	to bring	**g**	लेना	*lenā*	to take
d	लिखना	*likhnā*	to write	**h**	कहना	*kahnā*	to say

3 Now make up sentences using each of the passive verbs from Exercise 2, as in this example:

सारे समोसे खाए जाएँगे
sāre samosa khāe jāẽge. *All the samosas will be eaten.*

Language discovery 3

AGREEMENT ALL AROUND

Notice how all parts of the verb (the participle, e.g. दिया *diyā*, the form of जाना *jānā*, and the auxiliary होना *honā*) must agree with the subject. The subject has been underlined.

उनको पैसा दिया जाता है ।
unko paisā diyā jātā hai. — *Money is given to them.*

उनको अच्छी सलाह दी जाती है ।
unko acchī salāh dī jātī hai. — *Good advice is given to them.*

उनको कपड़े दिए जाते हैं ।
unko kapre die jāte haĩ. — *Clothes are given to them.*

ANY TENSE CAN HAVE A PASSIVE VERB

The passive can be used with all tenses:

उनको पैसा दिया जाता है ।	(Present imperfective)
unko paisā diyā jātā hai.	*Money is given to them.*
उनको पैसा दिया जा रहा है ।	(Present continuous)
unko paisā diyā jā rahā hai.	*Money is being given to them.*
उनको पैसा दिया गया ।	(Perfective)
unko paisā diyā gayā.	*Money was given to them.*
उनको पैसा दिया जाएगा ।	(Future)
unko paisā diyā jāegā.	*Money will be given to them.*
उनको पैसा दिया जाए ।	(Subjunctive)
unko paisā diyā jāe.	*Money should be given to them.*

The person by whom an action is done can be identified with से *se* (or, in more formal Hindi, with के द्वारा *ke dvārā*):

पैसा सरकार से (सरकार के द्वारा) दिया जाता है ।
paisā sarkār se (sarkār ke dvārā) diyā jātā hai.
Money is given by the government.

WHAT'S THE PASSIVE FOR?

We use a passive verb when the main focus is on the action done rather than the person doing it. In saying *this money was found under the chair*, we're more concerned with the act of finding than with the person who found it; if it had been the other way round, we would have said *So-and-so found this money under the chair*. In other words, passives offer a way of making impersonal statements: instead of saying *we use the passive* at the beginning of this paragraph, I could have adopted a more impersonal tone by saying *the passive is used* .... The passive is used a lot in Hindi.

Storyline

SHARMA JI IN HIS SHOP

11.05 ***Listen to and read the passage about Sharma ji in his shop, then answer the question.***

1 How many chores does Sharma ji give Gopal?

शर्मा जी अपनी दुकान में बैठकर सोच रहे थे । उन्होंने गोपाल को बुलाकर कहा, "बेटा, यह सारा सामान छोटे कमरे में रखो । फिर दुकान की सफ़ाई करो । मैं बहुत थका हूँ, थोड़ी देर के लिए घर जाकर सोऊँगा । आठ बजे दुकान को बंद करना । फिर दो सौ रुपये लो और धोबी के पास जाकर मेरे साफ़ कपड़े लाओ ।" पर गोपाल से कुछ नहीं सुना गया क्योंकि वह रेडियो सुन रहा था ।

Śarmā jī apnī dukān mẽ baiṭhkar soc rahe the. unhõne Gopāl ko bulākar kahā, beṭā, yah sārā sāmān choṭe kamre mẽ rakho. phir dukān kī safāī karo. maĩ bahut thakā hū̃, thoṛī der ke lie ghar jākar soū̃gā. āṭh baje dukān ko band karnā. phir do sau rupaye lo aur dhobī ke pās jākar mere sāf kapṛe lāo. par Gopāl se kuch nahī̃ sunā gayā kyõki vah reḍiyo sun rahā thā.

2 Listen to the passage again, then answer the questions.

a Why is Sharma ji going home?

b How much money should Gopal take to the dhobi to pay for Sharma ji's clothes?

3 11.06 **For an extra challenge, answer these questions about *Sharma ji in his shop* in Hindi. Speak in the pauses, then keep listening to check your answers.**

a गोपाल को किससे बुलाया गया ?
Gopāl ko kisse (by whom) *bulāyā gayā?*

b सामान कहाँ रखा जाएगा ?
sāmān kahā̃ rakhā jāegā?

c कमरे की सफ़ाई किससे की जाएगी ?
kamre kī safāī kisse kī jāegī?

d दुकान को कितने बजे बंद किया जाएगा ?
dukān ko kitne baje band kiyā jāega?

e शर्मा जी के साफ़ कपड़े कहाँ से लाए जाएँगे ?
Śarmā jī ke sāf kapṛe kahā̃ se lāe jāẽge?

f गोपाल से शर्मा जी की बातें क्यों नहीं सुनी गईं ?
Gopāl se Śarmā jī kī bātẽ kyõ nahī̃ sunī gaī̃?

Language discovery 4

OBLIGATIONS

Way back in Unit 5 we saw that चाहिए *cāhie*, used with को *ko*, meant *wanted, needed*. This construction relates to things, objects – *I want a newspaper*, and so on:

आपको क्या चाहिए ?
āpko kyā cāhie? *What do you need/want?*

मुझे (मुझको) आज का अख़बार चाहिए ।
mujhe mujhko āj kā akhbār cāhie. *I want today's newspaper.*

When चाहिए *cāhie* follows an infinitive verb (such as जाना *jānā to go*) it has a completely different meaning: it means *should, ought to*. Although the meaning of चाहिए *cāhie* has changed here, the word को *ko* remains an essential part of the construction:

मुझको घर जाना चाहिए ।
mujhko ghar jānā cāhie. *I should go home.*

आपको ध्यान से सुनना चाहिए ।
āpko dhyān se sunnā cāhie. *You should listen carefully.*

उनको समझना चाहिए ।
unko samajhnā cāhie. *They should understand.*

हमको चलना चाहिए ।
hamko calnā cāhie. *We should be on our way.*

तुमको यहाँ रहना चाहिए ।
tumko yahā̃ rahnā cāhie. *You should stay here.*

If there's a direct object involved, the infinitive verb agrees with it. In the next two sentences, the verbs बोलना *bolnā to speak* and सीखना *sīkhnā to learn* have to agree with its feminine object, उर्दू *urdū*:

तुमको उर्दू बोलनी चाहिए ।
tumko urdū bolnī cāhie. *You should speak Urdu.*

हमको थोड़ी उर्दू सीखनी चाहिए ।
hamko thoṛī urdū sīkhnī cāhie. *We should learn a little Urdu.*

You'll notice similar agreements in the following:

उन्हें मेरी बात सुननी चाहिए ।
unhẽ merī bāt sunnī cāhie. *They should listen to what I say.*

ड्राइवर को नक़्शा ख़रीदना चाहिए ।
ḍrāivar ko naqśā <u>kh</u>arīdnā cāhie. The driver should buy a map.

राजू को ये ख़त पढ़ने चाहिए ।
Rājū ko ye <u>kh</u>at paṛhne cāhie. Raju should read these letters.

आपको उनकी सलाह लेनी चाहिए ।
āpko unkī salāh lenī cāhie. You should take their advice.

Before going further, read the last four sentences again and make sure you understand what the infinitive verbs (सुननी *sunnī,* ख़रीदना *<u>kh</u>arīdnā,* पढ़ने *paṛhne,* and लेनी *lenī* respectively) agree with.

When we were doing the ने *ne* construction in Unit 10, we saw that the postposition को *ko* 'insulates' the verb, preventing agreement – हमने चिट्ठियाँ पढ़ीं *hamne ciṭṭhiyā̃ paṛhī̃,* but हमने चिट्ठियों को पढ़ा *hamne ciṭṭhiyõ ko paṛhā,* both meaning *we read the letters.* Similarly, with obligation expressions, the verb reverts to masculine singular when the direct object takes को *ko.* Confused? Look at the examples:

हमें चिट्ठियाँ पढ़नी चाहिए ।
hamẽ ciṭṭhiyā̃ paṛhnī cāhie. We should read the letters.

becomes …

हमें चिट्ठियों को पढ़ना चाहिए ।
hamẽ ciṭṭhiyõ ko paṛhnā cāhie. We should read the letters.

उन्हें मेरी बात सुननी चाहिए ।
unhẽ merī bāt sunnī cāhie. They should listen to what I say.

becomes …

उन्हें मेरी बात को सुनना चाहिए ।
unhẽ merī bāt ko sunnā cāhie. They should listen to what I say.

Finally, using चाहिए *cāhie* in the past is simplicity itself. Just add था, थे, थी, थीं *thā, the, thī, thī̃.*

हमको ये चिट्ठियाँ पढ़नी चाहिए थीं ।
hamko ye ciṭṭhiyā̃ paṛhnī cāhie thī̃. We should have read these letters.

उन्हें मेरी बात सुननी चाहिए थी ।
unhẽ merī bāt sunnī cāhie thī. They should have listened to what I said.

How would you say *You should drink milk* and *I should have come home yesterday*?

Listening and speaking

1 11.07 **Raju is asking for advice. Listen and answer *yes* to all of his questions. Then keep listening to check your answers. Give complete responses, as in the example:**

जी हाँ, आपको रहना चाहिए ।
jī hā̃, āpko rahnā cāhie. Yes, you should stay.

a क्या मुझे घर पर रहना चाहिए ?
kyā mujhe ghar par rahnā cāhie?

b क्या मुझे गीता की मदद करनी चाहिए ?
kyā mujhe Gītā kī madad karnī cāhie?

c क्या मुझको चाय बनानी चाहिए ?
kyā mujhko cāy banānā cāhie?

d क्या मुझको खाना भी बनाना चाहिए ?
kyā mujko khānā bhī banānā cāhie?

e क्या मुझे गीता की बात सुननी चाहिए ?
kyā mujhe Gītā kī bāt sunnī cāhie?

2 11.08 **Now give advice to Geeta, saying *no* or *yes* to her questions as you like. Will your advice be the same as ours?**

a क्या मुझे घर पर रहना चाहिए ?
kyā mujhe ghar par rahnā cāhie?

b क्या मुझे राजू की मदद करनी चाहिए ?
kyā mujhe Rājū kī madad karnī cāhie?

c क्या मुझे बाहर जाना चाहिए ?
kyā mujhe bāhar jānā cāhie?

d क्या मुझे अपनी सहेलियों को फ़ोन करना चाहिए ?
kyā mujhe apnī saheliõ ko fon karnā cāhie?

e क्या मुझे टैक्सी बुलानी चाहिए ?
kyā mujhe ṭaiksī bulānī cāhie?

f क्या मुझे राजू की बात सुननी चाहिए ?
kyā mujhe Rājū kī bāt sunnī cāhie?

3 11.09 **The Sharmas need your advice on various matters. Please respond:**

a गीता बहुत थकी है । उसको क्या करना चाहिए ?
Gītā bahut thakī hai. usko kyā karnā cāhie?

b मनोज के सिर में दर्द है। उसे क्या करना चाहिए ?
Manoj ke sir mẽ dard hai. use kyā karnā cāhie?

c राजू ने देखा है कि फ़र्श गंदी है। उसको क्या करना चाहिए ?
Rājū ne dekhā hai ki farś gandī hai. usko kyā karnā cāhie?

d मीना को भूख लगी है। उसको क्या करना चाहिए ?
Mīnā ko bhūkh lagī hai. usko kyā karnā cāhie?

e शर्मा परिवार का घर बहुत छोटा है। उन लोगों को क्या करना चाहिए ?
Śarmā parivār kā ghar bahut choṭā hai. un logõ ko kyā karnā cāhie?

LANGUAGE TIP

There can often be an overlap in meaning between a subjunctive and the use of चाहिए *cāhie*. Thus both आप आराम करें *āp ārām karẽ* and आपको आराम करना चाहिए *āpko ārām karnā cāhie* could be translated as *You should rest.*

Language discovery 5

STRONGER OBLIGATIONS

When *I should* gives way to *I have to* or *I must*, चाहिए *cāhie* gives way to stronger expressions. The first of these involves using the infinitive verb with है *hai*, as in मुझे जाना है *mujhe jānā hai I have to go* or *I am to go*.

Let us imagine that Raju's agenda for the day includes writing some letters, talking to Javed, and meeting his brother Mohan. He'd say:

मुझे पाँच ख़त लिखने हैं।
mujhe pā̃c khat likhne haĩ. — *I have to write five letters.*

मुझे जावेद से कुछ बातें कहनी हैं।
mujhe Jāved se kuch bātẽ kahnī haĩ. — *I have to say some things to Javed.*

मुझे मोहन से मिलना है।
mujhe Mohan se milnā hai. — *I have to meet Mohan.*

The sense of compulsion here isn't very strong: these are just ordinary things that are to be done in the normal course of events. The verb agreement follows the pattern of the चाहिए *cāhie* usage: लिखने हैं *likhne haĩ* agrees with पाँच ख़त *pā̃c khat*, etc.

What is the difference in meaning between मुझे घर की सफ़ाई करनी चाहिए *mujhe ghar kī safāī karnī cāhie* and मुझे घर की सफ़ाई करनी है *mujhe ghar kī safāī karnī hai*?

WHAT'S ON TODAY

The Sharma children have several things to do today. Taking as your model the sentence मनोज को जल्दी उठना है *Manoj ko jaldī uṭhnā hai Manoj has to get up early*, go through their lists.

MANOJ	MEENA	RAM
get up early	*make breakfast*	*read a story*
read the paper	*do some studying*	*write a letter*
go to the shops	*write two letters*	*make a picture*
phone Nani ji	*rest*	*sleep at 9 o'clock*

A stronger sense of compulsion involves the verb **पड़ना** *paṛnā*, literally meaning *to fall* but here meaning *to be compelled to, to really have to*. It's used when circumstances beyond your control make the action essential – as when the children broke their father's radio:

हमें पिताजी को बताना पड़ेगा ।
hamẽ pitājī ko batānā paṛegā.
We'll have to tell Father.

हमें नया रेडियो ख़रीदना पड़ेगा ।
hamẽ nayā reḍiyo kharīdnā paṛegā.
We'll have to buy a new radio.

पिताजी को हमें पैसे देने पड़ेंगे ।
pitājī ko hamẽ paise dene paṛẽge.
Father will have to give us the money.

In the imperfective (पड़ता है *partā hai,* or पड़ता था *paṛtā thā*), this same construction implies a compulsion that occurs regularly:

हमें रोज़ काम करना पड़ता है ।
hamẽ roz kām karnā paṛtā hai.
We have to work every day.

मुझे सात बजे उठना पड़ता था ।
mujhe sāt baje uṭhnā paṛtā thā.
I (always) had to get up at seven.

क्या तुम्हें अपने कपड़े ख़ुद धोने पड़ते हैं ?
kyā tumhẽ apne kapṛe khud dhone paṛte haĩ?
Do you have to wash your own clothes?

In the perfective (पड़ा *paṛā*), this same construction implies an unexpected compulsion, such as some kind of unforeseen event or emergency, as on discovering that Meena's car was stolen – complete with the children's toys! Keep an eye on the agreements: watch पड़ा *paṛā* changing to पड़ी *paṛī* or पड़े *paṛe* to match the object.

मुझे पुलिस को फ़ोन करना पड़ा ।
mujhe pulis ko fon karnā paṛā.
I had to phone the police.

घर जाने के लिए हमें टैक्सी लेनी पड़ी ।
ghar jāne ke lie hamẽ ṭaiksī lenī paṛī.
We had to take a taxi to get home.

मुझे बच्चों के लिए नए खिलौने ख़रीदने पड़े ।
mujhe baccõ ke lie nae khilaune kharīdne paṛe.
I had to buy new toys for the children.

How would you express these nuances: *We should say something, We have to say something,* and *We must say something*?

Practice 3

1 Someone's having a party on Sunday. Translate:

- **a** About 30 people will be invited.
- **b** The house will be cleaned on Saturday.
- **c** The food will be made on Sunday morning.
- **d** In the afternoon some relatives will be fetched from the station.
- **e** Presents will be given to the children.
- **f** Lamps will be lit in the garden at night.
- **g** Music will be played, too.
- **h** The neighbours will also be invited.

2 Things haven't gone too well at the Madhuban Hotel and you need to get the following points across to the long-suffering receptionist. Use passive verbs for the parts in bold print.

a Today's food wasn't fresh – it seems it was **made** yesterday.

b Your friends came to visit you last night, but you were not **told** that they had come.

c Someone's dirty clothes were **put** in your room.

d This evening you saw that the door of your room hadn't been **closed** properly ...

e .... and your luggage had been **opened**.

f You were not **given** hot water for bathing.

g You gave clothes for washing two days ago but they have not been **given back**.

h Your driver was **told** that he would (say 'will') have to sleep in the car.

3 11.10 **Enjoy (and translate) the receptionist's thoughts.**

ये लोग मुझे क्यों तंग करते हैं ? वे हर रोज़ किसी चीज़ की शिकायत करते हैं । लगता है उनको शिकायत करना बहुत पसंद है । मालूम नहीं वे किस देश से आए हैं । मेरे ख़याल से हमारे देश में आकर लोगों को हर चीज़ की शिकायत नहीं करनी चाहिए । उनको इस देश का आदर करना चाहिए । सच है कि उनके सामान को खोला नहीं जाना चाहिए था, लेकिन सारी दूसरी बातें तो मामूली-सी थीं । मुझे मैनेजर ('manager') को इसके बारे में बताना चाहिए पर मैं उन्हें बताना नहीं चाहता । नहीं बताऊँगा । ये लोग भाड़ में जाएँ !

ye log mujhe kyõ tang karte haĩ? ve har roz kisī cīz kī śikāyat karte haĩ. lagtā hai unko śikāyat karnā bahut pasand hai. mālūm nahī̃ ve kis deś se āe haĩ. mere khyāl se hamāre deś mẽ ākar logõ ko har cīz kī śikāyat nahī̃ karnī cāhie. unko is deś kā ādar karnā cāhie. sac hai ki unke sāmān ko kholā nahī̃ jānā cāhie thā, lekin sārī dūsrī bātẽ to māmūlī-sī thī̃. mujhe mainejar ko iske bāre mẽ batānā cāhie par maĩ unhẽ batānā nahī̃ cāhtā. nahī̃ batāū̃gā. ye log bhāṛ mẽ jāẽ!

Vocabulary builder

आगे	*āge*	*ahead*
आदर	*ādar* m.	*respect*
इमारत	*imārat* f.	*building*
उत्तर	*uttar*	*north*
उर्दू	*urdū* f.	*Urdu*
कहानी	*kahānī* f.	*story*

के द्वारा	*ke dvārā*	*by* (in formal passive sentences)
ख़याल	*khyāl* m.	*opinion, thought, idea*
खिलौना	*khilaunā* m.	*toy*
गरम	*garam*	*hot, warm*
चलते जाना	*calte jānā*	*to keep going*
चौड़ा	*cauṛā*	*wide, broad*
जलाना	*jalānā*	*to light*
टैक्सी	*ṭaiksī* f.	*taxi*
तंग	*taṅg*	*narrow*
तंग करना	*tang karnā*	*to annoy, harass*
तोहफ़ा	*tohfā* m.	*gift, present*
थकना	*thaknā*	*to get tired*
थाना	*thānā* m.	*police station*
दक्षिण	*dakṣiṇ*	*south*
दवाख़ाना	*davākhānā* m.	*pharmacy, chemist's shop*
दाहिना	*dāhinā*	*right* (not left)
देश	*deś* m.	*country*
धोबी	*dhobī* m.	*washerman*
नक़्शा	*naqśā* m.	*map*
निकलना	*nikalnā*	*to emerge, come/go out*
पचास	*pacās*	*fifty*
पड़ना	*paṛnā*	*to fall; to have to* (with preceding infinitive – मुझे जाना पड़ेगा *mujhe jānā paṛegā I'll have to go*)
पश्चिम	*paścim*	*west*
पार	*pār*	*across*
पार करना	*pār karnā*	*to cross* उस पार *us pār* on the other side (of के *ke*)
पुलिस	*pulis* f.	*police*
पुस्तकालय	*pustakālay* m.	*library*
पूर्व	*pūrv*	*east*
प्रदेश	*pradeś* m.	*state, region*
बजे	*baje*	*o'clock*
बटुआ	*baṭuā* m.	*purse, wallet*
बायाँ	*bāyā̃*	*left* (not right)
बुरा	*burā*	*bad*
भाड़ में जाए	*bhāṛ mẽ jāe*	*(he/she) can go to hell* (भाड़ *bhāṛ* m. *grain-parching oven)*
मंदिर	*mandir* m.	*temple*

मराठी	*marāṭhī* f.	*Marathi* (language of Maharashtra)
माफ़ी	*māfī* f.	*forgiveness*
माफ़ी माँगना	*māfī mā̃gnā*	*to apologize*
मामूली	*māmūlī*	*ordinary*
मार्ग	*mārg* m.	*road, street* (used in street names)
मैला	*mailā*	*dirty*
रिक्शेवाला	*rikśevālā* m.	*rickshaw driver*
रिश्तेदार	*riśtedār* m.	*relation, relative*
लगना	*lagnā*	*to seem; to be felt* (of hunger, thirst, etc.); *to take* (time); *to have an effect*; *to begin* (following an oblique infinitive)
सरकार	*sarkār* f.	*government*
सामान	*sāmān* m.	*goods, furniture, luggage*

Test yourself

1. रखना *rakhnā* means *to put* and रखा जाना *rakhā jānā* means *to be put*. So how would we say *to be spoken, to be eaten, to be said, to be asked*?
2. How would we say *It will take one hour, It will take two weeks*?
3. Explain the meaning and grammar of the sentence टैक्सी बुलाई जाए *ṭaiksī bulāī jāe*.
4. Would टैक्सी को बुलाया जाए *ṭaiksī ko bulāyā jāe* have a different meaning from this?
5. A friend says, लगता है तुमको भूख लगी होगी *lagtā hai tumko bhūkh lagī hogī*. What are the two different meaning of लगना *lagnā* here?
6. How would you say *It began raining*, using the f. noun बारिश *bāriś* *rain*?
7. चाय पीनी है ? *cāy pīnī hai?* Does this convey a sense of obligation to have tea?
8. Asked आज आपको काम करना ? *āj āpko kām karnā hai?*, a friend replies हाँ करना ही पड़ेगा ! *hā̃ karnā hī paṛegā!* What's the difference between these two kinds of 'compulsion', using है *hai* and पड़ेगा *paṛegā* respectively?
9. What's on your schedule? Name three things you have to do today, following the formula of मुझे खाना बनाना है *mujhe khānā banānā hai I have to prepare food*.
10. How would you say *I should give my friend a present*?

SELF CHECK

	I CAN...
○	... give directions.
○	... describe things being done.
○	... say *should* and *must*.

12 तबियत और शैली

tabiyat aur śailī

Health and style

In this unit you will learn how to:

- ***talk about getting things done by others.***
- ***add nuance to what you say.***
- ***speak about health matters.***
- ***use numbers.***
- ***tell the time.***

Language points

- *relative clauses*
- *causative verbs*
- *compound verbs*

Language discovery 1

J-WORDS AND RELATIVE CLAUSES

12.01 Earlier we saw a set of 'question words' beginning with *k-*.

कब *kab* when?   कहाँ *kahā̃* where?   कौन *kaun* who?

Now we meet a similar set of words, this time beginning with *j-*. These are used in 'relative clauses', where they introduce one clause that is 'related' or linked to a second one. Here are three members of this set:

जब *jab* when   जहाँ *jahā̃* where   जो *jo* who

जब *jab* is often partnered by तो *to* (or तब *tab then*) which ushers in a paired clause:

जब मैं छोटा था तो मुझे संगीत का बहुत शौक़ था ।
jab maĩ choṭā thā to mujhe sangīt kā bahut śauq thā.
When I was little I was very fond of music.

जब लता जी गाती थीं तब पिताजी भी सुनते थे ।
jab Latā jī gātī thī̃ tab pitājī bhī sunte the.
When Lata ji sang, even Father used to listen.

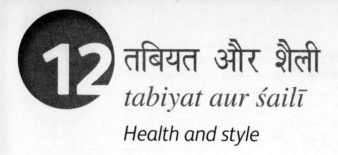

जब संगीत शुरू होता था तो सब लोग नाचने लगते थे ।
jab sangīt śurū hotā thā to sab log nācne lagte the.
When the music started everyone would begin to dance.

जहाँ *jahā̃* is often partnered by वहाँ *vahā̃* there:

जहाँ मैं रहता हूँ वहाँ कोई सिनेमा नहीं है ।
jahā̃ maĩ rahtā hū̃, vahā̃ koī sinemā nahī̃ hai.
Where I live, there's no cinema.

जहाँ सिनेमा पहले था वहाँ एक होटल बन रहा है ।
jahā̃ sinemā pahle thā vahā̃ ek hoṭal ban rahā hai.
Where the cinema was previously, a hotel is being built.

जहाँ लोग सो रहे हों वहाँ रेडियो मत बजाना ।
jahā̃ log so rahe hõ vahā̃ reḍiyo mat bajānā.
Don't play the radio where people may be sleeping.

जो *jo* who/which/what is often partnered by वह/वे *vah/ve:*

जो आदमी रेडियो में गाना गाता है वह सामने रहता है ।
jo ādmī reḍiyo mẽ gānā gātā hai vah sāmne rahtā hai.
The man who sings on the radio lives opposite.

जो गाना तुमने गाया, वह हमें बहुत पसंद आया ।
jo gānā tumne gāyā, vah hamẽ bahut pasand āyā.
We really liked the song you sang. (The song you sang, it pleased us.)

जो लोग गाना सीखना चाहते हैं उनको यह गाना सुनना चाहिए ।
jo log gānā sīkhnā cāhte haĩ unko yah gānā sunnā cāhie.
People who want to learn to sing should listen to this song.

जो *jo* has the oblique जिस *jis* (sing.) and जिन *jin* (pl.):

जिसने यह फ़िल्म बनाई वह मेरा पुराना दोस्त है ।
jisne yah film banāī vah mera purānā dost hai.
The person who made this film is my old friend.

जिस फ़िल्म में यह गाना आता है वह काफ़ी पुरानी है ।
jis film mẽ yah gānā ātā hai vah kāfī purānī hai.
The film in which this song comes is quite old.

जिन लोगों ने "शोले" फ़िल्म देखी है वे उसे कभी नहीं भूलेंगे ।
jin logõ ne 'śole' film dekhī hai ve use kabhī nahī̃ bhūlẽge.
People who have seen the film 'Sholay' will never forget it.

Supply the proper relative *j* words and their partner words in these two sentences:

a _______ नेहा छोटी थी _______ उसको पालक पसंद नहीं था ।
_______ *Nehā choṭī thī* _______ *usko pālak pasand nahī̃ thā.*

b _______ लोगों ने वह खाना खाया आज _______ बीमार हैं ।
_______ *logo ne vah khānā khāyā āj* _______ *bīmār haĩ.*

Storyline

THE LIFE OF A RICKSHAW DRIVER

12.02 *Now a narrative about Hiralal, the rickshaw driver, helps us get used to relative clauses. In addition to a couple of English words used here (artist, seat), you will need these new words:*

शानदार	*śāndār*	splendid	पहाड़	*pahāṛ* m.	hill
हीरा	*hīrā* m.	diamond	चढ़ाव	*caṛhāv* m.	rise, incline
चमकना	*camaknā*	to shine	भारी	*bhārī*	heavy
सवारी	*savārī* f.	passenger, rider	चढ़ना	*caṛhnā*	to climb, get into vehicle
जेब	*jeb* f.	pocket	वज़न	*vazan* m.	weight
थक जाना	*thak jānā*	to get tired	हो जाना	*ho jānā*	to become
मुफ़्त (का)	*muft (kā)*	cost-free	उतरना	*utarnā,*	
बारिश	*bāriś* f.	rain	उतर जाना	*utar jānā*	to get down, alight
ग़रीब	*ġarīb*	poor			
मौसम	*mausam* m.	weather	लेटना	*leṭnā*	to lie down

1 How many reasons are given to explain that the job of a rickshaw driver like Hiralal can be very hard? Can you list them in the order you hear them?

यह हीरालाल है, जो आगरे में रहता है । हीरालाल रिक्शेवाला है । जो रिक्शा हीरालाल चलाता है वह बहुत शानदार है । वह हीरे की तरह चमकता है ! जिसने यह रिक्शा बनाया हो[1] वह बहुत बड़ा आर्टिस्ट होगा ।[2]

जहाँ हीरालाल रहता है वहाँ बहुत-से दूसरे रिक्शेवाले भी रहते हैं । रिक्शे तो बहुत हैं लेकिन सवारियाँ कम आती हैं ।[3] जब एक भी सवारी नहीं आती तब हीरालाल की जेब ख़ाली रहती है । जब जेब ख़ाली रहती है तो पेट भी ख़ाली रहता है । मुफ़्त का खाना कहाँ मिलता है ?[4] और जब बारिश होती है तब भी हीरालाल को काम करना पड़ता है । जो लोग ग़रीब हैं उनको हर मौसम में काम करना पड़ता है ।

जहाँ पहाड़ या चढ़ाव हो वहाँ रिक्शा चलाना बहुत ही मुश्किल है । जब दो मोटे लोग अपने भारी सामान को लेकर[5] रिक्शे में चढ़ते हैं तो वज़न बहुत ज़्यादा हो जाता है । जब सवारियाँ उतर जाती हैं तो हीरालाल अपने रिक्शे की सीट पर लेटकर सोता है । जो लोग रिक्शे चलाते हैं उन्हें बहुत मेहनत करनी पड़ती है ।

yah Hīrālāl hai, jo āgre mẽ rahtā hai. Hīrālāl rikśevālā hai. jo rikśā Hīrālāl calātā hai vah bahut śāndār hai. vah hīre kī tarah camaktā hai! jisne yah rikśā banāyā ho[1] *vah bahut barā ārtist hogā.*[2]

jahā̃ Hīrālāl rahtā hai vahā̃ bahut-se dūsre rikśevale bhī rahte haĩ. rikśe to bahut haĩ lekin savāriyā̃ kam ātī haĩ.[3] *jab ek bhī savārī nahā̃ ātī tab Hīrālāl kī jeb khālī rahtī hai. jab jeb khālī rahtī hai to peṭ bhī khālī rahtī hai. muft kā khānā kahā̃ miltā hai?*[4] *aur jab bāriś hotī hai tab bhī Hīrālāl ko kām karnā paṛtā hai. jo log garīb haĩ unko har mausam mẽ kām karnā paṛtā hai.*

jahā̃ pahāṛ yā caṛhāv ho vahā̃ rikśā calānā bahut hī muśkil hai. jab do moṭe log apne bhārī sāmān ko lekar[5] *rikśe mẽ caṛhte haĩ to vazan bahuṭ zyādā ho jātā hai. jab savāriyā̃ utar jātī haĩ to Hīrālāl apne rikśe kī sīṭ par leṭkar sotā hai. jo log rikśe calāte haĩ unhẽ bahut mehnat karnī paṛtī hai.*

Notes

1 जिसने यह रिक्शा बनाया हो *jisne ya rikśā banāyā ho – the person who made this rickshaw;* हो *ho* is subjunctive to reflect the fact that the identity of the person is vague or unknown.

2 Remember that the future can express an assumption – *he must be a very great artist* (lit. *he will be ...*).

3 The noun सवारी *savārī* is feminine, even if the 'passenger' described is male.

4 मुफ़्त का खाना कहाँ मिलता है ? *muft kā khānā kahā̃ miltā hai? Where can you get food for free?* It's a rhetorical question – you can't get free food anywhere.

5 भारी सामान को लेकर *bhārī sāmān ko lekar taking heavy luggage* i.e. having heavy luggage with them.

2 Listen to Hiralal's story again, then answer the questions.

a What is his rickshaw like?

b Why is he sometimes not able to make any money?

c What does he do when it rains?

d What does he do after dropping his passengers off?

Practice 1

1 12.03 **Listen to and read these sentences. Then translate them into English.**

a जो आदमी रिक्शे में बैठा है वह बहुत मोटा है ।
jo ādmī rikśe mẽ baiṭhā hai vah bahut moṭā hai.

b जिस रिक्शे में वह बैठा है वह बहुत सुंदर है ।
jis rikśe mẽ vah baiṭhā hai vah bahut sundar hai.

c जो आदमी यह रिक्शा चला रहा है उसका नाम हीरालाल है ।
jo ādmī yah rikśā calā rahā hai uskā nām Hīrālāl hai.

d जिस औरत ने अभी हीरालाल से रास्ता पूछा वह कौन है ?
jis aurat ne abhī Hīrālāl se rāstā pūchā vah kaun hai?

e जहाँ मैं रहता हूँ वहाँ रिक्शे नहीं आते ।
jahā̃ maĩ rahtā hū̃ vahā̃ rikśe nahī̃ āte.

f जब मुझे स्टेशन जाना पड़ता है तो मुझे टैक्सी लेनी पड़ती है ।
jab mujhe sṭeśan jānā paṛtā hai to mujhe ṭaiksī lenī paṛtī hai.

2 And now for something completely different: a crossword puzzle.

Because the basic unit of the Devanagari script is the *syllable* (and not the individual letter, as in roman-script languages), each square will contain a complete syllable: so the word सोमवार *somvar Monday* would split up into four component units, सो | म | वा | र (*so* | *m* | *vā* | *r*). You will need to look up one or two words in the English–Hindi vocabulary.

ACROSS

1 brave
5 political party, group
6 teacher (female)
8 Madhuban (hotel name)
9 always (archaic/formal)
10 then
11 Tuesday
12 newspaper seller
17 don't ...!
18 ashtray
20 an Indian epic poem
22 straight
25 to bathe
26 singer

DOWN

1 ugly
2 condition, state
3 enemy
4 shopkeeper
6 now
7 concentration, attention
9 question
11 temple
12 American
13 danger
14 ancient city on Ganges
15 100,000
16 that is to say
19 lentils
21 to hit
23 thread
24 one

3 Are these statements right (सही *sahī*) or wrong (ग़लत *galat*)?

a हीरालाल दिल्ली से है ।
Hīrālāl dillī se hai.

b उसके पास बहुत पैसा है ।
uske pās bahut paisā hai.

c हीरालाल का रिक्शा काफ़ी सुन्दर है ।
Hīrālāl kā rikśā kāfī sundar hai.

d हीरालाल के घर के पास कोई दूसरा रिक्शेवाला नहीं रहता ।
Hīrālāl ke ghar ke pās koī dūsrā rikśevālā nahī̃ rahtā.

e सवारियों की कोई कमी नहीं है ।
savāriyõ kī koī kamī nahī̃ hai.

f बारिश के मौसम में हीरालाल काम नहीं करता ।
bāriś ke mausam mẽ Hīrālāl kām nahī̃ kartā.

g हीरालाल को खाना मुफ़्त में मिलता है ।
Hīrālāl ko khānā muft mẽ miltā hai.

h जब हीरालाल थक जाता है तो वह सोता है ।
jab Hīrālāl thak jātā hai to vah sotā hai.

Language discovery 2

GETTING THINGS DONE – CAUSATIVES

As you know, the Hindi for *to make* is बनाना *banānā* (हम चाय बनाएँगे *ham cāy banāẽge we'll make tea*). Extend this to बनवाना *banvānā* and you have a verb that means *to get made, to cause to be made.*

हम चाय बनवाएँगे ।	*ham cāy banvāẽge.*	*We'll get tea made.*
हम नौकर से चाय बनवाएँगे ।	*ham naukar se cāy banvāẽge.*	*We'll get tea made by the servant.*

These verbs with –वा- *-vā-* extensions are called 'causatives'. The word से *se* conveys the sense *by*: नौकर से *naukar se by the servant.*

Some causatives are less obviously connected to their base verb. For example, धोना *dhonā to wash* has the causative धुलवाना *dhulvānā to get washed*, and सीना *sīnā to sew* has सिलवाना *silvānā to get sewn.*

How many causatives can you spot in the following, in which Geeta talks about her annual preparations for Diwali?

सबसे पहले मैं दरज़ी से नए कपड़े सिलवाती हूँ । फिर धोबी को बुलवाकर मैं उससे सारे गंदे कपड़े धुलवाती हूँ । जो कपड़े मैंने ख़ुद धोए हों उनको मैं धोबी से प्रेस *['press']* करवाती हूँ । फिर घर को अच्छी तरह से साफ़ करवाती हूँ और रात का खाना बनवाती हूँ । रात को हम दीये जलाते हैं, या उनको बच्चों से जलवाते हैं ।

sabse pahle maĩ darzī se nae kapṛe silvātī hū̃. phir dhobī ko bulvākar maĩ usse sāre gande kapṛe dhulvātī hū̃. jo kapṛe maĩne k͟hud dhoe hõ unko maĩ dhobī se pres (press) karvātī hū̃. phir ghar ko acchī tarah se sāf karvātī hū̃ aur rāt kā khānā banvātī hū̃. rāt ko ham diye jalāte haĩ, yā unko baccõ se jalvāte haĩ.

First of all I get new clothes sewn by the tailor. Then I have the dhobi called and I get all the dirty clothes washed by him (*get him to wash…*). Whatever clothes I've washed myself I get ironed by him. Then I get the house cleaned thoroughly and I get dinner made. At night we light lamps, or get them lit by the children (*get the children to light them*).

There are *seven* causatives here (including two appearances of करवाना *karvānā to get done, cause to be done*):

सिलवाना	*silvānā*	*to get sewn*	(सीना *sīnā to sew*)
बुलवाना	*bulvānā*	*to get called, to summon*	(बुलाना *bulānā to call*)

धुलवाना	*dhulvānā*	to get washed	(धोना *dhonā* to wash)
प्रेस करवाना	*pres karvānā*	to get pressed, ironed	(प्रेस करना *pres karnā* to press, iron)
साफ़ करवाना	*sāf karvānā*	to get cleaned	(साफ़ करना *sāf karnā* to clean)
बनवाना	*banvānā*	to get made	(बनाना *banānā* to make)
जलवाना	*jalvānā*	to get lit	(जलाना *jalānā* to light)

VERB TRIPLETS

You'll often find triplets of related verbs like these sets:

बनना *bannā* to be made	बनाना *banānā* to make	बनवाना *banvānā* to get made
बोलना *bolna* to speak	बुलाना *bulānā* to call	बुलवाना *bulvānā* to summon
धुलना *dhulnā* to be washed	धोना *dhonā* to wash	धुलवाना *dhulvānā* to get washed
जलना *jalnā* to burn	जलाना *jalānā* to light	जलवाना *jalvānā* to get lit

The verb सीखना *sīkhnā* follows the same pattern as the four verbs shown above. How would you say *The children learn, Sandhya ji teaches the children*, and *Raju has the children taught by Sandhya ji*?

Writing

Now it's your turn to use causatives. Translate these sentences using the verbs provided.

a *We'll have the children taught Hindi by Sharma ji.*
(सिखवाना *sikhvānā* to have taught)

b *I got some food prepared by the servants.*
(तैयार करवाना *taiyār karvānā* to get prepared)

c *We have to get the car fixed.*
(ठीक करवाना *ṭhīk karvānā* *to get fixed*)

d *I want to get some kurtas sewn by Master ji.*
(सिलवाना *silvānā* *to get sewn*)

e *I got these letters written by someone.*
(लिखवाना *likhvānā* *to get written*)

Storyline

A VISIT TO THE DOCTOR

12.04 Sadly, Raju has been feeling unwell. Can the doctor help?

1 What seems to be wrong with Raju?

डाक्टर	आइए, आइए । क्या तकलीफ़ है आपको ?
राजू	डाक्टर साहब, मेरा सारा शरीर दर्द कर रहा है ।[1]
डाक्टर	आपकी तबियत कब से ख़राब है ?
राजू	दो दिन से । परसों मैं काम पर जानेवाला था[2] कि[3] सिर में दर्द होने लगा ।
डाक्टर	लगता है आपको फ़्लू हो गया है ।[4]
राजू	तो मुझे क्या करना चाहिए ?
डाक्टर	सिर्फ़ आराम करना चाहिए ।
राजू	कोई दवा या गोली तो दीजिए !
डाक्टर	आपको किसी गोली-वोली[5] की ज़रूरत नहीं है । आराम ही इलाज है ।
ḍākṭar	*āie, āie. kyā taklīf hai āpko?*
Rājū	*ḍākṭar sāhab, merā sārā śarīr dard kar rahā hai.*[1]
ḍākṭar	*āpkī tabiyat kab se kharāb hai?*
Rājū	*do din se. parsõ maĩ kām par jānevālā thā*[2] *ki*[3] *sir mẽ dard hone lagā.*
ḍākṭar	*lagtā hai āpko flū ho gayā hai.*[4]
Rājū	*to mujhe kyā karnā cāhie?*
ḍākṭar	*sirf ārām karnā cāhie.*
Rājū	*koī davā yā golī dījie!*
ḍākṭar	*āpko kisī golī-volī*[5] *kī zarūrat nahī̃ hai. ārām hī ilāj hai.*

Notes

1 दर्द करना *dard karnā to hurt*; also दर्द होना *dard honā to have a pain* (मेरे सिर में दर्द हो रहा है *mere sir mẽ dard ho rahā hai I have a headache*).

2 मैं जानेवाला था *maĩ jānevālā thā I was about to go*; -वाला *-vālā* added to a verb ending in *-ne* means *about to*. गीता अभी जानेवाली है *Gītā abhī jānevālī hai Geeta's just about to go*, मैं अभी आपको फ़ोन करनेवाला था *maĩ abhī āpko fon karnevālā thā I was just about to phone you*.

3 कि *ki* here means *when, when suddenly* in this construction with -वाला *-vālā* (see note 2).

4 हो जाना *ho jānā* is the simplest way of saying *to get* an illness etc. The patient takes को *ko*.

5 गोली-वोली *golī-volī tablet or anything like that* – वोली *volī* is a meaningless echo word. Echo words, usually beginning *v-*, generalize the sense of the preceding word, opening out the range of meaning from something specific (here, medicine) to a broader category (here, any kind of medication). Compare the following: चाय-वाय *cāy-vāy tea etc.*, खाना-वाना *khānā-vānā food, something to eat*, पानी-वानी *pānī-vānī water, something to drink*. The doctor's remark here has a disparaging touch: *You don't need any tablet or any such nonsense!*

2 Listen to the conversation again, then answer the questions.

a How long has Raju been feeling ill?
b What does he want from the doctor?
c What treatment does the doctor recommend?

Language discovery 3

PARTS OF THE BODY

In order to explain feelings of pain and sickness, etc. you need to know the main parts of the body. Ram has helpfully agreed to pose for us (for a substantial fee):

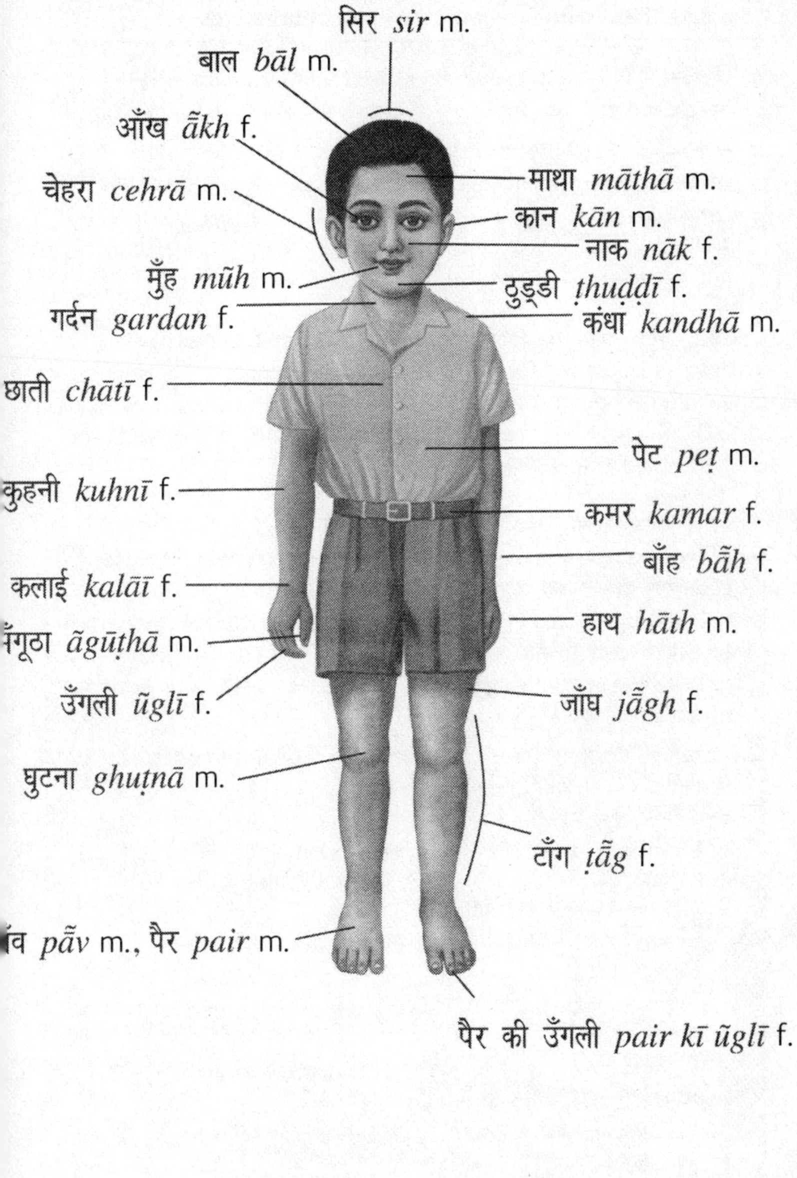
सिर sir m.
बाल bāl m.
आँख ā̃kh f.
चेहरा cehrā m.
माथा māthā m.
कान kān m.
नाक nāk f.
मुँह mũh m.
ठुड्डी ṭhuḍḍī f.
गर्दन gardan f.
कंधा kandhā m.
छाती chātī f.
पेट peṭ m.
कुहनी kuhnī f.
कमर kamar f.
बाँह bā̃h f.
कलाई kalāī f.
हाथ hāth m.
ँगूठा āgūṭhā m.
उँगली ũglī f.
जाँघ jā̃gh f.
घुटना ghuṭnā m.
टाँग ṭā̃g f.
ंव pā̃v m., पैर pair m.
पैर की उँगली pair kī ũglī f.

Complete these sentences with the appropriate words.

a एक हाथ की पाँच _______ होती हैं। *ek hāth kī pā̃c _______ hotī haĩ.*

b मैंने कुछ बुरा खाया, अब मेरा _______ ख़राब है। *maĩne kuch burā khāyā, ab merā _______ kharāb hai.*

c उस आदमी के _______ पर टोपी है। *us ādmī ke _______ par ṭopī hai.*

d कुत्ते के चार _______ होते हैं। *kutte ke cār _______ hote haĩ.*

Speaking

Role play: you go to the doctor because you've had a stomach ache, sickness, and diarrhoea for two days. You have a headache but your temperature is normal. Your alcohol consumption is moderate; you usually sleep OK. You have been careful about your food and the only water you drink is bottled water (बोतल का पानी *botal kā pānī*).

12.05 **Now answer the doctor's questions:**

a	आपकी तबियत कब से ख़राब है ? *āpkī tabiyat kab se kharāb hai?*	How long has your health been bad?
b	आपको बुख़ार तो नहीं है ? *āpko bukhār to nahī̃ hai?*	You don't have fever, do you?
c	क्या सिर में दर्द है ? *kyā sir mẽ dard hai?*	Do you have a headache?
d	आप बाहर का खाना खाते/खाती हैं, बाज़ार में ? *āp bāhar kā khānā khāte/khātī haĩ, bāzār mẽ?*	Do you eat food from outside, in the market?
e	आप नल का पानी पीते/पीती हैं ? *āp nal kā pānī pīte/pītī haĩ?*	Do you drink tap water?
f	उलटी हो रही है ? *ulṭī ho rahī hai?*	(Are you) Having vomiting attacks?
g	दस्त भी है ? *dast bhī hai?*	Is there diarrhoea too?
h	क्या आप शराब पीते/पीती हैं ? *kyā āp śarāb pīte/pītī haĩ?*	Do you drink alcohol?
i	क्या आपको नींद ठीक से आती है ? *kyā āpko nī̃d ṭhīk se ātī hai?*	Do you sleep properly?
j	आप कितने बजे सोते/सोती हैं ? *āp kitne baje sote/sotī haĩ?*	What time do you sleep?

k	कितने घंटे सोते/सोती हैं ?	
	kitne ghaṇṭe sote/sotī haĩ?	How many hours do you sleep?
l	और कोई तकलीफ़ है आपको ?	
	aur koī taklīf hai āpko?	Do you have any other symptoms?

Language discovery 4

SHADES OF MEANING

Different languages have different ways of adding shades of meaning to a statement. In English, for example, the basic verb *to write* underlies the variations *write down, write up, write out, write in* and so on. In Hindi, shades of meaning are often conveyed by a pairing of two verbs. Think of it being a bit like making lassi, the yoghurt drink: the first verb is the yoghurt that gives the basic meaning, while the second verb is the choice of sugar or salt that adds the flavouring. Here's an example with लिखना *likhnā to write* as first verb, and लेना *lenā to take* or देना *denā to give* as second verb:

मेरा पता लिख लो ।	*merā patā likh lo.*	Write down my address.
नहीं, तुम लिख दो ।	*nahī̃, tum likh do.*	No, you write (it) out.

लिख लो *likh lo* – this combines the basic sense of लिखना *likhnā to write* with a shade of meaning from लेना *lenā to take*; लेना *lenā* here suggests that the action is a 'taking' one – something done *for the benefit of the person who does the action*. So the implied meaning is *Take down my address (for your own use)*.

लिख दो *likh do* – this combines the basic sense of लिखना *likhnā* with a shade of meaning from देना *denā to give*; देना *denā* here suggests that the action is a 'giving' one – something done *for the benefit of someone else*. So the implied meaning is *Write it out for me*.

As well as लेना *lenā* and देना *denā*, another verb commonly used in this construction is जाना *jānā*, literally *to go*. In harmony with its literal meaning of movement from one place to another, it colours a preceding verb with a sense of a *completed action*, or a *change of state:*

अरे ! बिजली बंद हो गई !
are! bijlī band ho gaī! Hey! The electricity's gone off!

अच्छा ? मैं तो सो गया था ।
acchā? maĩ to so gayā thā. Really? I'd gone to sleep.

बिजली बंद हो गई *bijlī band ho gaī* – the main verb होना *honā to be* changes to हो जाना *ho jānā to become*, because a *change of state* has taken place.

मैं सो गया था *maī so gayā thā* – the verb सोना *sonā to sleep* changes to सो जाना *so jānā to go to sleep*, with the sense of *go* very similar in both English and Hindi.

Verbs of this kind are called 'compound verbs'. (Hindi has a better name for them – रंजक क्रिया *ranjak kriyā colouring verbs.*) There are many more combinations, some of which are given in the grammar summary, but लेना *lenā*, देना *denā*, and जाना *jānā* are by far the most common.

The ने *ne* construction is only used with compound verbs if *both* verbs in the compound are ने *ne* verbs (i.e. ones that are marked with ^{N} in the glossary at the end of the book).

Finally, a word of warning: compound verbs give a specific sense of the way in which a *particular* action is done. It therefore follows that *a sentence that's negative or general won't use them*; if no one drinks the lassi, its taste is irrelevant! Look closely at the use of a compound verb in the first of these two sentences, then at the *dropping* of the compound in the second (which is negative):

(राजू) मैंने खाना खा लिया है ।
(Rājū) maĩne khānā khā liyā hai. — *I've had my meal.*

(गीता) अच्छा ? मैंने तो नहीं खाया है ।
(Gītā) acchā? maĩne to nahī̃ khāyā hai. — *Really? I haven't.*

Raju stresses that he's had (and enjoyed or benefited from) his meal, a sense given by लेना *lenā*. But Geeta hasn't eaten yet, so her reply has no scope for the implication that लेना *lenā* brings.

How would you add लेना *lenā*, देना *denā*, and जाना *jānā* to these sentences to add nuance to their meanings? Can *all* the verbs here be converted to compound verbs?

---

a यह पानी पीजिए । — *yah pānī pījie.*
b हमने कुछ नहीं खाया । — *hamne kuch nahī̃ khāyā.*
c वह सेब मत खाओ, वह ज़मीन पर गिरा । — *vah seb mat khāo, vah zamīn par girā.*
d आप के लिए चाय बनाऊँ ? — *āp ke lie cāy banāū̃?*

I'VE ALREADY DONE THIS

12.06 The verb चुकना *cuknā* means *to have finished doing,* [illegible] *already done* and it's used in a structure identical to the one we've [illegible] been looking at – it follows the stem of the main verb:

मीना जा चुकी है ।
Mīnā jā cukī hai.
Meena has already gone.

राम अपना काम कर चुका है ।
Rām apnā kām kar cukā hai.
Ram has already done his work.

मनोज अपनी किताब पढ़ चुका है ।
Manoj apnī kitāb paṛh cukā hai.
Manoj has already read (or *finished reading*) *his book.*

राजू और गीता खाना खा चुके हैं ।
Rājū aur Gītā khānā khā cuke haĩ.
Raju and Geeta have already eaten (or *have finished eating*).

You'll be glad to hear that the ने *ne* construction is never used here!

Change these two sentences using चुकना *cuknā* to express that the actions have already been done.

मीना ने अपने कमरे की सफ़ाई की । *Mīnā ne apne kamre kī safāī kī.*
हम लोग वह फ़िल्म देखेंगे । *ham log vah film dekhẽge.*

Speaking

12.07 **Can you answer the following questions using चुकना *cuknā*? Remember the verb will agree with you in gender, whether you are male or female. Speak in the pauses and say *yes, I have already done it.* Then listen to check your answers.**

a क्या आपने शोले फ़िल्म देखी है ? *kyā āpne śole film dekhī hai?*
b क्या आपने खाना खाया है ? *kyā āpne khānā khāyā hai?*
c क्या आपने अपना काम किया है ? *kyā āpne apnā kām kiyā hai?*
d क्या आपने यह पूरी किताब पढ़ी है ? *kyā āpne yah pūrī kitāb paṛhī hai?*

DID YOU MANAGE TO DO THIS?

The same structure is used again with the verb पाना *pānā.* This literally means *to find, obtain,* but here it gives the meaning *to manage to, to be able to* (compare सकना *saknā*, met in Unit 6).

	… maĩ nahĩ jā pāyā.	*I didn't manage to go yesterday.*
	Gītā ṭikaṭ nahĩ <u>kh</u>arīd pāī.	*Geeta wasn't able to buy a ticket.*
	kyā tum yah kām akele kar pāoge?	*Will you manage to do this work alone?*

… with पाना *pānā* in these sentences to change the me… …*dn't* to *didn't manage to.*

कल हम आपके … नहीं जा सके । *kal ham āpke yahā̃ nahī̃ jā sake.*
मनीषा समय पर स्टेशन नहीं पहुँच सकी । *Maniśa samay par sṭeśan nahī̃ pahũc sakī.*

STYLE IN HINDI

The language used in this book reflects ordinary unselfconscious speech. But like all languages, Hindi has a variety of styles – formal, informal, colloquial, and so on. Formal Hindi uses a lot of loanwords from Sanskrit (India's main classical language) just as formal English uses words from Latin and Greek. For example, formal Hindi would use the Sanskrit loanword सहायता *sahāytā assistance* rather than the informal मदद *madad help*, which is a loanword from Arabic and which has an entirely natural place in informal Hindi. Many Arabic and some Turkish words came to India as part of the Persian language, from about the 11th century onwards – they are far from being newcomers!

The formal style of the language is called शुद्ध हिन्दी *śuddh hindī – pure Hindi*; but as this example of सहायता *sahāytā* shows, it is itself dependent on Sanskrit loanwords, which means that any claims to linguistic 'purity' have to be taken with a pinch of salt. In formal Hindi, especially in the written language but also in some people's preferred speaking style also, one *requires assistance*, one does not *need help*! When you start reading Hindi books and newspapers, you'll have to start adding Sanskritic vocabulary to the colloquial base you're learning here. But be careful about using it too much in everyday conversational contexts, because it could make your Hindi sound very bookish. People who learn Hindi from grammar books alone, especially those of the traditional variety, end up *requiring assistance*!

Today, informal Hindi uses words from a rich variety of sources, especially English, whose relentless spread throughout the world can be seen as a threat to so many languages.

Which English loanword do you see in this sentence referring to an illness? Can you guess its meaning?

मेरे दादा जी को शुगर है ।   *mere dādā jī ko śugar hai.*

12.08 *Go shopping with Geeta and you'll hear lots of familiar words. Here we catch up with her buying shoes in a shop in 'fashionable' South Extension, Delhi:*

गीता	आपके पास ग्रीन कलर का जूता है ?
दुकानदार	हाँ मैडम, देखिए, ये शूज़ ग्रीन कलर के हैं । और बहुत ही रीज़नेबुल हैं ।
गीता	नहीं, यह स्टाइल मैं लाइक नहीं करती ।
दुकानदार	पर इसकी लेदर बहुत ही सॉफ़्ट है ! और क्वालिटी भी देखिए इसकी ! ट्राई तो कीजिए !
Gītā	*āpke pās grīn kalar kā jūtā hai?*
dukāndār	*hā̃ maiḍam, dekhie, ye śūz grīn kalar ke haĩ. aur bahut hī rīzanebul haĩ.*
Gītā	*nahī̃, yah sṭāil maĩ lāik nahī̃ kartī.*
dukāndār	*par iskī ledar bahut hī sāfṭ hai! aur kvāliṭī bhī dekhie iskī! ṭrāī to kījie!*

And so on! As a learner of Hindi, you may find it rather depressing that it has allowed itself to be so heavily influenced by a language that is so foreign to its own character. But between the two extremes of heavily Sanskritized and heavily Anglicized versions of the language, Hindi remains a superbly subtle and vibrant language, full of expressiveness and life!

NUMBERS

Here are the cardinal numbers. You'll find it easier to get familiar with the higher ones (above 20) if you read them in 'decade' sequences such as 21, 31, 41, etc.

० शून्य *śūnya*

१ एक	११ ग्यारह	२१ इक्कीस	३१ इकत्तीस	४१ इकतालीस
1 ek	*11 gyārah*	*21 ikkīs*	*31 ikattīs*	*41 iktālīs*
२ दो	१२ बारह	२२ बाईस	३२ बत्तीस	४२ बयालीस
2 do	*12 bārah*	*22 bāīs*	*32 battīs*	*42 bayālīs*
३ तीन	१३ तेरह	२३ तेईस	३३ तैंतीस	४३ तैंतालीस
3 tīn	*13 terah*	*23 teīs*	*33 taĩtīs*	*43 taĩtālīs*
४ चार	१४ चौदह	२४ चौबीस	३४ चौंतीस	४४ चवालीस
4 cār	*14 caudah*	*24 caubīs*	*34 caũtīs*	*44 cavālīs*
५ पाँच	१५ पंद्रह	२५ पच्चीस	३५ पैंतीस	४५ पैंतालीस
5 pā̃c	*15 pandrah*	*25 paccīs*	*35 paĩtīs*	*45 paĩtālīs*
६ छह	१६ सोलह	२६ छब्बीस	३६ छत्तीस	४६ छियालीस
6 chah	*16 solah*	*26 chabbīs*	*36 chattīs*	*46 chiyālīs*
७ सात	१७ सत्रह	२७ सत्ताईस	३७ सैंतीस	४७ सैंतालीस
7 sāt	*17 satrah*	*27 sattāīs*	*37 saĩtīs*	*47 saĩtālīs*
८ आठ	१८ अठारह	२८ अट्ठाईस	३८ अड़तीस	४८ अड़तालीस
8 āṭh	*18 aṭhārah*	*28 aṭṭhāīs*	*38 aṛtīs*	*48 aṛtālīs*
९ नौ	१९ उन्नीस	२९ उनतीस	३९ उनतालीस	४९ उनचास
9 nau	*19 unnīs*	*29 untīs*	*39 untālīs*	*41 uncās*
१० दस	२० बीस	३० तीस	४० चालीस	५० पचास
10 das	*20 bīs*	*30 tīs*	*40 cālīs*	*50 pacās*

५१ इक्यावन	६१ इकसठ	७१ इकहत्तर	८१ इक्यासी	९१ इक्यानवे
51 *ikyāvan*	61 *iksaṭh*	71 *ik'hattar*	81 *ikyāsī*	91 *ikyānve*
५२ बावन	६२ बासठ	७२ बहत्तर	८२ बयासी	९२ बानवे
52 *bāvan*	62 *bāsaṭh*	72 *bahattar*	82 *bayāsī*	92 *bānve*
५३ तिरपन	६३ तिरसठ	७३ तिहत्तर	८३ तिरासी	९३ तिरानवे
53 *tirpan*	63 *tirsaṭh*	73 *tihattar*	83 *tirāsī*	93 *tirānve*
५४ चौवन	६४ चौंसठ	७४ चौहत्तर	८४ चौरासी	९४ चौरानवे
54 *cauvan*	64 *caũsaṭh*	74 *cauhattar*	84 *caurāsī*	94 *caurānve*
५५ पचपन	६५ पैंसठ	७५ पचहत्तर	८५ पचासी	९५ पचानवे
55 *pacpan*	65 *paĩsaṭh*	75 *pac'hattar*	85 *pacāsī*	95 *pacānve*
५६ छप्पन	६६ छियासठ	७६ छिहत्तर	८६ छियासी	९६ छियानवे
56 *chappan*	66 *chiyāsaṭh*	76 *chihattar*	86 *chiyāsī*	96 *chiyānve*
५७ सत्तावन	६७ सरसठ	७७ सतहत्तर	८७ सत्तासी	९७ सत्तानवे
57 *sattāvan*	67 *sarsaṭh*	77 *sat'hattar*	87 *sattāsī*	97 *sattānve*
५८ अट्ठावन	६८ अड़सठ	७८ अठहत्तर	८८ अट्ठासी	९८ अट्ठानवे
58 *aṭṭhāvan*	68 *aṛsaṭh*	78 *aṭhhattar*	88 *aṭṭhāsī*	98 *aṭṭhānve*
५९ उनसठ	६९ उनहत्तर	७९ उन्यासी	८९ नवासी	९९ निन्यानवे
59 *unsaṭh*	69 *unhattar*	79 *unyāsī*	89 *navāsī*	99 *ninyānve*
६० साठ	७० सत्तर	८० अस्सी	९० नब्बे	१०० सौ
60 *sāṭh*	70 *sattar*	80 *assī*	90 *nabbe*	100 *sau*

1.5	डेढ़	*ḍeṛh*
2.5	ढाई	*ḍhāī*
1000	हज़ार	*hazār*
100,000	लाख	*lākh*
10,000,000	करोड़	*karoṛ* (100 lakh, written 100,00,000)
150	डेढ़ सौ	*ḍeṛh sau*
1500	डेढ़ हज़ार	*ḍeṛh hazār*
150,000	डेढ़ लाख	*ḍeṛh lākh*
250	ढाई सौ	*ḍhāī sau*
2500	ढाई हज़ार	*ḍhāī hazār*
250,000	ढाई लाख	*ḍhāī lākh*

Write the following numbers as Hindi numerals:

पचहत्तर *pac'hattar*, डेढ़ लाख *ḍeṛh lākh*, उनतीस *untīs*

TIME

12.09 Listen to and read the time expressions.

बजे	*baje*	*o'clock*
बजना	*bajnā*	*to chime, resound*
डेढ़	*ḍeṛh*	*one and a half*
ढाई	*ḍhāī*	*two and a half*
पौन, पौने	*paun, paune*	*three quarters*
सवा	*savā*	*one and a quarter*
साढ़े	*sāṛhe*	*plus a half* (with 3 and upwards)
पौने एक बजा है ।	*paune ek bajā hai.*	*It's a quarter to one.*
एक बजा है ।	*ek bajā hai.*	*It's one o'clock.*
डेढ़ बजा है ।	*ḍeṛh bajā hai.*	*It's half past one.*
दो बजे हैं ।	*do baje haĩ.*	*It's two o'clock.*
ढाई बजे हैं ।	*ḍhāī baje haĩ*	*It's half past two.*
सवा सात बजे हैं ।	*savā sāt baje haĩ.*	*It's a quarter past seven.*
पौने दस बजे हैं ।	*paune das baje haĩ.*	*It's a quarter to ten.*
साढ़े ग्यारह बजे हैं ।	*sāṛhe gyārah baje haĩ.*	*It's half past eleven.*
हम दो बजे मिलेंगे ।	*ham do baje milẽge.*	*We'll meet at two o'clock.*
मैं डेढ़ बजे तक आऊँगा ।	*maĩ ḍeṛh baje tak āū̃gā.*	*I'll come by half past one.*
दस बज रहे हैं ।	*das baj rahe haĩ.*	*It's just ten* (ten is striking).
दस बजनेवाले हैं ।	*das bajnevāle haĩ.*	*It's nearly ten* (ten's about to strike).

Minutes before and after the hour are expressed by बजने में *bajne mẽ* and बजकर *bajkar* respectively.

एक बजनें में बीस मिनट हैं ।
ek bajne mẽ bīs minaṭ haĩ. *It's 12.40.*

आठ बजकर बीस मिनट हुए हैं ।
āṭh bajkar bīs minaṭ hue haĩ. *It's 8.20.*

WHAT'S THE TIME?

पौने एक बजा है *paune ek bajā hai*	एक बजा है *ek bajā hai*	डेढ़ बजा है *ḍeṛh bajā hai*	दो बजे हैं *do baje haĩ*
ढाई बजे हैं *ḍhāī baje haĩ*	साढ़े चार बजे हैं *sāṛhe cār baje haĩ*	पौने चार बजे हैं *paune cār baje haĩ*	सवा चार बजे हैं *savā cār baje haĩ*

Look at the time expressions and put these sentences in chronological order.

- **a** शाम को साढ़े पाँच बजे राजू जगदीश से मिला। *śām ko sāṛhe pā̃c baje Rājū Jagdiś se milā.*
- **b** सुबह सात बजे राजू जागा। *subah sāt baje Rājū jāgā.*
- **c** डेढ़ बजे दोपहर को राजू बाहर गया। *ḍeṛh baje dopahar ko Rājū bāhar gayā.*

MONTHS

India still uses its traditional calendar (with lunar months) for festival dates, and you can find plenty of information on this on the internet by searching for 'Hindu calendar'. But the 'western' (or global) calendar is usually preferred for mundane functions.

The month names are spelt in Hindi with dental consonants: this reflects their Portuguese ancestry (words from English being generally spelt with retroflexes).

जनवरी *janvarī*	फ़रवरी *farvarī*	मार्च *mārc*	अप्रैल *aprail*	मई *maī*	जून *jūn*
जुलाई *julāī*	अगस्त *agast*	सितंबर *sitambar*	अक्तूबर *aktūbar*	नवंबर *navambar*	दिसंबर *disambar*

Practice 2

1 Answer the questions about Hiralal:

a जो रिक्शा हीरालाल चलाता है, उसको किसने बनाया होगा ?
jo rikśā Hīrālāl calātā hai, usko kisne banāyā hogā?

b जहाँ हीरालाल रहता है वहाँ और कौन रहता है ?
jahā̃ Hīrālāl rahtā hai vahā̃ aur kaun rahtā hai?

c जिस शहर में हीरालाल रहता है, उसका नाम क्या है ?
jis śahar mẽ Hīrālāl rahtā hai, uskā nām kyā hai?

d जब बारिश होती है तो क्या हीरालाल घर जाता है ?
jab bāriś hotī hai to kyā Hīrālāl ghar jātā hai?

e रिक्शे का वज़न कब बहुत ज़्यादा हो जाता है ?
rikśe kā vazan kab bahut zyādā ho jātā hai?

f हीरालाल की जेब कब ख़ाली रहती है ?
Hīrālāl kī jeb kab <u>kh</u>ālī rahtī hai?

g जो लोग रिक्शे चलाते हैं उनकी ज़िन्दगी कैसी होती है ?
jo log rikśe calāte haĩ unkī zindagī kaisī hotī hai?

2 Complete the sentences meaningfully:

a जो लोग भारत के बारे में कुछ सीखना चाहते हैं, उनको ...
jo log bhārat ke bāre mẽ kuch sīkhnā cāhte haĩ, unko ...

b जब मैंने पहली बार ताज महल को देखा, मैंने सोचा कि ...
jab maĩne pahlī bār tāj mahal ko dekhā, maĩne socā ki ...

c जहाँ मेरे रिश्तेदार रहते हैं, वहाँ ...
jahā̃ mere riśtedār rahte haĩ, vahā̃ ...

d जो आदमी मेरे साथ काम करता है उसकी ...
jo ādmī mere sāth kām kartā hai uskī ...

e जो आदमी मेरे घर के सामने रहता है वह ...
jo ādmī mere ghar ke sāmne rahtā hai vah ...

f जिन लोगों के पास बहुत पैसा है, वे ...
jin logõ ke pās bahut paisā hai, ve ...

g जो कपड़े मैंने कल ख़रीदे ...
jo kapṛe maĩne kal <u>kh</u>arīde ...

3 Translate:

a When I go to Agra I often stay at Raju's place.
b The man who teaches us Hindi is Raju's brother.

c The present I gave to Ram today was quite cheap.
d When I gave it to him he showed it to his mother.
e When Raju's mother saw my present she began to laugh.
f I'll never forget the question she asked Raju about me.
g The answer Raju gave will always remain in my memory.

4 Here's a short letter to Manoj from a friend in the USA. Translate it, keeping an eye out for the compound verbs.

प्रिय मनोज,

तुम्हारा ख़त मिल गया, शुक्रिया । एक साल से कोई ख़त नहीं आया था तो मैं सोचने लगा था कि मेरे दोस्त मनोज को क्या हो गया है ?

यहाँ सब ठीक है । मेरे भाई की शादी हो गई है । उसने दिल्ली में एक छोटा-सा मकान किराये पर लिया है ।

मेरे पिताजी कहते हैं कि अब तुम भी शादी कर लो । पर मैंने उनको साफ़ बता दिया है कि मैं अभी शादी नहीं करूँगा । अभी जवान हूँ । जब तीस साल का हो जाऊँगा तो शायद इन बातों के बारे में सोचना शुरू करूँगा । लेकिन पिताजी मेरी बात नहीं सुनना चाहते । अभी थोड़ी देर पहले वे फिर से शादी के बारे में बात करने लगे । मैं थोड़ा नाराज़ हो गया । मैंने कहा, "हाँ पापा, मैंने सुन लिया !"

अपना ई-मेल का पता मुझे बता देना ।

तुम्हारा
मोटू

priy Manoj,

tumhārā <u>kh</u>at mil gayā, śukriyā. ek sāl se koī khat nahī̃ āyā thā to maĩ socne lagā thā ki mere dost Manoj ko kyā ho gayā hai?

yahā̃ sab ṭhīk hai. mere bhāī kī śādī ho gaī hai. usne dillī mẽ ek choṭā-sā makān kirāye par liyā hai.

mere pitājī kahte haĩ ki ab tum bhī śādī kar lo. par maĩne unko sāf kah diyā hai ki maĩ abhī śādī nahī̃ karū̃gā. abhī javān hū̃. jab tīs sāl kā ho jāū̃gā to śāyad in bātõ ke bāre mẽ socnā śurū karū̃gā. lekin pitājī merī bāt nahī̃ sunnā cāhte. abhī thoṛī der pahle ve phir se śādī ke bāre mẽ bāt karne lage. maĩ thoṛā nārāz ho gayā. maĩne kahā, 'hā̃ pāpā, maĩne sun liyā!'

apnā ī-mel ka patā mujhe batā denā.

tumhārā
Moṭū.

Vocabulary builder

अँगूठा	*ãgūṭhā* m.	*thumb*
आँख	*ãkh* f.	*eye*
उँगली	*ũglī* f.	*finger*
उगना	*ugnā*	*to grow* (of plants)
उतरना, उतर जाना	*utarnā, utar jānā*	*to get down, alight*
उलटी	*ulṭī* f.	*vomiting, sickness*
कटना	*kaṭnā*	*to be cut*
कमर	*kamar* f.	*waist*
कलाई	*kalāī* f.	*wrist*
करवाना	*karvānā*	*to cause to be done, to get done*
कान	*kān* m.	*ear*
कि	*ki*	*when, when suddenly; or*
कुहनी	*kuhnī* f.	*elbow*
खेल	*khel* m.	*game*
ग़रीब	*g̲arīb*	*poor*
गर्दन	*gardan* f.	*neck*
गाल	*gāl* f.	*cheek*
घास	*ghās* f.	*grass*
घुटना	*ghuṭnā* m.	*knee*
चढ़ना	*caṛhnā*	*to climb; to get into a vehicle*
चढ़ाव	*caṛhāv* m.	*rise, incline*
चमकना	*camaknā*	*to shine*
चुकना	*cuknā*	*to have already done* (with verb stem: वह जा चुका है *vah jā cukā hai He's already gone*)
छाती	*chātī* f.	*chest*
जब	*jab*	*when*
जलना	*jalnā*	*to burn*
जलवाना	*jalvānā*	*to cause to burn*
जवान	*javān*	*young*
जहाँ	*jahā̃*	*where*
जाँघ	*jā̃gh* f.	*thigh*
जेब	*jeb* f.	*pocket*
जैसा ... वैसा	*jaisā ... vaisā*	*as (one thing), so (another)*
टाँग	*ṭā̃g* f.	*leg*
टूटना	*ṭūṭnā*	*to break*
ठुड्डी	*ṭhuḍḍī* f.	*chin*

ताज महल	*tāj mahal* m.	*Taj Mahal*
दस्त	*dast* m.	*diarrhoea*
दस्त आना	*dast ānā*	*to have diarrhoea*
दाँत	*dā̃t* m.	*tooth*
दिल	*dil* m.	*heart*
दीया	*diyā* m.	*lamp*
धुलना	*dhulnā*	*to be washed*
धुलवाना	*dhulvānā*	*to cause to be washed*
नल	*nal* m.	*tap, pipe*
नाक	*nāk* f.	*nose*
नींद	*nī̃d* f.	*sleep*
नींद आना	*nī̃d ānā*	*(sleep to come) to get to sleep*
नौकर	*naukar* m.	*servant*
पता	*patā* m.	*address; whereabouts*
पहाड़	*pahāṛ* m.	*hill*
पाँव	*pā̃v* m.	*foot, leg*
पाना	*pānā*	*to find, obtain; to be able, to manage to* (with verb stem: मैं नहीं जा पाया *maĩ nahī̃ jā pāyā* I didn't manage to go)
पैर	*pair* m.	*foot*
पैर की उँगली	*pair kī ũglī* f.	*toe*
प्रेस करना	*pres karnā*	*to iron*
बनवाना	*banvānā*	*to cause to be made*
बहुत ज़्यादा	*bahut zyādā*	*very great, too much*
बाँह	*bā̃h* f.	*arm, upper arm*
बाल	*bāl* m.	*hair*
बुलवाना	*bulvānā*	*to cause to be called*
भरना	*bharnā*	*to be filled; to fill*
भारी	*bhārī*	*heavy*
माथा	*māthā* m.	*forehead*
मुँह	*mũh* m.	*mouth; face*
मुफ़्त (का)	*muft (kā)*	*free*
मुफ़्त में	*muft mẽ*	*for nothing, free*
मौसम	*mausam* m.	*weather*
रिक्शा	*rikśā* m.	*rickshaw*
लेटना	*leṭnā*	*to lie down*
वज़न	*vazan* m.	*weight*
विदेश	*videś*	*abroad*
विदेशी	*videśī* m.	*foreigner;* adj. *foreign*

शरीर	*śarīr* m.	*body*
शानदार	*śāndār*	*splendid, magnificent*
शुद्ध	*śuddh*	*pure*
शोला	*śolā* m.	*flame;* शोले *śole* 'Sholay', the title of a cult Hindi film (1975)
सवारी	*savārī* f.	*passenger, rider*
सहायता	*sahāytā* f.	*assistance*
सामने	*sāmne*	*opposite*
सिखवाना	*sikhvānā*	*to cause to be taught*
सिलवाना	*silvānā*	*to cause to be sewn*
सीना	*sīnā*	*to sew*
हर	*har*	*every, each*
हराम	*harām*	*forbidden*
हीरा	*hīrā* m.	*diamond*
हो जाना	*ho jānā*	*to become*

? Test yourself

1 An alien phones from a distant planet, wanting a description of a human body. Tell it, in three separate and simple sentences, how many hands, eyes, and heads you have.

2 After the clause जहाँ हम लोग रहते हैं ... *jahā̃ ham log rahte haĩ* ..., what is the next word likely to be?

3 What does जिस *jis* mean, and how could it be used in a sentence?

4 How would you say *The book I bought here is not available* (use मिलना *milnā*) in other shops?

5 अभी साढ़े चार बजे हैं । दो घंटे पहले कितने बजे थे ?
   abhī sāṛhe cār baje haĩ. do ghaṇṭe pahle kitne baje the?

6 What's the difference in meaning or implication between (a) मैं ने चाय पी है *maĩne cāy pī hai* and (b) मैं ने चाय पी ली है *maĩne cāy pī lī hai?*

7 If चाय बनाओ *cāy banāo* means *Make (some) tea*, how would you translate (a) चाय बना लो *cāy banā lo*; and (b) चाय बनवा लो *cāy banvā lo?*

8 Respond in the negative to this question: क्या आप चाय पी चुके/चुकी हैं ?
   kyā āp cāy pī cuke/cukī haĩ?

9 यूनिट १२ में जो रिक्शेवाला है, उसका नाम क्या है ?
   yūniṭ (unit) 12 mē̃ jo rikśevālā hai, uskā nām kyā hai?

10 इन सवालों का जवाब देने में आपको कितना समय लगा ?
   in savālõ kā javāb dene mē̃ āpko kitnā samay lagā?

SELF CHECK

	I CAN...
○	. . . talk about getting things done by others.
○	. . . add nuance to what I say.
○	. . . speak about health matters.
○	. . . use numbers.
○	. . . tell the time.

Key to the exercises

Bear in mind that there will often be several possible ways of answering questions and translating sentences. In the case of questions addressed to the reader, sample answers are given.

UNIT 1

Language discovery 1

Saying hello: Good morning or hello, goodbye
Introducing yourself: before the verb
Yes/No questions: क्या आप डाक्टर हैं ? *kyā āp ḍākṭar haĩ?*
You: हैं *haĩ* is plural

Language discovery 2

This and that: ये *ye,* वे *ve*
What? and Who? यह मेरा सितार है *yah merā sitār hai,* वह मेरा कुत्ता है *vah merā kuttā hai*

Listen and understand

a जी नहीं, मोती बिल्ली नहीं, कुत्ता है ।
jī nahī̃, Motī billī nahī̃, kuttā hai.

b जी हाँ, गीता डाक्टर है ।
jī hā̃, Gītā ḍākṭar hai.

c जी नहीं, मैं डाक्टर नहीं, अध्यापक हूँ ।
jī nahī̃, maĩ ḍākṭar nahī̃, adhyāpak hū̃.

d जी हाँ, राजू और गीता हिन्दुस्तानी हैं ।
jī hā̃, Rājū aur Gītā hindustānī haĩ.

e जी हाँ, हिन्दी बहुत आसान है !
jī hā̃, hindī bahut āsān hai!

What's this? क्या आप बीमार हैं ? *kyā āp bīmār haĩ ?*
क्या नेहा सुखी है ? *kyā Nehā sukhī hai ?*
क्या वह लड़की विद्यार्थी है ? *kyā vah laṛkī vidyārthī hai?*

Storyline

1 Javed says, मेरा नाम जावेद है **2a** The girl's name is Bano.
b Javed's full name is Javed Khan.

Practice

Exercise 1

जावेद	यह क्या है ?
Jāved	*yah kyā hai?*
मनोज	यह मेरा रेडियो है ।
Manoj	*yah merā reḍiyo hai.*
जावेद	वह लड़का कौन है ?
Jāved	*vah laṛkā kaun hai?*
मनोज	वह मेरा भाई है ।
Manoj	*vah merā bhāī hai.*
जावेद	उसका नाम क्या है ?
Jāved	*uskā nām kyā hai?*
मनोज	उसका नाम राम है ।
Manoj	*uskā nām Rām hai.*
जावेद	वह लड़की कौन है ?
Jāved	*vah laṛkī kaun hai?*
मनोज	उसका नाम मीना है ।
Manoj	*uskā nām Mīnā hai.*
जावेद	क्या वह बीमार है ?
Jāved	*kyā vah bīmār hai?*
मनोज	जी नहीं, वह बीमार नहीं है, वह ठीक है ।
Manoj	*jī nahī̃, vah bīmār nahī̃ hai, vah ṭhīk hai.*

Exercise 2

a जी नहीं, सुरेश शादी-शुदा नहीं है ।
jī nahī̃, Sureś śādī-śudā nahī̃ hai.

b जी हाँ, वह हिन्दुस्तानी है ।
jī hā̃, vah hindustānī hai.

c जी नहीं, वह अध्यापक नहीं है, विद्यार्थी है ।
jī nahī̃, vah adhyāpak nahī̃ hai, vidyārthī hai.

d उसका पूरा नाम सुरेश खन्ना है ।
uskā pūrā nām Suresh Khannā hai.

e जी हाँ, उमा हिन्दुस्तानी है ।
jī hā̃, Umā hindustānī hai.

f जी नहीं, वह डाक्टर नहीं है, वह अध्यापक है ।
jī nahī̃, vah ḍākṭar nahī̃ hai, vah adhyāpak hai.

g जी नहीं, वह शादी-शुदा नहीं है ।
jī nahī̃, vah śādī-śudā nahī̃ hai.

h जी हाँ, वह सुखी है ।
jī hā̃, vah sukhī hai.

i जी नहीं, विनोद अँग्रेज़ नहीं है, वह अमरीकन है ।
jī nahī̃, Vinod ãgrez nahī̃ hai, vah amrīkan hai.

j जी नहीं, वह अध्यापक नहीं है, वह डाक्टर है ।
jī nahī̃, vah adhyāpak nahī̃ hai, vah ḍākṭar hai.

k उसका पूरा नाम विनोद कुमार है ।
uskā pūrā nām Vinod Kumār hai.

l जी हाँ, वह शादी-शुदा है ।
jī hā̃, vah śādī-śudā hai.

m जी नहीं, सुरेश हिन्दुस्तानी है लेकिन विनोद अमरीकन है ।
jī nahī̃, Sureś hindustānī hai lekin Vinod amrīkan hai.

n जी नहीं, विनोद शादी-शुदा है लेकिन उमा शादी-सुदा नहीं है ।
jī nahī̃, Vinod śādī-śudā hai lekin Umā śādī-śudā nahī̃ hai.

o जी नहीं, उमा अध्यापक है लेकिन सुरेश विद्यार्थी है ।
jī nahī̃, Umā adhyāpak hai lekin Sureś vidyārthī hai.

Exercise 3

The doctor's name is Doctor Varma. His first name is Mohanlal and his son's name is Munna.

Test yourself

1 नमस्ते *namaste.*

2 At the end.

3 सुरेश ठीक है लेकिन उसका दोस्त बीमार है
Sureś ṭhīk hai lekin uskā dost ṭhīk nahī̃ hai.

4 By adding the word क्या *kyā* to the beginning of the sentence – as in क्या वह नेपाली है ? *kyā vah nepālī hai?* Is he/she Nepali?.

5 मेरा नाम रूपर्ट स्नेल है । *merā nām rūparṭ snel hai.*

6 That the 't' is dental, and that the 'e' is like French é, not like English 'ay' as in 'hay'.

7 यह *yah* refers to a person or thing near at hand (it also means 'this'), and वह *vah* refers to a person or thing who is not present, or is at some distance (it also means 'that').

8 किताब *kitāb* f. 'book'; मकान *makān* m. 'house'; मेज़ *mez* f. 'table'.

9 The sentence stays exactly the same: उसका *uskā* means 'his, her/hers, its', and its gender agrees with m. नाम *nām.*

10 जी हाँ *jī hā̃,* जी नहीं *jī nahī̃.*

UNIT 2

Language discovery 1

Gender matters: m, f, m, f, f
All nouns have a gender: छोटी बेटी *choṭī beṭī,* बड़ी मेज़ *baṛī mez,* मोटा कुत्ता *moṭā kuttā*

Speaking

a	जी हाँ, मैं गीता हूँ ।	*jī hā̃, maī̃ Gītā hū̃.*
b	मेरा पूरा नाम गीता शर्मा है ।	*merā pūrā nām Gītā Śarmā hai.*
c	जी हाँ, मैं शादी-शुदा हूँ ।	*jī hā̃, maī̃ śādī-śudā hū̃.*
d	राकेश मेरा भाई है ।	*Rākeś merā bhāī hai.*
e	सीता मेरी बहिन है ।	*Sītā merī bahin hai.*
f	जी नहीं, मेरी बहिन बीमार है ।	*jī nahī̃, merī bahin bīmār hai.*
g	जी नहीं, मेरा भाई ठीक है ।	*jī nahī̃, merā bhāī ṭhīk hai.*
h	जी नहीं, मैं बीमार नहीं हूँ, मैं ठीक हूँ ।	*jī nahī̃, maī̃ bīmār nahī̃ hū̃, maī̃ ṭhīk hū̃.*

Language discovery 2

Two types of masculine nouns: मकान *makān,* लड़के *laṛke,* कमरे *kamre,* पिता *pita*
Two types of feminine nouns: plural, plural, singular

Practice 1

a लंबी *lambī* **b** वे लड़के *ve laṛke* **c** बहुत पतला है *bahut patlā hai*
d कौन *kaun* क्या *kyā*

Language discovery 3

Some numbers: १४ = 14 and १८ = 18
Ordinal numbers: पहला पड़ोसी *pahlā paṛosī,* तीसरी बेटी *tīsrī beṭī,* दसवीं मंज़िल *dasvī̃ manzil*

Practice 2

Exercise 2

दसवाँ	*dasvā̃*
बारहवाँ	*bārahvā̃*

पंद्रहवाँ *pandrahvā̃*
उन्नीसवाँ *unnīsvā̃*
बीसवाँ *bīsvā̃*

Exercise 3

a जी हाँ, पहला लड़का मोटा है । *jī hā̃, pahlā laṛkā moṭā hai.*

b पहला लड़का गणेश है । *pahlā laṛkā Gaṇeś hai.*

c जी नहीं, तीसरा लड़का ख़ुश नहीं है । *jī nahī̃, tīsrā laṛkā <u>kh</u>uś nahī̃ hai.*

d पाँचवाँ लड़का राजेश है । *pā̃cvā̃ laṛkā Rājeś hai.*

e जी हाँ, चौथा लड़का बहुत पतला है । *jī hā̃, cauthā laṛkā bahut patlā hai.*

f चौथा लड़का दिनेश है । *cauthā laṛkā Dineś hai.*

g जी नहीं, दूसरा लड़का महेश नहीं, सुरेश है ।
jī nahī̃, dūsrā laṛka Maheś nahī̃, Sureś hai.

Language discovery 4

Getting familiar: आप *āp,* तुम *tum,* आप *āp,* तू *tū*
Listening: His name is Pratap. He is a student, and he lives next door to you. He says he's your neighbour.

Language discovery 5

Getting formal: a क्या आप राजू के भाई हैं ? *kyā āp Rājū ke bhāī haĩ?*
b मेरी बड़ी बहिन सुंदर हैं । *merī baṛī bahin sundar haĩ.*

Raju ji, Geeta ji: We are Raju's sisters. That cat is ours.

Storyline

1 Manoj, Meena, Ram, and Geeta.

2a Raju has two sons. **b** Geeta ji is Raju's wife. **c** He is a teacher.

Practice 3

Exercise 1

Manoj is his friend. His teacher is Sharma ji. He says Sharma ji is a very good teacher, but he doesn't seem too sure about it.

Exercise 2

a मेरा नाम मनोज है । राजू और गीता शर्मा मेरे माता-पिता हैं ।
merā nām Manoj hai. Rājū aur Gītā Śarmā mere mātā-pitā haĩ.

b मीना मेरी छोटी बहिन है और राम मेरा छोटा भाई है ।
Mīnā merī choṭī bahin hai aur Rām merā choṭā bhāī hai.

c मोती हमारा कुत्ता है । वह बहुत प्यारा है ।
Motī hamārā kuttā hai. vah bahut pyārā hai.

d यह मीना है । यह ठीक है । यह छोटी है ।
yah Mīnā hai. yah ṭhīk hai. yah choṭī hai.

e हमारा मकान बहुत बड़ा नहीं है । सिर्फ़ पाँच कमरे हैं ।
hamārā makān bahut baṛā nahī̃ hai. sirf pā̃c kamre haĩ.

f वह लड़का मेरा दोस्त है । उसका नाम प्रताप है ।
vah laṛkā merā dost hai. uskā nām Pratāp hai.

g जावेद साहब हमारे पड़ोसी हैं ।
Jāved sāhab hamāre paṛosī haĩ.

Exercise 3

a ये लड़के बहुत प्यारे हैं । *ye laṛke bahut pyāre haĩ.*

b ये कुत्ते हमारे नहीं हैं । *ye kutte hamāre nahī̃ haĩ.*

c वे लड़के कौन हैं ? *ve laṛke kaun haĩ?*

d ये आदमी कौन हैं ? *ye ādmī kaun haĩ?*

e मेरे दोस्त पंजाबी हैं । *mere dost panjābī haĩ.*

f क्या ये कुत्ते आपके हैं ? *kyā ye kutte āpke haĩ?*

g वे औरतें कौन हैं ? *ve auratẽ kaun haĩ?*

h हमारे बेटे अच्छे लड़के हैं । *hamāre beṭe acche laṛke haĩ.*

i मेरी बेटियाँ बीमार हैं । *merī beṭiyā̃ bīmār haĩ.*

j क्या ये किताबें महँगी हैं ? *kyā ye kitābẽ mahā̃gī haĩ?*

k ये मेज़ें गंदी हैं । *ye mezẽ gandī haĩ.*

Exercise 4

a आप कौन हैं ? *āp kaun haĩ?*

b आपका नाम क्या है ? *āpkā nām kyā hai?*

c आपके माता-पिता बहुत अच्छे लोग हैं । *āpke mātā-pitā bahut acche log haĩ.*

d आपका भाई सुंदर नहीं है । *āpkā bhāī sundar nahī̃ hai.*

e आप दोनों लड़के लंबे हैं । *āp donõ laṛke lambe haĩ.*

f आप कैसे हैं ? *āp kaise haĩ?*

g तुम्हारा नाम क्या है ? *tumhārā nām kyā hai?*

h क्या तुम ठीक हो ? *kyā tum ṭhīk ho?*

i तुम नाराज़ नहीं हो ? *tum nārāz nahī̃ ho?*

j तुम कैसी हो ? *tum kaisī ho?*

Test yourself

1 जी *jī.*

2 False. आदमी *ādmī* is an example of the many masculine -*ī* nouns.

3 दसवाँ *dasvā̃* 'tenth', बीसवाँ *bīsvā̃* 'twentieth'.

4 False. A common class of masculine nouns, such as मकान *makān* and आदमी *ādmī,* shows no change in the plural.

5 तुम हो *tum ho,* तू है *tū hai.*

6 दो लड़कियाँ *do laṛkiyā̃,* तीन लड़के *tīn laṛke,* चार तस्वीरें *cār tasvīrẽ,* पाँच आदमी *pā̃c ādmī.*

7 यह कमरा मेरा है । *yah kamrā merā hai.*

8 Nothing. The feminine agreement in पतली *patlī* and मेरी *merī* is with the noun किताब *kitāb.*

9 E.g.: ख़ाली *khālī,* ठीक *ṭhīk,* बीमार *bīmār,* साफ़ *sāf.*

10 Varanasi, Jaipur, Bhopal, London, Chicago.

UNIT 3

Language discovery 1

How much, how many? कितने विद्यार्थी हैं ? *kitne vidyārthī haĩ?* कैसा मकान है ? *kaisā makān hai?*

Speaking

a सिर्फ़ एक आदमी है । *sirf ek ādmī hai.*

b यह लंबा आदमी है । *yah lambā ādmī hai.*

c मेज़ छोटी है । *mez choṭī hai.*

d दो लड़कियाँ हैं । *do laṛkiyā̃ haĩ.*

e कुल मिलाकर तीन लोग हैं । *kul milākar tīn log haĩ.*

f जी नहीं, एक लड़की लंबी है, दूसरी छोटी है । *jī nahī̃, ek laṛkī lambī hai, dūsrī choṭī hai.*

g दो चूहे हैं । *do cūhe haĩ.*

h सिर्फ़ एक कुरसी है । *sirf ek kursī hai.*

i जी नहीं, चूहे छोटे हैं । *jī nahī̃, cūhe choṭe haĩ.*

j सिर्फ़ एक तोता है । *sirf ek totā hai.*

Speaking

a दिल्ली भारत में है *dillī bhārat mẽ hai*

b काठमांडु नेपाल में है *kāṭhmāṇḍu nepāl mẽ hai*

c कराची पाकिस्तान में है *karācī pākistān mẽ hai*

d मुम्बई भारत में है *mumbaī bhārat mẽ hai*

e लंदन इंग्लैंड में है *landan inglaiṇḍ mẽ hai*

f मैं ______ में हूँ *maĩ ______ mẽ hũ*

Language discovery 2

Word order: राम कहाँ है ? *Ram kahā̃ hai?*

Speaking

a बिल्ली बड़ी कुरसी पर है । *billī baṛī kursī par hai.*

b कुत्ता छोटी कुरसी पर है । *kuttā choṭī kursī par hai.*

c तस्वीर में दो कुरसियाँ हैं । *tasvīr mẽ do kursiyā̃ haĩ.*

d तस्वीर में सिर्फ़ एक बिल्ली है । *tasvīr mẽ sirf ek billī hai.*

e छोटी कुरसी पर कुत्ता है । *choṭī kursī par kuttā hai.*

f बड़ी कुरसी पर बिल्ली है । *baṛī kursī par billī hai.*

g मेज़ पर कुछ किताबें हैं । *mez par kuch kitābẽ haĩ.*

h जी हाँ, दोनों बहुत प्यारे हैं ! *jī hā̃, donõ bahut pyāre haĩ!*

Language discovery 3

Do you have… ? I have a picture of the hospital. Our house is next to the hospital.

Speaking

a जी हाँ, मेरे पास साइकिल है *jī hā̃, mere pās sāikil hai* / जी नहीं, मेरे पास साइकिल नहीं है *jī nahī̃, mere pās sāikil nahī̃ hai.*

b जी हाँ, मेरे पास बहुत पैसे हैं *jī hā̃, mere pās bahut paise haĩ* / जी नहीं, मेरे पास बहुत पैसे नहीं हैं *jī nahī̃, mere pās bahut paise nahī̃ haĩ.*

c जी हाँ, मेरे पास नया रेडियो है *jī hā̃, mere pās nayā reḍiyo hai* / जी नहीं, मेरे पास नया रेडियो नहीं है *jī nahī̃, mere pās nayā reḍiyo nahī̃ hai.*

d जी हाँ, मेरे पास नए हिन्दुस्तानी कपड़े हैं *jī hā̃, mere pās nae hindustānī kapṛe haĩ* / जी नहीं, मेरे पास नए हिन्दुस्तानी कपड़े नहीं हैं *jī nahī̃, mere pās nae hindustānī kapṛe nahī̃ haĩ.*

e जी हाँ, मेरे पास नई गाड़ी है *jī hā̃, mere pās naī gāṛī hai* / जी नहीं, मेरे पास नई गाड़ी नहीं है *jī nahī̃, mere pās naī gāṛī nahī̃ hai.*

Plural nouns in the oblique case: लंबे लड़कों को *lambe laṛkõ ko,* बड़ी मेज़ पर *baṛī mez par*

Reading

a घर आगरे में है । *ghar āgre mẽ hai.*

b नहीं, वह नया है । *nahī̃, vah nayā hai.*

c चार कमरे हैं – दो बड़े और दो छोटे । *cār kamre haĩ – do baṛe aur do choṭe.*

d हाँ, सब कमरों में खिड़कियाँ हैं । *hā̃, sab kamrõ mẽ khiṛkiyā̃ haĩ.*

e बड़े कमरों में पंखें हैं । *baṛe kamrõ mẽ pankhe haĩ.*

f बाहर बग़ीचा है । बग़ीचे में कुछ पेड़ हैं । *bāhar bag̲īcā hai. bag̲īce mẽ kuch peṛ haĩ.*

g किराया ५००० रुपये है । *kirāyā 5000 rupaye hai.*

Storyline

Geeta's home

a गीता वाराणसी से है । *Gītā vārāṇasī se hai.*

b जी हाँ, गीता शादी-शुदा है । *jī hā̃, Gītā śādī-śudā hai.*

c जी हाँ, राजू दिल्ली से है । *jī hā̃, Rājū dillī se hai.*

d जी नहीं, राजू डाक्टर नहीं, अध्यापक है । *jī nahī̃, Rājū ḍākṭar nahī̃, adhyāpak hai.*

e जी नहीं, यह घर दिल्ली में नहीं, आगरे में है । *jī nahī̃, yah ghar dillī mẽ nahī̃, āgre mẽ hai.*

f घर में पाँच कमरे हैं । *ghar mẽ pā̃c kamre haĩ.*

g बड़े कमरे में एक मेज़ है । *baṛe kamre mẽ ek mez hai.*

h कम्प्यूटर मेज़ पर है । *kampyūṭar mez par hai.*

i किताबें फ़र्श पर हैं । *kitābẽ farś par haĩ.*

j बग़ीचे में कुछ लंबे पेड़ हैं । *bag̲īce mẽ kuch lambe peṛ haĩ.*

At school 1a Ram's pen is on his chair. **2a** Ram isn't holding anything in his hands. **b** Ram's sister is at home because she is sick.

At home 1 Ram and Manoj are at school. **2a** Meena is in the garden. **b** Geeta doesn't know where Raju's brother is.

Practice

Exercise 1

a मेरी किताबें मेज़ पर पड़ी हैं । *merī kitābẽ mez par paṛī haĩ.*

b आपका भाई बग़ीचे में बैठा है । *āpkā bhāī bag̲īce mẽ baiṭhā hai.*

c मैं बड़े कमरे में खड़ा हूँ । *maĩ baṛe kamre mẽ khaṛā hū̃.*

d आपकी किताबें छोटी अलमारी में हैं । *āpkī kitābẽ choṭī almārī mẽ haĩ.*

e उसका मकान यहाँ से दूर नहीं है । *uskā makān yahā̃ se dūr nahī̃ hai.*

f आपके परिवार में कितने लोग हैं ? *āpke parivār mẽ kitne log haĩ?*

g आपके पति के पास कितना पैसा है ? *āpke pati ke pās kitnā paisā hai?*

h आज आपकी पत्नी कैसी हैं ? और आप कैसे हैं ?
āj āpkī patnī kaisī haĩ? aur āp kaise haĩ?

i बच्चे घर पर नहीं हैं, स्कूल पर हैं ।
bacce ghar par nahī̃ haĩ, skūl par haĩ.

j क्या यह छोटी लड़की तुम्हारी बहिन है ?
kyā yah choṭī laṛkī tumhārī bahin hai?

Exercise 2

a मेरा पूरा नाम श्रीमती गीता शर्मा है । *merā pūrā nām śrīmatī Gītā Śarmā hai.*

b जी हाँ, मैं डाक्टर हूँ । *jī hā̃, maĩ ḍākṭar hū̃.*

c जी नहीं, मेरे पति अध्यापक हैं । *jī nahī̃, mere pati adhyāpak haĩ.*

d जी हाँ, वे घर पर हैं । *jī hā̃, ve ghar par haĩ.*

e मेरे पति दिल्ली से हैं, लेकिन मैं वाराणसी से हूँ ।
mere pati dillī se haĩ, lekin maĩ vārāṇasī se hū̃.

f हमारे मकान में पाँच कमरे हैं । *hamāre makān mẽ pā̃c kamre haĩ.*

g हमारे परिवार में तीन बच्चे हैं । *hamāre parivār mẽ tīn bacce haĩ.*

h जी नहीं, वह बग़ीचे में है । *jī nahī̃, vah bag̱īce mẽ hai.*

i जी नहीं, उसका स्कूल यहाँ से दूर नहीं है ।
jī nahī̃, uskā skūl yahā̃ se dūr nahī̃ hai.

j दूसरे बच्चे भी बग़ीचे में हैं । *dūsre bacce bhī bag̱īce mẽ haĩ.*

k जी हाँ, कुत्ता हमारा है । *jī hā̃, kuttā hamārā hai.*

l उसका नाम मोती है । *uskā nām Motī hai.*

m जी हाँ, हमारे पास गाड़ी है । *jī hā̃, hamāre pās gāṛī hai.*

n जी हाँ, मेरे पास कम्प्यूटर है । *jī hā̃, mere pās kampyūṭar hai.*

Test yourself

1 कितनी कुरसियाँ *kitnī kursiyā̃,* कितने लोग *kitne log,* कितने पेड़ *kitne peṛ,* कितना पानी *kitnā pānī,* कितने पति *kitne pati.*

2 बूढ़ा *būṛhā refers* to 'old' people, पुराना *purānā* to 'old' things.

3 मेज़ पर क्या है ? *mez par kyā hai?* 'What's on the table?'

4 पैसा कहाँ है ? *paisā kahā̃ hai?* 'Where's the money?'

5 मकान में *makān mẽ,* कुरसी पर *kursī par,* घर पर *ghar par,* दिल्ली से *dillī se.*

6 **a** 'Near', as in मेरे घर के पास *mere ghar ke pās* 'near my home'; and **b** possession, as in मेरे पास पानी नहीं है *mere pās pānī nahī̃ hai* 'I don't have (any) water'.

7 For a noun that is followed by a postposition.

8 *-õ,* as in कमरों *kamrõ,* आदमियों *ādmiyõ,* घरों *gharõ.*

9 पड़ा *paṛā* refers to things, लेटा *leṭā* to people.

10 It comes immediately after the word it qualifies, as in मैं भी *maĩ bhī,* 'I too'.

UNIT 4

Language discovery 1

Commands and requests: **a** positive, **b** negative, **c** negative, **d** positive

Listening and speaking

Exercise 1

जाओ *jāo,* खाओ *khāo,* आओ *āo,* बैठो *baiṭho,* बोलो *bolo,* कहो *kaho,* दो *do,* लो *lo,* पियो *piyo,* करो *karo*

Exercise 2

जाइए *jāie,* खाइए *khāie,* आइए *āie,* बैठिए *baiṭhie,* बोलिए *bolie,* कहिए *kahie,* दीजिए *dījie,* लीजिए *lījie,* पीजिए *pījie,* कीजिए *kījie*

Exercise 3

a	मत जाओ । आओ, बैठो ।	*mat jāo! āo, baiṭho.*
b	बताओ, तुम कैसे हो ?	*batāo, tum kaise ho?*
c	समोसा खाओ, पानी पियो ।	*samosā khāo, pānī piyo.*
d	यह दूसरा समोसा भी लो ।	*yah dūsrā samosā bhī lo.*
e	मोती को समोसा न दो ।	*Motī ko samosā na do.*
f	और खाओ !	*aur khāo!*
g	खाली प्लेट मेज़ पर रखो ।	*k͟hālī pleṭ mez par rakho.*
h	अरे ! सिग्रेट न पियो !	*are! sigreṭ na piyo!*
i	और चाय लो ।	*aur cāy lo.*

Language discovery 2

Telling, saying, speaking, asking: **a** फिर से कहिए । *phir se kahie.* **b** मेरे भाई से पूछो । *mere bhāī se pūcho.* **c** धीरे-धीरे बोलिए । *dhīre-dhīre bolie.* **d** मेरी माता जी को मत बताओ ! *merī mātā jī ko mat batāo!*

Language Discovery 3

Routine events: वह पढ़ती है *vah paṛhtī hai,* वह पढ़ता है *vah paṛhtā hai,* वे पढ़ती हैं *ve paṛhtī haĩ,* हम पढ़ते हैं *ham paṛhte haĩ.*

Where do you live? What do you do? वह भारत में रहती है *vah bhārat mẽ rahtī hai,* मैं अंग्रेज़ी बोलती / बोलता हूँ *maĩ angrezī boltī/boltā hũ,* वह अस्पताल में काम करता है *vah aspatāl mẽ kām kartā hai*

Listen and understand

1 Her name is Urvashi and her husband is Banti. They live in Mumbai and work in a big bank there.

2 1d, 2c, 3a, 4f, 5e, 6g, 7b

Go further

वह स्कूल नहीं जाती *vah skūl nahī̃ jātī*

Storyline

1 The conversation is about work.

2a Javed teaches history (इतिहास *itihās*). **b** Javed's wife works in a hospital. **c** She is a doctor.

3 Raju and Javed both eat meat.

4 **a** Raju. **b** Javed. **c** Never, Geeta does not drink alcohol.

Practice

Exercise 1

a	घर में शराब मत पियो/पीजिए ।	*ghar mẽ śarāb mat piyo/pījie.*
b	ध्यान से सुनो/सुनिए ।	*dhyān se suno/sunie.*
c	यह पत्र मनोज को भेजो/भेजिए ।	*yah patr Manoj ko bhejo/bhejie.*
d	घर जाओ/जाइए ।	*ghar jāo/jāie.*
e	मुझको उसका नाम बताओ/बताइए ।	*mujhko uskā nām batāo/batāie.*
f	ये दो समोसे खाओ/खाइए ।	*ye do samose khāo/khāie.*
g	सितार बजाओ/बजाइए ।	*sitār bajāo/bajāie.*
h	मेरे पड़ोसी से पूछो/पूछिए ।	*mere paṛosī se pūcho/pūchie.*
i	यह पैसा मेरी पत्नी को दो/दीजिए ।	*yah paisā merī patnī ko do/dījie.*
j	आज गाड़ी मत चलाओ/चलाइए ।	*āj gāṛī mat calāo/calāie.*
k	धीरे धीरे बोलो/बोलिए ।	*dhīre dhīre bolo/bolie.*

Exercise 2

a	राम से पूछिए ।	*Rām se pūchie.*	Ask Ram.
b	बच्चों को मत बताना ।	*baccõ ko mat batānā.*	Don't tell the children.
c	चाचा जी से हिन्दी बोलो ।	*cācā jī se hindī bolo.*	Speak Hindi with Uncle.
d	मनोज से बात कीजिए ।	*Manoj se bāt kījie.*	Talk to Manoj.
e	गीता से पैसा माँगना ।	*Gītā se paisā mā̃gnā.*	Ask Geeta for money.

Exercise 3

a मेरा भाई दिल्ली में रहता है । मेरी बहिन दिल्ली में रहती है ।
merā bhāī dillī mẽ rahtā hai. merī bahin dillī mẽ rahtī hai.

b मैं हिन्दी समझता हूँ/समझती हैं । हम हिन्दी समझते हैं ।
maĩ hindī samajhtā hū̃/samajhtī haĩ. ham hindī samajhte haĩ.

c लड़का गाड़ी बहुत तेज़ चलाता है । लड़की गाड़ी बहुत तेज़ चलाती है ।
laṛkā gāṛī bahut tez calātā hai. laṛkī gāṛī bahut tez calātī hai.

d मेरा पति हिन्दी बोलता है । मेरी पत्नी हिन्दी बोलती है ।
merā pati hindī boltā hai. merī patnī hindī boltī hai.

e कौन अँग्रेज़ी बोलता है ? कौन अँग्रेज़ी बोलती है ?
kaun ãgrezī boltā hai? kaun ãgrezī boltī hai?

Exercise 4

Mahesh plays the sitar, Suresh plays the tabla, and Dinesh, the speaker, plays the sarangi.

Test yourself

1. बैठना *baiṭhnā*, stem बैठ *baiṭh;* भेजना *bhejnā* stem भेज *bhej;* खाना *khānā*, stem खा *khā.*
2. और *aur* can mean 'more', as in और चाय *aur cāy* 'more tea', और समय *aur samay* 'more time'.
3. The implication may be that the command is to be acted on later, not immediately.
4. धीरे धीरे बोलिए । *dhīre dhīre bolie.*
5. से *se.*
6. इसको क्या कहते हैं ? *isko kyā kahte haĩ?*
7. है *hai* (the auxiliary verb can optionally be dropped from negative sentences).
8. The speaker shows greater respect to Arun by calling him '*jī*' and using a plural verb.
9. फ़र्श पर न बैठो । *farś par na baiṭho.*
10. पढ़ना *paṛhnā* '*to study* (or *to read*)', पढ़ाना *paṛhānā* 'to teach'.

UNIT 5

Language discovery 1

More obliques: उन से पूछो, मुझ से मत पूछो ! *un se pūcho, mujh se mat pūcho!* मुझ को वह किताब दीजिए । *mujh ko vah kitāb dījie.*

Storyline

1 tidying the house

2a in the cupboard **b** clean the room **c** where the newspaper is

Language discovery 2

Liking things: जी हाँ, मुझ को पपीता पसंद है । *jī hā̃, mujh ko papītā pasand hai.*

Needing and wanting things: मीना को बिस्कुट चाहिए ? *Mīnā ko biskuṭ cāhie?*

Saying *I know*: मुझ को मालूम नहीं है कि कैसी गाड़ी है । *mujh ko mālūm nahī̃ hai ki kaisī gāṛī hai.* आप को मालूम है कि मेरे भाई को क्या पसंद है । *āp ko mālūm hai ki mere bhāī ko kyā pasand hai.*

Storyline

1 a convenience store

2a He wants to write something **b** a blue one **c** it's on the box

Speaking

मुझ को टार्च चाहिए	*mujh ko ṭārc cāhie*
मुझ को छोटा टार्च चाहिए	*mujh ko choṭā ṭārc cāhie*
मुझ को कलम चाहिए	*mujh ko kalam cāhie*
जी हाँ, यह मुझ को बहत पसंद है	*jī hā̃, yah mujh ko bahut pasand hai*
मुझ को मालूम नहीं	*mujh ko mālūm nahī̃*
नहीं धन्यवाद, उस को कुछ नहीं चाहिए	*nahī̃ dhanyavad, us ko kuch nahī̃ cāhie*

Language discovery 3

Writing

various answers are possible

The general and the particular: वह पेड़ लंबा है । *vah peṛ lambā hai.* पेड़ लंबे होते हैं । *peṛ lambe hote haĩ.*

Storyline

1 four days; he is leaving on Friday

2a a phone **b** 2000 rupees

3 It is dirty and the fan doesn't work.

4a There is no electricity. **b** बहुत अच्छा *bahut acchā* 'very good'

Language discovery 4

Quantities: मुझ को तीन किलो चावल चाहिए । *mujh ko tīn kilo cāval cāhie.* मुझ को एक चम्मच चीनी चाहिए । *mujh ko ek cammac cīnī cāhie.*

Practice

Exercise 1

a बहुत अच्छी है, धन्यवाद । *bahut acchī hai, dhanyavād.*

b जी हाँ, घर में सब लोग ठीक हैं । *jī hā̃, ghar mẽ sab log ṭhīk haĩ.*

c मुझको चावल चाहिए । *mujhko cāval cāhie.*

d पाँच किलो दीजिए । *pā̃c kilo dījie.*

e चीनी भी चाहिए । दो किलो देना । *cīnī bhī cāhie. do kilo denā.*

f हाँ, एक टिकिया साबुन । *hā̃, ek ṭikiyā sābun.*

g नहीं, वह सब नहीं चाहिए । *nahī̃, vah sab nahī̃ cāhie.*

h यहाँ से काफ़ी दूर है, लेकिन मेरे पास गाड़ी है ।
yahā̃ se kāfī dūr hai, lekin mere pās gāṛī hai.

i जी नहीं, ये मेरी नहीं हैं । *jī nahī̃, ye merī nahī̃ haĩ.*

j जी नहीं, गाड़ी दुकान के बहुत पास खड़ी है ।
jī nahī̃, gāṛī dukān ke bahut pās khaṛī hai.

Exercise 2

a मुझको तीन समोसे चाहिए ।
mujhko tīn samose cāhie.

b उनको यह मकान पसंद नहीं है, छोटा मकान पसंद है ।
unko yah makān pasand nahī̃ hai, choṭā makān pasand hai.

c मुझको यह कमरा पसंद नहीं है, कोई दूसरा कमरा दिखाइए ।
mujhko yah kamrā pasand nahī̃ hai, koī dūsrā kamrā dikhāie.

d आप कहाँ रहते हैं ? हम पुरानी दिल्ली में रहते हैं ।
āp kahā̃ rahte haĩ? ham purānī dillī mẽ rahte haĩ.

e आपका मकान हमारे मकान से बहुत दूर नहीं है । कल आना ।
āpkā makān hamāre makān se bahut dūr nahī̃ hai. kal ānā.

f मुझको मालूम है कि मेरे अध्यापक यहाँ नहीं रहते ।
mujhko mālūm hai ki mere adhyāpak yahā̃ nahī̃ rahte.

g मुझको मालूम है कि आपके अध्यापक कहाँ रहते हैं ।
mujhko mālūm hai ki āpke adhyāpak kahā̃ rahte haĩ.

h दिल्ली में मकान बहुत महँगे होते हैं । *dillī mẽ makān bahut mahã̄ge hote haĩ.*

i दादा जी बहुत सुन्दर हिन्दी बोलते हैं। *Dādā jī bahut sundar hindī bolte haĩ.*

j हमको ये काले जूते नहीं चाहिए। *hamko ye kāle jūte nahī̃ cāhie.*

Exercise 3

a इस कुर्सी पर मत बैठो। *is kursi par mat baiṭho.*

b मुझ को वह कलम दीजिए। *mujh ko vah kalam dījie.*

c कुछ और खाइए। *kuch aur khāie.*

d पानी पियो। *pānī piyo.*

e यहाँ आइए। *yahā̃ āie.*

Exercise 4

a मेरी कॉपी मेज़ पर पड़ी है। *merī kāpī mez par paṛī hai.*

b उस लड़के को कुछ मत बताओ। *us laṛke ko kuch mat batāo.*

c खाना इन डिब्बों में रखता हूँ। *khānā in ḍibbõ mẽ rakhtā hū̃.*

d ये फूल उन लड़कियों को दीजिए। *ye phūl un laṛkiõ ko dījie.*

e उस दूकान में अच्छे कपड़े मिलते हैं। *us dūkān mẽ acche kapṛe milte haĩ.*

Test yourself

1 'She speaks Hindi' is वह हिन्दी बोलती है *vah hindī boltī hai,* which works like the English, but 'She likes Hindi' becomes उसको हिन्दी पसंद है *usko hindī pasand hai* in which 'Hindi' (and not 'she') is the subject.

2 किसको *kisko* means 'to whom', किस *kis* being the oblique of कौन *kaun* 'who?'.

3 Because the subject of the verb is दिल्ली *dillī.*

4 मिलना *milnā* often means 'to get', and the thing 'got' is its subject. यहाँ फल मिलता है *yahā̃ phal miltā hai* 'You can get fruit here (fruit is available here).'

5 मुझको दो और चाबियाँ चाहिए। *mujhko do aur cābiyā̃ cāhie*

6 Because A is a *general* statement (talking about the house market overall), whereas B targets some *particular* houses.

7 हमको तीन कप काफ़ी दीजिए/देना। *hamko tīn kap kāfī dījie/denā.*

8 लाल साड़ियाँ *lāl sāṛiyā̃,* अच्छी चीज़ें *acchī cīzẽ,* छोटी-सी डिब्बियाँ *choṭī-sī ḍibbiyā̃,* सुन्दर हाथी *sundar hāthī* !

9 दरवाज़ा खोल ! *darvāzā khol!* (using the तू *tū* form of the command).

10 The first means 'Clean the room', the second 'Get the room cleaned'.

UNIT 6

Language discovery 1

Possession and to have: मुझ को उस लड़के के जूते पसंद हैं *mujh ko us laṛke ke jūte pasand haĩ,* मुझ को राम की किताबें दीजिए *mujh ko rām kī kitābẽ dījie*
Do you have brothers and sisters? मेरी तीन बहिनें हैं । मेरा कोई भाई नहीं है । *merā tīn bahinẽ haĩ. merā koī bhāī nahī̃ hai.*

Listen and understand

1a राम का पिता *Rām kā pita*

b राम की माता *Rām kī mātā*

c राम की बहिन *Rām kī bahin*

d राम की बहिन का नाम *Rām kī bahin kā nām*

e राम का भाई *Rām kā bhāī*

f राम के भाई का नाम *Rām ke bhāī kā nām*

g राम का कुत्ता *Rām kā kuttā*

h कुत्ते का नाम *kutte kā nām*

i आदमी का नाम *ādmī kā nām*

j इस आदमी का नाम *is ādmī kā nām*

k उस आदमी का नाम *us ādmī kā nām*

2 a false **b** true **c** true **d** false **e** false

Language discovery 2

How old are you?: a मैं तेरह साल की हूँ । *maĩ terah sāl kī hū̃.* **b** मैं नौ साल का हूँ । *maĩ nau sāl kā hū̃.*

Listening

1 a5, b1, d3, e2
2 Jyoti, ज्योति छह साल की है । *Jyoti chah sāl kī hai.*
Someone is there: a Please don't tell anyone anything. **b** कोई बात नहीं *koī bāt nahī̃*

Storyline

1 Raju addresses Pratap informally, using तुम *tum.*
2a Pratap is 21. **b** He doesn't have any sisters.

Listening and speaking

Answer the questions for yourself:

1 Sample answers:

मेरा कोई भाई नहीं है । *merā koī bhāī nahī̃ hai.*

मेरी दो बहिनें हैं । *merī do bahinẽ haĩ.*

जी हाँ, एक कुत्ता है । दो बिल्लियाँ भी हैं ।
jī hā̃, ek kuttā hai. do billiyā̃ bhī haĩ.

2 a3, b5, c1, d7, e2, f8, g4, h6

Storyline

1 Manoj wants to smoke.

2a Never; he doesn't smoke. **b** He doesn't have money to buy cigarettes. **c** He says it's Pratap's cigarette.

Listen and understand

a wrong, **b** correct, **c** correct, **d** wrong, **e** wrong, **f** wrong

Language discovery 4

Let me: राम की माँ उसको कॉफ़ी पीने नहीं देती *Rām kī mā̃ usko kāfī pine nahī̃ detī,* मुझ को सिनेमा जाने दीजिए *mujh ko sinemā jāne dījie*

Storyline

1 Geeta is talking to Manoj's father (Raju). **2a** because he is a good boy and he studies hard in school **b** America

Practice

Exercise 1

a मुझको अमरीका जाने दीजिए । *mujhko amrīkā jāne dījie.*

b मुझको गाड़ी चलाने दीजिए । *mujhko gāṛī calāne dījie.*

c मुझको खाना खाने दीजिए । *mujhko khānā khāne dījie.*

d मुझको काम करने दीजिए । *mujhko kām karne dījie.*

e मुझको आपसे बात करने दीजिए । *mujhko āpse bāt karne dījie.*

f उसको सिगरेट पीने दीजिए । *usko sigreṭ pīne dījie.*

g हमको अध्यापक से कुछ कहने दीजिए । *hamko adhyāpak se kuch kahne dījie.*

h उसको हिन्दी सीखने दीजिए । *usko hindī sīkhne dījie.*

i बच्चों को समोसे खाने दीजिए । *baccõ ko samose khāne dījie.*

j हमको यहाँ रहने दीजिए । *hamko yahā̃ rahne dījie.*

Exercise 2

a	फलवाला फल बेचता है !	*phalvālā phal bectā hai!*
b	अख़बारवाला अख़बार बेचता है !	*akhbārvālā akhbār bectā hai!*
c	दूधवाला दूध बेचता है !	*dūdhvālā dūdh bectā hai!*
d	अध्यापक पढ़ाता है ।	*adhyāpak paṛhātā hai.*
e	स्कूल में बच्चे पढ़ते हैं ।	*skūl mẽ bacce paṛhte haĩ.*
f	घर पर बच्चे खेलते हैं ।	*ghar par bacce khelte haĩ.*
g	ड्राइवर गाड़ी चलाता है ।	*ḍrāivar gāṛī calātā hai.*
h	दुकानदार माल बेचता है ।	*dukāndār māl bectā hai.*

Exercise 3

Sample answers:

a	मैं लन्दन में रहता हूँ ।	*maĩ landan mẽ rahtā hū̃.*
b	मैं हिन्दी पढ़ाता हूँ ।	*maĩ hindī paṛhātā hū̃.*
c	जी नहीं, मैं सितार नहीं बजाता, सिर्फ़ सुनता हूँ !	*jī nahī̃, maĩ sitār nahī̃ bajātā, sirf suntā hū̃!*
d	मैं कई अख़बार पढ़ता हूँ ।	*maĩ kaī akhbār paṛhtā hū̃.*
e	मैं चार भाषाएँ बोलता हूँ ।	*maĩ cār bhāṣāẽ boltā hū̃.*

Exercise 4

a जगदीश मनोज का अख़बार पढ़ता है ।
Jagdīś Manoj kā akhbār paṛhtā hai.

b मेरे दो भाई एक बड़े दफ़्तर में काम करते हैं ।
mere do bhāī ek baṛe daftar mẽ kām karte haĩ.

c मेरी बहिन मेरे भाई की गाड़ी चलाती है ।
merī bahin mere bhāī kī gāṛī calātī hai.

d वह सिर्फ़ हिन्दी बोलता है, अँग्रेज़ी नहीं बोलता ।
vah sirf hindī boltā hai, ãgrezī nahī̃ boltā.

e हमारे अध्यापक तीन भाषाएँ बोलते हैं ।
hamāre adhyāpak tīn bhāṣāẽ bolte haĩ.

f उसके बच्चे बग़ीचे में क्रिकेट खेलते हैं ।
uske bacce bagīce mẽ krikeṭ khelte haĩ.

g हमारे माता-पिता गोश्त नहीं खाते हैं ।
hamāre mātā-pitā gośt nahī̃ khāte haĩ.

h आप कहाँ काम करते हैं ? आप कहाँ रहते हैं ?
āp kahā̃ kām karte haĩ? āp kahā̃ rahte haĩ?

i आपका छोटा भाई क्या करता है ?
āpka choṭā bhāī kyā kartā hai?

j आपकी माता जी कितनी भाषाएँ बोलती हैं ?
āpkī mātā jī kitnī bhāṣāẽ boltī haĩ?

Exercise 5

a मुझ को रेडियो सुनने दीजिए । *mujh ko reḍio sunne dījie.*

b मुझ को सिग्रेट पीने दीजिए । *mujh ko sigreṭ pīne dījie.*

c मुझ को यहाँ बैठने दीजिए । *mujh ko yahā̃ baiṭhne dījie.*

d मुझ को क्रिकेट खेलने दीजिए । *mujh ko krikeṭ khelne dījie.*

e मुझ को आराम करने दीजिए । *mujh ko ārām karne dījie.*

Test yourself

1 उस *us* is oblique because of the postposition की *kī,* which in turn is feminine to agree with बिल्ली *billī.*

2 मेरी बहिन बारह साल की है *merī bahin bārah sāl kī hai;* or मेरी बहिन की उम्र बारह साल है *merī bahin kī umr bārah sāl hai.*

3 'Don't mention it', or (more likely today!) 'No problem!'.

4 किसी *kisī.*

5 किसी को पानी चाहिए *kisī ko pānī cāhie.*

6 'We can't ask the teacher!'; हैं *haĩ* is optionally dropped because the statement is negative. (The word जी *jī* is not really translatable here.)

7 'To smoke' (though only when सिग्रेट *sigreṭ* is stated or clearly implied).

8 दस मरीज़ *das marīz,* ग्यारह विद्यार्थी *gyārah vidyārthī,* बारह भाषाएँ *bārah bhāṣāẽ,* तेरह आवाज़ें *terah āvāzẽ,* चौदह बच्चे *caudah bacce.*

9 The verb for the 'permitted action' appears in the oblique infinitive: मुझे जाने दो *mujhe jāne do* 'let me go', in which जाने *jāne* is the oblique of the infinitive जाना *jānā* 'to go'.

10 'About, some'–'about twenty people, some twenty people'.

UNIT 7

Language discovery 1

In the past (1): a मेरे दो भाई दिल्ली में रहते थे । *mere do bhāī dillī mẽ rahte the.* **b** ज्योति अस्पताल में काम करती थी । *Jyoti aspatāl mẽ kām kartī thī.*

In the past (2): मेरी बहिन अंग्रेज़ी पढ़ाती थी *merī bahin angrezī paṛhātī thī,* मेरी बहिनें अंग्रेज़ी पढ़ाती थीं *merī bahinẽ angrezī paṛhātī thī̃*

Speaking

Sample answers:

a बचपन में मैं एक छोटे शहर में रहता था । *bacpan mẽ maĩ ek choṭe śahar mẽ rahtā thā.*

b जी हाँ, ज़रुर, मैं स्कूल जाता था । *jī hã̄, zarūr, maĩ skūl jātā thā.*

c मेरे पिता जी एक फ़ैक्ट्री में काम करते थे । *mere pita jī ek faikṭrī mẽ kām karte the.*

d मेरी माँ घर का काम करती थीं । *merī mā̃ ghar kā kām kartī thī̃.*

e मेरी माँ और मेरी बहिनें खाना बनाती थीं । *merī mā̃ aur merī bahinẽ khānā banātī thī̃.*

Listening and speaking

a जगदीश जी वाराणसी में रहते थे ।
Jagdīś jī vārāṇasī mẽ rahte the.

b उनके परिवार में सात बच्चे थे ।
unke parivār mẽ sāt bacce the.

c उनकी बहिनें स्कूल जाना चाहती थीं, लेकिन उस ज़माने में बहुत कम लड़कियाँ स्कूल जाती थीं ।
unkī bahinẽ skūl jānā cāhtī thī̃, lekin us zamāne mẽ bahut kam laṛkiyā̃ skūl jātī thī̃.

d उनका स्कूल उनके घर से काफ़ी दूर था ।
unkā skūl unke ghar se kāfī dūr thā.

e जी नहीं, वे पैदल नहीं जाते थे, साइकिल से जाते थे ।
jī nahī̃, ve paidal nahī̃ jāte the, sāikil se jāte the.

Language discovery 2

Getting specific: a वह अख़्बार पढ़ता है । *vah akhbār paṛhtā hai.* **b** वह इस अख़्बार को पढ़ता है । *vah is akhbār ko paṛhtā hai.* Use को *ko* in the second sentence to show specificity.

A shortcut: a किसे मालूम है कि गीता जी कहाँ है ? *kise mālūm hai ki Gītā jī kahā̃ hai?* **b** किसे चाई चाहिए ? *kise cāī cāhie?*

Speaking

a मुझे यह होटल पसंद है । *mujhe yah hoṭal pasand hai.*

b यह होटल किसे पसंद नहीं है ? *yah hoṭal kise pasand nahī̃ hai?*

c हमें कमरा चाहिए । *hamẽ kamrā cāhie.*

d उन्हें भी कमरा चाहिए । *unhẽ bhī kamrā cāhie.*

e उसे मालूम है कि हमें कमरा चाहिए । *use mālūm hai ki hamẽ kamrā cāhie.*

f क्या तुम्हें यह कमरा पसंद नहीं है ? *kyā tumhẽ yah kamrā pasand nahī̃ hai?*

g तुम्हें कैसा कमरा चाहिए ? *tumhẽ kaisā kamrā cāhie?*

Storyline

1 the Prime Minister

2a he had a fever **b** they didn't have the money **c** Raju didn't know if the Prime Minister enjoyed his letters, because he didn't reply.

Language discovery 3

Adding emphasis (1): मैं भी हिंदी बोलता/बोलती हूँ *maĩ bhī hindī boltā/boltī hū̃* and मैं हिंदी भी बोलता/बोलती हूँ *maĩ hindī bhī boltā/boltī hū̃*
Adding emphasis (2): हमारे घर में, हम हिंदी ही बोलते हैं *hamāre ghar mẽ, ham hindī hī bolte haĩ*
Adding emphasis (3): मैं तो ठीक हूँ, पर मेरी बहिन को बुख़ार है *maĩ to ṭhīk hū̃, par merī bahin ko bukhār hai.*

Practice

Exercise 1

a जगदीश मनोज का अख़बार पढ़ता था ।
Jagdīś Manoj kā akhbār paṛhtā thā.

b मेरे दो भाई एक बड़े दफ़्तर में काम करते थे ।
mere do bhāī ek baṛe daftar mẽ kām karte the.

c मेरी बहिन मेरे भाई की गाड़ी चलाती थी ।
merī bahin mere bhāī kī gāṛī calātī thī.

d वह सिर्फ़ हिन्दी बोलता था, अँग्रेज़ी नहीं बोलता था ।
vah sirf hindī boltā thā, ãgrezī nahī̃ boltā thā.

e हमारे अध्यापक तीन भाषाएँ बोलते थे ।
hamāre adhyāpak tīn bhāṣāẽ bolte the.

f उसके बच्चे बग़ीचे में क्रिकेट खेलते थे ।
uske bacce bagīce mẽ krikeṭ khelte the.

g हमारे माता-पिता गोश्त नहीं खाते थे ।
hamāre mātā-pitā gośt nahī̃ khāte the.

h आप कहाँ काम करते थे ? आप कहाँ रहते थे ?
āp kahā̃ kām karte the? āp kahā̃ rahte the?

i आपका छोटा भाई क्या करता था ?
āpka choṭā bhāī kyā kartā thā?

j आपकी माता जी कितनी भाषाएँ बोलती थीं ?
āpkī mātā jī kitnī bhāṣāẽ boltī thī̃?

Exercise 2

a In Jagdish's family only the boys used to go to school.

b His school was very far from his house.

c At school everyone called him 'Master ji', not just the children.

d In his job the actual pay wasn't very good.

e Jagdish's mother only spoke Hindi.

f In those days the children, at least, were very happy.

g There wasn't actually a garden, but there were lots of places for playing in.

h As for the children, they used to sleep on the roof.

i In his childhood, Raju was very fond of writing letters.

j The Prime Minister was kind, but he used to have a lot of work.

Exercise 3

Sample answer:

हम लोग वाराणसी के पास एक छोटे गाँव में रहते थे । मेरे पिताजी स्कूल में अध्यापक थे । लेकिन वे नेता बनना चाहते थे । वे प्रधान मंत्री बनने के सपने देखते थे । मेरी माँ उनको "प्रधान मंत्री जी" ही कहती थीं । हमारा घर गंगा के किनारे पर था । हम नदी के किनारे बहुत खेलते थे ।

उस ज़माने में हम हमेशा बड़े शहरों के बारे में बात करते थे । मैं अपने भाइयों और दोस्तों से कहता था कि बड़े लोग बड़े शहरों में ही रहते हैं । मैं भी बड़ा आदमी बनना चाहता था, मैं भी बड़े शहर में रहना चाहता था । मैं अब लंदन में रहता हूँ और मुझे मालूम है कि बड़े शहर की ज़िन्दगी कैसी होती है ... मैं एक छोटे गाँव में रहना चाहता हूँ !

ham log vārāṇasī ke pās ek choṭe gā̃v mẽ rahte the. mere pitājī skūl mẽ adhyāpak the. lekin ve netā bannā cāhte the. ve pradhān mantrī banne ke sapne dekhte the. merī mā̃ unko 'pradhān mantrī jī' hī kahtī thī̃. hamārā ghar gangā ke kināre par thā. ham nadī ke kināre bahut khelte the.

us zamāne mẽ ham hameśā baṛe śaharõ ke bāre mẽ bāt karte the. maĩ apne bhāiyõ aur dostõ se kahtā thā ki baṛe log baṛe śaharõ mẽ hī rahte haĩ. maĩ bhī baṛā ādmī bannā cāhtā thā, maĩ bhī baṛe śahar mẽ rahnā cāhtā thā. maĩ ab landan mẽ rahtā hū̃ aur mujhe mālūm hai ki baṛe śahar kī zindagī kaisī hotī hai ... maĩ ek choṭe gā̃v mẽ rahnā cāhtā hū̃!

Exercise 4

a He wants a job.

b He doesn't like working hard.

c She has a cold.
d She enjoys playing the sitar.
e He likes writing letters.
f They need a new house.
g He has a bit of a fever.

Test yourself

1 'was' – था *thā*, थी *thī*. 'were' – थे *the*, थीं *thī̃*.
2 On the last syllable of the auxiliary verb: थी *thī* becomes थीं *thī̃*.
3 It gives the sense 'all four'. 'All four children used to go to school'.
4 When the object of a verb is a person, it is 'specific' and requires को *ko*.
5 मुझे मालूम है कि तुम्हें कुछ पैसा चाहिए ।
mujhe mālūm hai ki tumhẽ kuch paisā cāhie.
6 Although Ram is OK, someone else may not be.
7 यहीं *yahī̃* is the emphatic form of यहाँ *yahā̃* 'here' and means 'right here'; यही *yahī* is the emphatic form of यह *yah* 'this, he, is, she, it' and means 'this very one' etc.
8 मुझे जुकाम है *mujhe zukām hai.*
9 'I know Hindi.'
10 फल खाइए, पानी पीजिए *phal khāie, pānī pījie.*

UNIT 8

Language discovery 1

Comparisons: a यह सबसे सुंदर साड़ी है । *yah sabse sundar sāṛī hai.*
b मनोज मीना से लंबा है । *Manoj Mīnā se lambā hai.*
c वह कमरा ज़्यादा बड़ा है । *vah kamrā zyādā baṛā hai.*

Listening and speaking

a जी हाँ, ओम शंकर से बड़ा है । *jī hā̃, Om Śankar se baṛā hai.*
b दो बच्चे रीता से छोटे हैं । *do bacce Rītā se choṭe haĩ.*
c सबसे बड़ा लड़का शिव है । *sabse baṛā laṛkā Śiv hai.*
d सबसे छोटा लड़का शंकर है । *sabse choṭā laṛkā Śankar hai.*
e ओम सिर्फ़ एक बच्चे से बड़ा है । *Om sirf ek bacce se baṛā hai.*
f जी नहीं, रीता शिव से छोटी है । *jī nahī̃, Rītā Śiv se choṭī hai.*
g जी नहीं, रीता ओम से छोटी नहीं है । *jī nahī̃, Rītā Om se choṭī nahī̃ hai.*
h जी नहीं, रीता शंकर से बड़ी है । *jī nahī̃, Rītā Śankar se baṛī hai.*
i मुझे तो सभी तस्वीरें बहुत पसंद हैं ! *mujhe to sabhī tasvīrẽ bahut pasand haĩ!*

Continuous tense: sentence **b** is continuous.

Storyline

1 the Taj Hotel **2a** having tea with some friends **b** talking to a girl **c** He is making dinner and he needs help

Speaking

1 जावेद पत्र लिख रहा है । *Javed part likh rahā hai.*

2 दो लड़कियाँ ताश खेल रही हैं । *do laṛkiyā̃ tāś khel rahī haĩ.*

3 कोई आदमी खाना तैयार कर रहा है । *koī ādmī khānā taiyār kar rahā hai.*

4 कुत्ता सो रहा है । *kuttā so rahā hai.*

5 सीता फ़ोन पर बात कर रही है । *Sītā fon par bāt kar rahī hai.*

6 गीता और राजू शराब पी रहे हैं । *Gītā aur Rājū śarāb pī rahe haĩ.*

7 राम बर्तन माँज रहा है । *Rām bartan mā̃j rahā hai.*

8 उषा दौड़ रही है । *Uṣā dauṛ rahā hai.*

Language discovery 2

One's own: a मैं अपने कुछ दोस्तों से बात कर रहा हूँ । *maĩ apne kuch dostõ se bāt kar rahā hū̃.* **b** गीता अपनी किताब पढ़ रही है । *Gītā apnī kitāb paṛh rahī hai.*

Language review: imperfectives

1 He wants to ask for a job.

2a sixteen **b** He is hard-working, reads and writes, and knows a little English. **c** Jagdish tells him to come back tomorrow, but he says not to ask about wages yet.

Practice 1

1 **a** wrong **b** right **c** wrong **d** right **e** wrong **f** right

2 1g, 2e, 3h, 4c, 5a, 6b, 7f, 8d

Storyline

1 He can't do anything for himself, but he can help others.

2a the Prime Minister's doctor **b** He asks that Raju write back to say how his brother is.

Language discovery 3

When and how: अगले हफ़्ते वह जयपुर जा रही है *agle hafte vah Jaipur jā rahī hai* and वह आराम करने घर जा रहा है *vah ārām karne ghar jā rahā hai*

Adverbs and postpositions: **a** वह बुलबुल की तरह गाती है *vah bulbul kī tarah gātī hai* **b** मंदिर की ओर जाइए । मेरा घर उस के नज़दीक है । *mandir kī or jāie. merā ghar us ke nazdīk hai.* **c** आप के जूते मेज़ के नीचे हैं । *āp ke jute mez ke nīce haĩ.*

Practice 2

Exercise 1

Sample answers: इस होटल के पीछे *is hoṭal ke pīche* 'behind this hotel', इन लोगों की तरह *in logo kī tarah* 'like these people', सोमवार के बाद *somvār ke bād* 'after Monday'

Exercise 2

a आप उनसे ज़्यादा होशियार नहीं हैं ।
āp unse zyādā hośiyār nahī̃ haĩ.

b मैं अपने भाई से बड़ी हूँ लेकिन आपसे छोटी हूँ ।
maĩ apne bhāī se baṛī hū̃ lekin āpse choṭī hū̃.

c मेरी दूसरी बहिन सबसे होशियार है ।
merī dūsrī bahin sabse hośiyār hai.

d कुछ लोग कहते हैं कि हिन्दी अँग्रेज़ी से ज़्यादा आसान है ।
kuch log kahte haĩ ki hindī ãgrezī se zyādā āsān hai.

e माँ सोचती हैं कि मेरी बहिन मुझसे ज़्यादा सुंदर है ।
mā̃ soctī haĩ ki merī bahin mujhse zyāda sundar hai.

f पिताजी माताजी से ज़्यादा जानते हैं लेकिन वे कुछ नहीं कह सकते हैं ।
pitājī mātājī se zyādā jānte haĩ lekin ve kuch nahī̃ kah sakte haĩ.

g उनका मकान हमारे मकान से ज़्यादा बड़ा और सुंदर है ।
unkā makān hamāre makān se zyādā baṛā aur sundar hai.

h मैं आपसे ज़्यादा होशियार हूँ ।
maĩ āpse zyādā hośiyār hū̃.

i आपकी भाषा मेरी भाषा से ज़्यादा मुश्किल है ।
āpkī bhāṣā merī bhāṣā se zyādā muśkil hai.

Exercise 3

a हम लोग अपने दोस्तों को खाना खाने बुला रहे हैं ।
ham log apne dostõ ko khānā khāne bulā rahe haĩ.
We're inviting our friends for a meal.

b मैं खाना तैयार कर रहा हूँ । *maĩ khānā taiyār kar rahā hū̃.*
I am preparing the food.

c वे लोग शाम को आ रहे हैं । *ve log śām ko ā rahe haĩ.*

They are coming in the evening.

d वे अपने बच्चों और दोस्तों को भी ला रहे हैं ।

ve apne baccõ aur dostõ ko bhī lā rahe haĩ.

They're bringing their children and friends, too.

e मेरी पत्नी कह रही है कि उनके बच्चे मोती को मार रहे हैं ।

merī patnī kah rahī hai ki unke bacce Motī ko mār rahe haĩ.

My wife is saying that their children are hitting Moti.

f दादी जी हमारी मदद नहीं कर रही हैं, सिर्फ़ रेडियो सुन रही हैं ।

dādī jī hamārī madad nahī̃ kar rahī haĩ, sirf reḍiyo sun rahī haĩ.

Grandma isn't helping us, she's only listening to the radio.

g हमारा कुकर ठीक से काम नहीं कर रहा है ।

hamārā kukar ṭhīk se kām nahī̃ kar rahā hai.

Our cooker isn't working properly.

h हमारे दोस्त कह रहे हैं कि बाथरूम में पानी नहीं आ रहा है ।

hamāre dost kah rahe haĩ ki bāthrūm mẽ pānī nahī̃ ā rahā hai.

Our friends are saying that there isn't any water ['coming'] in the bathroom.

Exercise 4

Sample answers:

a अपने ख़ाली समय में मैं अपने दोस्तों से मिलता हूँ ।

apne khālī samay mẽ maĩ apne dostõ se miltā hū̃.

b मुझे दोनों पसंद हैं – घर पर रहना भी और बाहर जाना भी !

mujhe donõ pasand haĩ – ghar par rahnā bhī aur bāhar jānā bhī. (Note भी… भी *bhī … bhī* 'both … and'.)

c क्योंकि मेरे बहुत-से हिन्दुस्तानी दोस्त हैं ।

kyõki mere bahut-se hindustānī dost haĩ.

d जी नहीं, मेरे ख़याल में दोनों भाषाएँ काफ़ी मुश्किल हैं !

jī nahī̃, mere khyāl se donõ bhāṣāẽ kāfī muśkil haĩ!

e जी हाँ, मेरे हिन्दुस्तानी दोस्त हिन्दी बोलते हैं ।

jī hā̃, mere hindustānī dost hindī bolte haĩ.

f आज मैं यह किताब लिख रहा हूँ !

āj maĩ yah kitāb likh rahā hū̃!

g अपनी छुट्टियों में मैं भारत या ग्रीस [Greece] जाता हूँ ।

apnī chuṭṭiyõ mẽ maĩ bhārat yā grīs jātā hū̃.

h मैं अभी सोच रहा हूँ कि यह पाठ [lesson] बहुत लंबा है !

maĩ abhī soc rahā hū̃ ki yah pāṭh bahut lambā hai!

Test yourself

1 The hardworking postposition से *se*.

2 The first means 'she speaks Hindi' and is habitual; the second means 'she is speaking Hindi' and refers to what is happening at the present time.

3 की तरफ़ *kī taraf* means 'towards', and की तरह *kī tarah* means 'like, in the manner of'.

4 We are doing our work is हम अपना काम कर रहे हैं *ham apnā kām kar rahe haĩ.* Any possessive pronoun is replaced by अपना *apnā* when referring to the subject of the clause (i.e.'our' and 'we' both refer to the same people).

5 प्रिय *priy.*

6 Various adverbial expressions, such as इन दिनों *in dinõ* 'these days' and इस साल 'this year', use the oblique case without postposition.

7 कितने दिन, कितने हफ़्ते, कितने महीने, कितने साल
kitne din, kitne hafte, kitne mahīne, kitne sāl

8 (a) बजाना *bajānā,* (b) खेलना *khelnā.*

9 क्या वाराणसी भारत का सबसे पुराना शहर है ?
kyā Vārāṇasī Bhārat kā sabse purānā śahar hai?

10 It is oblique: destinations of verbs of motion take the oblique case.

UNIT 9

Language discovery 1

The future tense: a मैं चाय पिऊँगी *maĩ cāy piū̃gī* **b** मैं चाय पिऊँगा *maĩ cāy piū̃gā*

Storyline

1 what they will do tomorrow

2a they will work **b** they don't have work tomorrow

Listening and speaking

Sample answers:

a आज रात को मैं हिन्दुस्तानी खाना खाऊँगा ।
āj rāt ko maĩ hindustānī khānā khāū̃gā.

b मैं शायद बीयर पिऊँगा ।
maĩ śāyad bīyar piū̃gā.

c आज मैं काम करूँगा और अपने बड़े बेटे से मिलने जाऊँगा ।
āj maĩ kām karũgā aur apne baṛe beṭe se milne jāũgā.

d कल सुबह मैं ब्रिटिश लाइब्रेरी [British Library] जाऊँगा ।
kal subah maĩ briṭiś lāibrerī jāũgā.

e अगर आप परसों लंदन आएँगे/आएँगी, तो आपसे ही मिलूँगा !
agar āp parsõ landan āẽge/āẽgī, to āpse hī milũgā!

Language discovery 2

Future verb endings (1):
वे मेहनत करेंगे *ve mehnat karẽge,* अगले हफ़्ते वह घर आएगा *agle hafte vah ghar āegā*

Future verb endings (2):
Tomorrow they (feminine) will come to our place *or* Tomorrow she (respectful) will come to our place.

Reported speech: मैं गोपाल की मदद करूँगी *maĩ Gopāl kī madad karũgī*

Storyline

The days ahead: 1 Monday **2a** go and meet his father **b** Saturday **c** study

Geeta's diary:

सोमवार *somvār*	घर पर रहना ghar par rahnā
मंगलवार *mangalvār*	दिल्ली जाना *dillī jānā*
बुधवार *budhvār*	कुछ चीज़ें ख़रीदना *kuch cīzẽ kharīdnā*
गुरुवार *guruvār*	घर वापस आना *ghar vāpas ānā*
शुक्रवार *śukravār*	आराम करना *ārām karnā*
शनिवार *śanivār*	सीता के यहाँ जाना *Sītā ke yahā̃ jānā*
रविवार *ravivār*	अगले हफ़्ते की तैयारियाँ करना *agle hafte kī taiyāriyā̃ karnā*

Language discovery 3

Ifs and maybes (1): The speaker could be male or female; you can't tell because the verb is subjunctive and therefore has no gender marker.

Ifs and maybes (2):
अगर आप रजनी को बताएँ तो वह नाराज़ होगी *agar āp Rajnī ko batāẽ to vah nārāz hogī,* अगर राम कुत्ते को खिलाए तो वह वापस आएगा *agar Rām kutte ko khilāe to vah vāpas āegā*

Storyline

1 at home
2a He suggests making tea. **b** They will stay at home.

Language discovery 4

A suggestion or a command? On a road; it means *please drive slowly.*
I want to…/I want you to… गीता चाहती है कि उसकी बेटी पढ़े *Gītā cāhtī hai ki uskī beṭī paṛhe,* वह पढ़ना चाहता है *vah paṛhnā cāhtā hai*

Listening and speaking

Sample answers:

मैं चाहता हूँ कि तुम हमारे यहाँ ठहरो ।
maĩ cāhtā hū̃ ki tum hamāre yahā̃ ṭhaharo.

हम चाहते थे कि तुम्हारा दोस्त भी आए ।
ham cāhte the ki tumhārā dost bhī āe.

वे चाहते हैं कि वह अपना काम करें ।
ve cāhte haĩ ki vah apnā kām kare.

वह चाहता है कि तुम जाने की तैयारियाँ करो ।
vah cāhtā hai ki tum jāne kī taiyāriyā̃ karo.

मैं चाहती थी कि आप आराम करें ।
maĩ cāhtā thī ki āp ārām karẽ.

मेरी बहिन चाहती है कि तुम खाना बनाओ ।
merī bahin cāhtī hai ki tum khānā banāo.

Language discovery 5

So that, in order that: राहुल मेट्रो से जाता है ताकि वह जल्दी पहुँचे । *Rahul meṭro se jātā hai tāki vah jaldī pahũce.*

How long does it take? स्टेशन पहुंचने में आधा घंटा लगता है *sṭeśan pahũcne mẽ ādhā ghanṭā lagtā hai,* रात का खाना तैयार करने में तीन घंटे लगेंगे *rāt kā khānā taiyār karne mẽ tīn ghanṭā lagẽge*

Practice 2

Exercise 1

1e If the vegetable market is closed, get ('take') the vegetables tomorrow morning.

2d If you don't know the way, buy a map.

3c If you don't know the meaning of some/any word, look in a dictionary.

4b If you don't find a policeman at the roundabout, go to the police station.

5a If you don't get a room at the hotel, stay at my place.

6f If you turn into that narrow lane you'll see the café on your left ('the café will appear…').

Exercise 2

a दो लोगों के लिए कमरा चाहिए । हम दो दिन रहेंगे ।
do logõ ke lie kamrā cāhie. ham do din rahẽge.

b आज शाम को हमारे कुछ दोस्त हमसे मिलने आएँगे ।
āj śam ko hamāre kuch dost hamse milne āẽge.

c नाश्ते में क्या मिलेगा ?
nāśte mẽ kyā milegā?

d क्या रात का खाना भी मिलेगा ?
kyā rāt kā khānā bhī milegā?

e यहाँ से सिनेमा जाने में कितना समय लगेगा ? हम पैदल जाना चाहते हैं ।
yahā̃ se sinemā jāne mẽ kitnā samay lagegā? ham paidal jānā cāhte haĩ.

f मैं लंदन फ़ोन करना चाहता हूँ । क्या मैं अपने कमरे से ही फ़ोन कर सकता हूँ ?
maĩ landan fon karnā cāhtā hū̃. kyā maĩ apne kamre se hī fon kar sak tā hū̃?

g अगले हफ़्ते हम लोग आगरे और दिल्ली जाएँगे ।
agle hafte ham log āgre aur dillī jāẽge.

h क्या आज रात को हमारे दोस्त हमारे साथ खाना खा सकते हैं ?
kyā āj rāt ko hamāre dost hamāre sāth khānā khā sakte haĩ?

Exercise 3

a4, b6, c1, d2, e5, f3

Test yourself

1. You (numerical plural – more than one of you!) are being asked to your friend's place for dinner tomorrow night.
2. आएँगे *āẽge* can be used with हम *ham* 'we' and ये/वे *ye/ve* 'they'.
3. परसों शुक्रवार होगा । *parsõ śukravār hogā.*
4. The first is a straightforward 'polite' command; the second is more circumspect, because the subjunctive verb indicates a suggestion rather than a direct command.

5 वे चाहती हैं कि आप भी आएँ । *ve cahtī haĩ ki āp bhī āẽ.*

6 वे चाहती हैं कि तुम भी आओ । *ve cahtī haĩ ki tum bhī āo.*

7 मिले *mile* is subjunctive, as required by ताकि *tāki* 'so that'. सीट *sīṭ* is its subject.

8 क्या हमको नाश्ता मिलेगा ? *kyā hamko nāśtā milegā?* (हमको *hamko* would probably be dropped.)

9 How long will it take to clean the room?

10 हमारा कमरा आपके कमरे से थोड़ा बड़ा है ।
hamārā kamrā tumhāre kamre se thoṛā baṛā hai.

UNIT 10

Language discovery 1

The past tense: वह बोला *vah bola,* वह बोली *vah bolī,* वे बोलीं *ve bolī̃,* and हम बोले *ham bole*

Coming and going: Sentence **b** contains an irregular verb: गया *gayā*

Speaking

Exercise 1

Sample answers:

मीना स्टेशन पहुँची ।	*Mīnā sṭeśan pahũcī.*
राम हँसा ।	*Rām hãsā.*
गीता आई ।	*Gītā āī.*
मनोज घर गया ।	*Manoj ghar gayā.*
हम उठे ।	*ham uṭhe.*
प्रताप दौड़ा ।	*Pratāp dauṛā.*

Exercise 2

a	मनोज घर गया ।	*Manoj ghar gayā.*
b	राजू और राम बांहर गए ।	*Rājū aur Rām bāhar gae.*
c	सीता दिल्ली गई ।	*Sītā dillī gaī.*
d	कुछ नहीं हुआ ।	*kuch nahī̃ huā.*
e	मीना कल पहुँची ।	*Mīnā kal pahũcī.*
f	दादीजी परसों आईं ।	*Dādījī parsõ āī̃.*
g	मनोज मंगलवार को आया ।	*Manoj mangalvār ko āyā.*

Language discovery 2

Transitivity: **c** needs ने *ne*; the sentence should read: मनोज ने नई गाड़ी खरीदी । *Manoj ne naī gāṛī kharīdī.* The verbs उठना *uṭhnā,* जाना *jānā,* and पहुँचना *pahũcnā* are intransitive and never take the _ *ne* construction.

Practice 1

Exercise 1

a बनाया *banāyā*

b आईं *āī̃*

c आए *āe*

d बजाया *bajāyā*

e भौंका *bhaũkā*

f खाए *khāe*

g रहे *rahe*

h उठे *uṭhe*

Exercise 2

1 मैंने दो किताबें देखीं । *maĩne do kitābẽ dekhī̃.*
2 मैंने एक सिग्रेट देखा । *maĩne ek sigreṭ dekhā.*
3 मैंने एक अख़बार देखा । *maĩne ek akhbār dekhā.*
4 मैंने दो गाड़ियाँ देखीं । *maĩne do gāṛiyā̃ dekhī̃.*
5 मैंने एक गिलास देखा । *maĩne ek gilās dekhā.*
6 मैंने एक ट्रेन देखी । *maĩne ek ṭren dekhī.*
7 मैंने दो जूते देखे । *maĩne do jūte dekhe.*
8 मैंने तीन चाबियाँ देखीं । *maĩne tīn cābiyā̃ dekhī̃.*
9 मैंने दो हाथी देखे । *maĩne do hāthī dekhe.*
10 मैंने एक मकान देखा । *maĩne ek makān dekhā.*
11 मैंने दो कुत्ते देखे । *maĩne do kutte dekhe.*
12 मैंने एक बंदर देखा । *maĩne ek bandar dekhā.*
13 मैंने एक बिल्ली देखी । *maĩne ek billī dekhī.*
14 मैंने एक क़मीज़ देखी । *maĩne ek qamīz dekhī.*
15 मैंने एक दरवाज़ा देखा । *maĩne ek darvāzā dekhā.*
16 मैंने तीन बोतलें देखीं । *maĩne tīn botalẽ dekhī̃.*

Language discovery 3

Some special verbs: **a** उन्होंने इंतज़ार किया । *unhõne intazār kiyā.* **b** मैंने चाय पी । *maĩne cāy pī.*

Listen and understand

a गीता ने एक नई फ़िल्म देखी । *Gītā ne ek naī film dekhī.*
b राजू ने दो अख़बार ख़रीदे । *Rājū ne do akhbār kharīde.*
c मोती ने दस चपातियाँ खाईं । *Motī ne das capātiyā̃ khāī̃.*
d मीना ने दो कहानियाँ पढ़ीं । *Mīnā ne do kahāniyā̃ paṛhī̃.*
e हमने चार कुरते ख़रीदे । *hamne cār kurte kharīde.*
f उन्होंने मेज़ पर कुछ किताबें रखीं । *unhõne mez par kuch kitābẽ rakhī̃.*
g मैंने दीवार पर अपना नाम लिखा । *maĩne dīvār par apnā nām likhā.*
h मैंने कई बातें सुनीं । *maĩne kaī batẽ sunī̃.*
i मैंने एक ही भाषा सीखी । *maĩne ek hī bhāṣā sīkhī.*

Language discovery 4

A particular object: मैंने उन लड़कों को देखा । *maĩne un laṛkõ ko dekhā.*
Other perfective tenses: b, c, a

Storyline

1 He was in a good mood.
2a The night before it rained; this morning it was clear. **b** waking up Geeta **c** There was too much sugar in it.

Writing

a आज मैं जल्दी उठा/उठी । *āj maĩ jaldī uṭhā / uṭhī.*

b मेरे पिता जी ने मुझे छह बजे जगाया । *mere pitā jī ne mujhe chah baje jagāyā.*

c उन्होंने मेरे लिए नाश्ता तैयार किया । *unhõne mere lie naśtā taiyār kiyā.*

d फिर मैं अख़बार खरीदने बाहर गया/गई । *phir maĩ akhbār kharīdne bāhar gayā/gaī.*

e दूकान के पास मैं ने अपने चाचा जी की गाड़ी देखी । *dūkān ke pās maĩ ne apne cācā jī kī gāṛī dekhī.*

f मेरे चाचा जी दूकान में गए थे । *mere cācā jī dūkān mẽ gae the.*

g मेरे चाचा जी ने मुझे देखा और मुझसे पूछा कि तुम कैसे/कैसी हो । *mere cācā jī ne mujhe dekhā aur mujhse pūchā ki tum kaise/kaisī ho.*

h वे मेरे साथ घर आए और मैंने उनके लिए काफ़ी बनाई । *ve mere sāth ghar āe aur maĩne unke lie kāfī banāī.*

i मेरे पिता जी ने मुझसे पूछा कि अख़बार कहाँ है । *mere pitā jī ne mujhse pūchā ki akhbār kahā̃ hai.*

j मैंने कहा कि मैं अख़बार नहीं लाया/लाई हूँ, मैं चाचा जी लाया / लाई हूँ । *maĩne kahā ki maĩ akhbār nahī̃ lāyā/lāī hū̃, maĩ cācā jī lāyā/lāī hū̃.*

Storyline

1 She doesn't like toast and there was too much sugar in the tea. **2a** Shahrukh Khan **b** She had a headache so she took two pills.

Writing

a wrong; सबसे पहले राजू उठा *sabse pahle Rājū uṭhā* **b** right **c** right **d** wrong; गीता ने शिकायत की कि चाई में चीनी ज़्यादा थी *Gītā ne śikāyat kī ki cāī mẽ cīnī zyādā thī* **e** right **f** wrong; गीता ने गोलियाँ खाईं *Gītā ne goliyā̃ khāī̃.* **g** right

Speaking

a राजू ने चाई बनाई। *Rājū ne cāī banāī.*

b उसने गीता को जगाया। *usne Gītā ko jagāyā.*

c वह नीचे आई। *vah nice āī.*

d उसने केला खाया। *usne kelā khāyā.*

e उसने दो गोलियाँ भी खाईं। *usne do goliā̃ bhī khāī̃.*

f राजू ने चाय में बहुत ज़्यादा चीनी डाली थी।
Rājū ne cāy mẽ bahut zyādā cīnī ḍālī thī.

g क्या राजू ने कुछ खाया ? *kyā Rājū ne kuch khāyā?*

Language discovery 5

Linking two actions: सीता खाकर बाहर गई। *Sītā khākar bāhar gaī.*

Storyline

1 negative **2a** toast and oranges **b** tea and toast **c** Raju

Practice 2

Exercise 1

a जावेद ने मुझे फ़ोन करके बताया कि मेरी तबियत ख़राब है।
Jāved ne mujhe fon karke batāyā ki merī tabiyat kharāb hai.

b मैं जावेद के घर जाकर उसके कमरे में गया।
maĩ Jāved ke ghar jākar uske kamre mẽ gayā.

c जावेद का हाल देखकर मैंने डाक्टर को बुलाया।
Jāved kā hāl dekhkar maĩne ḍākṭar ko bulāyā.

d थोड़ी देर में आकर डाक्टर ने कहा कि जावेद बहुत ही कमज़ोर है।
thoṛī der mẽ ākar ḍākṭar ne kahā ki Jāved bahut hī kamzor hai.

e जावेद को कुछ गोलियाँ देकर डाक्टर ने कहा कि रोज़ दो गोलियाँ लेना।
Jāved ko kuch goliyā̃ dekar ḍākṭar ne kahā ki roz do goliyā̃ lenā.

f जावेद ने मुस्कराकर डाक्टर से धन्यवाद कहा ।
Jāved ne muskarākar ḍākṭar se dhanyavād kahā.

g डाक्टर ने मेरी तरफ़ देखकर कहा कि "अच्छा, तो मैं चलता हूँ ।"
ḍākṭar ne merī taraf dekhkar kahā ki 'acchā, to maĩ caltā hū̃'.

h मैंने कहा कि चाय पीकर जाइए । *maĩne kahā ki cāy pīkar jāie.*

i डाक्टर ने हँसकर कहा कि मैं चाय नहीं लूँगा, अपनी फ़ीस लूँगा !
ḍākṭar ne hãskar kahā ki maĩ cāy nahī̃ lū̃gā, apnī fīs lū̃gā!

Exercise 2

कल सुबह मैं छह बजे उठा । नाश्ता करके मैंने अपने भाई को फ़ोन किया । वह सो रहा था । मेरी आवाज़ सुनकर उसने कहा, "तुमने मुझे इतनी जल्दी क्यों जगाया ?" । मैंने कहा, "तुमको याद नहीं ? आज हम जयपुर जा रहे हैं !" उसने पूछा, "हम कितने बजे जा रहे हैं ?" । मैंने जवाब दिया, "हम दस बजे की गाड़ी पकड़ेंगे । तुम जल्दी तैयार हो जाओ !" उसने जँभाई लेकर कहा कि रात में उसने सपना देखा था । सपने में एक बूढ़ी औरत ने उससे कहा था कि आज तुम कहीं मत जाना ! घर पर ही रहना ! मैंने हँसकर कहा, "यह तो सपना ही था । उठो न ! तैयार हो जाओ ।"

गाड़ी ठीक दस बजे स्टेशन से चलने लगी । पर बीस-पच्चीस मिनट बाद वह रुकी । इंजन ख़राब हो गई थी । सुनसान जगह थी; पास में कोई गाँव या मकान नहीं था । जुलाई की गरमी में सारे यात्रियों ने गाड़ी से उतरकर कई घंटों तक कुछ छोटे पेड़ों के साये में इंतज़ार किया । भयंकर गरमी थी । तीन बजे एक दूसरी गाड़ी आकर रुकी । यह दूसरी गाड़ी यात्रियों को वापस दिल्ली ले आने आई थी ।

गाड़ी की कहानी हमने रेडियो पर ही सुनी । हमने उस बूढ़ी औरत की सलाह ली थी ! हम जयपुर कल जाएँगे ...

kal subah maĩ chah baje uṭhā. nāśtā karke maĩne apne bhāī ko fon kiyā. vah so rahā thā. merī āvāz sunkar usne kahā, 'tumne mujhe itnī jaldī kyõ jagāyā?' maĩne kahā, 'tumko yād nahī̃? āj ham jaypur jā rahe haĩ!' usne pūchā, 'ham kitne baje jā rahe haĩ?'. maĩne javāb diyā, 'ham das baje kī gāṛī pakaṛẽge. tum jaldī taiyār ho jāo!' usne jãbhāī lekar kahā ki rāt mẽ usne sapnā dekhā thā. sapne mẽ ek būṛhī aurat ne usse kahā thā ki āj tum kahī̃ mat jānā! ghar par hī rahnā! maĩne hãskar kahā, 'yah to sapnā hī thā. uṭho na! taiyār ho jāo.'
gāṛī ṭhīk das baje sṭeśan se calne lagī. par bīs-paccīs minaṭ bād vah rukī. injan <u>kh</u>arāb ho gaī thī. sunsān jagah thī; pās mẽ koī gā̃v yā makān nahī̃ thā. julāī kī garmī mẽ sāre yātriyõ ne gāṛī se utarkar kaī ghaṇṭõ tak kuch choṭe peṛõ ke sāye mẽ intazār kiyā. bhayankar garmī thī. tīn baje ek dūsrī gāṛī ākar rukī. yah dūsrī gāṛī yātriyõ ko vāpas dillī le āne āī thī. gāṛī kī kahānī hamne reḍiyo par hī sunī. hamne us būṛhī aurat kī salāh lī thī! ham jaypur kal jāẽge ...

Test yourself

1 We run every day: हम रोज़ दौड़ती हैं । *ham roz dauṛtī haĩ.*
We are running: हम दौड़ रही हैं । *ham dauṛ rahī haĩ.*
We shall run: हम दौड़ेंगी । *ham dauṛẽgī.*
We may perhaps run: हम शायद दौड़ें । *ham śāyad dauṛẽ*
We ran: हम दौड़ीं । *ham ḍauṛī̃.* Phew!

2 Did you have fun? Did you enjoy yourself?

3 The verb is feminine plural, so the subject must be either a group of females or a single female who is shown respect with an 'honorific' plural.

4 The first uses the ने *ne* construction because its verb is transitive and the verb agrees with its object (masculine खाना *khānā*); the second is intransitive ('to come' takes no object) and the verb agrees with its subject (feminine सीता *Sītā*).

5 मैंने कुछ हिन्दी सीखी । *maĩne kuch hindī sīkhī.* Or थोड़ी-सी *thoṛī-sī* instead of कुछ *kuch.*

6 मैंने खाना खाया, तुमने चाय पी, और पिताजी ने दो सिग्रेटें पीं । *maĩne khānā khāyā, tumne cāy pī, aur pitājī ne do sigreṭẽ pī̃.*

7 'Wash your hands and eat (your meal)' (or 'Wash your hands before you eat').

8 इधर आकर बैठो । *idhar ākar baiṭho.*

9 की *kī* is both the feminine possessive (मोहन की किताब *Mohan kī kitāb* 'Mohan's book'), and the feminine form of the past tense of करना *karnā* (सीता ने शिकायत नहीं की *Sītā ne śikāyat nahī̃ kī* 'Sita didn't complain').

10 **a** गोपाल ने किताब पढ़ी है *Gopāl ne kitāb paṛhī hai,* 'Gopal has read ...'
b गोपाल ने किताब पढ़ी थी *... paṛhī thī,* 'had read ...'
c गोपाल ने किताब पढ़ी होगी *...paṛhī hogī,* 'will/must have read ...'
d गोपाल ने किताब पढ़ी हो *...paṛhī ho,* 'may have read ...'.

UNIT 11

Language discovery 1

A verb with many meanings: लड़के बोलने लगे *laṛke bolne lage,* आज रश्मी खुश लगती है *āj Raśmī khuś lagtī hai.*

Storyline

1 Three landmarks are mentioned: a school, a cinema, a roundabout.

2a Chandrashekhar Azad Road **b** 8–10 minutes **c** 20–25 rupees; not more than 25 rupees

Practice 1

Exercise 1

Sample answers:

a मंदिर से निकलकर आप चंद्रशेखर आज़ाद रोड पर आगे जाइए। पुलिस स्टेशन के पास महात्मा गांधी मार्ग पर बाएँ मुड़िए। गोलचक्कर आएगा, आगे चलते जाइए। डाकख़ाना दाहिने हाथ पर होगा। *mandir se nikalkar āp Candraśekhar āzād roḍ par āge jāie. pulis steśan ke pās Mahātmā Gāndhī Marg par bāẽ muṛie. golcakkar āegā; āge calte jāie. ḍākkhānā dāhine hāth par hogā.*

b सिनेमा से निकलकर आप दाहिने मुड़िए। चंद्रशेखर आज़ाद रोड आएगा, वहाँ दाहिने मुड़िए। फिर महात्मा गांधी मार्ग पर बाएँ मुड़िए। सब्ज़ी मंडी बाएँ हाथ पर होगी। *sinema se nikalkar āp dāhine muṛie.Candraśekhar āzād Roḍ āegā; vahā̃ dāhine muṛie. phir Mahātmā Gāndhī Marg par bāẽ muṛie. sabzī manḍī bāẽ hāth par hogī.*

c स्टेशन से निकलकर दाहिने मुड़िए। थोड़ी दूरी पर बाएँ हाथ पर एक तंग गली आएगी। इस गली में मुड़ना। आगे चलकर एक चौड़ी सड़क आएगी जिसे चंद्रशेखर आज़ाद रोड कहते हैं। बाएँ मुड़िए। फिर महात्मा गांधी मार्ग को पारकर पुलिस स्टेशन दाहिने हाथ पर होगा। *sṭeśan se nikalkar dāhine muṛie. thoṛī dūrī par bāyẽ hāth par ek taṅg galī āegī. is galī mẽ muṛnā. āge calkar ek cauṛī saṛak āegī jise 'Candraśekhar Āzād roḍ' kahte haĩ. bāẽ muṛie. phir Mahātmā Gandhī Mārg ko pārkar pulis steśan dāhine hāth par hogā.*

Exercise 2

a wrong **b** right **c** right **d** right **e** right **f** wrong **g** right **h** wrong **i** wrong **j** right

Language discovery 2

The passive voice: मेज़ पर **किताबें** रखी गईं। *mez par **kitābẽ** rakhī gaĩ.* उन लोगों को **खाना** दिया जाएगा। *un logo ko **khānā** diyā jāegā.*

Practice 2

Exercise 1

a तमिल तमिलनाडू में बोली जाती है।
tamil tamilnāḍu mẽ bolī jātī hai.

b मराठी महाराष्ट्र में बोली जाती है।
marāṭhī mahārāṣṭra mẽ bolī jātī hai.

c केरल में मलयालम बोली जाती है।
keral mẽ malayālam bolī jātī hai.

d हिन्दी दस प्रदेशों में बोली जाती है।
hindī das pradeśõ mẽ bolī jātī hai.

e दिल्ली और बिहार के बीच उत्तर प्रदेश पाया जाता है ।
dillī aur bihār ke bīc uttar pradeś pāyā jātā hai.

Exercise 2

a खाया जाना *khāyā jānā*

b पिया जाना *piyā jānā*

c लाया जाना *lāyā jānā*

d लिखा जाना *likhā jānā,*

e डाला जाना *ḍālā jānā*

f बताया जाना *batāyā jānā*

g लिया जाना *liyā jānā*

h कहा जाना *kahā jānā*

Language discovery 3

Any tense can have a passive verb: किताब राजू से पढ़ी गई *kitāb Rājū se paṛhī gayī,* मोहित को मुझसे पैसा दिया जाएगा *Mohit ko mujhse paisa diyā jāegā*

Storyline

1 He gives him four chores: store the goods in the little room, clean the shop, close up at 8 o'clock, and get the clean clothes from the cleaner's.

2a He is tired. **b** 200 rupees

3a गोपाल को शर्मा जी से बुलाया गया ।
Gopāl ko Śarmā jī se bulāyā gayā.

b सामान छोटे कमरे में रखा जाएगा ।
sāmān choṭe kamre mẽ rakhā jāegā.

c कमरे की सफ़ाई गोपाल से की जाएगी ।
kamre kī safāī Gopāl se kī jāegī.

d दुकान को आठ बजे बंद किया जाएगा ।
dukān ko āṭh baje band kiyā jāegā.

e शर्मा जी के साफ़ कपड़े धोबी के यहाँ से लाए जाएँगे ।
Śarmā jī ke sāf kapṛe dhobī ke yahā̃ se lāe jāẽge.

f क्योंकि गोपाल रेडियो सुन रहा था !
kyõki Gopāl reḍiyo sun rahā thā!

Language discovery 4

Obligations: आपको दूध पीना चाहिए *āpko dūdh pīnā cāhie,* कल मुझे पढ़ना चाहिए था *kal mujhe paṛhnā cāhie thā*

Listening and speaking

Exercise 1

a जी हाँ, आपको रहना चाहिए । *jī hā̃, āpko rahnā cāhie.*

b जी हाँ, आपको गीता की मदद करनी चाहिए ।
jī hā̃, āpko Gītā kī madad karnī cāhie.

c जी हाँ, आपको चाय बनानी चाहिए । *jī hā̃, āpko cāy banānī cāhi.*

d जी हाँ, आपको खाना बनाना चाहिए । *jī hā̃, āpko khānā banānā cāhie.*

e जी हाँ, आपको गीता की बात सुननी चाहिए । *jī hā̃, āpko Gītā kī bāt sunnī cāhie.*

Exercise 2

a जी नहीं, आपको घर पर नहीं रहना चाहिए ।
jī nahī̃, āpko ghar par nahī̃ rahnā cāhie.

b जी नहीं, आपको राजू की मदद नहीं करनी चाहिए ।
jī nahī̃, āpko Rājū kī madad nahī̃ karnī cāhie.

c जी हाँ, आपको बाहर जाना चाहिए । *jī hā̃, āpko bāhar jānā cāhie.*

d जी हाँ, आपको अपनी सहेलियों को फ़ोन करना चाहिए ।
jī hā̃, āpko apnī saheliyõ ko fon karnā cāhie.

e जी हाँ, आपको टैक्सी बुलानी चाहिए । *jī hā̃, āpko ṭaiksī bulānī cāhie.*

f जी नहीं, आपको राजू की बात नहीं सुननी चाहिए ।
jī nahī̃, āpko Rājū kī bāt nahī̃ sunnī cāhie.

Exercise 3

a गीता को आराम करना चाहिए । *Gītā ko ārām karnā cāhie.*

b मनोज को गोली लेनी चाहिए और पानी पीना चाहिए ।
Manoj ko golī lenī cāhie aur pānī pīnā cāhie.

c राजू को फ़र्श को साफ़ करना चाहिए । *Rājū ko farś ko sāf karnā cāhie.*

d मीना को कुछ खाना चाहिए । *Mīnā ko kuch khānā cāhie.*

e उन लोगों को नया घर लेना (या ख़रीदना) चाहिए ।
un logõ ko nayā ghar lenā (yā <u>kh</u>arīdnā) cāhie.

Language discovery 5

Stronger obligations: मुझे घर की सफ़ाई करनी चाहिए *mujhe ghar kī safāī karnī cāhie* I **should** clean the house; मुझे घर की सफ़ाई करनी है *mujhe ghar kī safāī karnī hai* I **have to** clean the house

What's on today? हमको कुछ कहना चाहिए *hamko kuch kahnā cāhie,* हमको कुछ कहना है *hamko kuch kahnā hai,* हमको कुछ कहना पड़ेगा *hamko kuch kahnā paṛegā.*

Practice 3

Exercise 1

a कोई तीस लोग बुलाए जाएँगे । *koī tīs log bulāe jāẽge.*

b शुक्रवार को घर को साफ़ किया जाएगा । *śukravār ko ghar ko sāf kiyā jāegā.*

c रविवार की सुबह को खाना बनाया जाएगा ।
ravivār kī subah ko khānā banāyā jāegā.

d दोपहर को कुछ रिश्तेदारों को स्टेशन से लाया जाएगा ।
dopahar ko kuch riśtedārõ ko sṭeśan se lāyā jāegā.

e बच्चों को तोहफ़े दिए जाएँगे । *baccõ ko tohfe die jāẽge.*

f रात को बग़ीचे में बत्तियाँ जलाई जाएँगी । *rāt ko bag̱īce mẽ battiyā̃ jalāī jāẽgī.*

g संगीत भी बजाया जाएगा । *sangīt bhī bajāyā jāegā.*

h पड़ोसियों को भी बुलाया जाएगा । *paṛosiyõ ko bhī bulāyā jāegā.*

Exercise 2

a आज का खाना ताज़ा नहीं था । लगता है वह कल ही बनाया गया था ।
āj kā khānā tāzā nahī̃ thā. lagtā hai vah kal hī banāyā gayā thā.

b कल रात को हमारे दोस्त हमसे मिलने आए थे लेकिन हमें नहीं बताया गया कि वे आए हैं । *kal rāt ko hamāre dost hamse milne āe the lekin hamẽ nahī̃ batāyā gayā ki ve āe haĩ.*

c किसी के गंदे कपड़े मेरे कमरे रखे गए थे ।
kisī ke gande kapṛe mere kamre mẽ rakhe gae the.

d आज शाम को मैंने देखा कि हमारे कमरे के दरवाज़े को ठीक से बंद नहीं किया गया था । *āj śām ko maĩne dekhā ki hamāre kamre ke darvāze ko ṭhīk se band nahī̃ kiyā gayā thā.*

e एक बात और – हमारे सामान को खोला गया था ।
ek bāt aur – hamāre sāmān ko kholā gayā thā!

f हमको नहाने के लिए गरम पानी नहीं दिया गया ।
hamko nahāne ke lie garam pānī nahī̃ diyā gayā.

g मैंने परसों कुछ कपड़े दिए थे धोने के लिए, लेकिन अभी तक वे वापस नहीं दिए गए ।
maĩne parsõ kuch kapṛe die the dhone ke lie, lekin abhī tak ve vāpas nahī̃ die gae.

h मेरे ड्राइवर को बताया गया कि उसे गाड़ी में ही सोना होगा ।
mere ḍrāivar ko batāyā gayā ki use gāṛī mẽ hī sonā hogā.

Exercise 3

Why do these people hassle me? Every day they complain about something. It seems they're very fond of complaining. I don't know which country they're from [they've come from]. In my opinion when people come to our country they shouldn't complain about everything. They should respect this country. It's true that their luggage shouldn't have been opened, but all the other matters were quite minor. I should tell the manager about this but I don't want to tell him. I won't tell him. These people can go to hell!

Test yourself

1 बोला जाना, खाया जाना, कहा जाना, पूछा जाना ।
bolā jānā, khāyā jānā, kahā jānā, pūchā jānā.

2 'It will take one hour': एक घंटा लगेगा *ek ghaṇṭā lagegā.*
'It will take two weeks': दो हफ़्ते लगेंगे *do hafte lagẽge.*

3 'A taxi should be called': the verb is passive and जाना *jānā* is in the subjunctive to give the sense 'should'. The verb बुलाई *bulāī* is feminine to agree with टैक्सी *ṭaiksī.*

4 Slightly: adding को *ko* that a specific taxi is meant, so it may be translated as 'The taxi should be called'.

5 'To seem' and 'to strike': लगता है *lagtā hai* 'it seems' तुमको भूख लगी होगी *tumko bhūkh lagī hogī* 'You must be feeling hungry'.

6 बारिश होने लगी । *bāriś hone lagī.*

7 It's not really an obligation – the infinitive (here पीनी *pīnī*) simply refers to something that is expected or due to happen, an intention of something to be done.

8 काम करना है *kām karnā hai* has a fairly neutral tone, with little urgency; but the use of पड़ना *paṛnā* implies that something *must* be done, probably because of some outside influence, some third party.

9 E.g. मुझे बैंक जाना है, घर साफ़ करना है, और एक दोस्त से मिलना है ।
mujhe baink jānā hai, ghar sāf karnā hai, aur ek dost se milnā hai – 'I have to go to the bank, clean the house, and meet a friend'.

10 मुझे अपने/अपनी दोस्त को तोहफ़ा देना चाहिए ।
mujhe apne/apnī dost ko tohfā denā cāhie.

UNIT 12

Language discovery 1

J-words and relative clauses: a जब नेहा छोटी थी तब उसको पालक पसंद नहीं था । ***jab*** *Nehā choṭī thī* ***tab*** *usko pālak pasand nahī̃ thā.*

b जिन लोगों ने वह खाना खाया आज वे बीमार हैं । ***jin*** *logo ne vah khānā khāyā āj ve bīmār haĩ.*

Storyline

1 Five reasons are given: there is a lot of competition; sometimes there aren't any passengers; Hiraral has to work even in the rain; it's hard to drive a rickshaw up and down hills; and sometimes the rickshaw can be very heavy **2a** beautiful; it 'shines like a diamond' **b** sometimes there are no passengers **c** he still works in the rain **d** he sleeps on the seat of his rickshaw

Practice 1

Exercise 1

a The man who is sitting in the rickshaw is very fat.

b The rickshaw he is sitting in is very fine.

c The man who is driving this rickshaw is called Hiralal.

d Who is the woman who just asked Hiralal the way?

e Rickshaws don't come where I live.

f When I have to go to the station, I have to take a taxi.

Exercise 2

1 ब	2 हा	3 दु	र				4 दु
5 द	ल	श		6 अ	7 ध्या	पि	का
सू		8 म	धु	ब	न		न
र		न				9 स	दा
10 त	ब		11 मं	ग	ल	वा	र
			दि			ल	
12 अ	13 ख़	बा	र	14 वा	15 ला		16 या
17 म	त			18 रा	ख	19 दा	नी
री	20 रा	21 मा	य	ण		ल	
क		र		22 सी	23 धा		24 ए
25 न	हा	ना			26 गा	य	क

Exercise 3

a wrong **b** wrong **c** right **d** wrong **e** wrong **f** wrong **g** wrong **h** right

Language discovery 2

Verb triplets: बच्चे सीखते हैं *bacce sīkhte haĩ,* संध्या जी बच्चों को सिखाती है *Sandhyā jī baccõ ko sikhātī hai,* राजू संध्या जी से बच्चों को सिखवाता है *Rājū Sandhyā jī se baccõ ko sikhvātā hai*

Writing

a हम शर्मा जी से बच्चों को हिन्दी सिखवाएँगे ।
ham Śarmā jī se baccõ ko hindī sikhvāẽge.

b मैंने नौकरों से कुछ खाना बनवाया ।
maĩne naukarõ se kuch khānā banvāyā.

c हमें गाड़ी को ठीक करवाना है ।
hamẽ gāṛī ko ṭhīk karvānā hai.

d मैं मास्टरजी से कुछ कुरते सिलवाना चाहता हूँ ।
maĩ māsṭarjī se kuch kurte silvānā cāhtā hū̃.

e मैंने इन पत्रों को किसी से लिखवाया ।
maĩne in patrõ ko kisī se likhvāyā.

Storyline

1 He has the flu. **2a** two days **b** pills or medicine **c** rest

Language discovery 3

Parts of the body:

a उँगलियाँ *ungliā̃* **b** पेट *peṭ* **c** सिर *sir* **d** पैर *pair*

Speaking

a मेरी तबियत दो दिन से ख़राब है । *merī tabiyat do dinse kharāb hai.*

b जी नहीं, बुख़ार नहीं है । *jī nahī̃, bukhār nahī̃ hai.*

c जी हाँ, सिर में दर्द है । *jī hā̃, sir mẽ dard hai.*

d जी नहीं, मैं बाहर का खाना कभी नहीं खाता हूँ ।
jī nahī̃, maĩ bāhar kā khānā kabhī nahī̃ khātā hū̃.

e जी नहीं, मैं बोतल का पानी ही पीता हूँ ।
jī nahī̃, maĩ botal kā pānī hī pītā hū̃.

f जी हाँ, उलटी हो रही है । *jī hā̃, ulṭī ho rahī hai.*

g हाँ, दस्त भी है । *hā̃, dast bhī hai.*

h मैं शराब पीता तो हूँ लेकिन बहुत ज़्यादा नहीं ।
maĩ śarāb pītā to hū̃ lekin bahut zyādā nahī̃.

i आम तौर पर नींद ठीक से आती है ।   *ām taur par nī̃d ṭhīk se ātī hai.*

j मैं ग्यारह-बारह बजे सोता हूँ ।   *maĩ gyārah-bārah baje sotā hū̃.*

k मैं कम से कम [at least] सात घंटे सोता हूँ ।
maĩ kam se kam [at least] sāt ghaṇṭe sotā hū̃.

l जी नहीं, और कोई तकलीफ़ नहीं है ।   *jī nahī̃, aur koī taklīf nahī̃ hai.*

Language discovery 4

Shades of meaning: a यह पानी पी लीजिए । *yah pānī pī lījie.* **c** वह सेब मत खाओ, वह ज़मीन पर गिर गया । *vah seb mat khāo, vah zamīn par gir gayā.* **d** आप के लिए चाय बना दूँ ? *āp ke lie cāy banā dū̃?* Sentence **b** should not use a compound verb because it is a negative sentence.

I've already done this: मीना अपने कमरे की सफ़ाई कर चुकी है । *Mīnā apne kamre kī safāī kar cukī hai.* हम लोग वह फ़िल्म देख चुके हैं । *ham log vah film dekh cuke haĩ.*

Speaking

a जी हाँ, मैं उससे देख चुका हूँ/जी हाँ मैं उससे देख चुकी हूँ
jī hā̃, maĩ usse dekh cukā hā̃/jī hā̃, maĩ usse dekh cukī hū̃

b जी हाँ, मैं खाना खा चुका हूँ/जी हाँ मैं खाना खा चुकी हूँ
jī hā̃, maĩ khānā khā cukā hū̃/jī hā̃, maĩ khānā khā cukī hū̃

c जी हाँ, मैं अपना काम कर चुका हूँ/जी हाँ मैं अपना काम कर चुकी हूँ
jī hā̃, maĩ apnā kām kar cukā hū̃/jī hā̃, maĩ apnā kām kar cukī hū̃

d जी हाँ, मैं यह पूरी किताब पढ़ चुका हूँ/जी हाँ मैं यह पूरी किताब पढ़ चुकी हूँ
jī hā̃, maĩ yah pūrī kitāb paṛh cukā hū̃/jī hā̃, maĩ yah pūrī kitāb paṛh cukī hū̃

Did you manage to do this? कल हम आपके यहाँ नहीं जा पाए । *kal ham āpke yahā̃ nahī̃ jā pāe.* मनीषा समय पर स्टेशन नहीं पहुंच पाई । *Manīṣā samay par sṭeśan nahī̃ pahũc pāī.*

Style in Hindi: The English word is sugar and the sentence means: My grandfather has diabetes. In idiomatic Hindi, to 'have sugar' means to have diabetes.

Numbers: ७५ 75, १५० ००० 150,000, २६ 29

What's the time? b, c, a

Practice 2

Exercise 1

a किसी बड़े आर्टिस्ट ने उसको बनाया होगा ।
kisī baṛe ārṭisṭ ne usko banāyā hogā.

b जहाँ हीरालाल रहता है वहाँ कई दूसरे रिक्शेवाले भी रहते हैं ।
jahā̃ Hīrālāl rahtā hai vahā̃ kaī dūsre rikśevāle bhī rahte haĩ.

c उस शहर का नाम आगरा है । *us śahar kā nām āgrā hai.*

d जी नहीं, बारिश में भी हीरालाल को काम करना पड़ता है ।
jī nahī̃, bāriś mē̃ bhī Hīrālāl ko kām karnā paṛtā hai.

e रिक्शे का वज़न तब बहुत ज़्यादा हो जाता है जब मोटे लोग
अपने भारी सामान को लेकर रिक्शे में चढ़ते हैं ।
*rikśe kā vazan tab bahut zyādā ho jātā hai jab moṭe log apne bhārī
sāmān ko lekar rikśe mē̃ caṛhte haĩ.*

f हीरालाल की जेब तब ख़ाली रहती है जब कोई सवारी नहीं आती ।
Hīrālāl kī jeb tab k͟hālī rahtī hai jab koī savārī nahī̃ ātī.

g जो लोग रिक्शे चलाते हैं उनकी ज़िन्दगी मुश्किल होती है ।
jo log rikśe calāte haĩ unkī zindagī muśkil hotī hai.

Exercise 2

Sample answers:

a जो लोग भारत के बारे में कुछ सीखना चाहते हैं उनको हिन्दी सीखनी चाहिए ।
jo log bhārat ke bāre mē̃ kuch sīkhnā cāhte haĩ unko hindī sīkhnī cāhie.

b जब मैंने पहली बार ताज महल को देखा तो मैंने सोचा कि मैं भी एक ऐसी इमारत
बनाऊँगा !
*jab maĩne pahlī bār tāj mahal ko dekhā to maĩne socā ki maĩ bhī ek
aisī imārat banāū̃gā!*

c जहाँ मेरे रिश्तेदार रहते हैं, वहाँ पहुँचने में कई घंटे लगते हैं ।
jahā̃ mere riśtedār rahte haĩ, vahā̃ pahũcne mē̃ kaī ghaṇṭe lagte haĩ.

d जो आदमी मेरे साथ काम करता है उसकी पत्नी मेरी पत्नी की सहेली है ।
jo ādmī mere sāth kām kartā hai uskī patnī merī patnī kī sahelī hai.

e जो आदमी मेरे घर के सामने रहता है वह कोई बड़ा नेता है ।
jo ādmī mere ghar ke sāmne rahtā hai vah koī baṛā netā hai.

f जिन लोगों के पास बहुत पैसा है वे ही लंदन में बड़ा मकान ख़रीद सकते हैं ।
*jin logõ ke pās bahut paisā hai ve hī landan mē̃ baṛā makān kharīd
sakte haĩ.*

g जो कपड़े मैंने कल ख़रीदे उनको तुमने कहाँ रखा ?
jo kapṛe maĩne kal k͟harīde unko tumne kahā̃ rakhā?

Exercise 3

a जब मैं आगरे जाता हूँ तो अक्सर राजू के यहाँ रहता हूँ ।
jab maĩ āgre jātā hū̃ to aksar Rājū ke yahā̃ rahtā hū̃.

b जो आदमी हमको हिन्दी पढ़ाता है वह राजू का भाई है ।
jo ādmī hamko hindī paṛhātā hai vah Rājū kā bhāī hai.

c जो तोहफ़ा मैंने आज राजू को दिया वह काफ़ी सस्ता था ।
jo tohfā maĩne āj Rājū ko diyā vah kāfī sastā thā.

d जब मैंने उसे उसको दिया तो उसने उसे अपनी माँ को दिखाया ।
jab maĩne use usko diyā to usne use apnī mā̃ ko dikhāyā.

e जब राजू की माँ ने मेरा तोहफ़ा देखा तो वे हँसने लगीं ।
jab Rājū kī mā̃ ne merā tohfā dekhā to ve hãsne lagī̃.

f जो सवाल उन्होंने राजू से मेरे बारे में पूछा मैं उसको कभी नहीं भूलूँगा ।
jo savāl unhõne Rājū se mere bāre mẽ pūchā maĩ usko kabhī nahī̃ bhūlū̃gā.

g जो जवाब राजू ने दिया वह हमेशा याद रहेगा ।
jo javāb Rājū ne diyā vah hameśā yād rahegā.

Exercise 4

Dear Manoj,

I got your letter, thanks. I hadn't had a letter for a year so I'd begun wondering what had happened to my friend Manoj.

Everything's fine here. My brother has married. He's rented a small house in Delhi.

My father says I should get married, too, now. But I've told him clearly that I won't get married yet. I'm still young. When I turn thirty then maybe I'll start thinking about these things. But Father doesn't want to listen to what I say. Just a little while ago he again began talking about marriage. I got a bit angry. I said, 'Yes Papa, I heard!'

Tell me your email address.

Yours, Motu

Test yourself

1 जी, मेरे दो हाथ हैं *jī, mere do hath haĩ.* मेरी दो आंखें भी हैं *merī do ãkhẽ bhī haĩ.* लेकिन मेरा सिर्फ़ एक सिर है *lekin merā sirf ek sir hai.*

2 वहाँ *vahã.*

3 जिस *jis* is the oblique of जो *jo,* as in जिस आदमी को तुमने पैसे दिए थे, वह तुमसे मिलने आया है । *jis ādmī ko tumne paise diye the, vah tumse milne āyā hai* (The man you gave money has come to meet you).

4 जो किताब मैंने यहाँ ख़रीदी थी वह दूसरी दुकानों में नहीं मिलती । *jo kitāb maĩne yahã kharīdī thī vah dūsrī dukānõ mẽ nahī̃ miltī.*

5 दो घंटे पहले ढाई बजे थे । *do ghaṇṭe pahle ḍhāī baje the.*

6 Approximately – (a) 'I've had tea'; (b) 'I've had my tea'.

7 (a) 'Make yourself some tea'; (b) 'Get yourself some tea made'.

8 जी नहीं मैंने चाय नहीं पी है । *jī nahī̃, maĩne cāy nahī̃ pī hai.* (It's a negative sentence, so चुकना *cuknā* is dropped; है *hai* could also be dropped.)

9 यूनिट १२ में जो रिक्शेवाला है, उसका नाम हीरालाल है ।
yūniṭ 12 mẽ jo rikśevālā hai, uskā nām Hīrālāl hai.

10 इन सवालों का जवाब देने में मुझे तीस मिनट लगे / एक घंटा लगा ।
in savālõ kā javāb dene mẽ mujhe tīs minaṭ lage / ek ghaṇṭā lagā.

Storyline transcripts

UNIT 1

01.10

Raju	Hello. I am Raju. Who are you?
Javed	Hello. My name is Javed.
Raju	Are you OK?
Javed	Yes, thank you, I am OK.
Raju	Who is that girl?
Javed	Her name is Bano.
Raju	What is your full name?
Javed	My full name is Javed Khan.

UNIT 2

02.12

Javed	Raju ji, who is Manoj?
Raju	Manoj is our elder (big) son.
Javed	Right. Who are Meena and Ram?
Raju	Meena is our daughter and Ram is our second son.
Javed	And Geeta ji is your wife?
Raju	Yes, Geeta is my wife.
Javed	Is your brother a doctor?
Raju	No, he's a teacher.
Javed	What kind of teacher is he? (i.e. 'is he good?')
Raju	He's a very good teacher.

UNIT 3

03.07

My name is Geeta – Mrs Geeta Sharma. I'm from Varanasi. My husband is Mr Rajkumar Sharma. He's from Delhi. Raju is a teacher. This is our house. Our house is in Agra. In the house there's one big room and four small rooms. This is our big room. In the room there's one big table. On the table is my computer. There's a fan too. Some books are lying on the floor. In the garden there are two or three tall trees.

03.09

Teacher	Ram, where are your books?
Ram	Sir, my books are lying here on the table.
Teacher	What's lying on your chair?
Ram	Sir, my pens are on my chair.
Teacher	What's in your hands?
Ram	There's nothing in my hands.
Teacher	Where is your sister Meena today?
Ram	Sir, she's at home. She's unwell.

03.10

Raju	Geeta, where's Manoj?
Geeta	He's at school.
Raju	And where's Ram?
Geeta	He's at school too.
Raju	I see! And Meena?
Geeta	Meena's sitting in the garden.
Raju	Where's my brother?
Geeta	Don't know!

UNIT 4

04.09

Javed	Raju ji, you teach in a college, don't you?
Raju	Yes, I teach history.
Javed	And your wife? Does she work too?
Raju	Yes, of course, we both work.
Javed	What work does she do?
Raju	She works in a hospital. She's a doctor.

04.10

Javed	Tell me this, Raju ji, do you eat meat?
Raju	Yes, sometimes I do. And you?
Javed	I do too. But I don't drink alcohol.
Raju	You don't drink? I do, but very little.
Javed	Does Geeta drink too?
Raju	No, she doesn't drink.

UNIT 5

05.01

Manoj, son, put these books in the cupboard. Which books? Yes these, the ones (lit. 'which are lying') on my table. Where's Meena? Call her.

Oh, Meena, you're here? You clean this room. Ram, ask Father where the newspaper is. Tell him that Uncle is waiting (lit. 'sitting').

05.05

Pratap I need a torch too.
Shopkeeper Not *ṭorc, ṭārc*! What else?
Pratap I ... what's it called ... a little book ... I want to write something.
Shopkeeper Oh, you need an exercise book.
Pratap Yes, an exercise book! Give me a pen too.
Shopkeeper What kind of pen do you want?
Pratap Not black ... 'blue' ...
Shopkeeper Here you are, a blue pen. What else?
Pratap I need that thing too ...
Shopkeeper Which thing? This box?
Pratap No no, that red thing (lit. 'that's lying') on the box.
Shopkeeper Oh, a penknife! You need a penknife. Here you are.

05.08

Shankar Please come (in), sir, what do you want?
Raju I need a room. Show me some decent room.
Shankar Very good. What kind of room do you want?
Raju I want a big room.
Shankar Very good. How many days do you want it for?
Raju For four days – that is, until Friday.
Shankar Very good. We have a very good room vacant from today until Friday.
Raju Is there a phone in the room? There needs to be a phone.
Shankar Yes, there is. It's a very good room. Such rooms are hard to find in this town.
Raju How much is it (lit. 'the rent')?
Shankar Only seven hundred rupees.
Raju Show me the room.
Shankar Very good, sir. Come, I'll show (you) the room.

05.09

(Both men go upstairs. Shankar opens a door.)

Shankar Please come in, sir.
Raju This room isn't clean.
Shankar Very good, sir. I'll get the room cleaned at once.
Raju Does this old fan work?

Shankar Yes, the fan works. It's a very good fan. You can't get fans like this these days.

Raju Turn it on.

(Shankar switches on the fan, but the fan doesn't turn.)

Raju The fan doesn't turn.

Shankar Yes, sir *(he agrees that it doesn't)*, because there's no 'light' – no electricity.

Raju What's your name?

Shankar Sir, I'm called Shankar. And what is your good name?

Raju My name is Sharma. Mr Rajkumar Sharma.

Shankar It's a very good name, sir. I like your name very much.

Raju Shankar, you say 'very good' very much. But this room isn't very good. Show me some other room.

Shankar Very good, Sharma ji. Please come.

UNIT 6

06.05

Manoj Pratap, meet my father.

Pratap Hello, ji.

Raju Hello, Pratap, how are things?

Pratap Fine, thank you.

Raju How old are you, Pratap?

Pratap I'm twenty-one.

Raju How many brothers and sisters do you have?

Pratap I have one brother, I don't have any sisters.

06.10

Manoj Have a cigarette, Pratap! There's no one in the house.

Pratap No, I don't smoke. You can.

Manoj Yes, I smoke two or three cigarettes every day.

Pratap These cigarettes are yours?

Manoj No, they're my dad's.

Pratap Why do you smoke his cigarettes?

Manoj I don't have any money. I can't buy cigarettes.

Raju [from another room] Manoj! Oh Manoj! Where are you?

Pratap Your father's voice!

(Raju comes into the room.)

Raju Hey, what's this? What's that in your hand, Manoj?

Manoj Father! Look, this is Pratap's cigarette ...

Raju	Manoj, don't talk nonsense. Pratap, you can go.
Manoj	But ... but ...

06.12

Manoj's dream

Geeta – 'Manoj's father, let Manoj smoke, and let him drink too. He's a very good boy; he studies very hard at school. Why don't you let him drive the car? Oh and yes, let him go to America in the holidays!'

UNIT 7

07.03

We used to live in Varanasi. Our house was on the bank of the Ganges. It was a biggish house. We were three brothers and four sisters. All three of us boys used to go to school; the girls used to stay at home. In those days very few girls went to school. Money was short and people used to think that women's place was in the home.

Father taught in a school – but not in our school. His school was quite far from our house. He used to go to school by bicycle. Everyone called him 'Master ji'. We called him 'Papa' and we called mother 'Ma'.

What a beautiful house we had! There wasn't a garden, but we children used to play to our hearts' content in the courtyard. Sometimes we would play on the roads or on the riverbank. In the evening we used to take a ride in a boat on the river. A cool breeze would blow. At night we used to sleep on the roof. I think of those days a lot.

07.06

In childhood I was very fond of writing letters. Sometimes I would even write letters to the Prime Minister. I didn't know if he liked my letters or not, because he never replied (lit. 'used not to reply'). One time my younger brother was ill for several months. He had a high fever and so we were very worried. I knew that he needed medicine but we didn't have the money (lit. 'where was the money?'). People used to say that the Prime Minister was a very kindly man. So ...

Dear (lit. 'respected') Prime Minister ji,

Respectful greetings. I know that you have a lot of work but we are very anxious because my younger brother has fever. We don't have any money. Can you do something? We have full trust in you.

With best wishes, yours, Rajkumar Sharma.

UNIT 8

08.02

Geeta	Hello, Raju, this is Geeta speaking.
Raju	Where are you speaking from?
Geeta	From the Taj Hotel.
Raju	What are you doing there?
Geeta	I'm having tea with some friends!
Raju	What are the children doing?
Geeta	They're playing in the garden here.
Raju	So is Manoj playing too?
Geeta	No, he's talking to some girl.
Raju	Oho! When are you all coming home?
Geeta	We're just coming in a little while. Why?
Raju	Because I'm making dinner. I need help.
Geeta	Why? Is someone coming tonight?
Raju	Yes, Javed's coming. Some of his friends are coming too.
Geeta	Oh my God! OK, I'm on my way (lit. 'I'm just coming').
Raju	Don't spend too much money there in the Taj!

08.04

Gopal	Hello Sharma ji.
Jagdish	Hello. What do you want, son?
Gopal	Sir, I need a job in your shop.
Jagdish	Yes, I **do** need a hard-working lad.
Gopal	I work very hard, Sharma ji!
Jagdish	How old are you?
Gopal	Sir, I'm sixteen.
Jagdish	Where do you live?
Gopal	Nearby. Our house isn't far from here.
Jagdish	Do you know how to read and write?
Gopal	Yes, and I know a little English too.
Jagdish	All right, come from tomorrow.
Gopal	Thank you very much. Sharma ji, please tell me one thing.
Jagdish	Speak, what is it?
Gopal	The wages ...?
Jagdish	Don't ask this just now!

08.06

Dear Raju,

Do you know what a Prime Minister's life is like? He can't do anything for himself but he can do something for others! Don't worry about your brother. I'm getting some medicine sent by my very own doctor. In your next letter write how he is. And take care of your own health too!

Yours (...)

UNIT 9

09.01

Raju What will you do tomorrow?

Javed Tomorrow I'll work. What will you do?

Raju I shall stay at home.

Javed Why will you stay at home? Won't you go to work?

Raju No, I won't go to work. Tomorrow's a holiday.

The same dialogue is spoken between Geeta and Usha. Take this opportunity to listen to, and practise, masculine and feminine endings.

09.04

Manoj Pratap, will you tell [me] the names of the days of the week?

Pratap Yes, they are … *somvār, mangalvār, budhvār,* then ... then ...

Manoj *guru* ...

Pratap Yes! *guruvār* or *bṛhaspativār, śukravār, śanivār, ravivār.*

Manoj Bravo! What day will it be tomorrow?

Pratap Tomorrow will be Tuesday.

Manoj What will you do the day after tomorrow?

Pratap The day after tomorrow, that is on Wednesday, I'll go to meet Father.

Manoj Where will you go on Thursday?

Pratap On Thursday I'll stay at home.

Manoj What will you do on Friday?

Pratap On Friday I'll do my studying.

Manoj And on Saturday you'll rest?

Pratap No, on Saturday I'll go out and enjoy myself!

09.05

Today is Monday; today I'll stay at home. Tomorrow, i.e. on Tuesday, we'll go to Delhi. The day after, i.e. on Wednesday, we'll go to buy some things for our house. On Thursday we'll come back home. On Friday I'll rest. On Saturday night we'll go to Sita's. On Sunday I'll get ready for next week.

09.06

Javed	May I come in?
Raju	Yes, yes, of course you may come in! (Do come in!)
Javed	Where should I sit?
Raju	Please sit over here. Should I make tea?
Javed	If you wish. Or should we go out?
Raju	No, let's stay at home.

UNIT 10

10.04

This morning I got up at five o'clock. For a little while I sat in the courtyard. Yesterday evening when we went to the cinema to see Shahrukh Khan's new film it had rained; but today I saw that the sky was clear. In the mornings it's peaceful all around. I'm very fond of the morning time.

I made tea for myself. After having tea I woke up my wife. Making tea is two minutes' work but waking up the memsahib is another matter. Finally, when she came down I got her breakfast ready. Me, I never eat breakfast, but Geeta does of course. I made two pieces of toast for her. She had tea and ate half a banana too. She complained that there was too much sugar in the tea. I said that she needed a bit of sweetness in her life.

10.05

Usually Raju wakes me late but today he woke me very early. I was sleeping peacefully and dreaming about Shahrukh Khan (an actor). It was such a sweet dream! When I heard my husband's voice I thought Shahrukh himself had come to wake me. But this was just a dream. I went down into the kitchen. My husband had made two pieces of toast for me. How many times have I told him that I don't like toast, but him, he doesn't listen. He'd put far too much sugar in the tea. I had a headache so I took two pills. Raju must have had breakfast before waking me because he didn't eat anything with me. I asked him why he woke me up so early but he didn't answer. Shahrukh, where art thou?

10.07

Today Raju got up and went downstairs. Then he made tea and went to sit in the courtyard. After drinking his tea he began to think about his dreams. He had dreamed of Shahrukh Khan. Shahrukh had broken down the door and come into the room, but Raju had picked up a heavy dictionary from the table and had given Shahrukh a good thrashing.

At seven o'clock Raju called out Geeta's name and tried to wake her, but she was sleeping deeply. Raju made himself four or five pieces of toast and ate them. Then he ate three or four oranges. At eight o'clock he shook Geeta's shoulder and woke her. Then he made tea for her, and two pieces of toast as well. Geeta yawned and said 'Give me an orange', and Raju laughed and said, 'Manoj must have got up early and eaten all the oranges, he loves oranges!'

UNIT 11

11.02

Emerging from the station, turn right. At a short distance you'll come to a narrow alley. Turn into this alley. Going straight on you'll reach a wide road which is called Chandrashekhar Azad Road. Turning left and crossing the road, keep going. A school will be seen on the right. After this turn right. I don't remember the name of this road but you'll see a cinema on your left. Then a little further on you'll come to another big road which is called maybe 'Nai Sarak' (New Road). Turn left. Then you'll come to a roundabout. On the other side of the roundabout you'll see your Madhuban Hotel.

The Madhuban Hotel isn't far from the station. It's barely an eight- or ten-minute trip. If you've got a lot of luggage it would be better to take a rickshaw. Tell the rickshaw driver that the hotel is on 'M. G. Road'. The rickshaw driver will take 20 or 25 rupees. You shouldn't give him more than 25.

11.05

Sharma ji was sitting in his shop thinking. He called Gopal and said, 'Son, put all this stuff in the little room. Then clean the shop. I'm very tired, I'll go home and sleep for a little while. Close the shop at eight o'clock. Then take 20 rupees and go to the dhobi and bring my clean clothes.' But none of this was heard by Gopal because he was listening to the radio.

UNIT 12

12.02

This is Hiralal, who lives in Agra. Hiralal is a rickshaw driver. The rickshaw that Hiralal drives is very fine. It shines like a diamond! Whoever made this rickshaw must be a very great artist.

Where Hiralal lives many other rickshaw drivers live too. There are lots of rickshaws but few passengers come. When not a single passenger comes, Hiralal's pocket remains empty. When the pocket remains empty the stomach also remains empty. Where can one get free food? And when it rains, even then Hiralal has to work. People who are poor have to work in all weathers (lit. 'in every weather').

Where there's a hill or a slope it's very difficult to drive a rickshaw. When two fat people get onto the rickshaw with their heavy luggage the weight gets too much. When the passengers get down Hiralal lies down on the seat of his rickshaw and sleeps. People who drive rickshaws have to work very hard.

12.04

Doctor Come in, come in. What's your complaint?
Raju Doctor sahib, my whole body is aching.
Doctor How long has your health been bad?
Raju For two days. The day before yesterday I was just about to go to work when my head started to ache.
Doctor It seems you've caught flu.
Raju So what should I do?
Doctor You should just rest.
Raju Please give (me) some medicine or tablet!
Doctor You don't need any tablet or anything like that. Rest itself is the cure.

12.08

Geeta Do you have a green colour shoe?
Shopkeeper Yes, madam, please look, these shoes are green. And they're very reasonable.
Geeta No, I don't like this style.
Shopkeeper But its leather is very soft. And see its quality, too! Try it at least!

Hindi–English vocabulary

KEY

adj.	adjective	m., f.	used for both sexes
f.	feminine	m./f.	used in either gender
m.	masculine	pl.	plural

DICTIONARY ORDER

The order of the characters in the Devanagari script follows the chart given in the introduction. Vowels precede consonants; nasalized vowels precede unnasalized vowels; plain consonants precede conjunct consonants.

अँगूठा *ãgūṭhā* m. *thumb*

अँग्रेज़ *ãgrez* m., f. *English person*

अँग्रेज़ी *ãgrezī* f. *English (language);* and adj.

अंदर *andar* *inside*

अख़बार *a<u>kh</u>bār* m. *newspaper*

अख़बारवाला *a<u>kh</u>bārvālā* m. *newspaper seller*

अकेला *akelā* *alone*

अकेलापन *akelāpan* m. *loneliness*

अगर *agar* *if*

अगला *aglā* *next*

अच्छा *acchā* *good, nice*

अध्यापक *adhyāpak* m. *teacher*

अध्यापिका *adhyāpikā* f. *teacher*

अपना *apnā* *one's own (my own, etc.)*

अभी *abhī* *right now; still*

अमरीकन *amrīkan* *American*

अरे *are* *hey! oh!*

अलमारी *almārī* f. *cupboard*

अस्पताल *aspatāl* m. *hospital*

आँख *ā̃kh* f. *eye*

आँगन *ā̃gan* m. *courtyard*

आकाश *ākāś* m. *sky*

आगे *āge* *ahead*

आज *āj* *today;* आजकल *ājkal* *nowadays, these days;* आज रात को *āj rāt ko* *tonight;* आज शाम को *āj śām ko* *this evening*

आठ *āṭh* *eight*

आदमी *ādmī* m. *man*

आदर *ādar* m. *respect*

आदरणीय *ādaraṇīy* *respected* (used for *Dear* in formal correspondence)

आधा *ādhā* m. *half*

आना *ānā* *to come*

आप *āp* *you*

आपका *āpkā* *your, yours*

आम *ām*[1] m. *mango*

आम *ām*² ordinary; आम तौर पर *ām taur par* usually

आराम *ārām* m. rest; आराम करना *ārām karnā* to rest; आराम से *ārām se* comfortably, easily

आवाज *āvāz* f. voice; sound

आशा *āśā* f. hope

आसान *āsān* easy

इंजन *injan* m. engine (train)

इंतज़ार *intazār* m. waiting, expecting का इंतज़ार करना *kā intazār karnā* to wait for

इतना *itnā* so much, so

इतिहास *itihās* m. history

इधर *idhar* here, over here

इमारत *imārat* f. building

इलाज *ilāj* m. cure, treatment

इसका *iskā* his, her/hers, its

इसलिए *islie* so, because of this

उँगली *ũglī* f. finger

उगना *ugnā* to grow (of plants)

उठना *uṭhnā* to get up, rise

उठाना *uṭhānā* to pick up, raise

उतरना, उतर जाना *utarnā, utar jānā* to get down, alight

उत्तर *uttar* north

उधर *udhar* there, over there

उम्र *umra, umar* f. age

उर्दू *urdū* f. Urdu

उलटी *ulṭī* f. vomiting, sickness

उसका *uskā* his, her/hers, its

ऊपर *ūpar* up, upstairs

ऋण *ṛṇ* m. debt

एक *ek* one; a

ऐसा *aisā* such, of this kind

ओ *o* oh!

ओर *or* f. side, direction

और *aur* and; more

औरत *aurat* f. woman

कंधा *kandhā* m. shoulder

कई *kaī* several

कटना *kaṭnā* to be cut

कपड़ा *kapṛā* m. cloth; garment

कब *kab* when?

कभी *kabhī* ever; कभी कभी *kabhī kabhī* sometimes; कभी नहीं *kabhī nahī̃* never

कम *kam* little, less

कमज़ोर *kamzor* weak

कमर *kamar* f. waist

कमरा *kamrā* m. room

कमी *kamī* f. lack, shortage

क़मीज़ *qamīz* f. shirt

कम्प्यूटर *kampyūṭar* m. computer

करना *karnā* to do

करवाना *karvānā* to get done (by someone else)

कराची *karācī* f. Karachi

कल *kal* yesterday; tomorrow

क़लम *qalam* m./f. pen

कलाई *kalāī* f. wrist

कहना *kahnā* to say

कहाँ *kahā̃* where?

कहानी *kahānī* f. story

कहीं *kahī̃* anywhere, somewhere

का–की–के *kā-kī-ke* (shows possession, like English apostrophe + s, 's)

काठमांडु *kāṭhmāṇḍu* m. Kathmandu

कान *kān* m. ear

कॉफ़ी *kāfī*¹ f. coffee

काफ़ी *kāfī*[2] quite, very; enough

काम *kām* m. work; job, task; काम करना *kām karnā* to work; to function

काला *kālā* black

कालेज *kālej* m. college

कि *ki* that (conjunction); कि *ki* when, when suddenly; or

कितना *kitnā* how much/many?

किताब *kitāb* f. book

किनारा *kinārā* m. bank, edge

किराया *kirāyā* m. rent; fare

किलो *kilo* m. kilo, kilogram

किसी *kisī* oblique of कोई *koī*

की ओर *kī or* towards

की तरफ़ *kī taraf* towards

की तरह *kī tarah* like

कुछ *kuch* some; something; कुछ और *kuch aur* some more; कुछ नहीं *kuch nahī̃* nothing

कुत्ता *kuttā* m. dog

कुरता *kurtā* m. kurta, loose shirt

कुरसी *kursī* f. chair

कुल मिलाकर *kul milākar* all together, in total

कुहनी *kuhnī* f. elbow

कृपया *kṛpayā* please (formal)

के अंदर *ke andar* inside

के अलावा *ke alāvā* as well as

के ऊपर *ke ūpar* above, on top of

के चारों तरफ़ *ke cārõ taraf* all around

के द्वारा *ke dvārā* by (in formal passive sentences)

के नज़दीक *ke nazdīk* near

के नीचे *ke nīce* below, under

के पास *ke pās* near; in the possession of

के बाहर *ke bāhar* outside

के यहाँ *ke yahā̃* at the place of

के लिए *ke lie* for

के साथ *ke sāth* with, in the company of

के सामने *ke sāmne* opposite

केला *kelā m.* banana

कैसा *kaisā* how?

को *ko* to (also marks an individualized direct object: पानी को पियो *pānī ko piyo* Drink the water)

कोई *koī* some, any, a; (with number) about; कोई दूसरा *koī dūsrā* some other, another; कोई नहीं *koī nahī̃* nobody

कौन *kaun* who?

कौनसा *kaunsā* which?

क्या *kyā* what?; and question marker

क्यों *kyõ* why?

क्योंकि *kyõki* because

क्रिकेट *krikeṭ* m. cricket

खड़ा *khaṛā* standing

ख़त *khat* m. letter (correspondence)

ख़त्म *khatm* finished; ख़त्म करना *khatm karnā* to finish

ख़याल *khyāl*, m. opinion, thought, idea

ख़राब *kharāb* bad ख़राब हो जाना *kharāb ho jānā* to break down

ख़रीदना *kharīdnā* to buy

ख़र्च *kharc* m. expenditure; ख़र्च करना *kharc karnā* to spend

ख़ाली *khālī* empty, free, vacant

खाना *khānā*[1] m. food

खाना *khānā*[2] to eat

खिड़की *khiṛkī* f. window

खिलौना *khilaunā* m. *toy*

ख़ुद *khud* *oneself (myself, etc.)*

ख़ुश *khuś* *pleased, happy*

ख़ूब *khūb* *a lot, freely*

खेल *khel* m. *game*

खेलना *khelnā* *to play* (a game)

खोलना *kholnā* *to open*

गंगा *gangā* f. *Ganges*

गंदा *gandā* *dirty*

गरम *garam* *hot, warm*

गरमी *garmī* f. *heat;* गरमियाँ *garmiyā̃* f. pl. *summer*

ग़रीब *garīb* *poor*

गर्दन *gardan* f. *neck*

गली *galī* f. *lane, narrow street*

गाँव *gā̃v* m. *village*

गाड़ी *gāṛī* f. *car; train; vehicle*

गाना *gānā* m. *song, singing*

गाना *gānā* *to sing*

गाल *gāl* f. *cheek*

गिलास *gilās* m. *tumbler*

गुजराती f. *Gujarati*

गुरुवार *guruvār* m. *Thursday*

गोलचक्कर *golcakkar* m. *roundabout*

गोली *golī* f. *tablet, pill; bullet*

गोश्त *gośt* m. *meat*

घंटा *ghaṇṭā* m. *hour*

घर *ghar* m. *house, home*

घास *ghās* f. *grass*

घुटना *ghuṭnā* m. *knee*

घुसना *ghusnā* *to enter, sneak in*

घूमना *ghūmnā* *to turn, revolve*

घोड़ा *ghoṛā* m. *horse;* घोड़े बेचकर सोना *ghoṛe beckar sonā* *to sleep like a log*

चढ़ना *caṛhnā* *to climb, get into a vehicle*

चढ़ाव *caṛhāv* m. *rise, incline*

चपाती *capātī* f. *chapati*

चमकना *camaknā* *to shine*

चम्मच *cammac* m. *spoon*

चलना *calnā* *to move, blow, flow;* चलते जाना *calte jānā* *to keep going*

चलाना *calānā* *to drive*

चश्मा *caśmā* m. *glasses, spectacles*

चाक़ू *cāqū* m. *knife, penknife*

चाचा *cācā* m. *uncle* (father's younger brother)

चाबी *cābī* f. *key*

चाय *cāy* f. *tea*

चार *cār* *four;* चारों ओर *cārõ or* *all around*

चालू करना *cālū karnā* *to turn on*

चावल *cāval* m. *rice*

चाहना *cāhnā* *to want, wish*

चाहिए *cāhie* *(is) wanted, needed*

चिंता *cintā* f. *anxiety*

चिट्ठी *ciṭṭhī* f. *letter, note*

चीज़ *cīz* f. *thing*

चीनी *cīnī* f. *sugar*

चुकना *cuknā* *to have already done* (with verb stem: वह जा चुका है *vah jā cukā hai* *He's already gone)*

चूहा *cūhā* m. *mouse, rat*

चेहरा *cehrā* m. *face*

चौड़ा *cauṛā* *wide, broad*

चौथा *cauthā* *fourth*

छठा *chaṭhā* *sixth*

छत *chat* f. *roof*

छह *chah* *six*

छाती *chātī* f. chest

छुट्टी *chuṭṭī* f. holiday; free time

छोटा *choṭā* small

जँभाई *jãbhāī* f. yawn

जगह *jagah* f. place

जगाना *jagānā* to awaken

जब *jab* when

ज़माना *zamānā* m. period, time

ज़रूर *zarūr* of course

ज़रूरत *zarūrat* f. need; मुझको X की ज़रूरत है *mujhko X kī zarūrat hai* I need X

जलना *jalnā* to burn

जलवाना *jalvānā* to cause to burn

जलाना *jalānā* to light, burn

जल्दी *jaldī* quickly, early; f. hurry

जवान *javān* young

जवाब *javāb* m. answer, reply; जवाब देना *javāb denā* to reply

जहाँ *jahā̃* where

जाँघ *jā̃gh* f. thigh

जान *jān* f. life, soul

जानना *jānnā* to know

जाना *jānā* to go

ज़िंदगी *zindagī* f. life

ज़िंदा *zindā* (invariable -ā ending) alive

जी *jī* word of respect used after names, etc. and as a short form of जी हाँ *jī hā̃* yes

जी नहीं *jī nahī̃* no

जी हाँ *jī hā̃* yes

जीतना *jītnā* to win, conquer

जीवन *jīvan* m. life

ज़ुकाम *zukām* m. head cold

जूता *jūtā* m. shoe

जेब *jeb* f. pocket

जैसा ... वैसा *jaisā ... vaisā* as (one thing), so (another)

जो *jo* who, which

ज़ोर से *zor se* with force, loudly

ज़्यादा *zyādā* more, much

झूठ *jhūṭh* m. lie

टाँग *ṭā̃g* f. leg

टार्च *ṭārc* m. torch, flashlight

टिकट *ṭikaṭ* m./f. ticket; stamp

टिकिया *ṭikiyā* f. cake (e.g. of soap)

टूटना *ṭūṭnā* to break

टैक्सी *ṭaiksī* f. taxi

टोस्ट *ṭosṭ* m. toast, piece of toast

ट्रेन *ṭren* f. train

ठंड *ṭhaṇḍ* f. cold; ठंड लगना *ṭhaṇḍ lagnā* to feel cold

ठंडा *ṭhaṇḍā* cold

ठीक *ṭhīk* OK, all right; exactly

ठुड्डी *ṭhuḍḍī* f. chin

डाक *ḍāk* f. post; डाक घर *ḍāk ghar* m. post office; डाक की टिकट *ḍāk kī ṭikaṭ* f. stamp

डाक्टर *ḍākṭar* m. doctor

डालना *ḍālnā* to put, pour

डिब्बा *ḍibbā* m. box

ड्राइवर *ḍrāivar* m. driver

ढाबा *ḍhābā* m. roadside café

तंग *tang* narrow, confined; तंग करना *tang karnā* to harass

तक *tak* up to, until, as far as

तकलीफ़ *taklīf* f. suffering, pain, discomfort, inconvenience, trouble

तनख़्वाह *tankhvāh*, तनख़ाह *tankhāh* f. pay, wages

तब *tab* then

तबला *tablā* m. tabla (drum)

तबियत *tabiyat* f. *health, disposition*

तमिल f. *Tamil*

तस्वीर *tasvīr* f. *picture*

ताकि *tāki* *so that, in order that*

ताज महल *tāj mahal* m. *Taj Mahal*

ताज़ा *tāzā* (-ā ending sometimes treated as invariable) *fresh*

ताश *tāś* m. *playing cards*

तीन *tīn* *three*

तीसरा *tīsrā* *third*

तुम *tum* *you* (familiar)

तुम्हारा *tumhārā* *your, yours*

तू *tū* *you* (intimate)

तैयार *taiyār* *ready, prepared;* तैयार करना *taiyār karnā* *to prepare;* तैयार हो जाना *taiyār ho jānā* *to get ready*

तैयारी *taiyārī* f. *preparation*

तो *to* *so, then; as for ...*

तोड़ना *toṛnā* *to break, smash*

तोता *totā* m. *parrot*

तोहफ़ा *tohfā* m. *gift, present*

थकना *thaknā* *to get tired*

थाना *thānā* m. *police station*

थोड़ा *thoṛā* *(a) little;* थोड़ी देर *thoṛī der* f. *a little while*

दक्षिण *dakṣiṇ* *south*

दफ़्तर *daftar* m. *office*

दयालु *dayālu* *kind, merciful*

दरवाज़ा *darvāzā* m. *door*

दर्ज़ी *darzī* m. *tailor*

दर्द *dard* m. *pain*

दवा *davā* f. *medicine*

दवाख़ाना *davākhānā* m. *pharmacy, chemist's shop*

दस *das* *ten*

दस्त *dast* m. *diarrhoea;* दस्त आना *dast ānā* *to have diarrhoea*

दाँत *dā̃t* m. *tooth*

दादा *dādā* m. *grandfather* (father's father)

दादी *dādī f.* *grandmother* (father's mother)

दाल *dāl* f. *daal, lentil*

दाहिना *dāhinā* *right* (direction)

दिखाना *dikhānā* *to show*

दिन *din* m. *day*

दिल *dil* m. *heart*

दिल्ली *dillī* f. *Delhi*

दीया *diyā* m. *lamp*

दीवार, दीवाल *dīvār, dīvāl* f. *wall*

दुकान *dukān* f. *shop*

दुकानदार *dukāndār* m. *shopkeeper*

दुखी *dukhī* *sad*

दुर्घटना *durghaṭnā* f. *accident*

दूध *dūdh* m. *milk*

दूधवाला *dūdhvālā* m. *milkman*

दूर *dūr* *far, distant*

दूसरा *dūsrā* *second; other*

देखना *dekhnā* *to look, to see*

देना *denā* *to give; to allow to, let* (with oblique infinitive: हमको जाने दो *hamko jāne do* Let us go)

देर *der* f. *a while, length of time; delay;* देर से *der se* late

देरी *derī* f. *delay*

देश *deś* m. *country*

दो *do* *two*

दोनों *donõ* *both, the two*

दोस्त *dost* m., f. *friend*

दौड़ना *dauṛnā* to run

धन्यवाद *dhanyavād* thank you

धीरे धीरे *dhīre dhīre* slowly

धुलना *dhulnā* to be washed

धुलवाना *dhulvānā* to get washed

धोना *dhonā to* wash

धोबी *dhobī* m. washerman

ध्यान *dhyān* m. attention; ध्यान से *dhyān se* attentively; ध्यान रखना *dhyān rakhnā* to pay attention to, look after

न *na* don't; isn't that so?

नक़्शा *naqśā* m. map, plan

नदी *nadī* f. river

नमस्कार *namaskār* hello; goodbye

नमस्ते *namaste* hello; goodbye

नया *nayā* (f. नई *naī;* m. pl. नए *nae)* new

नर्स *nars* m., f. nurse

नल *nal* m. tap, pipe

नहाना *nahānā* to bathe

नहीं *nahī̃* not, no

नाक *nāk* f. nose

नाम *nām* m. name

नाराज़ *nārāz* angry, displeased

नाव *nāv* f. boat

नाश्ता *nāśtā* m. breakfast, snack; नाश्ता करना *nāśtā karnā* to have breakfast

निकलना *nikalnā* to emerge, come/go out नीचे *nīce* down, downstairs

नींद *nī̃d* f. sleep; नींद आना *nī̃d ānā* (sleep to come) to get to sleep

नीला *nīlā* blue

नेता *netā* m. leader; politician

नेपाल *nepāl* m. Nepal

नौ *nau* nine

नौकर *naukar* m. servant

नौकरी *naukarī* f. job, employment

पंखा *pankhā* m. fan

पकड़ना *pakaṛnā* to catch

पचास *pacās* fifty

पड़ना *paṛnā* to fall; to have to (with preceding infinitive: मुझे जाना पड़ेगा *mujhe jānā paṛegā I'll have to go)*

पड़ा *paṛā* lying

पड़ोसी *paṛosī* m., पड़ोसिन *paṛosin* f. neighbour

पढ़ना *paṛhnā* to read, to study

पढ़ाई *paṛhāī* f. studies, studying

पढ़ाना *paṛhānā* to teach

पतला *patlā* thin

पता *patā* m. address; whereabouts

पति *pati* m. husband

पत्नी *patnī* f. wife

पत्र *patr* m. letter (correspondence)

पर *par*[1] but

पर *par*[2] on; at (at home, etc.)

परसों *parsõ* two days away (the day after tomorrow; the day before yesterday)

परिवार *parivār* m. family

पश्चिम *paścim* west

पसंद *pasand* pleasing (यह मुझको पसंद है *yah mujhko pasand hai I* like this); पसंद आना *pasand ānā* to appeal to, to be liked

पहला *pahlā* first

पहाड़ *pahāṛ* m. hill

पहुँचना *pahũcnā* to reach, arrive

पाँच *pā̃c* five; पाँचवाँ *pā̃cvā̃* fifth

पाँव *pā̃v* m. *foot, leg*

पाकिस्तान *pākistān* m. *Pakistan*

पागल *pāgal* *mad, crazy*

पाना *pānā* *to find, obtain; to be able, to manage to* (with verb stem: मैं नहीं जा पाया *maĩ nahī̃ jā pāyā* *I didn't manage to go*)

पानी *pānī* m. *water*

पापा *pāpā* m. *papa, father*

पार *pār* across; पार करना *pār karnā* to cross; उस पार *us pār* on the other side (of के *ke*)

पार्टी *pārṭī* f. party

पास में *pās mẽ* *nearby*

पिछला *pichlā* *previous, last*

पिता *pitā* m. *father*

पीटना *pīṭnā* *to beat, thrash*

पीना *pīnā* *to drink; to smoke*

पीला *pīlā* *yellow*

पुकारना *pukārnā* *to call out*

पुराना *purānā* *old* (for inanimates, not for people)

पुल *pul* m. bridge

पुलिस *pulis* f. police; पुलिसवाला *pulisvālā* m. policeman

पुस्तकालय *pustakālay* m. *library*

पूछना *pūchnā* *to ask*

पूरा *pūrā* *full, complete*

पूर्व *pūrv* *east*

पेट *peṭ* m. stomach

पेड़ *peṛ* m. *tree*

पैदल *paidal* *on foot*

पैर *pair* m. *foot;* पैर की उँगली *pair kī ũglī* f. *toe*

पैसा *paisā* m. *money*

प्यारा *pyārā* *dear, sweet, cute*

प्यास *pyās* f. *thirst;* प्यास लगना *pyās lagnā* *(thirst to strike) to feel thirsty*

प्रदेश *pradeś* m. *state, region*

प्रधान मंत्री *pradhān mantrī* m., f. *prime minister*

प्रिय *priy* *dear; Dear* (in informal letter writing)

प्रेस करना *pres karnā* *to iron*

प्लेट *pleṭ* f. *plate*

फ़र्श *farś* m./f. *floor*

फल *phal* m. *fruit*

फलवाला *phalvālā* m. *fruitseller*

फिर, फिर से *phir, phir se* again

फ़िल्म *film* f. *film*

फ़ीस *fīs* f. *fee, fees*

फूल *phūl* m. *flower*

फ़ोन *fon* m. *phone;* फ़ोन करना *fon karnā* *to phone*

बंद *band* *closed, shut*

बकवास *bakvās* f. *nonsense, idle chatter*

बग़ीचा *bagīcā* m. *garden*

बचपन *bacpan m* *childhood*

बच्चा *baccā* m. *child*

बजना *bajnā* *to play, resound, chime*

बजाना *bajānā* *to play* (music)

बजे *baje* *o'clock*

बड़ा *baṛā* *big*

बटुआ *baṭuā* m. *purse, wallet*

बढ़िया *baṛhiyā* (invariable *-ā* ending) *excellent, really good, fine*

बताना *batānā* *to tell*

बत्ती *battī* f. *light, lamp*

बनवाना *banvānā* *to cause, to be made*

बनाना *banānā* *to make*

बरतन *bartan* m. *dish, utensil*

बस *bas* f. *bus*

बहिन *bahin* f. *sister*

बहुत *bahut* *very;* बहुत ज़्यादा *bahut zyādā* *very great, too much*

बाँह *bā̃h* f. *arm, upper arm*

बाज़ार *bāzār* m. *market, bazaar*

बात *bāt* f. *thing said, idea;* बात करना *bāt karnā* *to talk*

बाप *bāp* m. *dad;* बाप रे बाप ! *bāp re bāp!* *Oh God!*

बायाँ *bāyā̃* *left* (direction)

बार *bār* f. *time, occasion;* इस बार *is bār* *this time;* कितनी बार *kitnī bār* *how many times?;* कई बार *kaī bār* *several times*

बारिश *bāriś f* *rain;* बारिश होना *bāriś honā* *to rain*

बाल *bāl* m. *hair*

बाहर *bāhar* *outside*

बिजली *bijlī* f. *electricity*

बिलकुल *bilkul* *quite, completely*

बिल्ली *billī* f. *cat*

बिस्कुट *biskut* m. *biscuit, cookie*

बीमार *bīmār* *ill, sick*

बीयर *bīyar* f. *beer*

बुख़ार *bu<u>kh</u>ār* m. *fever*

बुधवार *budhvār* m. *Wednesday*

बुरा *burā* *bad*

बुलवाना *bulvānā* *to cause to be called*

बुलाना *bulānā* *to call, invite, summon*

बूढ़ा *būṛhā* *elderly*

बेचना *becnā* *to sell*

बेटा *betā* m. *son*

बेटी *betī* f. *daughter*

बेहतर *behtar* *better*

बैठना *baithnā* *to sit*

बैठा *baiṭhā* *seated, sitting*

बोतल *botal* f. *bottle*

बोलना *bolnā* *to speak*

भयंकर *bhayankar* *terrible*

भरना *bharnā* *to be filled*

भरोसा *bharosā* m. *trust, reliance*

भाई *bhāī* m. *brother*

भाड़ में जाए *bhāṛ mẽ jāe* (he/she) *can go to hell* (भाड़ *bhār* m. *grain-parching oven)*

भारत *bhārat* m. *India*

भारी *bhārī* *heavy*

भाषा *bhāṣā* f. *language*

भिजवाना *bhijvānā* *to have sent, to cause to be sent*

भी *bhī* *also; even*

भूख *bhūkh* f. *hunger;* भूख लगना *bhūkh lagnā* *(hunger to strike) to feel hungry*

भेजना *bhejnā* *to send*

मंगलवार *maṅgalvār* m. *Tuesday*

मंदिर *mandir* m. *temple*

मकान *makān* m. *house*

मज़ा *mazā* m. *enjoyment, fun;* मज़े करना *maze karnā* *to enjoy oneself, have fun*

मत *mat* don't

मतलब *matlab* m. *meaning*

मदद *madad* f. *help;* किसी की मदद करना *kisī kī madad karnā* *to help someone*

मराठी *marāṭhī* f. *Marathi*

मरीज़ *marīz* m. *patient*

महँगा *mahā̃gā* *expensive*

महसूस करना ***mahsūs karnā*** *to feel;* महसूस होना ***mahsūs honā*** *to be felt, experienced*

महिला ***mahilā*** f. *lady*

महीना ***mahinā*** m. *month*

माँ ***mā̃*** f. *mother;* माँ-बाप ***mā̃-bāp*** m. pl. *parents*

माँगना ***mā̃gnā*** *to ask for, demand*

माँजना ***mā̃jnā*** *to scour, clean, cleanse*

माता ***mātā*** f. *mother*

माता-पिता ***mātā-pitā*** m. pl. *parents*

माथा ***māthā*** m. *forehead*

माफ़ी ***māfī*** f. *forgiveness;* माफ़ी माँगना ***māfī mā̃gnā*** *to apologize*

मामूली ***māmūlī*** *ordinary*

मारना ***mārnā*** *to hit, beat, strike*

माल ***māl*** m. *goods, stuff*

मालूम ***mālūm*** *(is) known;* मालूम नहीं ***mālūm nahī̃*** *(I) don't know*

मार्ग ***mārg*** m. *road, street* (used in street names)

मिठाई ***mithāī*** f. *sweet, sweetmeat*

मिठास ***miṭhās*** f. *sweetness*

मिलना ***milnā*** *to meet, to be available*

मीठा ***mīṭhā*** *sweet*

मुंबई ***mumbaī*** f. *Mumbai, Bombay*

मुँह ***mũh*** m. *mouth; face*

मुड़ना ***muṛnā*** *to turn*

मुफ़्त (का) ***muft (kā)*** *free;* मुफ़्त में ***muft mẽ*** *for nothing, free*

मुश्किल ***muśkil*** *difficult;* मुश्किल से ***muśkil se*** *with difficulty, hardly*

मुस्कराना ***muskarānā*** *to smile*

में ***mẽ*** *in*

मेज़ ***mez*** f. *table*

मेमसाहब ***memsāhab*** f. *memsahib, lady of the house*

मेरा ***merā*** *my, mine*

मेहनत ***mehnat*** f. *hard work;* मेहनती ***mehntī*** *hard working*

मैं ***maĩ*** *I*

मैला ***mailā*** *dirty*

मोटा ***moṭā*** *fat*

मौसम ***mausam*** m. *weather*

यह ***yah*** *he, she, it, this*

यहाँ ***yahā̃*** *here*

यहीं ***yahī̃*** *right here*

या ***yā*** *or*

यात्री ***yātrī*** m. *traveller, passenger*

याद ***yād*** f. *memory*

यानी ***yānī*** *in other words, that is to say*

ये ***ye*** *they, these*

रखना ***rakhnā*** *to put, place, keep*

रविवार ***ravivār*** m. *Sunday*

रसोई ***rasoī*** f. *kitchen*

रहना ***rahnā*** *to live, to stay*

राजा ***rājā*** m. *king, raja*

रात ***rāt*** f. *night, PM;* रात का खाना ***rāt kā khānā*** m. *dinner*

रास्ता ***rāstā*** m. *road*

रिक्शा ***rikśā*** m. *rickshaw*

रिक्शेवाला ***rikśevālā*** m. *rickshaw driver*

रिश्तेदार ***riśtedār*** m. *relation, relative*

रुपया ***rupayā*** m. *rupee*

रेडियो ***reḍiyo*** m. *radio*

रोज़ ***roz*** *every day*

रोना ***ronā*** *to cry, weep*

लंबा ***lambā*** *tall*

लगना ***lagnā*** *time to be taken;* घर जाने में १० मिनट लगते हैं/एक घंटा

लगता है *ghar jāne mẽ 10 minaṭ lagte haĩ/ek ghaṇṭā lagtā hai* It takes 10 minutes/one hour to get home; लगना *lagnā* to seem; to be felt (of hunger, thirst, etc.); to have an effect; to begin (following an oblique infinitive)

लड़का *laṛkā* m. boy

लड़की *laṛkī* f. girl

लन्दन *landan* m. London

लाइट *lāiṭ* f. light, electric power

लाना *lānā* to bring

लाल *lāl* red

लिखना *likhnā* to write

लेकिन *lekin* but

लेखक *lekhak* m. writer

लेटना *leṭnā* to lie down

लेटा *leṭā* lying, lying down

लेना *lenā* to take

लोग *log* m. pl. people

लौटना *lauṭnā* to return

व *va* and

वग़ैरह *vagairah* etc., and so on

वज़न *vazan* m. weight

वह *vah* he, she, it, that

वहाँ *vahā̃* there

वापस *vāpas* 'back' in वापस आना/जाना/देना *vāpas ānā/jānā/denā* to come/go/give back

वाराणसी *vārāṇasī* f. Varanasi, Banaras

विदेश *videś* abroad

विदेशी *videśī* m. foreigner; adj. foreign

विद्यार्थी *vidyārthī* m. student

वे *ve* they, those

शक्ति *śakti* f. power

शनिवार *śanivār* m. Saturday

शब्द *śabd* m. word

शब्दकोश *śabdkoś* m. dictionary

शराब *śarāb* f. alcoholic drink, liquor

शरीर *śarīr* m. body

शहर *śahar* m. town, city

शांति *śānti* f. peace

शादी *śādī* f. wedding, marriage; शादी करना *śādī karnā* to marry

शादी-शुदा *śādī-śudā* (*ā* ending invariable) married

शानदार *śāndār* splendid, magnificent

शाबाश *śābāś* bravo!, well done!

शाम *śām* f. evening

शायद *śāyad* maybe, perhaps

शिकायत *śikāyat* f. complaint; शिकायत करना *śikāyat karnā* to complain

शुक्रवार *śukravār* m. Friday

शुक्रिया *śukriyā* thank you

शुद्ध *śuddh* pure

शुभ *śubh* good, auspicious

शुभकामना *subhkāmnā* f. good wish

शोला *śolā* m. flame

शौक़ *śauq* m. liking, hobby, interest

श्री *śrī* Mr; श्रीमती *śrīmatī* Mrs

संगीत *saṅgīt* m. music

संगीतकार *saṅgītkār* m. musician

संतरा *santarā* m. orange

सकना *saknā* to be able (with verb stem: तुम जा सकते हो *tum jā sakte ho* You can go)

सच *sac* m. truth; adj. true

सड़क *saṛak* f. road, street

सपना *sapnā* m. dream; सपना देखना *sapnā dekhnā* to dream, to have a dream

सब *sab* all; सब कुछ *sab kuch* everything; सबसे *sabse* of all (in superlatives, e.g. सबसे अच्छा *sabse acchā* best, best of all)

सब्ज़ी *sabzī* f. vegetable(s); सब्ज़ी मंडी *sabzī maṇḍī* f. vegetable market; सब्ज़ीवाला *sabzīvālā* m. vegetable seller

समझना *samajhnā* to understand

समय *samay* m. time

समोसा *samosā* m. samosa

सरकार *sarkār* f. government

सलाह *salāh* f. advice

सवारी *savārī* f. passenger, rider

सस्ता *sastā* cheap

सहायता *sahāytā* f. assistance

सहित *sahit* with (formal)

सही *sahī* correct, true, exact

सहेली *sahelī* f. *female's* female friend

-सा *-sā* -ish (suffix that qualifies an adjective, as in बड़ा-सा *baṛā-sā* biggish)

साइकिल *sāikil* f. bicycle

साड़ी *sāṛī* f. sari

सात *sāt* seven

सादर *sādar* respectful

साफ़ *sāf* clean, clear; साफ़ करना *sāf karnā* to clean

साबुन *sābun* m. soap

सामने *sāmne* opposite

सामान *sāmān* m. goods, furniture, luggage

साया *sāyā* m. shade, shadow

साल *sāl* m. year

साहब *sāhab* m. sahib

सिखवाना *sikhvānā* to cause to be taught

सिखाना *sikhānā* to teach

सिग्रेट *sigreṭ* m./f. cigarette

सितार *sitār* m. sitar

सिनेमा *sinemā* m. cinema

सिर *sir* m. head

सिर्फ़ *sirf* only

सिलवाना *silvānā* to have sewn

सीना *sīnā* to sew

सीखना *sīkhnā* to learn

सुंदर *sundar* beautiful, handsome

सुखी *sukhī* happy

सुनना *sunnā* to hear, to listen

सुनसान *sunsān* desolate, empty

सुबह *subah* f. morning

से *se* from

सैर *sair* f. trip

सोचना *socnā* to think

सोना *sonā* to sleep

सोमवार *somvār* m. Monday

सौ *sau* m. hundred

स्कूल *skūl* m. school

हँसना *hãsnā* to laugh

हफ़्ता *haftā* m. week

हम *ham* we, us

हमारा *hamārā* our, ours

हमेशा *hameśā* always

हर *har* every, each

हवा *havā* f. air, breeze

हाँ *hā̃* yes

हाथ *hāth* m. hand

हाथी *hāthī* m. elephant

हाल *hāl* m. condition, state (in क्या हाल है ? *kyā hāl hai?* How's things? How are you?)

हिन्दी *hindī* f. Hindi

हिन्दुस्तानी ***hindustānī*** *Indian*

हिलाना ***hilānā*** *to move, shake*

ही ***hī*** *only* (emphatic)

हीरा ***hīrā*** m. *diamond*

हुआ ***huā*** (past tense of होना ***honā***) *happened*

हूँ ***hū̃*** *am*

हैं ***haĩ*** *are*

है ***hai*** *is*

हो ***ho*** *are* (with तुम ***tum***)

होटल ***hotal*** m. *hotel, restaurant, café*

होना ***honā*** *to be;* हो जाना ***ho jānā*** *to become*

होशियार ***hośiyār*** *clever*

English–Hindi vocabulary

KEY

adj. adjective (only stated to resolve ambiguities)

adv. adverb

f. feminine

m. masculine

m., f. used for both sexes

m./f. used in either gender

N regularly uses the ने ne construction in perfective tenses

n sometimes uses the ने ne construction in perfective tenses

pl. plural

a एक *ek* कोई *koī*

able, to be सकना *saknā* (after verb stem – मैं जा सकता हूँ *maĩ jā saktā hū̃* *I can go*)

about (approx.) क़रीब *qarīb* लगभग *lagbhag;* (with number) कोई *koī* (कोई दस लोग *koī das log* *some ten people*);

(concerning) के बारे में *ke bāre mẽ*

above ऊपर *ūpar*

abroad विदेश *videś*

accept, to स्वीकार करना *svīkār karnā*[N]; मानना *mānnā*[N]

accident हादसा *hādsā* m., दुर्घटना *durghaṭnā* f.

actually वैसे *vaise*

add, to जोड़ना *joṛnā*[N]

address पता *patā* m.

advice सलाह *salāh* f.

aeroplane हवाई जहाज़ *havāī jahāz* m.

affection प्यार *pyār* m.

after के बाद *ke bād*

again फिर *phir*, फिर से *phir se*

age (of person) उम्र f. *umra, umar*

Agra आगरा *āgrā* m.

ahead (of) (के) आगे *(ke) āge*

air हवा *havā* f.

airmail हवाई डाक *havāī ḍāk* f.

alcoholic drink शराब *śarāb* f.

all सब *sab*, सभी *sabhī;* whole सारा *sārā*

allow, to oblique inf. + देना *denā*[N] (मुझे जाने दो *mujhe jāne do* *'let me go'*)

alone अकेला *akelā;* (adv.) अकेले *akele*

also भी *bhī*

although हालाँकि *hālā̃ki*

always हमेशा *hameśā*

America अमरीका *amrīkā* m.; *American* अमरीकन *amrīkan*

among के बीच *ke bīc; among themselves* आपस में *āpas mẽ*

and और *aur*

anger गुस्सा *gussā* m.

angry नाराज़ *nārāz*

answer जवाब *javāb* m.; *to answer* जवाब देना *javāb denā*ᴺ

anxiety परेशानी *pareśānī* f.; चिंता *cintā* f.

anyone (at all) कोई (भी) *koī (bhī)*

anywhere (at all) कहीं (भी) *kahī̃ (bhī)*

apart from के सिवा/सिवाय *ke sivā/sivāy;* को छोड़कर *ko choṛkar*

apologize, to (से) माफ़ी माँगना *(se) māfī mā̃gnā*ᴺ

appear, to दिखना *dikhnā* दिखाई देना *dikhāī denā; to seem* लगना *lagnā*

area, district इलाक़ा *ilāqā* m.

arm बाँह *bā̃h* f.

around, in the vicinity of के आस-पास *ke ās-pās*

arrange, to का इंतज़ाम करना *kā intazām karnā*ᴺ

arrangement इंतज़ाम *intazām* m.

arrive, to पहुँचना *pahũcnā*

as if, as though जैसे *jaise,* मानों *mānõ*

as soon as जैसे ही *jaise hī*

ask, to पूछना *pūchnā*ᴺ; *ask Ram* राम से पूछो *Rām se pūcho*

at को *ko;* पर *par*

at least कम से कम *kam se kam*

attention ध्यान *dhyān* m.; *to pay attention (to)* (पर) ध्यान देना *(par) dhyān denā*ᴺ

attentively ध्यान से *dhyān se*

August अगस्त *agast* m.

available, to be मिलना *milnā*

back (in sense 'return') वापस *vāpas*

back (part of body) पीठ *pīṭh* f.

bad ख़राब *kharāb,* बुरा *burā*

bag, cloth bag थैला *thailā* m.

Banaras बनारस *banāras* m., वाराणसी *vārāṇasī* f.

bathe, to नहाना *nahānā*

be, to होना *honā,* बनना *bannā*

beat, to मारना *mārnā*ᴺ

beautiful सुन्दर *sundar*

because क्योंकि *kyõki*

because of की वजह से *kī vajah se,* के कारण *ke kāraṇ*

become, to बनना *bannā*

before (के/से) पहले *(ke/se) pahle*

begin to, to oblique inf. + लगना *lagnā* (पानी पड़ने लगा *pānī paṛne lagā* it began to rain); शुरू करना *śurū karnā*ᴺ (हम काम शुरू करें *ham kām śurū karẽ* let's begin work)

beginning शुरू *surū* m.

behind (के) पीछे *(ke) pīche*

bell घंटी *ghaṇṭī* f.

below, beneath (के) नीचे *(ke) nīce*

between के बीच *ke bīc; between*

themselves आपस में *āpas mẽ*

bicycle साइकिल *sāikil* f.

big बड़ा *baṛā*

bird चिड़िया *ciṛiyā* f.

birth जन्म *janm* m.

birthday जन्मदिन *janmdin* m.

blanket कंबल *kambal* m.

boil, to उबलना *ubalnā*, उबालना *ubālnā*N

book किताब *kitāb* f.; पुस्तक *pustak* f.

bored, to be ऊबना *ūbnā*

born, to be पैदा होना *paidā honā* (पैदा *paidā* inv.); का जन्म होना *kā janm honā*

both दोनों *donõ*

bottle बोतल *botal* f.

boy लड़का *laṛkā* m.

bread रोटी *roṭī* f.; (loaf) डबल रोटी *ḍabal roṭī* f.

break, to तोड़ना *toṛnā*N

breakfast नाश्ता *nāśtā* m.

bridge पुल *pul* m.

bring, to लाना *lānā*, ले आना *le ānā*

broken, to be टूटना *ṭūṭnā*

brother भाई *bhāī* m.

brother-in-law (husband's younger brother) देवर *devar* m.; (wife's brother) साला *sālā* m.

building इमारत *imārat* f.

bullet गोली *golī* f.

burn, to जलना *jalnā;* जलाना *jalānā*N

bus बस *bas* f.

but लेकिन *lekin,*पर *par,* मगर *magar*

butter मक्खन *makkhan* m.

buy, to ख़रीदना *kharīdnā*N

by से *se; by means of* (के) द्वारा *(ke) dvārā*

call, to (invite) बुलाना *bulānā*N

camera कैमरा *kaimrā* m.

can: see *able, to be*

capital city राजधानी *rājdhānī* f.

car गाड़ी *gāṛī* f., कार *kār* f.

care (about), to (की) परवाह करना *(kī) parvāh karnā*N

cat बिल्ली *billī* f.

catch, to पकड़ना *pakaṛnā*N; (fire or illness) लगना *lagnā*

cause कारण *kāraṇ* m.

certainly ज़रूर *zarūr*

chair कुरसी *kursī* f.

chance मौक़ा *mauqā* m.

change, to बदलना *badalnā*n

chapatti चपाती *capātī* f.

cheap सस्ता *sastā*

child बच्चा *baccā* m.

childhood बचपन *bacpan* m.

choose, to चुनना *cunnā*N

cigarette सिग्रेट *sigreṭ* m./f.

cinema सिनेमा *sinemā* m.

city शहर *śahar* m.

class क्लास *klās* m./f.

clean साफ़ *sāf; to clean* साफ़ करना *sāf karnā*N

cleaning सफ़ाई *safāī* f.

clear साफ़ *sāf;* (evident) ज़ाहिर *zahir*

clever (intelligent) होशियार *hośiyār;* (cunning) चतुर *catur*

closed बंद *band*

close, to बंद करना *band karnā*N

cloth कपड़ा *kaprā* m.

clothing, garment कपड़ा *kaprā* m.

cloud बादल *bādal* m.

coffee काफ़ी *kāfī* f.

cold ठंड *ṭhaṇḍ* f.; (adj.) ठंडा *ṭhaṇḍā;* (illness) ज़ुकाम *zukām* m.

come, to आना *ānā*

come out, to निकलना *nikalnā*

comfort आराम *ārām* m.; *comfortably* आराम से *ārām se*

companion साथी *sāthī* m.

complain, to शिकायत करना *śikāyat karnā*N*; to complain to Sita about Ram* सीता से राम की शिकायत करना *Sītā se Rām kī śikāyat karnā*N

complaint शिकायत *śikāyat* f.

computer कम्प्यूटर *kampyūṭar* m.

concern चिंता *cintā* f.

condition (state) हाल *hāl* m., हालत *hālat* f.

congratulations बधाई *badhāī* f.

conversation बातचीत *bātcīt* f.

copy (of book, etc.) प्रति *prati* f.

corner कोना *konā* m.

correct सही *sahī*

cough, to खाँसी आना *khā̃sī ānā*

country देश *deś* m.

cow गाय *gāy* f.

cross, to (road etc.) पार करना *pār karnā*N

crowd भीड़ *bhīṛ* f.

cup प्याला *pyālā* m.

cupboard अलमारी *almārī* f.

cure इलाज *ilāj* m.

curtain परदा *pardā* m.

cut, to be कटना *kaṭnā*

cut, to काटना *kāṭnā*N

daal, lentils दाल *dāl* f.

daily (adverb) रोज़ *roz*

dance नृत्य *nṛtya* m., नाच *nāc* m.; *to dance* नाचना *nācnā*

dark अँधेरा *ā̃dherā;* (of colour) गहरा *gahrā; darkness* अँधेरा *ā̃dherā* m.

date तारीख़ *tārīkh* f.

daughter बेटी *beṭī* f.

daughter-in-law बहू *bahū* f.

day दिन *din* m.; *all day* दिन भर *din bhar; day before yesterday/after tomorrow* परसों *parsõ*

dear प्रिय *priy*

death मौत *maut* f., मृत्यु *mṛtyu* f.

degree (academic) डिगरी *ḍigrī* f.

delay देर f. *der*

Delhi दिल्ली *dillī* f.

deliberately जान-बूझकर *jān-būjhkar*

description वर्णन *varṇan* m.; to describe का वर्णन करना *kā varṇan karnā*N

despair निराशा *nirāśā* f.

Devanagari (the Hindi script)

देवनागरी *devnāgarī* f.

dhobi, washerman धोबी *dhobī* m.

dialect बोली *bolī* f.

dictionary शब्दकोश *śabdkoś* m.

die, to मरना *marnā*

difference फ़र्क़ *farq* m.; *it makes no difference* कोई फ़र्क़ नहीं पड़ता *koī farq nahī̃ paṛtā*

different भिन्न *bhinn;* (separate) अलग *alag*

difficult मुश्किल *muśkil*

difficulty मुश्किल *muśkil* f.

direction तरफ़ *taraf* f., ओर *or* f.

dirty गंदा *gandā,* मैला *mailā*

disappointment निराशा *nirāśā* f.; *disappointed* निराश *nirāś*

distant दूर *dūr*

do, to करना *karnā*^N

doctor डाक्टर *ḍākṭar* m.

dog कुत्ता *kuttā* m.

don't (in commands) न *na,* मत *mat*

door दरवाज़ा *darvāzā* m.

doubt शंका *śankā* f.

down, downstairs नीचे *nīce*

draw, to खींचना *khī̃cnā*^N

drawer दराज़ *darāz* f.

dream सपना *sapnā* m.; *to dream* सपना देखना *sapnā dekhnā*^N

drink, to पीना *pīnā*^N

drive, to चलाना *calānā*^N

driver ड्राइवर *ḍrāivar* m.

each हर *har,* हरेक *harek*

ear कान *kān* m.

early जल्दी *jaldī*

earn, to कमाना *kamānā*^N

easily आसानी से *āsānī se,* आराम से *ārām se*

easy आसान *āsān*

eat, to खाना *khānā*^N

edge किनारा *kinārā* m.

either ... or या तो ... या *yā to ... yā*

electricity बिजली *bijlī* f.

email ई-मेल *ī-mel* f./m.

emerge, to निकलना *nikalnā*

employment नौकरी *naukrī* f.

end अंत *ant* m.; *in the end, after all* आख़िर (में) *ākhir (mẽ)*

English person अँग्रेज़ *ãgrez* m., f.

enough! that's all! बस! *bas!*

envelope लिफ़ाफ़ा *lifāfā* m.

escape, to बचना *bacnā*

etc. वग़ैरह *vagairah,* इत्यादि *ityādi*

evening शाम *śām* f.

everything सब *sab,* सब कुछ *sab kuch*

exactly, precisely ठीक *ṭhīk*

examination परीक्षा *parīkṣā* f.; *to take (sit) an exam* परीक्षा देना *parīkṣā denā*^N; *to examine* की परीक्षा लेना *kī parīkṣā lenā*^N

except for (को) छोड़कर *ko choṛkar,* के सिवाय *ke sivāy*

expensive महँगा *mahãgā*

experience अनुभव *anubhav* m.

explain, to समझाना *samjhānā*^N

extremely बहुत ही *bahut hī*

face मुँह *mũh* m.; चेहरा *cehrā* m.

facing, opposite (के) सामने *(ke) sāmne*

fall, to गिरना *girnā*

family परिवार *parivār* m.

famous मशहूर *maśhūr*, प्रसिद्ध *prasiddh*

fan पंखा *pankhā* m.

far away दूर *dūr*

fare (taxi, etc.) किराया *kirāyā* m.

fat मोटा *moṭā*

father पिता *pitā* m. (inv.), बाप *bāp* m.

fault (guilt) कसूर *kasūr* m.

fear डर *ḍar* m.; *to fear* (से) डरना *(se ḍarnā)*

feel, to महसूस करना *mahsūs karnā*[N]; *to be felt* महसूस होना *mahsūs honā*

fetch, to लाना *lānā*, ले आना *le ānā*

fever बुख़ार *bukhār* m.

fight, to (से) लड़ना *(se) laṛnā*[N]

film फ़िल्म *film* f.

find, to पाना *pānā*[N]

finger उँगली *ũglī* f.

finish, to ख़त्म करना *khatm karnā*[N]

finished ख़त्म *khatm*

fire आग *āg* f.

first पहला *pahlā*; (adverb) पहले *pahle*

fix, to ठीक करना *ṭhīk karnā*[N]

floor फ़र्श *farś* m./f.

flower फूल *phūl* m.

fly (insect) मक्खी *makkhī* f.

fly, to उड़ना *uṛnā*

follow, to का पीछा करना *kā pīchā karnā*[N]

food खाना *khānā* m.

for के लिए *ke lie*

forbidden मना *manā* (inv.)

force, strength ज़ोर *zor* m.

foreign country विदेश *videś* m.

foreigner विदेशी *videśī* m.

forget, to भूलना *bhūlnā*, भूल जाना *bhūl jānā*

forgive, to माफ़ करना *māf karnā*[N]

forgiveness माफ़ी *māfī* f.

fork (utensil) काँटा *kā̃ṭā* m.

free (vacant) ख़ाली *khālī*; (of cost) मुफ़्त *muft*; *free time* फ़ुरसत *fursat* f.

fresh ताज़ा *tāzā*

friend दोस्त *dost* m., f., मित्र *mitr* m., f.; (girl's girlfriend) सहेली *sahelī* f.

from से *se*

fruit फल *phal* m.

full पूरा *pūrā*, भरा *bharā*

fun मज़ा *mazā* m.

furniture सामान *sāmān* m.

future भविष्य *bhaviṣya* m.

Ganges गंगा *gangā* f.

garden बग़ीचा *bagīcā* m.

get up, to उठना *uṭhnā*

ghost भूत *bhūt* m.

gift तोहफ़ा *tohfā* m., भेंट *bhẽṭ* f.

girl लड़की *laṛkī* f.

give, to देना *denā*[N]; *to give up* छोड़ना *choṛnā*[N]

glasses चश्मा *caśmā* m.

go, to जाना *jānā*

gold सोना *sonā* m.

good अच्छा *acchā;* (decent) भला *bhalā*

goodbye नमस्ते *namaste,* नमस्कार *namaskār*

government सरकार *sarkār* f.; *governmental* सरकारी *sarkārī*

grandfather (father's father) दादा *dādā* m. (invariable -*ā* ending); (mother's father) नाना *nānā* m. (invariable -*ā* ending)

grandmother (father's mother) दादी *dādī* f.; (mother's mother) नानी *nānī* f.

grass घास *ghās* f.

guest मेहमान *mehmān* m.

guru गुरु *guru* m.

half आधा *ādhā* adj. & m.

hand हाथ *hāth* m.

happiness ख़ुशी *<u>kh</u>uśī* f.

happy ख़ुश *khuś*

harass, to तंग करना *tang karnā*[N]

hard, difficult मुश्किल *muśkil*

hard-working मेहनती *mehntī*

harm नुक़सान *nuqsān* m.

hate नफ़रत *nafrat* f.; *to hate* (से) नफ़रत करना *(se) nafrat karnā*[N]

he वह *vah*

head सिर *sir* m.

health तबियत *tabiyat* f.

hear, to सुनना *sunnā*[N]

heart दिल *dil* m.

heat गरमी *garmī* f.

heaven स्वर्ग *svarg* m.

heavy भारी *bhārī*

height लंबाई *lambāī* f.

hello नमस्ते *namaste,* नमस्कार *namaskār;* (on phone) हलो *halo*

help मदद *madad* f.; *to help him* उसकी मदद करना *uskī madad karnā*[N]

here यहाँ *yahā̃,* इधर *idhar*

high ऊँचा *ū̃cā*

hill पहाड़ *pahāṛ* m.

Hindi हिन्दी *hindī* f.

Hindu हिन्दू *hindū*

history इतिहास *itihās* m.

hit, to मारना *mārnā*[N]

holiday छुट्टी *chuṭṭī* f.

home घर *ghar* m.; *at home* घर पर *ghar par*

hope आशा *āśā* f., उम्मीद *ummīd* f.

hospital अस्पताल *aspatāl* m.

hot गरम *garam*

hotel होटल *hoṭal* m.

hour घंटा *ghaṇṭā* m.

house मकान *makān* m.

how much/many कितना *kitnā; how much does that come to?* कितना हुआ ? *kitnā huā?*

hunger भूख *bhūkh* f.

hungry भूखा *bhūkhā; to feel hungry* भूख लगना *bhūkh lagnā*

husband पति *pati* m.

I मैं *maĩ*

ice बर्फ़ *barf* f.

idea विचार *vicār* m., ख़याल *khyāl* m.

if अगर *agar*

ill बीमार *bīmār*

immediately तुरंत *turant*

important ज़रूरी *zarūrī*

impossible असंभव *asambhav*, नामुमकिन *nāmumkin*

in में *mẽ*

in front (of) (के) आगे *(ke) āge*

increase, to बढ़ना *baṛhnā*, बढ़ाना *baṛhānā*ᴺ

India हिन्दुस्तान *hindustān* m., भारत *bhārat* m.; *Indian* हिन्दुस्तानी *hindustānī*, भारतीय *bhāratīy*

individual (person) व्यक्ति *vyakti* m.

inside (के) अंदर *(ke) andar*

instead of के बजाय *ke bajāy*

intelligent होशियार *hośiyār*, तेज़ *tez*

intention इरादा *irādā* m.

interesting दिलचस्प *dilcasp*

invite, to बुलाना *bulānā*ᴺ

-ish –सा *-sā*

it वह *vah*

job, employment नौकरी *naukrī* f.

joke मज़ाक़ *mazāq* m.; *joking, fun* हँसी-मज़ाक़ *hãsī-mazāq* m.

journey यात्रा *yātrā* f., सफ़र *safar* m.

jungle जंगल *jangal* m.

keep, to रखना *rakhnā*ᴺ

key चाबी *cābī* f.

kill, to मारना *mārnā*ᴺ, मार डालना *mār ḍālnā*ᴺ

kind (type) तरह *tarah* f., प्रकार *prakār* m.

king राजा *rājā* m. (inv.)

kitchen रसोईघर *rasoīghar* m.

knife छुरी *churī* f.

know, to जानना *jānnā*ᴺ; मालूम होना *mālūm honā*

kurta कुरता *kurtā* m.

lack कमी *kamī* f.

lady महिला *mahilā* f.

lamp (light) बत्ती *battī* f.

land ज़मीन *zamīn* f.

lane गली *galī* f.

language भाषा *bhāṣā* f., ज़बान *zabān* f.

last (previous) पिछला *pichlā*

late (delayed) देर से *der se*

later बाद (में) *bād (mẽ)*, आगे चलकर *āge calkar*

laugh, to हँसना *hãsnā*ⁿ; *to make laugh* हँसाना *hãsānā*ᴺ

lazy आलसी *ālsī*; (workshy) कामचोर *kāmcor*

leader; politician नेता *netā* m.

learn, to सीखना *sīkhnā*ᴺ; *to study* पढ़ना *paṛhnā*

leave, to छोड़ना *choṛnā*ᴺ

left (opp. of right) बायाँ *bāyā̃*; *to the left (hand side)* बायें/उलटे (हाथ) *bāyẽ/ulṭe (hāth)*

left (remaining) बाक़ी *bāqī*

length लंबाई *lambāī* f.

lentil(s) दाल *dāl* f.

less कम *kam*

letter ख़त *<u>kh</u>at* m., पत्र *patr* m., चिट्ठी *ciṭṭhī* f.

lie झूठ *jhūṭh* m.; *to lie* झूठ बोलना *jhūṭh bolna*N

lie, to (recline) लेटना *leṭnā*

life ज़िंदगी *zindagī* f., जीवन *jīvan* m.

lift, to उठाना *uṭhānā*N

light (brightness) रोशनी *rośnī* f.; (lamp, electric light) बत्ती *battī* f.

light (in weight) हल्का *halkā*

like की तरह *kī tarah;* (equal to) (के) समान *ke samān;* (such as) जैसा *jaisā*

like, to पसंद करना *pasand karnā*N, पसंद होना *pasand honā*

listen, to सुनना *sunnā*N

little, a थोड़ा-सा *thoṛā-sā*

live, to (reside) रहना *rahnā;* (be alive) जीना *jīnā*

lock ताला *tālā* m.

London लंदन *landan* m.

loneliness अकेलापन *akelāpan* m.

look, to देखना *dekhnā*N

look for, to ढूँढ़ना *ḍhū̃ṛhnā*N, की तलाश करना *kī talāś karnā*N

lose, to खोना *khonā*N

love प्रेम *prem* m., प्यार *pyār* m.; *to love us* हमसे प्रेम/प्यार करना *hamse prem/pyār karnā*N

luggage सामान *sāmān* m.

lunch दोपहर का खाना *dopahar kā khānā* m.

luxury ऐश *aiś* m.

lying (for inanimate things) पड़ा *paṛā;* (for people, 'lying down') लेटा *leṭā*

Ma माँ *mā̃* f.

mad पागल *pāgal*

mail (post) डाक f.

make, to बनाना *banānā*N

man (person) आदमी *ādmī* m.

mango आम *ām* m.

market बाज़ार *bāzār* m.

married शादी-शुदा *śādī-śudā* (invariable *-ā* ending)

marry, to शादी करना *śādī karnā*N*; to marry Ram* राम से शादी करना *Rām se śādī karnā*N*; to marry Ram to Sita* राम की शादी सीता से करना *Rām kī śādī Sītā se karnā*N

matter बात *bāt* f.; *it doesn't matter* कोई बात नहीं *koī bāt nahī̃*

mean (miserly) कंजूस *kanjūs*

meaning मतलब *matlab* m., अर्थ *arth* m.

meat गोश्त *gośt* m., माँस *mā̃s* m.

medicine दवा *davā* f.

meet, to (से) मिलना *(se) milnā*

meeting मुलाक़ात *mulāqāt* f., भेंट *bhẽṭ* f.

memory याद *yād* f.

midnight आधीरात *ādhīrāt* f.

milk दूध *dūdh* m.

mine मेरा *merā*

minute मिनट *minaṭ* m.

mistake ग़लती *<u>g</u>altī* f., भूल *bhūl* f.; *to make a mistake* ग़लती/भूल करना *<u>g</u>altī/bhūl karnā*N

Monday सोमवार *somvār* m.

money पैसा *paisā* m.

monkey बंदर *bandar* m.

month महीना *mahīnā* m.

moon चाँद *cā̃d* m.

more और *aur,* ज़्यादा *zyādā,* अधिक *adhik*

morning सुबह *subah* f.

mosquito मच्छर *macchar* m.

most ज़्यादा *zyādā,* अधिक *adhik; at the most* अधिक से अधिक *adhik se adhik,* ज़्यादा से ज़्यादा *zyādā se zyādā*

mostly ज़्यादातर *zyādātar*

mother माता *mātā* f., माँ *mā̃* f.

mountain पहाड़ *pahāṛ* m.

mouth मुँह *mũh* m.

move, to चलना *calnā;* हिलना *hilnā; to move house* शिफ़्ट करना *śifṭ karnā*[N], घर बदलना *ghar badalnā*[N]

much ज़्यादा *zyādā,* अधिक *adhik*

Muslim मुसलमान *musalmān* adj. and m.

my मेरा *merā*

narrow तंग *tang*

near (के) नज़दीक *(ke) nazdīk,* (के) पास *(ke) pās*

necessary ज़रूरी *zarūrī*

neck गर्दन *gardan* f.

need ज़रूरत *zarūrat* f.

needed चाहिए *cāhie*

neighbour पड़ोसी *paṛosī* m.

neither ... nor न ... न *na ... na*

new नया (नए, नई) *nayā (nae, naī)*

news ख़बर *k͟habar* f., समाचार *samācār* m.

newspaper अख़बार *ak͟hbār* m.

next अगला *aglā*

next to (close by) की बग़ल में *kī bagal mẽ*

night रात *rāt* f.

no नहीं *nahī̃;* जी नहीं *jī nahī̃*

no one कोई नहीं *koī nahī̃*

nobody कोई नहीं *koī nahī̃*

noise शोर *śor* m.

noon (afternoon) दोपहर *dopahar* f.

nose नाक *nāk* f.

not नहीं *nahī̃,* न *na*

nothing कुछ नहीं *kuch nahī̃*

now अब *ab*

nowadays आजकल *ājkal*

nowhere कहीं नहीं *kahī̃ nahī̃*

o'clock बजे *baje*

of का *kā*

of course ज़रूर *zarūr,* अवश्य *avaśya*

office दफ़्तर *daftar* m.

often अक्सर *aksar*

old (of people) बूढ़ा *būṛhā;* (of things) पुराना *purānā*

old man बूढ़ा *būṛhā* m.

old woman बुढ़िया *buṛhiyā* f.

on पर *par*

on top (of) के ऊपर *ke ūpar*

one एक *ek; one and a half* डेढ़ *ḍeṛh; one and a quarter* सवा *savā oneself* खुद *khud*, स्वयं *svayam*

only सिर्फ़ *sirf*, केवल *keval*, ही *hī*

open खुला *khulā*; *to open* खुलना *khulnā*, खोलना *kholnā*N

opinion राय *rāy* f., ख़याल *khyāl* m.; *in my opinion* मेरे ख़याल में/से *mere khyāl mẽ/se*

opportunity मौक़ा *mauqā* m.

or या *yā*

order, to मँगवाना *mãgvānā*N

ordinary आम *ām*, साधारण *sādhāraṇ*

other (second) दूसरा *dūsrā*

otherwise नहीं तो *nahī̃ to*

our(s) हमारा *hamārā*

out बाहर *bāhar*

out of (from among) में से *mẽ se*

outside (के) बाहर *(ke) bāhar*

own (one's own) अपना *apnā*

pain दर्द *dard* m.; (mental) दुःख *duḥkh* m.

paper काग़ज़ *kāgaz* m.

park, to (car) खड़ा करना *khaṛā karnā*N

particular ख़ास *khās*, विशेष *viśeṣ*

party (political) दल *dal* m.

party (social event) पार्टी *pārṭī* f.

passenger यात्री *yātrī* m., मुसाफ़िर *musāfir* m., सवारी *savārī* f.

pearl मोती *motī* m.

pen क़लम *qalam* m./f.

pencil पेंसिल *pensil* f.

people लोग *log* m. pl.; *the people*, *public* जनता *jantā* f. (used in singular)

perhaps शायद *śāyad*

period (age) ज़माना *zamānā* m.

person (individual) व्यक्ति *vyakti* m.

phone, to फ़ोन करना *fon karnā*N

photo(graph) फ़ोटो *foṭo* m.; *to take a photo* फ़ोटो खींचना *foṭo khī̃cnā*N

pick up, to उठाना *uṭhānā*N

picture तस्वीर *tasvīr* f., चित्र *citr* m.

piece (bit) टुकड़ा *ṭukṛā* m.

pill गोली *golī* f.

place जगह *jagah* f.

play, to (game) खेलना *khelnā*N

play, to (music) बजाना *bajānā*N

please कृपया *kṛpayā*, मेहरबानी करके *meharbānī karke*

pocket जेब *jeb* f.

poem, poetry कविता *kavitā* f.

police पुलिस *pulis* f. (used in singular)

politician नेता *netā* m. (inv.)

poor ग़रीब *garīb*

possible मुमकिन *mumkin*, संभव *sambhav*

post (mail) डाक *ḍāk* f.

post office डाकघर *ḍākghar* m.

pour, to डालना *ḍālnā*N

power शक्ति *śakti* f.

practice अभ्यास *abhyās* m.

praise तारीफ़ *tārīf* f.; *to praise* की तारीफ़ करना *kī tārīf karnā* N

prepare, to तैयार करना *taiyār karnā*N

present (gift) तोहफ़ा *tohfā* m., उपहार *uphār* m.

presentation भेंट *bheṭ* f.

previous पिछला *pichlā; previously* पहले *pahle*

price दाम *dām* m., क़ीमत *qīmat* f.

pride गर्व *garv* m.

problem समस्या *samasyā* f.

profession पेशा *peśā* m.

properly ठीक से *ṭhīk se*

public (the people) जनता *jantā* f. (used in singular)

pure (unmixed) शुद्ध *śuddh*

put on, to पहनना *pahannā*^N

put, to रखना *rakhnā*^N

quarrel झगड़ा *jhagṛā* m.

question सवाल *savāl* m., प्रश्न *praśn* m.

quick तेज़ *tez*

quickly जल्दी *jaldī*

quite (fairly) काफ़ी (completely) बिलकुल *bilkul*

radio रेडियो *reḍiyo* m.

rain बारिश *bāriś* f.; *to rain* बारिश होना *bāriś honā*, पानी पड़ना *pānī paṛnā*

reach, to पहुँचना *pahũcnā*

read, to पढ़ना *paṛhnā*^N

ready तैयार *taiyār*

real असली *aslī*

reason कारण *kāraṇ* m., वजह *vajah* f.

recognize, to पहचानना *pahcānnā*^N

red लाल *lāl*

refuse (to), to (से) इनकार करना *(se) inkār karnā*^N

relative रिश्तेदार *riśtedār* m., f.

remain, to रहना *rahnā*

remaining बाक़ी *bāqī*

remember, to याद करना *yād karnā*^N; याद होना *yād honā*

remind, to याद दिलाना *yād dilānā*^N

rent किराया *kirāyā* m.; *to rent* किराये पर लेना/देना *kirāye par lenā/denā*^N

reply जवाब *javāb* m.; *to reply* जवाब देना *javāb denā*^N

rest (ease) आराम *ārām* m.; *to rest* आराम करना *ārām karnā*^N

return, to लौटना *lauṭnā*

rice चावल *cāval* m.

rich (wealthy) अमीर *amīr*

rickshaw रिक्शा *rikśā* m.

right (correct) ठीक *ṭhīk*, सही *sahī*

right (opp. of left) दाहिना *dāhinā; to the right (handside)* दाहिने (हाथ) *dāhine (hāth)*

river नदी *nadī* f.

robbery चोरी *corī* f.

room कमरा *kamrā* m.

run, to दौड़ना *dauṛnā; to run away* भागना *bhāgnā*

rupee रुपया *rupayā* m.

salt नमक *namak* m.

samosa समोसा *samosā* m.

sandal चप्पल *cappal* f.

Sanskrit संस्कृत *sanskṛt* f.

sari साड़ी *sāṛī* f.

Saturday शनिवार ***śanivār*** m.

save, to बचाना ***bacānā***[N]

say, to (से) कहना ***(se) kahnā***[N]

scold, to डाँटना ***ḍā̃ṭnā***[N]

script (alphabet) लिपि ***lipi*** f.

sea समुद्र ***samudra*** m.

search तलाश ***talāś*** f.; *to search for* की तलाश करना ***kī talāś karnā***[N]

seated बैठा ***baiṭhā***

see, to देखना ***dekhnā***[N]

seem, to लगना ***lagnā;*** मालूम होना ***mālūm honā***

sell, to बेचना ***becnā***[N]

send, to भेजना ***bhejnā***[N]

sentence वाक्य ***vākya*** m.

separate(ly) अलग ***alag***

servant नौकर ***naukar*** m.

several कई ***kaī***

she वह ***vah***

shoe जूता ***jūtā*** m.

shop दुकान ***dukān*** f.; shopkeeper दुकानदार ***dukāndār*** m.

should चाहिए ***cāhie*** (after infinitive: 'I should go' मुझको जाना चाहिए ***mujhko jānā cāhie***)

shout, to चिल्लाना ***cillānā***[N]

shut बंद ***band;*** *to shut* बंद करना ***band karnā***[N]

side (direction) तरफ़ ***taraf*** f., ओर ***or*** f.

silent चुप ***cup,*** ख़ामोश ***khāmoś***

simple सरल ***saral***

since the time when … since then जब से … तब से ***jab se … tab se***

sing, to गाना ***gānā***[N]

sister बहिन ***bahin*** f.

sit, to बैठना ***baiṭhnā***

sitar सितार ***sitār*** m.

sky आकाश ***ākāś*** m., आसमान ***āsmān*** m.

sleep नींद ***nīd̃*** f.; *to sleep* सोना ***sonā***

small छोटा ***choṭā***

smile, to मुस्कराना ***muskarānā***[n]

smoke, to (सिग्रेट) पीना ***(sigreṭ) pīnā***[N]

so (then) तो ***to,*** सो ***so;*** *so much* इतना ***itnā***

soap साबुन ***sābun*** m.

sold, to be बिकना ***biknā***

some (with single countable noun) कोई ***koī;*** (with uncountable) कुछ ***kuch;*** *something else* कुछ और ***kuch aur;*** *something or other* कुछ न कुछ ***kuch na kuch***

somehow कहीं ***kahī̃***

someone कोई ***koī;*** *someone else* और कोई ***aur koī,*** कोई और ***koī aur;*** *someone or other* कोई न कोई ***koī na koī***

some time कभी ***kabhī;*** *sometimes* कभी कभी ***kabhī kabhī***

somewhere कहीं ***kahī̃;*** *somewhere else* कहीं और ***kahī̃ aur;*** *somewhere or other* कहीं न कहीं ***kahī̃ na kahī̃***

son बेटा ***beṭā*** m.

song गाना ***gānā*** m., गीत ***gīt*** m.

soon जल्दी ***jaldī***

sound आवाज़ ***āvāz*** f.

south दक्षिण *dakṣiṇ* m.
speak, to बोलना *bolnā*[N]
spoon चम्मच *cammac* m.
stair (case) सीढ़ी *sīṛhī* f.
stamp टिकट *ṭikaṭ* m./f.
standing खड़ा *khaṛā*
state (province) प्रदेश *pradeś* m.
station स्टेशन *sṭeśan* m.
stay, to रहना *rahnā*
steal, to चोरी करना *corī karnā*[N]
still (up to now) अभी *abhī*
stomach पेट *peṭ* m.
stone पत्थर *patthar* m.
stop, to रुकना *ruknā;* रोकना *roknā*[N]
story कहानी *kahānī* f.
straight (forward) सीधा *sīdhā*
strange अजीब *ajīb*
stranger अजनबी *ajnabī* m.
street सड़क *saṛak* f.
string रस्सी *rassī* f.
stroll, to टहलना *ṭahalnā*
strong मज़बूत *mazbūt,* तेज़ *tez*
student विद्यार्थी *vidyārthī* m., f.
studies पढ़ाई *paṛhāī* f.
study, to पढ़ना *paṛhnā*
stupid बेवकूफ़ *bevaqūf;* stupid person उल्लू *ullū* m.
subject (topic) विषय *viṣay* m.
success सफलता *saphaltā* f.; successful सफल *saphal,* कामयाब *kāmyāb*
suddenly (unexpectedly) अचानक *acānak,* एकाएक *ekāek*
suggestion सुझाव *sujhāv* m.; to suggest सुझाव देना *sujhāv denā*[N]
summer गरमियाँ *garmiyā̃* f. pl; summer holidays गरमी की छुट्टियाँ *garmī kī chuṭṭiyā̃* f. pl
sun सूरज *sūraj* m.; sunlight, sunshine धूप *dhūp* f.
Sunday रविवार *ravivār* m.
surprise आश्चर्य *āścarya* m.; *I'm surprised* मुझे आश्चर्य है *mujhe āścarya hai*
sweet मीठा *mīṭhā;* sweet dish मिठाई *miṭhāī* f.
swim, to तैरना *tairnā*[N]
tabla तबला *tablā* m.
table मेज *mez* f.
tablet गोली *golī* f.
tailor दर्ज़ी *darzī* m.
take, to (receive) लेना *lenā*[N]*;* (deliver) ले जाना *le jānā*
take away, to ले जाना *le jānā*
take care of, to का ख़याल/ध्यान रखना *kā khyāl/dhyān rakhnā*[N]
talk, to (से) बात/बातें करना *(se) bāt/bātẽ karnā*[N]
tall लंबा *lambā;* (high) ऊँचा *ū̃cā*
tap नल *nal* m.
taxi टैक्सी *ṭaiksī* f.
tea चाय *cāy* f.
teach, to (a subject) पढ़ाना *paṛhānā*[N], (a skill) सिखाना *sikhānā*[N]

teacher अध्यापक *adhyāpak* m.

tell, to बताना *batānā*[N]

temple मंदिर *mandir* m.

thank you शुक्रिया *śukriyā*, धन्यवाद *dhanyavād*

that (conjunction) कि *ki*

that (pronoun) वह *ah*

that is to say यानी *yānī*

theft चोरी *corī* f.

then फिर *phir*, तब *tab*

there वहाँ *vahā̃; right there* वहीं *vahī̃; over there* उधर *udhar*

these ये *ye*

they ये *ye*, वे *ve*

thick (coarse) मोटा *moṭā*

thief चोर *cor* m.

thin पतला *patlā;* (lean) दुबला-पतला *dublā-patlā*

thing चीज़ *cīz* f.; (abstract, 'matter') बात *bāt* f.

think, to सोचना *socnā*[N]

thirst प्यास *pyās* f.; *to feel thirsty* प्यास लगना *pyās lagnā*

this यह *yah*

those वे *ve*

thought विचार *vicār* m., ख़याल *khyāl* m.

throat गला *galā* m.

throw, to डालना *ḍālnā*[N], फेंकना *phẽknā*[N]

ticket टिकट *ṭikaṭ* m./f.

time समय *samay* m., वक़्त *vaqt* m.; (occasion) बार *bār* f., दफ़ा *dafā* f.

tired थका *thakā; to be tired* थकना *thaknā*

to को *ko*

today आज *āj*

together (in the company of) एक साथ *ek sāth*, के साथ *ke sāth*

tomorrow कल *kal*

too (also) भी *bhī;* (excessive) बहुत ज़्यादा *bahut zyādā*

touch, to छूना *chūnā*[N]

towards की तरफ़/ओर *kī taraf/or*

town शहर *śahar* m.

toy खिलौना *khilaunā* m.

train ट्रेन *ṭren* f., गाड़ी *gāṛī* f., रेलगाड़ी *relgāṛī* f.

translation अनुवाद *anuvād* m.; *to translate* (का) अनुवाद करना (*kā*) *anuvād karnā*[N]

travel यात्रा *yātrā* f., सफ़र *safar* m.; *to travel* यात्रा/सफ़र करना *yātrā/safar karnā*[N]

traveller यात्री *yātrī* m., मुसाफ़िर *musāfir* m.

tree पेड़ *peṛ* m.

true सच *sac*

trust भरोसा *bharosā* m., विश्वास *viśvās* m.

truth सच्चाई *sacāī* f.

try, to की कोशिश करना *kī kośiś karnā*[N]

turn (bend) मोड़ *moṛ* m.

turn, to मुड़ना *muṛnā*, मोड़ना *moṛnā*[N]

two दो *do;* two and a half ढाई *ḍhāī*

uncle (father's younger brother) चाचा *cācā* m. (inv.)

understand, to समझना *samajhnā*ⁿ

understanding समझ *samajh* f.

until तक *tak*

up, upstairs ऊपर *ūpar*

up to तक *tak*

upset परेशान *pareśān*

Urdu उर्दू *urdū* f.

urgent ज़रूरी *zarūrī*

us हम *ham*

useless बेकार *bekār*

usually आम तौर पर *ām taur par*

vacant ख़ाली *khālī*

vacate, to ख़ाली करना *khālī karnā*ᴺ

valuable क़ीमती *qīmtī*

Varanasi वाराणसी *vārāṇasī* f.

vegetable(s) सब्ज़ी *sabzī* f.

very बहुत *bahut*

via से होकर *se hokar*

village गाँव *gā̃v* m.

visible, to be दिखाई देना *dikhāī denā*

voice आवाज *āvāz* f.

wait(ing) इंतज़ार *intazār* m.; *to wait (for)* (का) इंतज़ार करना *(kā) intazār karnā*ᴺ

walk, to पैदल चलना/जाना *paidal calnā/jānā*

wall दीवार *dīvār* f.

want, to चाहना *cāhnā*ᴺ (in past, use imperfective – मैं चाहता था *maī̃ cāhtā thā* – rather than perfective)

warm गरम *garam*

wash, to धोना *dhonā*ᴺ (bathe) नहाना *nahānā; to wash dishes* बरतन माँजना *bartan mā̃jnā*ᴺ

washed, to be धुलना *dhulnā*

watch (wristwatch) घड़ी *ghaṛī* f.

water पानी *pānī* m.

way (manner) ढंग *ḍhang* m., तरह *tarah* f., प्रकार *prakār* m.

we हम *ham*

weak कमज़ोर *kamzor*

wear, to पहनना *pahannā*ᴺ

weather मौसम *mausam* m.

wedding शादी *śādī* f.

week हफ़्ता *haftā* m., सप्ताह *saptāh* m.

weep, to रोना *ronā*ᴺ

well (anyway) ख़ैर *khair*

well (in a good way) अच्छा *acchā*, अच्छी तरह (से) *acchī tarah (se)*

wet (soaked) भीगा *bhīgā;* (damp) गीला *gīlā*

what? क्या *kyā*

what like? (what kind of?) कैसा *kaisā*

when? कब *kab*

when … then जब … तब *jab … tab*

where? कहाँ *kahā̃*, किधर *kidhar*

where … there जहाँ … वहाँ *jahā̃ … vahā̃*

which (the one which) जो *jo; which/what ever* जो भी *jo bhī*

which? कौनसा *kaunsā*

while (on the other hand) जब कि *jab ki*

white सफ़ेद *safed; white person* गोरा *gorā* m.

who (the one who) जो *jo; whoever* जो भी *jo bhī*

who? कौन *kaun*

why? क्यों *kyõ*

wife पत्नी *patnī* f.

wind हवा *havā* f.

window खिड़की *khiṛkī* f.

with से *se;* (in company of) के साथ *ke sāth*

without के बिना *ke binā; without doing/saying/thinking* बिना किए/बोले/सोचे *binā kie/bole/soce*

woman औरत *aurat* f.

wood लकड़ी *lakṛī* f.

word शब्द *śabd* m.

work काम *kām* m.; (occupation) धंधा *dhandhā* m.; (employment) नौकरी *naukrī* f.

world दुनिया *duniyā* f.

write, to लिखना *likhnā*[N]

writer लेखक *lekhak* m.

wrong (incorrect) ग़लत *galat*

year साल *sāl* m., वर्ष *varṣ* m.; (of calendar, era) सन् *san* m.

yes हाँ *hā̃*, जी हाँ *jī hā̃*

yesterday कल *kal*

you (intimate) तू *tū;* (familiar) तुम *tum;* (formal) आप *āp*

young छोटा *choṭā*, जवान *javān*

your(s) (intimate) तेरा *terā;* (familiar) तुम्हारा *tumhārā;* (formal) आपका *āpkā*

Glossary of grammatical terms

absolutive A form of the verb such as पहुँचकर *pahũckar having arrived,* whose phrase is independent of the grammar of the rest of the sentence: घर पहुँचकर मैं आराम करूँगा *ghar pahũckar maĩ ārām karũgā having arrived home I'll rest (I'll rest when I get home).*

adjective A word that describes: *green, small, nice.*

adverb A word or phrase that describes the way in which something happens: *quickly, carefully, immediately, next week.*

agreement Having the same number, gender, and case: in *we go*, the verb *go* agrees with *we*; in *he goes, goes* agrees with *he*.

case A way of showing the relationship of a word to other words in a sentence: *she hit her* distinguishes aggressor and victim by having *she* and *her* in different cases. In Hindi, the main distinction is between 'direct case' and 'oblique case'.

causative A category of verbs that describe an action that the subject does not perform but rather causes to be performed: कमरा साफ़ करवाऊँगा *kamrā sāf karvāũgā I'll have the room cleaned (by someone else).*

conjunction A link word between parts of a sentence, such as *that* and *but* in *I heard that my brother was ill but I did nothing.*

continuous The tense that describes things going on at a particular time, conveyed in English by an *-ing* verb and in Hindi by a रहा *rahā* construction: वह बोल रहा है *vah bol rahā hai he is speaking.*

direct The case used by default for nouns (and pronouns and adjectives); it is replaced by the 'oblique' when a noun (etc.) is followed by a postposition and in some adverbial phrases.

gender The status of a noun as being either masculine or feminine. For animates, grammatical gender follows sexual gender (आदमी *ādmī man* is masculine, औरत *aurat woman* is feminine), but for inanimates the allocation of gender is not easily predictable (कान *kān ear* is masculine, नाक *nāk nose* is feminine).

imperfective A verb tense whose action is not a completed, one-off event: मैं हिन्दी बोलता हूँ *maĩ hindī boltā hū̃ I speak Hindi*; see also **perfective.**

infinitive The form of the verb listed in dictionaries: in Hindi, it ends in –ना *-nā*, as in करना *karnā*; in English, it features the word *to*, as in *to do*. An infinitive is used in many constructions such as मुझको जाना चाहिए *mujhko jānā cāhie I ought to go.*

intransitive verb One that cannot take a direct object. Verbs of motion are typical examples: आना *ānā to come*, जाना *jānā to go*.

noun A word that names something: *mouse, love, brother, Ram.*

number The status of a word as being either singular or plural.

object The part of the sentence that is affected by the verb or to which the action is done. In वह राम को पैसा देगा *vah Rām ko paisā degā He'll give money to Ram*, वह *vah he* is the subject, पैसा *paisā money* is the direct object, राम *Rām Ram* the indirect object.

oblique The case that is used before a postposition. In मेरे कमरे में *mere kamre mẽ in my room*, मेरे कमरे *mere kamre* is made oblique by में *mẽ*. An oblique also appears (without postposition) in some adverbs such as इन दिनों *in dinõ these days.*

participle A form of the verb used as the basis for various tenses: जाता *jātā* is the imperfective participle from जाना *jānā to go* and is used to form वह जाता है/था *vah jātā hai/thā he goes/used to go.*

passive A verb whose focus is on the action being done rather than the person doing it: *the food is being cooked* is passive, *I am cooking the food* is active.

perfective A verb tense that describes a completed, one-off action, as in हमने गाड़ी ख़रीदी *hamne gāṛī <u>kh</u>arīdī we bought a car.*

possessive Having a meaning that indicates ownership: *my* and *our* are possessive pronouns.

postposition Words like में *mẽ in*, पर *par on*, and के लिए *ke lie for*, expressing a relationship to the word or phrase preceding it, as in मेज़ पर *mez par on the table*, आप के लिए *āp ke lie for you*; a postposition is the Hindi equivalent of an English preposition.

pronoun A word that stands for a noun: *Manoj read a book* uses nouns, *he read it* uses pronouns.

relative A relative pronoun such as *who* giving further information about something already mentioned, as in *Find the boy who took my jacket*: such a word introduces a relative clause.

stem The base form of a verb, to which endings are added: कर *kar* in करना *karnā to do.*

subject That person or thing who acts or is: हम *ham we* in हम खाना तैयार करेंगे *ham khānā taiyār karẽge we will prepare food*.

subjunctive A form of the verb that typically expresses possibility or suggestion rather than definitive actions.

transitive A transitive verb is one that can take a direct object: *to eat, to write, to ask* (*to eat food, to write letters, to ask questions*).

verb A word or phrase that denotes an action or a state of being: *ate* in *I ate the banana*; or *am* in *I am unwell*. It usually has a subject (*I*) and may also take an object (*the banana*).

Index

References indicate the unit, followed by the corresponding **Language discovery** section number.